RISE AND FALL

A Discourse Upon the Phenomena
of Civilisation and Decline

SILAS GAUTHIER

Rise and Fall: A Discourse Upon the Phenomena of Civilisation and Decline

1st Edition

Copyright © 2021 Silas Gauthier

All rights reserved.

ISBN: 978-1-7397548-0-8

Table of Contents

Chapter I: Introduction	1
Overview of the Seven Stages	5
Chapter II: Cultural and Social Mores	9
Cultural and Sexual Norms	10
Pessimism and Religious Osmosis	18
Heroes and Celebrities	24
Foreign Migration	27
Democratisation of Enfranchisement	32
Belief in Eternal Pre-eminence	38
Chapter III: Economic and Political State	41
The Economic Machine	43
Reasons for Debasement	46
How is the Modern Currency Supply Created?	48
Inflation and Deflation	51
Political Polarisation and Turmoil	55
Normalisation of the Radical	59
Political Ideology or Emerging Religious Movement?	61
The Lack of Resolve to Resolve	64
Supply Chain Breakdown and Food Shortages	65
Indisputable Corruption	67
Refugee Crises	73
Usury	76
Chapter IV: Religion and Belief	81
Legal Arbitrariness and Juris Prudence	84
Atheism and Nihilism	91
An Abundance of Inaction	97
Inequality of Everything	99
Radically Superficial	103
Contrived Beliefs and Manufactured Ideas	105
Bread and Circuses	108

Chapter V: Military — 111

- Foreign Cohorts — 112
- Terrorist, The New Barbarian? — 115
- Offence Makes Way for Defence — 118
- Pax Americana — 121
- Rise of the Upstarts — 125
- Thucydides's Trap — 127
- Build the Wall — 129
- Populist Caesars — 132
- Inability to Absorb Defeat — 135
- Putting Man Before God — 137
- Inward Search for War — 140
- The Plastic Man — 143
- Oikophobia — 146
- Ideological Subversion — 155

Chapter VI: Plato's Five Regimes — 161

- Oligarchy — 162
- Democracy — 165
- Tyranny — 166
- Aristocracy — 169
- Timocracy — 179
- Polybius's Anacyclosis — 183

Chapter VII: The Trappings of Democracy — 187

- Ancient Examples of Flaws in Democracy — 188
- Thomas Hobbes and Democracy — 191
- The God that Failed — 212
- Inconsequential Constitutions — 219
- Anomalies in the Democratic Machine — 223
- Crossing the Rubicon — 230
- Caesarism — 234
- E Pluribus Unum — 246

Chapter VIII: Opinions upon the Contemporary — 253

- The Modus Operandi of Capital and the State — 255
- Rebellions: Threat or a Tool? — 260

The Milgram Experiments	266
The Problematic Condition of Man	270
On Coercion	274
On Corruption	276
On Critical Thought	278
Merchants of the Revolution	279
On Domestication	288
On Hate Crime Legislation	289
A Thousand Points of Light	291
The Strange Light of Hope	294
The Piper Comes a Calling	299
The Cult of Covid	307
The Children of Saturn	321
A Silent Overthrow	324
Jahr Null (Year Zero)	330
On Propaganda	336
On Escapism	337
The Global Plantation	338
The Postmodern "Meta-truth"	341
Temptation, the Key to Power	343
Fear, The Initiator of New Paradigms	349
The Panopticon Cometh Forth	353
Incremental Digitisation	362
The Atlantean Myth	366
Silent Weapons for Quiet Wars	369
On Control Functions Within Society	387
The Cybernetic Truth	388
Epilogue	**409**
Bibliography	**417**

Chapter I

Introduction

The West has long enjoyed an unrivalled era of peace and prosperity in recent history. Its culture has come to dominate and influence every other; its military, a shining example of strength and unparalleled might; its metropolises, a beacon of freedom and modernity. However, under the veneer of this seemingly unmatched hegemony is a festering rot that is beginning to crack the very edifice of Western civilisation itself. It is self-evident and undeniable; posing a grave dilemma to us all and to our posterity.

However, is this ensuing decline unique to the modern context or is this simply a cycle that has played itself out, countless times, throughout the history of mankind? Seemingly futile to run from and impossible to change.

Some readers may be surprised to realise, but the recent bouts of rioting, social upheaval, new radical changes in socio-sexual mores, and the climate of economic and monetary instability, is nothing new and is not to be unexpected. This has been experienced within every major civilizational decline from the noble Republic and eventual Empire of Rome, to the grand Abbasid Caliphate. They, too, all experienced very similar symptoms of decline and in the same pattern of succession.

Within this abridged examination of the decline of the modern West, and the parallels exhibited by its historical counterparts, I will include eye-witness accounts from the varied historical periods of civilisational deterioration, and I will delve into much of the source material that underpins this sociological theory; and the various author's insights into their findings on the rise and fall of empires and civilisations. Furthermore, for sake of clarity and digestibility for the reader, I will categorise these parallels into compartmentalised chapters or sections, based upon similarity. For example, all parallels that share a similar socio-economic theme will be grouped. Thus, the parallels of decline will be categorised in the following manner:

- Cultural and Social Mores
- Economic and Political State
- Religion and Belief
- Military

I will include a brief description as to the various fundamental source material I am utilising to aid me in this examination, for sake of prior intellectual transparency and so you may be encouraged to use this as a guide to applying these works to a modern context, too. The two main sources of information I will be utilising for my inquiry's underpinnings are *"The Fate of Empires and Search for Survival"* by *Sir John Glubb* and *"The Decline of the West"*, both volumes, by *Oswald Spengler*. The former establishing the timescale of the seven ages of empire; and the notable characteristics of each. In contrast, *Oswald Spengler*'s work is far more unorthodox in terms of the way he approaches historical categorisations, of the major civilisations and major historical epochs. For example, he openly dismisses the traditional academic periodisation of history based on epochs of time; ancient, medieval, and modern. Alternatively, he advocates that history, as a philosophy, should be understood from the perspective of acknowledging that there have been eight major cultures.

Chapter I

Thus, we should see history through this lens. These he describes as "High History".

The similarity between both scholarly pieces of work is encapsulated within both authors shared acknowledgment of the truth that each civilisation, or culture, from Spenglerian thinking, has each its period of youth, growth, maturity and decay. This mirrors a symbiosis with nature and thus is the cyclical pattern of all biological life and, by extension, the lifecycle of the social constructs of Humanity itself. What's more, each described the lifecycle of a civilisation thusly; a cycle of rise and fall, a pioneer period of warfare and empire building and at the end a disintegration of the old order by a resulting deluge of irreligiosity, intellectual scepticism, materialism, greed and the search for diversions.

> "What experience and history teach is this – that people and governments never have learned anything from history, or acted on principles deduced from it."

Each author steadfastly believed in the notion that, for us to break the cyclical vision of history – to step off the proverbial hamster wheel, so to say - we must ensure we view history in its totality. *G. W. F. Hegel* famously and poignantly stated, "What experience and history teach is this – that people and governments never have learned anything from history, or acted on principles deduced from it." Education in the idea that Western civilisation, though how unassailable to entropy it may seem, is a fragile flower and at any moment may wither to the bitter devices of Human greed, and our acute nature for self-destruction. The irony of this cycle of civilisation is thus, that when we are in the decline phase, and I posit we are, we believe ourselves to be at the apex of our development; sophisticated and above our plebiscite ancestors – within all areas, most assuredly that of virtue and morality. This is what quickens the spiralling degeneration within the decline phase, the seventh and last stage, that is that we think while at our lowest, we are at our height. This is what makes it so difficult to convey to our fellow citizenry, even to the astute paragons of academia, of the grave implications of the present situation; and they will resist, vehemently so, the idea that we are at anything other than the zenith of everything that has preceded us. Therefore, this is the paradoxical nature of the issue that faces us – how does one reverse an agglomerate decay that seems to be naturally destined to occur? However, at the very least, we may educate ourselves upon this pressing matter and position ourselves accordingly to weather the storm, so to say.

Additionally, as well as discussing the social or civilisational cycles, I will also summarily discuss the governmental cycles and what can be expected after the inexorable collapse of this period of experimentation in Democracy. This was well understood by some of the greatest philosophers and political theorists of antiquity; while observing, firsthand, the political petri-dish known as classical Hellenic civilisation. That is, that Democracies, once rotten beyond all repair, create the fertile breeding ground for a different governmental type to take hold; and thus, that different governmental type makes way for another governmental type, once the former has imploded - and so on, and so forth. The cycle eventually circulating back to its original stage.

I will detail, beginning on page seven, a brief overview of the various stages of empire and their general characteristics; as purported by *Sir John Glubb*. This will be a succinct guide to the other material within the rest of the book and will map clearly, for the reader's understanding, the important subject matter of which we are about to discuss. Therefore, without further ado, let us begin our journey to understand the past and how it reconnects with our troubled present.

CHAPTER I

Overview of the Seven Stages

1. *The Age of Pioneers (Outburst)* – A nation starts out with a sound money supply; gold or silver; its population has a sense of duty, are hardy and enterprising; it has a homogenous culture; there is a youthful vigour within the population; it will have rapid expansion within this period too; i.e., Macedonian conquests, the Islamic Arabic conquests, the Spanish colonial acquisitions, the Mongolian and Nomadic outbursts, British colonial conquests and America's "Manifest Destiny".

2. *The Age of Conquests* – The nation begins to expand its sphere of influence through alliances and cements and solidifies their newly acquired land; it begins to build a greater degree of public works and thus more future economic burden is sown, as a result; typically, there is a stark population growth; creation of mass infrastructural installations and transportation links; adoption of a greater degree of rigid military and governmental organisation.

3. *The Age of Commerce* – The vast conquest of land leads to a natural economic stimulus and a greater variety of trade goods are available to the empire; the desire to make money slowly begins to erode the original militarism that birthed the empire; glory and honour, as concepts, become less fashionable to the newly emerging merchant elite; it will still fund its military massively though, and see to new conquests and acquisition of more land; the youth still have a sense of patriotism inculcated in them, by education.

4. *The Age of Affluence* – The merchant class grow immensely rich from the wealth pouring into the nation; Wealth becomes more abundant, but the decentralisation of that wealth is lacking;

gradual shift to defensiveness; rise of the merchant banker and beginning of currency debasement; the object of the youth changes from honour or adventure to how best to acquire money; money becomes God; education transforms too, and slowly stops its teachings of patriotism to the youth.

5. *The Age of Intellect* – At this stage, luxury is still pervasive but there is ample surplus of capital in circulation to allow for private capital injection into intellectual pursuits; the merchant class, aristocratic in nature, but potentially not in name, by this time, begin to give patronage to intellectual thinkers, inventors and to the founding of universities and colleges; education begins to become more democratised and institutes of higher-learning become ubiquitous throughout the land; the youth, of whose attentions were already turned from military glory, are now swayed from the acquisition of wealth to academic pursuits and accumulation of academic honours (this will pervade throughout the *age of decadence*); Intellectual scepticism, with all its inescapable trappings, will manifest during this period; secular or opposing religious ideologies and, in all but name, cults will begin to form; a period of intellectual and technological expansion, within all areas of science and academic thought; the *age of intellect* brings with it the general consensus of the populace, or at least of the educated classes, that, as *Sir John Glubb* states, "Perhaps the most dangerous by-product of the *Age of Intellect* is the unconscious growth of the idea that the human brain can solve the problems of the world. Even on the low-level of practical affairs this is patently untrue.", and this leads to all manner of ridiculous notions taking root – of which they hold to the general pattern that they diminish the idea of self-sacrifice to the nation or empire,

within the civil zeitgeist; establishment of formal centralised issuers of credit or dangerous levels of debasement of the money supply (this typically begins, as aforementioned, within stage 4, respectively).

6. *The Age of Decadence* – Swelling of political hatreds; beginning of a loss of faith of the currency supply caused by incessant devaluation or sporadic economic fluxes; a section of the population will begin to horde tangible assets that retain their value – gold, silver, land, etc; increasing reliance upon diversions, such as sports teams, which become of national significance; growth of an all-encompassing welfare state; massive tax burden; influx of foreigners; demographic decline; pessimism; irreligiosity; pluralism; sexual aberrancy; cults gain political clout.

7. *The Age of Decline & Collapse* – Disintegration of the old order; "founding peoples" lose political power and may become marginalised but that is dependent upon the initial reason for collapse; moral and cultural conservatism begins to take hold again after a few generations proceeding the collapse; the collapse may be caused by a number or combination of factors – political instability, foreign invasion, economic woes, etc; bankruptcy of the nation ensues within this period; military fracturing and a weakening of internal stability; cults, be them secular or religious, may take hold and sweep away the old religious priesthood or doctrine; a cultural and intellectual stagnation may occur but may also begin within the *age of decadence;* slow or precipitous decline in living standards and GDP; foreign occupation and/or cultural or ethnic assimilation into the invading peoples (if the collapse is due to internal or external agitation via a foreign contingent).

Chapter II

Cultural and Social Mores

I am writing from the assumption that, as of right now in the West, we are firmly in the *Age of Decadence*. I pontificate this as largely self-evident, as we can see from recent events and moreover from the historical pattern of our sharp decline in the attitudes of the youth – generation after generation. For example, we can observe that much of the youth, in the modern West, subscribe to ideas and attitudes that many in preceding ages certainly would have called obscene and would have objected to. However, on that fact alone we cannot call these ideas and attitudes an example of a decline, simply because preceding generations would object. But they certainly can be called an objective illustration of decline because they induce, into the mind of the populace, or youth, an unfavourable or unpropitious view of self-sacrifice for the group, or country, and an adherence to beliefs that induce pessimism or nihilism. These are the behaviours of *decline*, or *decadence*; as established by *Sir John Glubb* and other concurrent thinkers upon the topic.

Now, with that said, I will begin to examine the historical parallels between the West's cultural and social mores and how they factor into historical instances of other empires, of who were embroiled in the throngs of the *Age of Decadence*, too.

"Hard times create strong men, strong men create good times, good times create weak men, and weak men create hard times." - *G. Michael Hopf.*

The cultural and social mores, to anyone with eyes to see, have slowly corrupted since the advent of the sexual revolution in the 1960's; however, the gradual signs of putrefaction were beginning to rear their ugly heads even at the advent of the 20th century. The Western society that has formed since this radical divergence, is one in which democratised institutions of education instruct the youth to openly hold disdain for their civilisation and loath its founding principles and people; one in which copious amounts of alcohol, drugs and mindless diversions are the universally favoured pastimes; one in which the institution of marriage has been so thoroughly eroded that many marriages swiftly end in divorce and by virtue, we are in demographic freefall; one in which patriotism has become a dirty word and a pessimistic outlook, nihilistic in principle, has taken hold. However, we are not historically alone in experiencing these overt hallmarks of decline, they are commonplace in most late-period civilisations and, though they still pose an existential threat to our civilisation's existence, we can use these as points of reference to educate our fellow citizens on the gravity of the situation.

Cultural and Sexual Norms

Let us now investigate the late-period Roman Empire and see if we can ascertain the cultural and social equivalents between the decline of the modern West and that of the Roman Empire. What is very explicit within the cultural decline we see, or the cultural divergence one could say, is this general emancipation of what was traditionally regarded as deviant sexual proclivities. This has been a slow and gradual transformation but is nonetheless a pronounced one. Though this is, however, nothing new and was found within the Roman Empire during its likewise decay. Homosexuality, adultery, and cross-dressing became rife after the latter

Chapter II

years of the 1st century AD; a liberalisation of sexuality became prominent throughout the society but most acutely with the gentry, as is the case today[1]. Prior to the social acceptance of these behaviours, Roman society had witnessed an increasingly widespread acceptance and commonplace occurrence of prostitution; as we can see from the wonderfully ornate and graphic late 1st century AD frescos in Pompeii[2]. However, we must understand that prostitution was prevalent throughout Roman society since its founding presumably, but what we find, especially during the later years of the empire, prior to the division of it, is an increasing prevalence of divergent sexual practises becoming more commonplace. *Cato the Elder*, a statesman, soldier and senator, was openly opposed to what he saw as "Hellenisation" through the increase in a type of free sexuality[3]. He described it as having the effect of making Roman men "too feminine".

Homosexual marriage became part of the social fabric too during the later imperial-era. Though, it was attacked and ridiculed during its introduction, it became not too uncommon for the era. Here is evidence from satirists and poets of the radical changes to Roman marriage custom;

Martial, the first-century AD, in one epigram writes discontentedly, of a man who "played the bride yesterday." In another he says mockingly, "Bearded Callistratus gave himself in marriage to…Afer, in the manner in which a virgin usually gives herself in marriage to a male. The torches shone in front, the bridal veils covered his face, and wedding toasts were not absent, either. A dowry was also named. Does that not seem

---

[1] John Pollini, *"The Warren Cup: Homoerotic Love and Symposial Rhetoric in Silver,"* Art Bulletin 81.1 (1999) 21–52. John R. Clarke, *Looking at Lovemaking: Constructions of Sexuality in Roman Art* 100 B.C.–A.D. 250 (University of California Press, 1998, 2001), p. 61, asserts that the Warren cup is valuable for art history and as a document of Roman sexuality precisely because of its "relatively secure date."
[2] Angelika Dierichs: *Erotik in der Römischen Kunst. von Zabern, Mainz 1993* (Zaberns Bildbände zur Archäologie) [[ISBN 3-8053-1540-6]].
[3] Hubbard, T. *Historical Views of Homosexuality: Roman Empire. Oxford Research Encyclopedia of Politics.* Retrieved 28 Jun. 2021, from https://oxfordre.com/politics/view/10.1093/acrefore/9780190228637.001.0001/acrefore-9780190228637-e-1243.

enough yet for you, Rome? Are you waiting for him to give birth?"[4] The way in which he states cynically "Does that not seem enough yet for you, Rome?" relays a sense that this was a rising systemic issue he was complaining about; we have to recall as well that Martial was born in provincial Hispania, so he may have seen all of this cultural shift from a very contrasting perspective, as to say cosmopolitan Rome.

In *Juvenal's* Second Satire (117AD), we hear of one Gracchus, "arraying himself in the flounces and train and veil of a bride," now a "new-made bride reclining on the bosom of her husband."[5]

Tacitus writes "Nero was already corrupted by every lust, natural and unnatural. But he now refuted any surmises that no further degradation was possible for him. For…he went through a formal wedding ceremony with one of the perverted gang called Pythagoras. The emperor, in the presence of witnesses, put on the bridal veil. Dowry, marriage bed, wedding torches, all were there. Indeed, everything was public which even in a natural union is veiled by night."[6]

As can be seen, it was very common for one of the partners to wear the bridal veil or stola – this would have been shocking to witness for Romans as they saw sexuality in terms of active and passive roles, masculine and feminine, and for one to take the passive role and adorn themselves in the clothes of women, would be to be seen as weak or without personal honour[7]. Apropos of the aforementioned quotes, we can find the historical Roman record of the period is replete with these types of writings. However, this slow cultural osmosis occurring during the late 1st and 2nd century AD became far more accepted, even commonplace, during the 3rd century AD. One Emperor, *Elagabalus* (218-222AD), married and

---

[4] Howell, Peter, editor. *Martial: The Epigrams, Book V* (XLII. ON CALLISTRATUS AND AFER.). Liverpool University Press, 1995. JSTOR, www.jstor.org/stable/j.ctv1228h00. Accessed 28 June 2021.
[5] Juvenal. *The satires of Juvenal*. As translated by G.G. Ramsay (1918). Satire 2 ("Moralists Without Morals"). London.
[6] Tacitus, Cornelius. *The Annals of Tacitus, Book XV, Chapter XXXVIII*. LCL 322: 270-271, London: Methuen & Co. Ltd., 1939. DOI: 10.4159
[7] Williams, *Roman Homosexuality*, p. 200.

then divorced five women. But he considered his male chariot driver to be his "husband," and he also married one *Zoticus*, a male athlete[8]. *Elagabalus* loved to dress up as the queen at public events; this would have been unthinkable to preceding Roman generations and would have led to large-scale public condemnation. Tangentially, in a more general sense, we take note that at least two of the Roman Emperors were in same-sex unions; and in fact, thirteen out of the first fourteen Roman Emperors are recorded to have been bisexual or exclusively homosexual[9]. The first Roman emperor to have married a man was *Nero*, who was reported to have married two other men on different occasions[10].

This type of sexual liberalisation that became rather quotidian, in its scope, had a noticeable effect upon the birth rates within the empire; naturally, a society of people lusting after every type of sexual gratification imaginable are less likely to have a stable family and raise well-rounded offspring. We know this to be apparent because Rome's population alone was declining by about 2% per decade from the 2nd to 4th centuries AD, of which intensified to 5% per decade from the 4th to 6th centuries AD[11]; alarmingly, we actually see higher rates than these within certain Western cities at present. The priest class of Rome tried to assuage this by regularly broadcasting and disseminating Paeans, to the glory of marriage; a Paean being a glorious song in the honour of something – typically, religious in nature. A considerable sum of other pro-marriage edicts was issued, but these all failed to stem the tide of demographic contraction. This being an acutely terrible problem for Rome as their volunteer military had a smaller pool to draw recruits from – and by the 4th century, *Foedus*, established treaties of mutual assistance, were being signed with barbarian tribes on the frontier of the empire to swell the Roman ranks. These barbarians would be drafted into the Roman military and in turn, once their period

---

[8] Scott, *Emperors and Usurpers*, p. 137.
[9] Hinsch, Bret. (1990). *Passions of the Cut Sleeve*. University of California Press. pp. 35–36.
[10] Cassius Dio. *"Roman History - Epitome of Book LXII"*. University of Chicago.
[11] Kevin Twine. (1992). *The City In Decline: Rome In Late Antiquity*. Middle States Geographers. Volume 25, pg. 135.

of service was complete, would receive land or citizenship, or both. At the inception of the practise these tribes were used as a type of mercenary auxiliary force but by the 5th century AD the *foederati* comprised a vast majority of the Roman military, and had assumed positions of power at the top military echelons in the empire; most notable of these was the late-Roman general *Stilicho*, of whom was of Vandal extraction and whose parents were both from the ranks of *foederati*[12].

In connection with the modern West, we have seen a similar disintegration of traditional sexual and cultural mores and, as a result, have witnessed decreased marriage rates, decreased birth rates and an increase in divorce rates[13]. Now, the West does not particularly rely on brute force to win military conflicts anymore – Western militaries have a greater array of capabilities at their disposal than their ancient counterparts, naturally – and as such the problem of decreased birth rates does not directly hamper our martial power, but it is debilitating to our economic potential. Just as the Roman empire of old federated and incorporated large swathes of foreign peoples into their empire to bolster their military, we invite a large swathe of immigrant workers to bolster our economy. You see, the issue with a declining population is that our civilisation is faced with the many complicated repercussions of such decline, that in turn feed into the initial problem. For example, population decline signals the onset of declining economic productivity, negative economic growth, and a contraction of the available domestic market base – all due to decreased participation in the labour market. The other issue is that less engineers and scientists will emerge within our societies; thus, creativity and technological advancement stalls – further damaging economic growth. However, I will touch upon this subject in detail in the economic section of the book, further on.

---

[12] Jones, *The Later Roman Empire, 284-602: A Social Economic and Administrative Survey*, 1986 (1964), pg. 620

[13] Esteban Ortiz-Ospina and Max Roser (2020) - *"Marriages and Divorces"*. Published online at OurWorldInData.org. Retrieved from: 'https://ourworldindata.org/marriages-and-divorces' [Online Resource]

Chapter II

A social acceptance of traditionally sexually prohibited behaviour, in a moral or legal sense, is not the issue in and of itself. The crux of the problem arises from the terminal affects felt by increased promiscuity and a mass societal acceptance of traditionally-viewed perverse behaviours; that is, the distraction and negative effect it poses to beginning a family and thus having a healthy number of well-rounded offspring, of whom you may impart your culture and the ideals of the civilisation to. We can see that from our present situation and the historical accounts previously stated. This is one of the quintessential markings of a civilisation in decline and the effects of which are debilitating for the promulgation of the traditional culture and civilisation, as a whole.

We can further see this type of decadency from the historical record in the of the era of the Abbasid Caliphs (750–1258). Now, for the first century and a half of Islamic rule over most of the Middle East, there was no evidence of deviation from sexual norms, but after the Abbasid Revolution of the 8th century AD, morals began to slip overtime[14]. Since the Abbasids were ruling over a vast swathe of territory, most of

> "Does that not seem enough yet for you, Rome?
> Are you waiting for him to give birth?"

it non-Islamic and non-Arabic, they had to make many concessions or face overthrow like that of the Umayyad Caliphate, which they had just ousted. Slowly foreign customs began to take hold in the royal court and then the capital city; Baghdad. *Al-Jahiz*, the famous Arabic author, explains at this period of time there was a vast array of lude music and dance practiced by *mukhannathun* (feminine men), and there was a great

---

[14] Rowson, Everett K. (30 December 2012) [15 December 2004]. *"HOMOSEXUALITY ii. IN ISLAMIC LAW"*. Encyclopædia Iranica. XII/4. New York: Columbia University. pg. 441–445. ISSN 2330-4804. Accessed 29/06/2021.

degree of "corruption of the morals" in the holy cities of Mecca and Medina – implying sexual deviancy was rife there[15]. We see from other records, there were around four thousand *ghulamiyyat* (females who dress as males) at the court of *Harun al-Rashid*, an Abbasid Caliph of the late 8th century[16]. *Salah Al-Din Al-Munajjid*, a modern Islamic scholar, discusses the way the commercialisation of such practises in this time took place – through the trading of slave boys and singing girls – and he comments as well upon the proliferation of these in the public discourse, in *ghazal* poetry[17]. Moreover, one of the famous Arabian poets, *Abu Nawas*, wrote many of these poems *Al-Munajjid* was most likely referring to. An excerpt from one of his more famous poems goes thus;

"My eyes are fixed upon his delightful body
And I do not wonder at his beauty.
His waist is a sapling, his face a moon,
And loveliness rolls off his rosy cheek"

These types of poems existed throughout the ostensible Islamic Golden Age (sometimes referred to by modern Islamic scholars as the *al-Jahiliyyah*, or the "age of ignorance") usually considered from the 8th to 13th century AD, approximately. This broad age brought with it much technological advancement and cultural works but replete throughout this age, specifically in the Abbasid Caliphate, was a proliferation of many, what would be considered by Islamic societies today, eccentric and forbidden (*Haram*) behaviours; most of all the social acceptance of the consumption of alcohol[18]. Many of the Golden Age Islamic rulers

---

[15] Bosworth, C. E.; van Donzel, E. J.; Heinrichs, W. P.; Lewis, B.; Pellat, Ch., eds. (1986). "Liwāṭ". *Encyclopaedia of Islam, Second Edition*. 5. Leiden: Brill Publishers. doi:10.1163/1573-3912_islam_SIM_4677. ISBN 978-90-04-16121-4.

[16] El-Feki. 2013. *Sex and the Citadel: Intimate Life in a Changing Arab World*, pg. 262

[17] Joseph A. Massad (2008). *Desiring Arabs*. Chicago: The University of Chicago Press Chicago and London. pg. 60.

[18] Harb, F. (1990). Wine poetry (khamriyyāt). In J. Ashtiany, T. Johnstone, J. Latham, & R. Serjeant (Eds.), *Abbasid Belles Lettres* (The Cambridge History of Arabic Literature, pp. 219-234). Cambridge: Cambridge University Press. doi:10.1017/CHOL9780521240161.015

– be them Abbasid, Umayyad, Aghlabid or Ghaznavid – were openly practising homosexuality and even pederasty[19]; in the case of *Emir Ibrahim II Aghlabid*[20]. For example, the Abbasid ruler *Al-Amin* (809–813AD) was said to have required slave women to be dressed in masculine clothing so he could be persuaded to have sex with them, and thus fulfil his monarchical duty and produce an heir[21]. The same was said of Andalusian *Caliph al-Hakam II* (915–976AD). Many great Arabic historians, poets and scholars would retrospectively remark upon the degeneration of the Arabic Caliphates of old, expressing "They deeply deplored [Arabs] the degeneracy of the times in which they lived, emphasising particularly the indifference to religion, the increasing materialism and the laxity of sexual morals. They lamented also the corruption of the officials of the government and the fact that the politicians always seemed to amass large fortunes while they were in office."[22]

The Abbasid Caliphate would collapse in the end, in 1258AD, but would go through extreme bouts of civil war, followed by power vacuums and the Caliphate becoming a weaker geo-political player in the later periods. The actual *age of decline* or *collapse* occurred after the culmination of the *Fourth Fitna* or Great Abbasid Civil War (811AD), I would argue, wherein the old political order was shattered, and precipitous territorial loss occurred, succeeding this moment. Leading up to the conclusion of the Golden Age of Islam, we find many theologians begin to become dogmatic and puritanical in their exhortations against the secular cultural fabric and especially of scientific inquiry[23]. Eventually, with the growing

---

[19] Boronha, M.A. (2014). *Male homosexuality in Islamic normative and in the mujun literature of al-Andalus and the Maghreb between the 10th and 13th centuries.*
[20] C.E. Bosworth, ed. et al., *"Liwat," The Encyclopedia of Islam*, New Edition. (Lei den: E.J. Brill, 1986), 5:777.
[21] Joubin, R. (2020). *The Multifarious Lives of the Sixth 'Abbasid Caliph Muhammad al-Amin: Collective Memory Construction, Queer Spaces, and Historical Television Drama in Egypt and Syria.* International Journal of Middle East Studies, 52(4), 643-663. doi:10.1017/S0020743820000793
[22] GLUBB, J. B., & GLUBB, J. B. (1978). *The Fate of Empires and Search for survival.* Edinburgh, Blackwood. Pg. 15.
[23] Hillel Ofek. (2011). *Why the Arabic World Turned Away from Science: On the lost Golden Age and the rejection of reason.* Available: https://www.thenewatlantis.com/publications/why-the-arabic-world-turned-away-from-science. Last accessed 02/07/2021.

number of *madrasas* and decreased versatility of the Islamic economies, post-Mongol invasion, it became far more politically sensible to provide patronage to religious works and knowledge, rather than scientific.

Conversely, we witnessed a similar type of puritanism at the end of the Roman empire, and we find ourselves with similar cults – though, secular in tone – in our modern society. I could mention the moral decline of the Athenian empire, encapsulated after the outright control over the Delian League, and Ottoman empire but I would not wish to belabour the point.

Pessimism and Religious Osmosis

On the idea of pessimism and the infectivity of it, within a society that is experiencing *en masse* degradation, within the sixth and seventh ages, that of *decadence* and *collapse*, is truly fascinating to witness, but terrifying in the rapid ruination it reaps. This type of pathological disease takes hold of its host, spreading like an aggressive cancer, it greedily consumes the entirety of its victim, until all that remains is a befouled shell of what once was. We can see the effects widespread pessimism is having upon our society at present; where once we stood for something, had a sense of natural right and wrong, and strived for something better for our progeny. Now, where are we? Our values have been boiled down to politically charged buzzwords, our political careerist elite are interested in nothing else than amassing illicit wealth pilfered from the coffers of the nation and conspicuously displaying it, and our societal landscape is one mired in disunity, and ensuing political and racial balkanisation. However, if you speak to many, especially the educated and idealistic among us, and they are becoming more numerous by the day, they believe us to be at a period of history where we are by far the most sophisticated, morally righteous, cosmopolitan, and progressive generation to ever have walked the Earth. Consequently, the irony is almost poetic, as you will see this type of vain hubris is not the mark of a people living at a civilisational

Chapter II

zenith, but a people who are living in the bearish phase of what was once a great nation. Accordingly, this illustrated set of behaviour is archetypical of an empire, or civilisation, busily in the midst of deconstructing itself.

We can see from the historical record that, for example, the Roman republic was robust and confident within its abilities and were unyielding to invaders. I draw the reader's attention to the disastrous Battle of Cannae where *Hannibal* and his force of Carthaginians, and their mercenary allies, slaughtered an estimated twenty percent of every fighting man Rome could muster, between the ages of eighteen and fifty[24]. The Romans proceeding this became even more determined and emboldened in their resistance, and new senatorial armies were mustered en masse; citizens would also destroy their crops to deny the marauding Carthaginian raiders supplies[25]. Another example was at the early breathes of the republic, in which it was repeatedly on the verge of extinction from its northern rivals of Etruscan kings and Gallic chieftains, and the southern adversaries of the Samnites and other opposing Italic tribes. In 390BC, Rome was sacked by *Brennan*, likely a title meaning a Gallic King, and just narrowly escaped utter extirpation by way of bribing the invading Gauls (*Senones*) to leave; the Gauls would meet their demise at the hands of the Romans some four centuries later, in a strange twist of fate[26]. What was apparent from these early defeats is that Rome bounced back from them stronger than ever, displaying an indomitable spirit that could not be broken – they were an example of an optimistic people, whose leadership was working within their interests to preserve their civilisation; to learn from their moments of failure. Juxtaposed to this, we can see later in the imperial period at the cataclysmic battle of Edessa, in 260AD, where emperor *Valerian* and 70,000 Roman troops were captured or killed by Persian *Shahanshah Shapur I*, and this, instead of unifying

---

[24] Gabriel, *Scipio Africanus,* pg. 49.
[25] Strauss, Barry (2013). *Masters of Command: Alexander, Hannibal, Caesar, and the Genius of Leadership.* Simon and Schuster. p. 88. ISBN 9781439164495.
[26] Livy (1924) *The History of Rome,* Benjamin Oliver Foster, ed., Cambridge, Massachusetts, USA: Harvard University Press, Book 5, chapter 48.

and emboldening the empire with resolve and vigour for vengeance, it fractured and nearly collapsed it into chaos until the *Restitutor Orbis*, restorer of the world, arrived in the form of emperor *Aurelian*[27]. Later catastrophic military defeats at the hands of former *foederati* Goths and Alans at the battle of Adrianople, 378AD, also signify this cultural weakening. As in the aftermath of Adrianople, with the luxury we possess of historical distance, we witness the weak response to this by the Roman leadership. Did they attempt to assimilate, exterminate or fight tooth-and-nail to extinguish this threat – which were once ostensible allies – from their frontier? No, under *Theodosius I*, they were once again hailed as allies and embraced as such in a spirit of peace[28]. They would later pick apart the empire like vultures, establishing kingdoms of their own from the carcass of their former masters, Western Rome. Likely so, this was caused by a multivariable and systemic issue within the empire – be it political instability, deep-rooted cultural and moral rot, a pessimism within the empire, a populace of whose attentions were diverted to trivial pastimes, or a false sense of security in that they could never fall no matter how much was taken from the empire – whatever the reason, we see similarities within our own civilisation's slow demise. For example, our leaders too seem unable to act resilient and defiant in the face of attacks upon our civilisation by foreign foes and subversive revolutionaries, amassed on and within our borders; some leaders even side with them and further the cause championed by them[29][30]; at the detriment of our own civilisation, mind you. At the same time, within our educational institutions and expressed within governmental policy is a growing

---

[27] Edward Gibbon and J.B. Bury. 1914. *The history of the decline and fall of the Roman empire.* New York, (NY: Macmillan), pg. 294.
[28] Williams, Stephen; Friell, Gerard. Theodosius: *The Empire at Bay* (First American ed.). Yale University Press. ISBN 978-0-300-06173-4. Pg. 32
[29] AFP. (2021). *New Zealand has duty to support Muslim community, says Jacinda Ardern.* Available: https://www.thenews.com.pk/latest/803742-new-zealand-has-duty-to-support-muslim-community-says-jacinda-ardern. Last accessed 09/07/2021.
[30] Andrew Gleeson. (2020). *Seattle's Summer of Love.* Available: https://quillette.com/2020/06/16/seattles-summer-of-love/. Last accessed 09/07/2021.

resentment to our traditional culture and religious traditions; churches, marriage and Western traditions are mocked and ridiculed, in the media apparatus, as relics of a by-gone age of intolerance and bigotry[31].

Interestingly, *Theodosius I* was also famous or infamous, depending upon one's opinion, for the wide-scale intolerance for and militant attacks to Graeco-Roman and other pagans throughout the empire[32]. He oversaw and permitted the destruction of Roman temples, disbanding of the Vestal Virgins, the outlawing of pagan rituals on punishment of death, legislating that traditional Roman holidays were to be reassigned as workdays, and the refusal to restore the *Alter of Victory* in the Senate. His actions were profane to traditional Romans and indicated that he was fanatical in his Nicene faith, as he oversaw the total deculturisation of Rome. He did everything mortally possible to ensure the empire would be crippled beyond all repair and be without any resolve to resist the future barbarian threats that would be arrayed against it. It collapsed less than fifty years later. Our history and images of veneration too are being destroyed, similarly; though, how long shall we outlive the consequences of this cultural dissolution and transformation?

Moreover, as a final point upon Theodosius I, a very interesting character indeed, would be to state that our current generation of political leaders have very much been canonised or baptised, if you will, into the modern-day equivalent of the Nicene cult, that being Marxism. Both the Nicene Cult and Marxism are and were urban phenomenon until they grew in power[33]. This modern-day incarnation of the early militant form of Christianity, has the same modus operandi and incumbent virtues as its historical predecessor. That is, it seeks to acquire political power to thus ensure it can remake society in its own unnatural image; it is

---

[31] PHAROS. (2019). *"Western Civilization" means Classics…and White Supremacy.* Available: https://pharos.vassarspaces.net/2019/01/25/western-civilization-means-classics-and-white-supremacy/. Last accessed 09/07/2021.
[32] Hughes, Philip (1949), "6", *A History of the Church*, I (rev ed.), Sheed & Ward.
[33] Stark, R. (1991). *Christianizing the Urban Empire: An Analysis Based on 22 Greco-Roman Cities*. Sociological Analysis, 52(1), 77-88. doi:10.2307/3710716: "Christianity was first and foremost an urban movement…"

puritanical in its philosophy and openly hostile to the society at large, of whom it sees as immoral actors; it believes itself to be righteous above all and propagates moral virtues, even while conducting heinous acts; it calls for the deculturisation and dismantling of traditional forms of culture and morality; it holds any who would oppose it as heretics and thus to be dealt with violently (we can see this from the current riotous behaviour in the West, circa 2020); and finally, it has infiltrated the hierarchy of the state and bureaucracy, imposing draconian and unpopular sweeping rectifications upon society.

> They would later pick apart the empire like vultures, establishing kingdoms of their own from the carcass of their former masters, Western Rome

However, the question could be posed, what did the Romans do whilst their civilisation and culture was being plainly demolished before their own eyes? The answer is they drunk, were perpetually merry and cared for little other than the spectacle of gladiatorial battles and the green and blue chariot races. In fact, the Nika riots of 532AD is a prime example of the fervour surrounding these sporting events. The divisiveness of the Green versus Blue chariot teams, within the Hippodrome, became the focus of social and political issues and a visceral form of urban balkanisation. *Justinian I*, the Byzantine Emperor at the time, supported the Blue team. On 531AD, some men from the Blue and Green team were wanted in connection with hooligan like murders that occurred at a chariot race some months back. The murderers were to be executed and most were but in January, 532AD, two of them escaped and were taking refuge in a local church, where they were being defended by a large mob. *Justinian I*, whilst seeking peace with the Persians following the Iberian war, did not wish for civil strife to ensue within his city. Therefore, he commuted the sentence of the criminals to imprisonment and held chariot games for later on in the month. The mob, Blues and Greens, being emboldened by the mollification of the mob by *Justinian I*, wished for nothing less than the complete pardoning of the criminals. This entire riot bears striking resemblance to what is unfolding in the West, circa 2020.[34]

The chariot race began in earnest on January 13th 532AD. The crowd were hurling insults at Justinian I all day, but the partisan chants of "Blues" and "Greens" quickly transformed into "*Nika!*", meaning "Victory" or "Conquer". The crowd then began storming the imperial palace which was located next to the Hippodrome. The palace was then besieged for the next five days and political rivals to *Justinian I*, seeing this as an opportunity to depose the emperor, demanded the removal of certain court officials and, in the resultant power vacuum, crowned a new emperor, *Hypatius*. Whilst this was occurring, the Hagia Sophia was made asunder and half of the city was put to the torch; looting and mayhem was occurring. Later the situation was stabilised and within the Hippodrome, the Blues and Greens were slaughtered indiscriminately under the command of the generals Mundus and Belisarius; 30,000 in total are said to have lost their life. Thus, we may conclude that this situation of riotous behaviour, was caused by the overall unorthodox reforms of *Justinian I*.[35]

The riots and civil turmoil that plagued Nika fifteen-hundred years ago, now plagues us. The current situation of riots is caused by similar divisive political and social strife – the main focal point or villain being an unorthodox populist reformer – and churches and private property are being attacked and destroyed. The ones who oppose the mob are beaten and, sometimes, murdered as we have seen. These types of riots, as were seen in Nika, were not new to Roman society, but Nika was by far the bloodiest, and many of the other riots occurred prior to the collapse of Western Rome and within the crisis of the third century; that period having widespread peasant revolts – but they were largely conducted

---

[34] J. B. Bury, "The Nika Revolt", chapter XV part 5, *History of the Later Roman Empire* (1923).
[35] Heather, P. J. (Peter J.) (2018). *Rome resurgent: war and empire in the age of Justinian.* New York, NY. Pg. 1.

because of socio-economic concerns rather than religious, political or social divisions, as we see now. Riots, we must recall, are not in and of themselves a sign of decline or collapse – *Justinian I* would oversee the largest expansion of Roman territory, since the time of Caesar and Augustus, nonetheless – but they do herald a potentiality for further decline if left unresolved and, with other compounding factors, may be the spark that lights the tinderbox.

Another poignantly illustrative example akin to *Justinian*'s populist reformations, and the resultant societal division sown from such acts, would be the short and spontaneous rebellion instigated by *Tiberius Gracchus*, a People's Tribune, who attempted to bring about radical land reforms – which naturally empowered the plebeians at the expense of the patrician and senatorial classes. Thus, he met a grizzly and brutal end when he was cut down in the street and unceremoniously dumped in the river Tiber[36]. I will discuss the idea of revolutions being unquestionably a tool primarily employed by the merchant or aristocratic classes in a later section. Naturally, rebellions of peasants – without capital backing them – rarely succeeds.

HEROES AND CELEBRITIES

What is very interesting is that in the depths of modernity, of which we find ourselves in, we see "celebrities" - or those worthy of celebration - as actors, reality TV personalities, chefs, and sports stars; whereas in past centuries it was statesmen, generals, or genius inventors. What has caused this overall shift in our thinking on this matter? Are the *Kardashians* really worthy of the same acclamation as say, a brilliant statesman or a genius inventor? What worth do they provide to the civilisation, besides mindless entertainment for an audience of cognitively puerile troglodytes? The answer is nothing, to the contrary they provide a detrimental effect upon society as a whole, one may argue.

---

[36] Plutarch, *The Parallel Lives'*, *"The Life of Tiberius Gracchus,"*, pg. 4.

Chapter II

Why are these people then touted as wondrous and glamorous individuals, worthy of exaltation, a type of apotheosis if you will, above all of us lowly mortals? The answer is that this is what declining societies cling to at the terminus of their lifecycle. It may be subconscious even, but they are diligently scurrying about attempting to find what made the civilisation great, what were its endearing values, and how can they recapture the magic of old. The answer, by and large, always falls to "Celebritising" entertainers and chefs during the *age of decadence*. As *Sir John Glubb* stated, "frivolity is the frequent companion of pessimism"[37]. During the declining phases of the Roman, Spanish and even Ottoman Empires, chefs began to be almost exalted as semi-divine deities and glorified as geniuses[38]. This is due to the peculiar pattern of pessimism within a dishevelled civilisation, on the long road of descent. That is, they universally do not feel great anymore – however they might feel virtuous or morally progressive, but that is different – and they feel less powerful, and less accomplished, than their ancestors. Therefore, though they cannot create great works of artistic splendour, technological innovations or even conquer vast swathes of land as their ancestors had once done, they alternatively search for it in areas of culinary delight, fashion, Avant-Garde "art", music, theatre or movies, or even literary works such as magazines or fiction books. However, this will not satiate people and they will constantly push the boundaries of these various mediums of culture, in a vain attempt to rekindle the discoveries and exploits of old[39]. This ultimately finds its end in these forms of media becoming corrupted and morally repugnant, as would be perceived by older generations. This entire chaotic situation always ends in perversion, of some description, and the peoples of a decaying civilisation will always be addicted to perversion and sex; as I have previously discussed. They

---
[37] Glubb, J. (1978). The Fate of Empires and Search for Survival. Edinburgh: Blackwood. Pg. 14.
[38] (2016). *Why Celebrity Chefs Herald the End of Empire*. Available: https://www.ask-therightquestion.org/politicians-have-discovered-a-new-role-that/. Last accessed 22/07/2021.
[39] Joseph Epstein. (2015). *Empire, Erudition and Entertainment*. Available: https://www.wsj.com/articles/empire-erudition-and-entertainment-1448661415. Last accessed 22/07/2021.

will lose their spiritual compass, will become morally bankrupt, and will seek escapism within superficial materialism. What have we seen in these avowed modern days? Just like the Roman plebiscites of old - with their demands for free meals, public games, gladiatorial shows, chariot racing, and athletic events – the modern mob's passions lie in the demand for free money (UBI and the enlarging of the welfare state), public sporting events of national significance, reality TV and feebleminded game shows, and every type of addictive substance, sexual perversion and ignorance-inducing amusement modern man may fathom; all nicely endorsed by the media and approved by the government. We have become anaesthetised by infantile entertainment and a reliance upon that which makes us the sick man of the world. Moreover, these aforementioned issues compound to create a citizenry of who are irreligious, lacking in spirituality and who resemble one-dimensional beings rather than complex actors with agency.

Friedrich Nietzsche described his idea of the "last man", of whom would inhabit the twilight of Western civilisation, as an animal without dignity or uniqueness. "*En masse*, he represents the multiplication of zero by zero. That he is more insect than man"; obeying his short-term impulses for pleasure; he is thus a slave to pleasure. *Herbert Marcuse* stated something similar concerning the future "one-dimensional man". We have condensed the idea of individuality, in current times, into boorish axioms such as "everyone has their own truth" and "you only live once", these have become almost widely accepted and fashionable epistemic maxims of our age. The Romans had "Carpe Diem" and the oldest surviving musical composition, from 2nd century AD Greek Anatolia, part of the Roman empire at the time of its creation, the lyrics read: "While you live, shine; have no grief at all; life exists only for a short while; and Time demands his due". Similar in tenor to the biblical adage, stated by *Isaiah*, "let us eat and drink, for tomorrow we die."[40]

---

[40] Anna Mar. (2019). *6 Characteristics of The Last Man*. Available: https://simplicable.com/new/last-man-nietzche. Last accessed 22/07/2021.

Chapter II

Alas, many individuals in the modern West today, while having a world of literature and information at their finger-tips, pride themselves on not knowing anything concerning politics, history, geo-political events, and even current news events – however, ask them of the latest *Kardashian* scandal and they could relay to you an in-depth report upon it. Correspondingly, the citizens of Rome, passionately transfixed to their own forms of entertainment, relaxing their once vivacious spirit, were totally oblivious to the fact that the entire empire was collapsing around them.

Foreign Migration

One of the central reasons an empire or civilisation becomes weaker is through the effects of mass-migration[41]. The effect being that of reduced social cohesion, economic burdens (due to a dependence upon a universal welfare state), and the opening up of new theatres of division – be them ethnic, political, or religious. We can currently see a great deal of imported political, religious and ethnic division within modern Western nations. For example, the Sunni and Shi'a divide which has become increasingly sectarian in the modern-era has been imported here, the persecuted religious minority groups – such as the Yazidi, Assyrian Nestorian Christians, the Alawites, and Muʿtazilism, but to name a few – are considered heretical by Sunni and Shi'a alike, and major ethno-religious divisions such as Jews and Muslims, Kurds and Turks, Armenians and Turks, Kurds and other Muslims, and Alawites and Sunni, are all now present here. This growing plethora of divisive issues leads to the fracturing of a society, the disintegration of its social cohesion, and the growing localisation of power, within distinct ethno-religious enclaves and communities; for example, a growing push for Islamic law

---

[41] *How immigration destroyed Rome.* Oxford historian Peter Heather has re-examined the *Fall of Rome*. His new book, *The Fall of the Roman Empire*, holds many lessons for today… (n.d.) >The Free Library. (2014). Retrieved Jul 22 2021 from https://www.thefreelibrary.com/How+immigration+destroyed+Rome.+Oxford+historian+Peter+Heather+has…-a0141907543

to overtake the various common or civil law structures within European nations.[42]

To elucidate my point further, in the Roman empire, with the mass migration of so many diverse peoples, each with their own sectarian issues and tribal affiliations, into the territorial area of the empire, be them barbarians or eastern nomads, the over-stretched legions found themselves unable to maintain the passivity and control of them. Moreover, the growing localisation of power, within the late-imperial period of the empire, translated into an increasing multitude of Roman Citizens being unwilling to care to remain spiritually or nationally connected to the capital or the Italian heartland, from which borne the famous superstate. This ensured that the increasingly large numbers of federated barbarians (*foederati*), who were becoming regional internal powers in and of themselves, could better provide for the citizenry than an overtaxing, bloated relic such as late-period Rome. That being said, as we can bear witness to, mass-immigration quickly saturates a population with a foreign culture, or a weak cosmopolitan mishmash of one, and most importantly foreign priorities. Since most of the Roman military was no longer made up of men from the areas of Latin culture, of the "founding peoples" of the empire, the priorities of the military were vastly different; they were far more centred around increasing political power for their various tribes or religious denominations. Additionally, barbarian recruits could be paid less, and could be swayed to fight against anyone; and were thus less loyal to the empire in times of emergency; the Hunnic invasions being the most salient example.[43]

Immigration, more precisely, is not what administers the *coup de grâce* but is a symptom of a weakening of the pre-eminence of the national spirit amongst the various other bordering nations, or barbarians amassing at the borders – biding their time for the final rush for wealth and land once the

---

[42] Damon Embling & Aissa Boukanoun. (2018). *Islam Party stirs controversy ahead of Belgian elections*. Available: https://www.euronews.com/2018/04/26/islam-party-stirs-controversy-ahead-of-belgian-elections. Last accessed 22/07/2021.

[43] Peter Heather, *The Fall of the Roman Empire*, Pan Books, 2005, 158ff.

empire is in an infirmed state, that of forlorn hope. Immigration is simply a symptom that magnifies the greater illness afflicting the civilisation, it magnifies the already growing political or religious divide, heightening the potential for civil strife, the cultivation of internal enmities. *J.P. Rushton's Theory of Ethnic Nepotism*, a study which sheds light upon the link between social cohesion, the increased propensity for violence, social trust and isolationism in relation to national ethnic diversity; the link shown was more ethnic diversity equates to a lessening of social cohesion[44]. *Sir John Glubb* stated, in his work "*Fate of Empires and Search for Survival*", that, I quote, "One of the oft-repeated phenomena of great empires is the influx of foreigners to the capital city."[45] As we can see as of the present day, great Western capitals such as London, Berlin and Paris are comprised of either majority foreign-born or of individuals of second-generation foreign extraction. As to the process of transformation of the ethnic landscape, the statistical projections of such demographic change within Western nations and cities warrants it a likely outcome. *Sir John Glubb* goes on to detail his point on foreign influx, as a symptom of a civilisation in decline, he states,

"Second - or third-generation - foreign immigrants may appear outwardly to be entirely assimilated, but they often constitute a weakness in two directions. First, their basic Human nature often differs from that of the original imperial stock. If the earlier imperial race was stubborn and slow-moving, the immigrants might come from more emotional races, thereby introducing cracks and schisms into the national policies, even if all were equally loyal."

We can witness this type of migrant behaviour begin to manifest itself within Western countries right now. We can see this in countries such as France, Germany, Netherlands and the UK, where a sizeable contingent of second or third generation European-born Muslims began flooding

---

[44] Salter, F., & Harpending, H. *J.P. Rushton's theory of ethnic nepotism*. Personality and Individual Differences (2012); http://dx.doi.org/10.1016/j.paid.2012.11.014
[45] Glubb, J. (1978). The Fate of Empires and Search for Survival. Edinburgh: Blackwood. Pg. 13.

the ranks of the Islamic State; whilst, even after this, a growing number continue to be radicalised and instructed to hold very opposing views to general Western enlightenment values. In addition, *Trevor Philips*, former chair of the Equality and Human Rights Commission, stated in 2016 that Muslims are "becoming a nation within a nation"[46]. However, we typically find that this is not unique to Muslim migrants solely, but a trait observed within every migrant group or minority – that being said, it is only natural for these peoples to self-segregate, evolutionarily speaking.

Sir John Glubb goes on to express "Second, while the nation is still affluent, all the diverse races may appear equally loyal. But in an acute emergency, the immigrants will often be less willing to sacrifice their lives and their property than will be the original descendants of the founder race." This was witnessed within the federated barbarian tribes of the Roman empire, the foreign Mameluke overthrow of the Ayyubid dynasty and from the growing instability we are seeing in the modern West. Where, it has been a slowly ascending trend for, foreign migrant communities are seeking either reparation for historical transgressions or greater degrees of, what has been termed, affirmative action. Moreover, we seem to see homegrown terrorist attacks on a monthly basis, too.

Glubb expounds the issue further: "Third, the immigrants are liable to form communities of their own, protecting primarily their own interests, and only in the second degree that of the nation as a whole. Fourth, many of the foreign immigrants will probably belong to races originally conquered by and absorbed into the empire. While the empire is enjoying its "High Noon" (*age of commerce and affluence*) of prosperity, all these people are proud and glad to be imperial citizens. But when decline sets in, it is extraordinary how the memory of ancient wars, perhaps centuries before, is suddenly revived, and local or provincial movements appear demanding secession or independence."[47] We can see this in the context

---

[46] Phillips, Trevor (2016-04-10). *What do British Muslims really think?* The Times. Last Accessed: 22/07/2021

[47] Glubb, J. (1978). *The Fate of Empires and Search for Survival.* Edinburgh: Blackwood. Pg. 13-14.

of the USA at present, where the African diaspora population, with contingents of cultish Marxist revolutionaries, are becoming increasingly overtly hostile to the majority "founding peoples" and actively seek reparations for past injustices, wish to remake the historical and religious iconography within their own image, and demand a greater degree of societal prominence; be it in the sphere of education or in the realm of popular culture.[48]

We can see in this excerpt from the satirist and populist of 2nd century AD Rome, *Juvenal*, that there was a general disdain for the growing "Hellenisation" of Rome; via Greek and eastern immigration. He stated, "Now let me say something about that race that most appals me. I just can't stand our city full of Greeks. For too long now the East has dumped this scum into our beloved Tiber, carrying with them their language and habits, their flutes and ridiculous stringed instruments. What a travesty! Foreigners just blown into Rome get a better deal than I do; I, who drew my first breath in the city."[49] These are quintessential murmurs of discontent so often heard in the beginnings of a waning civilisation, and ominously these are sentiments all too familiar to the ears of the modern Westerner. Like *Juvenal*, more than two millennia ago, Westerners too feel a growing sense of disenfranchisement; like they are being undermined by their very leaders and nepotism, in favour of the foreigner, is becoming growingly apparent to them. This only broadens the ever-present myriad of internal issues and divisions extant within society. However, the majority of the parent culture and ethnicity are wilfully enthralled in the base excitements of the bread and circuses on display for them; they remain comfortably numb in their complacent assumption that they will remain masters of the world, until the end of time. Naturally, they are obviously mad in this assumption and will succumb to it, unless it is discarded swiftly.

---

[48] Prager, J. (2017), *Do Black Lives Matter? A Psychoanalytic Exploration of Racism and American Resistance to Reparations. Political Psychology*, 38: 637-651. https://doi.org/10.1111/pops.12436

[49] Juvenal, & translation by Ramsay, G. (1918). *The Satires of Juvenal*. London. Satire III.

As a final concluding notion, I harken back to the words of *Sir John Glubb*, in which he summarises the major characteristics of the previous ages of civilisational outburst and conquest. He articulates this sentiment, and I find it fitting to end on, "In the age of the first outburst and the subsequent *Age of Conquests*, the race is normally ethnically more or less homogeneous. This state of affairs facilitates a feeling of solidarity and comradeship. But in the *Ages of Commerce and Affluence*, every type of foreigner does flood into the great city, the streets of which are reputed to be paved with gold"[50]. In the modern age, we hear several migrants, especially those within the migrant or refugee crisis of late, talk about Europe as though it is a magical place where no one need work and the streets are, quite literally, paved with fine gold[51]. I truly wish this was the case, for them and for myself, but it is not and delivers a distressing sentiment to us: what happens when these impoverished people come to realise that Europe does not have streets paved with gold and the houses are not lavishly adorned, Romanesque marble palaces? What type of societal tension occurs when it is learned that Europe is an economically deteriorating continent, collapsing under the weight of a mismanaged monetary system and an unpropitious and infinitely expanding welfare state? One shudders to think.

Democratisation of Enfranchisement

What we find, be it an aspect that furthers decline or be it just a symptom of the *age of decadence*, is that enfranchisement and liberties is extended

---

[50] Glubb, J. (1978). *The Fate of Empires and Search for Survival*. Edinburgh: Blackwood. Pg. 13.
[51] David Smith. (2009). *Letter from Africa: land of opportunity turns out to be another dead end*. Available: https://www.theguardian.com/world/2009/jul/07/letter-from-africa-johannesburg. Last accessed 22/07/2021. "I came to America because I heard the streets were paved with gold. When I got here, I found out three things: first, the streets weren't paved with gold; second, they weren't paved at all; and third, I was expected to pave them."

to every aspect of the society[52]. The clamour for impossible equality, as deluded and unnatural as it may be, is something that defines the spirit of this age. We typically find traditional gender roles within society are undermined and the patriarchal order has been inverted[53]. Female empowerment is not the crux of the affliction during this period - the actual danger for the society stems from the indication that the male populace has become less assertive and overly apathetic. Thus, females have commandeered the role, within this power vacuum, of becoming the socio-political dominant sex[54]. Moreover, with the greater degree of power and influence women gain – be it in their individual vocations, or in the external political and societal environment – they become less and less reliant upon a husband. One can easily prove this point by simply bearing witness to the parallel rise of divorce rates and female labour participation; and thus, personnel income increases [55]. Needless to say, this then has a discordant causal effect upon not just birth rates, but the quality of the generations that postdate this societal shift. As a side note, as you will be aware, I have made numerous allusions to the fact that all of these aggregate issues that arise within an aging society not just hasten the eventual civilisational death, but further instigate the accumulation of more fissures forming within the civilisational fabric, so to say; thus, creating the compounding effect that leads to a cacophony of disarray within the conventional order.

It is analogous to a fly within the web of a spider. The fly, symbolic of civilisation, is flying, strong and free, throughout its domain. Then,

---

[52] Being Human, God and science, History, Religion. (2015). *Rome and America: Feminism destroys*. Available: http://blogmekrystle.com/2015/04/rome-and-america-feminism-destroys/. Last accessed 07/08/2021.

[53] Brandon Marlon. (2015). *The Decline and Fall of Modern Civilization: 8 Simple Steps to Squandering It All*. Available: https://www.algemeiner.com/2015/01/22/the-decline-and-fall-of-modern-civilization-8-simple-steps-to-squandering-it-all/. Last accessed 07/08/2021.

[54] Glubb, J. (1978). *The Fate of Empires and Search for Survival*. Edinburgh: Blackwood. Pg. 15.

[55] Bremmer, D., Kesselring, R. *Divorce and female labour force participation: Evidence from times-series data and cointegration*. Atlantic Economic Journal 32, 175–190 (2004). https://doi.org/10.1007/BF02299436

without warning, it finds itself caught within the ensnaring web strings of the spider. The sticky strands of the web, symbolic of the varied issues arising from a waning civilisation, latch onto the fly with an unbreakable grip. The more the, now fragile, fly thrashes and resists, the greater the grip intensifies and the more strands of the web it becomes latched to. The fly, aware of impending doom, glimpses the merciless spider – symbolic of collapse or the essence of decay. The spider slowly creeps to the fly; all the whilst the fly becomes more and more tired and disparaged from its incessant struggling with the innumerable and enshrouding tendrils of the web. The spider then arrives at the tired and worn-out body of the fly. Towering ominously over the fly, and in absence of any mercy, it administers its poisonous death blow to its defenceless victim. The spider, once satiated with this meal, hides and awaits the arrival of a new meal to its trap – and thus, the cycle repeats, ad infinitum.

This trap of the spider is as unavoidable to the fly, as civilisational entropy is to us. No civilisation in history has outlived these cyclical patterns. However, I disagree with *Sir John Glubb*'s assertion that empires can only survive for a set period of ten generations, or two-hundred and fifty years approximately. I would argue that with structured populist reformations, such as in Rome and later Byzantine Rome, we find a civilisation that constantly evolved and adapted to the new geopolitical order – until internal political strife and external enemies became too much for it to bear.

Digressing, if we take a look also at the famous *Calhoun Experiment*, we find that another mammalian species, namely mice, also seem to suffer from the same collective decay derived from either overpopulation or lack of harshness, or predation within their environment. *Dr. Calhoun*'s "Mouse Utopia Experiment", in 1973, attempted to see the sole effects overpopulation had on a mammalian societal grouping; hoping to infer findings that could be pertinent to Humanities future. He created a colony in which could, theoretically, be housed three-thousand mice - he kept the rodent inhabitants of this colony well-fed, well-nourished and they had a sizeable area to explore, too.[56]

He began to notice several alarming patterns of negative behaviour, in the late-period colony, of which he called "Behavioural Sinks", and he also identified four phases of growth and decline within the colony. Phases A-D; Phase A was typified with exploration and acclimatisation to the surrounding environment; Phase B was characteristic of a population boom and the population doubled every sixty-days, fledgling social hierarchies were formed here too; Phase C was the phase of equilibrium, where the mouse population plateaued at two-thousand two-hundred, and the territorial and social orders were all well-established; Phase D, the final stage, exhibited a period of precipitous putrescence, titled the "Behavioural sink", and ultimately leading to self-extinction. More than that, during the final phase, *Calhoun* witnessed a peculiar series of behaviours amongst the mouse population - including everything from sexual deviation to cannibalism. Furthermore, some mice displayed introverted behaviour and self-isolated from the others, only coming out to feed when the other mice were sleeping. There were also two behaviourally distinct variants of mice that became apparent – one, titled the "beautiful ones", whose life was devoted to grooming, eating, sleeping and being perfect representations of the species, and the other becoming unpredictably violent, especially to mice deemed to be extramural to the established social clique. Interestingly too, the "Beautiful ones" seemed to be unable to cope properly with abnormal stimuli and lacked the inquisitiveness inherent in the species; they were, for all intents and purposes, extraordinarily stupid. However, both variants had males within them that became rejected by the females of the group, who had taken a more dominant role within the hierarchy at this point, and consequently withdrew from the group dynamic; indicating a loss

---

[56] Calhoun, John B. (1962). *"Population density and social pathology"*. Scientific American. 206 (3): 139–148. doi:10.1038/scientificamerican0262-139 (inactive 31 May 2021). PMID 13875732.

of purpose within them. What is also fascinating to behold from this experiment too, is what *Calhoun* also noted about the females within the last phase, and this has direct parallels with our modern society, that they begin to ignore or abandon their offspring and that they begin to project masculine traits; such as aggression and territoriality. *Calhoun*, further noted, regarding the more youthful members of the society, that they vie with the more established, and older members, for social occupancy; this subsequently leads to the near total breakdown of the social order. These correlations are seen within the intragroup behaviours of our modern society; divorce rates are skyrocketing, declining birth-rates, a breakdown of the hierarchical order, an elite who narcissistically flaunt conspicuous displays of wealth and their own self-assuredness, to a growing feminist movement who openly despise males and encourage female hostility to any sort of tradition, and a youth who hold the wisdom of their elders in a state of total disregard and insolently rebel against the ideals of every preceding generation.[57]

The historical precedence for these types of behaviours and shift in power dynamics between the sexes in the stages of civilisation can be seen in the Abbasid Caliphate and Roman empire. The Roman empire, postdating the 2nd century AD, was described in complaint by Roman citizens, and in jest by barbarians, that "Rome rules the world, but women ruled Rome". Moreover, in the Arab Empire of the 10th century, *Sir John Glubb* writes, "In the tenth century, a similar tendency was observable in the Arab Empire, the women demanding admission to the professions hitherto monopolised by men. 'What,' wrote the contemporary historian, *Ibn Bassam*, 'have the professions of clerk, tax-collector or preacher to do with women? These occupations have always been limited to men alone.' Many women practised law, while others obtained posts as university professors. There was an agitation for the appointment of female

---

[57] Hall, Edward, T. (1966). *The Hidden Dimension: An Anthropologist Examines Humans' Use of Space in Public and in Private.* Anchor Books. p. 25.

judges..."⁵⁸. We can corroborate this by the long list of female champions in education, medicine and legal fields at the end of the 9th and turn of the 10th century. I would like to stress again; this is not to demean the role of women in society or in these fields, they breathe literal life into civilisation after all, but this is actually an indication of a seismic shift in cultural attitudes and an indication of the lessening forthrightness and hardiness of the males within the society; of which they typically held the traditional role of dominance and were responsible for the initial outbursts of conquest. Some of the most notable women during this period include *Fatima al-Fihri*, an Arab educator credited with founding the oldest existing, continually operating and first degree-awarding university in the world, the University of al-Qarawiyyin in Fez, Morocco in 859AD⁵⁹. Moreover, *Sutayta al-Mahamili*, who was a polymath from Baghdad, was credited with creating the algebraic formula of inheritance and furthered the development of mathematics⁶⁰. Additionally, *Mariam "Al-Astrolabiya" Al-Ijliya*, who was employed at the Hamdanid court in the 10th century, who created astrolabes, a type of analogue computer of inclinometer, which is utilised to solve several astronomical problems⁶¹. There is a plethora of female poets and authors too, beginning from approximately the 8th century, and this shows the beginning of a shift towards a weakening of the religious orthodoxy. Ironically, this is considered a Golden Age of Islam, but it seems the period was populated with a greater adherence to Greek and classical philosophy rather than rigid Islamism; a pre-Renaissance if you will.

---

⁵⁸ Glubb, J. (1978). *The Fate of Empires and Search for Survival*. Edinburgh: Blackwood. Pg. 15.

⁵⁹ Iroegbu Chinaemerem. (2017). *MEET FATIMA AL-FIHRI: THE FOUNDER OF THE WORLD'S FIRST LIBRARY*. Available: https://venturesafrica.com/meet-fatima-al-fihri/. Last accessed 07/08/2021.

⁶⁰ Dale Debakcsy. (2017). *The Algebraist of Baghdad: Sutayta Al-Mahamali's Medieval Mathematics*. Available: https://womenyoushouldknow.net/sutayta-al-mahamalis-mathematics/. Last accessed 07/08/2021.

⁶¹ Mohamed Soliman. (2019). *Maryam Al-Astrolabiya: Arab Astronomer Pioneer*. Available: http://bibalex.org/SCIplanet/en/Article/Details?id=12463. Last accessed 07/08/2021.

Belief in Eternal Pre-eminence

This section will briefly cover the archetypal belief of a major civilisation or, empire, that it will be masters of the world forever. I have alluded to this prior in the book, but I thought it fitting to dedicate a section to it solely. I find it a very interesting, though peculiar, belief that declining civilisations hold to – it is almost supremacist and hyper-nationalistic in sentiment – but can occur at a time when intellectual scepticism, and criticalness of the empire, is at its most intense. The belief, I feel, stems from the wish of the waning civilisation to still emulate the greatness of their ancestors by conquering the new frontiers; even if they may be attempting to conquer and subvert nature herself. As we can bear witness to today, the new movement towards gender fluidity, pluralism, endless growth, consumerism, technocracy, infanticide and narcissism stem, or are adopted at least, from the vain attempt of the modern generations to conquer the unknown; like their forefathers conquered uncharted horizons or discovered new and profound technologies and scientific insights. In likeness, it is the same reason we see a lot of declining empires cling to their chefs or entertainers, as celebrity figures, because there really is a diminutive quantity of things the society has left to achieve[62]. Therefore, such is the self-destructive nature of the Human condition - we, as benefactors, squander the inheritance bestowed upon us by our forebears in an enervated attempt to still remain relevant and symbolise ourselves as the leaders of the world; even if the metric for that be, how much virtue we exude.

It was said of the British empire that the "the sun would never set" on it; it deconstructed itself shortly after such foolish rhetoric. The Romans believed in the almost supernatural legitimacy of their system; however, they too fell. The Arab empires thought themselves to be divinely chosen by Allah, to proclaim *Dar-al-Islam* across the entire world, and then to

---

[62] Glubb, J. (1978). *The Fate of Empires and Search for Survival*. Edinburgh: Blackwood. Pg. 14.

lead that divine super-state until the day of judgement; they too fell into a dark-age stupor. We too will fall, and it will come as a shock to us; even if we have citizens, ironically, while living in the luxury afforded to them by the system, decrying the said system as evil incarnate. Furthermore, luxury seems to create a weak and impotent populace who seem more inclined to gravitate towards beliefs that, should be, antithetical to their interests – these beliefs also have a subtle aura of self-assured superiority to them. For example, the British believed they were "civilising the savage" when they were colonising and building up these various colonial nations; they saw it as a sign of their virtuousness and altruism towards the other. However, with historical distance it is clear it came forth from the belief of superiority. The Empire of Charlemagne believed they were saving the heathen when they directed the massacre at Verden and subsequent deculturalisation of the Saxon lands; with historical distance, this is obviously an act borne out of malice, rather than love.

We also believe that we are the most superior peoples, we have by consequence created our modern and fashionable value system – sometimes referred to as "woke" culture – from the premise that "white" people have an unfair advantage, compared to other races, from birth by virtue of their skin colour[63]. This postulation comes from a position of supremacy. Simply subscribing to the belief that the founding peoples of the Western system have an advantage, over incomers, by virtue of their melanin-deficiency is definitionally supremacist in its fundamental assertion, and in addition, espouses a deeply flawed and almost patronising idea of people of a different skin tone. Moreover, Westerners of a fair complexion must, because of this unfair advantage, accommodate incomers by holding themselves back – educationally, economically and politically. I find this a highly racialist stance that "woke" culture has tried to catapult into the Western ethos, and I find this flawed fundamental

---

[63] Yadon, N., Ostfeld, M.C. *Shades of Privilege: The Relationship Between Skin Color and Political Attitudes Among White Americans*. Polit Behavior, 42, 1369–1392 (2020). https://doi.org/10.1007/s11109-020-09635-0

assertion that fair-skinned peoples are inherently better by virtue of their skin tone to be something akin to the Ku Klux Klan's rhetoric, or some other white-nationalist organisation. Seemingly, the only apparent difference between the "woke" culture and the white nationalists, is that "woke" culture demands forcible inclusion via segregation and impractical equality, based on the aforementioned flawed assertion, while white nationalists obviously demand a quixotic ethno-state. This is prototypical behaviour of a decadent people, who believe themselves invincible; and in this hubris it typically falls, in a spectacularly surprising manner, too.

Indeed, this type of civilisational arrogance was awash in Rome [64], and their culture and civilisation are now long distant relics of a by-gone age; now all that is left is a dead language and a dead people, of whom once believed they would be forever the mistress of the world.

---

[64] Balsdon, J. P. (1979). *Romans and Aliens*. Chapel Hill: University of North Carolina Press. Pg. 24-28.

CHAPTER III

ECONOMIC AND POLITICAL STATE

The economic and political state of a declining nation is one marred in internal political strife, rising balkanisation and an abrupt weakening of the value of the currency or money[65]. There is typically a transition into a monetary system in which it is either colossally debased, or is coercively flung into a currency by fiat. The current financial oligarchy is hellbent on ensuring this economic and monetary system, built on the accruing of insurmountable and unpayable debt, survives for as long as possible, even if they must collateralise our potential productivity and future generation's prosperity to do so. Of which they are already doing, as per their nature.

Lest people forget, in 2008, the great financial crisis or credit crunch was not the first occasion in which it looked very possible that the present global financial paradigm could implode; in March 2000 another artificially created bubble popped and almost took the entire economic ship down with it – the dotcom bubble. The Federal Reserve, the central bank which is empowered to issue credit on behalf of the US government, but independent of them, under *Greenspan*, created the dotcom bubble of the new millennia[66]. Firstly, by bailing out Mexican bondholders and

---
[65] Mommsen, T. 1992. *A History of Rome under the Emperors*, London. Pg. 216
[66] Luka Nikolic. (2019). *A Tale of Two Bubbles: How the Fed Crashed the Tech and the Hous-*

the US banks that held those, by this time, negative yielding bonds, due to the precipitous decline of the Peso. *Greenspan* and *Clinton* would both organise a bailout, entitled the Mexican Stabilisation Act. However, it was euphemistically worded as it neither was interested in stabilisation or Mexico and it was created with the plain intent of using the American tax-payer as collateral for the losses of banks of whom *Greenspan* and *Clinton* were friendly, too – nepotism and overt corruption, something near and dear to the heart of a dying civilisation[67]. The second reason was the outright repeal of the Glass-Steagall act in 1999, which guarded against investment and retail banks acting in similar capacities, and this only added to the speculative bubble in the sector of tech stocks[68]. Thirdly, and finally, was the rate cut following LTCM's collapse – which ensured that credit would easily flood the market and take the speculative bubble to new heights[69]. Similar irresponsible acts occurred leading up to and after the 2008 housing bubble – and similar levels of idiocy are seen in this major bull-run in the stock market, all artificial of course and all extremely fragile.

The political environment is another that fairs not much better than the economic and financial one. We see a stark political divide that is becoming more and more apparent after every election cycle, and the centrists and moderates are being swept away by the rising tide of political extremism, on both sides[70]. The recent bouts of political violence and riotous behaviour only reinforces the gravity of the situation and

---

ing Markets. Available: https://fee.org/articles/a-tale-of-two-bubbles-how-the-fed-crashed-the-tech-and-the-housing-markets/. Last accessed 11/08/2021.

[67] Peter Schiff. (2019). *A Look Back: How the Greenspan Fed Helped Blow Up the Dot-Com Bubble*. Available: https://schiffgold.com/guest-commentaries/a-look-back-how-the-greenspan-fed-helped-blow-up-the-dot-com-bubble/. Last accessed 11/08/2021.

[68] J.B. Maverick. (2019). *Consequences of The Glass-Steagall Act Repeal*. Available: https://www.investopedia.com/ask/answers/050515/did-repeal-glasssteagall-act-contribute-2008-financial-crisis.asp. Last accessed 11/08/2021.

[69] The 92'ers. *Derivatives and the Financial Crisis - An Introduction to the Timeline*. Available: http://www.the92ers.com/dunce/alan-greenspan. Last accessed 11/08/2021.

[70] Heltzel, G., & Laurin, K. (2020). *Polarization in America: two possible futures*. Current opinion in behavioural sciences, 34, 179–184. https://doi.org/10.1016/j.cobeha.2020.03.008

the untenableness of the current political order. As of right now, the former political centrists are straying further to the respective extremes of their political affiliations, and what was once considered fringe ideas – "defund the police" and "eat the rich" – have of late became sacred ideals disseminated by the establishment figureheads of the day. Moreover, the political hatred that has been permitted to fester and materialise into bloodlust and rage, for the political or racial opposition, can do absolutely no good for the individual, or national situation. The unbelievable insanity of it all persists in the fact that none of this was designed to heal divisions, it was designed to sow them.

THE ECONOMIC MACHINE

The reason for the sporadic and devastating cycles of booms and busts – especially in recent history – is fiat currency; and the problems it poses to the long-term stability of the economy, and the integrity of the political system, are immeasurable[71]. As can be witnessed in every great civilisation, from Rome to Mongolia, we see that in the stages of early *conquest* and *pioneering* that the monetary system is typically a silver, gold or bi-metallic system – a sound money supply that had minimal inflation, per annum, and ensures long-term stability. Rome started with the Roman denarius, and aureus, that was first introduced in 211BC, following the culmination of the second Punic war. The Roman denarius began with nearly <95% silver content, but following *Nero's* reign there was excessive and successive devaluation of the coinage, and by the year 274AD the denarius was only 5% fineness and half the weight of the original[72]; by the end of the Western Roman empire,

---

[71] Kallmes, Kevin. *"Imperial Monetary Policy and Social Reaction in Third Century Rome"*. Journal des Économistes et des Études Humaines, vol. 24, no. 1, 2018, pp. 20170002. Available here: https://doi.org/10.1515/jeeh-2017-0002

[72] Butcher, K., Ponting, M., Evans, J., Pashley, V., & Somerfield, C. (2015). *Provincial silver coinages*. In *The Metallurgy of Roman Silver Coinage: From the Reform of Nero to the Reform of Trajan* (Pg. 461-700). Cambridge: Cambridge University Press. doi:10.1017/CBO9781139225274.033.

the denarius was just 0.002% fineness[73]. We find too, that within the reign of *Diocletian*, as was conducted within the USA during the *Nixon* regime (Executive Order 11615), there was issued an *Edict of Maximum Prices* or a price control pursuant to combating inflation; naturally, this policy always falls short of its mark. As a tangential point, notice the Roman Emperors issued "edicts" and now American Presidents issue "Executive Orders"; both are exactly the same political command and thus both political systems are extremely similar, in terms of the degree of power entrusted within the executive. Digressing, following from the general maxim introduced to us by *Exeter's Pyramid*, the pre-reform denarius (the higher percentage of fineness denarius) became less and less circulated. In fact, at the end of the Western Roman empire, archaeologists, especially in Britain, have found extensive hoarding of coins dating to the end of Western Rome[74]; we find similar growing levels of precious metal hoarding today. However, they are now referred to and refer to themselves as "stackers".

In historical terms, the denarius at the end of the Western Roman empire was worth four-million six-hundred-thousandth of an original gold aureus coin; there was virtually no silver content left and was comprised mainly of various metal alloys, with a wash of silver[75]. Conversely, the modern US dollar has lost 92% of its original purchasing power; that equates to the contemporary dollar being worth four cents in 1913 terms[76]. The British pound has comparatively lost 99.8% of its original purchasing power, but it is much older than the dollar at

---

[73] Alan W. Pense (1992). *The decline and fall of the roman denarius*. Materials Characterization, Volume 29, Issue 2, Pages 213-222.

[74] Guest, Peter 2014. *The hoarding of Roman metal objects in fifth-century Britain*. In: Haarer, Fiona K., Collins, Rob, Fitzpatrick-Matthews, Keith J., Moorhead, Sam, Petts, David and Walton, Philippa J. eds. *AD 410: The History and Archaeology of Late and Post-Roman Britain*. London: Society for the Promotion of Roman Studies, pp. 117-129.

[75] Money Museum. (2019). *The Fall of the Roman denarius*. Available: https://www.moneymuseum.com/en/for-sunflower/the-fall-of-the-roman-denarius-460?slbox=true. Last accessed 12/08/2021.

[76] Arsen J. Darnay, editor, *Economic Indicators Handbook* (Detroit, London: Gale Research Inc., 1992), p. 232 and Survey of Current Business, vol. 75, February 1995, p. C-5.

around four hundred years[77]. As you can see a precipitous decline in the monetary standard is something that plagues this ailing civilisation, too. With the devaluation of the currency, we find a rise of prices, increasing localisation of trade (trade wars), a fractured economic structure, progressively heavier tax burdens and financial crises as was seen in the late-period Rome. As can be seen today, we have extraordinarily high tax rates and the regulatory red tape that surrounds every economic activity we undertake is stifling. Moreover, coupled with this bureaucratic nightmare, we find that every ten years, or at least twice a generation now, there is a protracted period, succeeding a speculative bubble bursting, of economic stagnation. Preceding this event, we are encouraged to, by lower interest rates, borrow obscene amounts of capital to fund personal economic projects or general consumeristic impulses – this is called an "economy", in modern academic parlance. However, this growth and activity is entirely artificial and contrived and the proof of that is witnessed within the bursting of every speculative bubble – from housing, to tech stocks, to general stocks, to the pharmaceutical industry, to foreign bond markets, to the commodities market, etc. Speculation does not equal long-term and meaningful economic growth, no matter how much the global Keynesian wishes to believe the contrary. It was much the same in Rome too, the gargantuan and cumbersome fiscal burden of attempting to pay for a massive military, bureaucracy, welfare state, infrastructural developments, great works – and couple that with generalised inefficiency due to corruption and skimming from the coffers – was too much to bear and the Romans looked for ways in which to circumvent these issues[78]. Problematically so, though, we find that most civilisations, even though ample historical precedent is available to caution the current generation,

---

[77] Toby Baxendale. (2010). *HOW MUCH IS YOUR POUND OR DOLLAR ACTUALLY WORTH SINCE GOVERNMENT HAS BEEN IN CONTROL OF MONEY?* Available: https://www.cobdencentre.org/2010/02/how-much-is-your-pound-or-dollar-actually-worth-since-government-has-been-in-control-of-money/. Last accessed 12/08/2021.

[78] Jeff Clark. (2018). *The Past Allows Us to Predict the Future: Brand New Hidden Secrets of Money Episode 9.* Available: https://goldsilver.com/blog/the-past-allows-us-to-predict-the-future-brand-new-hidden-secrets-of-money-episode-9/. Last accessed 12/08/2021.

they persist in taking the path of least resistance and short-term gain by debasing the currency. Obviously, everything I have just stated is occurring today and with great ferocity, too. I will now delve into a detailed overview of the side-effects of the debasement of the currency or monetary standard, and why it is politically pragmatic and expedient for elites to engage in it, and also the subsequent long-term net effects of such a monetary policy.

Reasons for Debasement

The reasons for the consensus for adopting a policy of debasement are many, and they vary between each political faction of the hierarchy. However, the main reason, specifically for the leader or political leadership, is to attempt to ease the burden of either military spending, infrastructural spending or welfare spending[79]. It reduces the overall burden in the short-term and allows a greater volume of currency to enter circulation, and thus stimulate economic activity, or allow the ruler to pay the troops far more easily. However, once the market revaluates the intrinsic value of the currency accordingly, based on supply and demand, it typically leads, in the long-term, to higher prices, increased governmental or military wages, trade and economic imbalances; and thus, the only way to solve the issues arising from the original debasement is to debase more[80]. Contrastingly, the alternative would be to reign in public expenditure and induce a short-term economic contraction to rebalance the economy, but that would be political and military suicide because of the necessities posed by a constantly increasing military budget and expanding government welfare system to a burgeoning empire. However, some of the more idiosyncratic reasons for debasement would simply be

---

[79] Friedman, M. (1990). *Free to choose: a personal statement*. Houghton Mifflin Harcourt. Pg. 269
[80] Stephen Michael Maclean. (2013). *The inexorable lessons of currency debasement*. Available: https://iea.org.uk/blog/the-inexorable-lessons-of-currency-debasement. Last accessed 16/08/2021.

a reactionary pressure through the depriving of bullion or capital assets relied upon, by either subterfuge or piracy; we see this within the Spanish Empire, at approximately at the turn of the 17th century.[81]

Typically, historically speaking, the need for deficit spending through debasement is enacted due to military urgency – Rome in the Punic wars or Athens in the Peloponnesian War[82]. This is what drives the first thrusts into debasement of the currency, however, in the modern context we find that the Federal Reserve was created in 1913 in the vacuum of no war, no financial gyration and no necessity. In fact, it seems to have been brought about by the lobbying and conspiring of large financial and business interests, in the pursuit of a cartel or monopoly; in a bid to maintain dominance of their particular sector of the economy. This entire conspiracy was hatched on Jekyll Island, a small and quaint country club retreat on the coast of Georgia[83].

Another reason for the general political push for debasement occurs within democracies, specifically. That is, the elected leader, to become elected, promised more than the confines of the national coffers permitted and therefore, deficit spending is thence required[84]. To begin deficit spending, one must debase their monetary standard or opt for the employment of some form of currency by fiat. This allows the politician to far more easily attain their election promises, but it has the consequential effect of creating a system in which ever greater heights of debt will be required, in perpetuity, to simply ensure the system survives. Therefore, this is one of the major flaws of the fiat currency system.

---

[81] Ryan Miller. (2020). *Spain's Lesson in Hubris: Tracing Spain's Financial Collapse to the Beginning of its New World Empire*. Available: https://theclassicjournal.uga.edu/index.php/2020/05/07/spains-lesson-in-hubris-tracing-spains-financial-collapse-to-the-beginning-of-its-new-world-empire/. Last accessed 27/09/2021.

[82] Bransbourg, G. (2015). *Currency Debasement and Debt Management at the Time of the Second Punic War*. Fides, Contributions to Numismatics in Honour of Richard B. Witschonke, New York, 2015. Pg. 150-154.

[83] GRIFFIN, G. E. (1995). *The creature from Jekyll Island: a second look at the Federal Reserve*. Appleton, Wis, American Opinion.

[84] Gordon, David. *"No Safety in Numbers."* Review of Democracy: The God That Failed, by Hans-Hermann Hoppe. The Mises Review 8, No. 1 (Spring 2002).

How is the Modern Currency Supply Created?

I think I should preface this discussion of the economic and monetary tendencies of a declining empire with how our modern currency supply is created and issued; there are striking parallels between the debasement strategies of old and the strategies we use, nowadays. One could say that the strategy we employ today, through the adoption of the *credit theory of money*[85], is, in a way, far more destructive than the strategies of old. As you see, our modern method is not limited by the finite supply of alloys or metals, that could be used for debasement, it is limited only by the numbers we can fathom and the artificial "growth" we can stimulate via irresponsible and infinite lending[86]. As some economist said a few years ago, I forget specifically who, in regard to our modern currency system, "the only difference between a million and a trillion is six zeroes". The exact profundity of the statement is clear, that our currency system is illusory, and the currency created does not symbolise value, nor does it create value. A greater degree of zeroes equates not to value. It is analogous to one attempting to create the illusion of a greater length on the metre stick by representing the one metre by the greater numbers contained within the sub-units of measurement. For example, one metre becomes one-hundred centimetres, we move on from centimetres and one metre becomes one-thousand millimetres, and so on. This does not mean that the value of the original metre has changed but that the representation of that metre has. This will all become clear in the next section, and I will discuss just how the fraud of fiat is perpetuated.

According to "*Can banks individually create money out of nothing? — The theories and the empirical evidence*", a study conducted in December 2014, in the International Review of Financial Analysis, that empirically

---

[85] Mitchell Innes, 2004. *"The Credit Theory of Money,"* Chapters, in: L. Randall Wray (ed.), Credit and State Theories of Money, chapter 3, Edward Elgar Publishing.
[86] Robert P. Murphy, review of *The Deficit Myth: Modern Monetary Theory and the Birth of the People's Economy*, by Stephanie Kelton, Quarterly Journal of Austrian Economics 23, no. 2 (Summer 2020): 232–51. Pg. 233-234.

established the fact that currency is created from nothing, and apart from the prevailing confidence in its integrity or the floating price on the market, it denotes no set standard of value[87]. I will largely be basing my assessment of currency creation upon this scholarly study. I will also use the fantastic series on this, entitled *Hidden Secrets of Money* by *Mike Maloney* – please do digest the information found within this documentary series, it is very informative.

So how is currency truly created and distributed into circulation? The answer will shock the ones uninitiated among the readers, and it will seem that our Western currency system acts somewhat like a complex and convoluted Ponzi-scheme. Well, that's because it is. I will discuss in terms of the American context, just for clarity and because it finds itself at the heart of the Anglo-American empire. Therefore, to begin, the first stage of currency creation begins with a demand for deficit spending and this demand is met by the Treasury issuing a bond. That begs the question, what is a bond? A bond is a promissory note to make good on a debt; the principle of the debt, plus a percentage of interest, in a set time period. The treasury will then hold a bond auction and these bonds are subsequently sold to large global banks; who are bidding to buy a part of the national debt of the US, in this case, and subsequently earn interest on it, backed by a certain percentage of future tax revenue depending on the bond yield. Furthermore, the banks will then be allowed the option to sell those bonds to the Federal Reserve in a process called *open market operations*, for profit naturally. To pay for the price for these bonds, the Federal Reserve will simply make an accounting entry, mark up the account, of which it is infinite in scope, and will then use that created fiat bank reserve – magicked out of nothing – to buy the aforementioned bonds. The Federal Reserve will then hand those newly created bank reserves to the bank, in exchange for the bond, and the bank will then use that newly created currency to buy new bonds at the next Treasury

---

[87] Richard A. Werner. (2014). *Can banks individually create money out of nothing? — The theories and the empirical evidence.* International Review of Financial Analysis, Volume 36.

bond auction. The repetition of this cycle is what increases the threshold of the national debt and thus, these "money men", use your future potential productivity and creativity as collateral for this burgeoning debt threshold. Fantastic is it not? I told you it may shock you.[88]

However, it does not end there and that is only the first part of the entire scheme. The Treasury bonds bought by these intermediary banks, then sold to the Federal Reserve for more currency, then creates a concentration of bonds at the Federal Reserve and currency at the Treasury. This concentration at the Treasury is then subsequently utilised on government projects, typically, they fall into three categories: public works, war and welfare. These employees of the government will then typically deposit a portion of these wages within a bank account, these deposits are not actually deposits but a type of loan the account holder makes to the bank – provable by the fact that your ostensible deposit is actually registered as an asset on the asset sheet of the bank. We must recall too, since the repealing of the Glass-Steagall Act, the line between commercial and investment banking has blurred, and thus the bank may use your deposit to trade securities such as stocks, commodities, etc, or lend it out to accrue the interest from such a financial endeavour – such is the conventional idea. However, the old theory of fractional reserve lending is actually wholly incorrect, and what the banks actually utilise is what has been termed *the credit creation theory*. This aforementioned theory is, in short, a way in which the bank's lending capacity is not determined by the number of deposits it holds[89]. In short, it creates money itself and credits the borrower's account with a deposit that came from nowhere – it is the literal manifesting of something from nothing. This results in the bank's ability to expand the currency supply being limited by very little, save the availability of demand for liquidity in the

---

[88] GoldSilver (w/ Mike Maloney). (2013-2018). *Hidden Secrets of Money (ALL EPISODES)*. Available: https://www.youtube.com/playlist?list=PLE88E9ICdiphYjJkeeLL2O09e-JoC8r7Dc. Last accessed 17/08/2021.

[89] Maurice Starkey. (2018). *Credit Creation Theory of Banking*. Available: https://www.economicsnetwork.ac.uk/archive/starkey_banking. Last accessed 17/08/2021.

market. Thus, this is another reason why bubbles are created so easily, and the boom-and-bust cycles, have become so unbelievable in recent decades. This further currency the bank then creates on top of the "base currency", from the real or artificially created deposits and also from the sales of treasury bonds, is added to by this "bank credit", I have detailed above, that is issued via lending. Therefore, this really equates to a system in which the banks are powers in and of themselves, via the issuance of any amount they so deem, and hold great sway over the reins of power; it is staggering to believe such a system was devised and has been allowed to operate for so long, unimpeded.

The entire system has been likened to a Ponzi-scheme, for obvious reasons. It is far more nuanced than what I have detailed above and needlessly so, but what I have detailed above is the general synopsis of the monetary system that is dominant in most nations today – more acutely so in some.

INFLATION AND DEFLATION

As *Julius Paulus Prudentissimus*, a Roman Jurist, once stated "For there was once a time when no such thing as money existed...a material was selected which, being given a stable value by the state, avoided the problems of barter by providing a constant medium of exchange. That material, struck in due form by the mint, demonstrates its utility and title not by its substance as such but by its quantity"[90].

The Romans famously clipped their coins and utilised the art of revaluation of their medium of exchange[91]; the Athenians melted down

---

[90] Paulus served as chief legal advisor to the Roman emperor *Severus Alexander* (222-235 C.E.), during a period of multiple revisions to the designated purity and weight in silver of the Roman denarius. He was granted the honorific "Prudentissimus" and his commentaries were later included in the *Digest*, a legal compendium produced by the Byzantine emperor *Justinian*. The excerpt shown here is taken from section 18.1 of the *Digest*; the translation from the original Latin is that of Watson (2010), pg. 55.

[91] Burnett, A. (1984). *Clipped Siliquae and the End of Roman Britain. Britannia*, 15, pg. 163-168. doi:10.2307/526589

and added alloys and worthless base metals to theirs, at the height of their golden age[92]. Now, in the midst of the grandiose Anglo-American experiment, in republican-style empire, we coin clip too, through the means of reapportioning our serving sizes on packaged foods and through the exporting of our inflation through running trade deficits with developing rentier-states; this is how we limit consumer inflation[93]. We are conducting the exact same policy of general debasement today, however, with the use of modern technologies, unavailable to the ancients, we can now attempt to hide these inflationary effects through companies adopting clever marketing and convoluted global trade strategies, as previously mentioned. These machinations allow the Western economist to exclaim, with much glee, "But we haven't had consumer inflation for [insert number of years]". We have, in the specific example of the gradually reducing portion sizes of food items, we find that the rising cost of prices was felt at the production stage, and that the company developed appropriate counter-measures to ensure that the inflated production cost was not passed onto the consumer; that is one of the reasons why we see no significant rise in consumer inflation as of 2020. In terms of inflation within the general economy, and the loss of substantial purchasing power in a relatively short span of time, we do not find that yet, because of the fact that the Federal Reserve's packages of quantitative easing has not yet exceeded the amount of currency that was created by the intermediary banks during the recent record low-interest rates and irresponsible lending[94]. That money was essentially sucked out of circulation once these banks began

---

[92] Kroll, J., & Walker, A. (1993). *The Greek Coins*. The Athenian Agora, 26, pg. 9: "The law specified that if the dokimastes determined that any coin of Athenian type had a bronze or lead core or that its silver was debased, it was to be mutilated and removed from circulation by being cut across, dedicated to the Mother of the Gods, and turned over to the Council (Stroud, 1974)."

[93] Sylvain Charlebois. (2018). *Shrinkflation: When less is not more at the grocery store*. Available: https://theconversation.com/shrinkflation-when-less-is-not-more-at-the-grocery-store-97240. Last accessed 23/08/2021.

[94] Barraza, J. & Lee, Wayne & Yeager, Timothy. (2014). *Financial Crisis and the Supply of Corporate Credit*. SSRN Electronic Journal. 10.2139/ssrn.2422678.

imploding, and a lot of these negative positions were then covered by the central bank bailout. Although, the deficit is to increase to levels that will exceed this initial supply of credit, by banks in the financial crisis, and this transition will be the sounding of the beginning of the increase of higher levels of inflation – theoretically speaking. This is set to occur at the end of 2021.

However, that being said, depression-era deflation would have occurred if the quantitative easing was not enacted by the Federal Reserve; I am not in support of the Federal Reserve, I am just stating the fact of the matter. Furthermore, a great deal of inflation or dreaded hyperinflation was not felt because of the fact the US economy was already in a deflationary state – around -2% per annum at its lowest, if I recall correctly – and thus the QE stimulus being utilised for the buying of toxic assets and government bonds did not enter circulation as generally as it would have done, if say, it was utilised for lending purposes. It was simply a means of covering positions, insularly circulating liquidity, if you will[95].

Additionally, we must recall that these types of QE stimulus bills cannot occur indefinitely and the advantage of reducing interest rates any further to facilitate large spikes in currency creation, is becoming less and less feasible; though, negative-interest rates have been suggested as a means of propping up the ailing system a little longer[96]. Will we have hyperinflation? Yes, the US dollar will eventually succumb to some form of rapid devaluation during the stage of collapse, similar to other fiat currencies or debased monetary standards of old, but before that occurs there will most likely be a large-scale global conflict induced by the US to maintain their dominance and their golden goose – the dollar. The dollar, as of right now though, is highly sought after due to many countries either holding vast quantities of US debt, securities

---

[95] Adam Hayes. (2021). *Why Didn't Quantitative Easing Lead to Hyperinflation?* Available: https://www.investopedia.com/articles/investing/022615/why-didnt-quantitative-easing-lead-hyperinflation.asp. Last accessed 23/08/2021.
[96] Matheus R. Grasselli & Alexander Lipton (2018). *"On the Normality of Negative Interest Rates,"*. Papers 1808.07909, arXiv.org.

and dollars and some, like China, relying very heavily upon the US-China trade imbalance to continue to exert economic and industrial importance on the global stage[97]. However, the US rely on the US-China trade imbalance too, to expedite access to cheap consumer products thus circumventing one of the causes of consumer inflation[98]. For the dollar to precipitously collapse, the $13 Trillion of US debt that is currently held by other nations, would need to be dumped at serious cost and potential economic ruin for the countries that hold this "asset". Naturally, this will be unlikely to occur and the event that will more likely occur, in contrast, will be a steep rise in the value of the dollar, as compared to other fiat currencies, spurred on by a currency crisis, or some other catastrophic economic or global market issue, which will channel worried and fearful foreign and domestic investors into, what is considered, the one safe-haven asset in the global financial landscape – namely that of the dollar. This will then consequently drive US asset prices up and thus the dollar value higher, acting as a massive deflationary weight on the rest of the world via the extremely high demand for the US dollar and US securities, and out of this carnage will arise a new consensus on either revaluing the dollar downwards or adopting a new reserve currency via a currency reset or transition to a digital, or crypto, form[99]. This is a potential outcome, but whatever occurs in the economic future the USA's geopolitical and economic position will steadily weaken and eventually their hegemony, much like Rome's perceived eternal economic and geopolitical hegemony, will come to a decidedly abrupt end.

---

[97] Yen Nee Lee. (2020). *5 charts show how much the U.S. and Chinese economies depend on each other*. Available: https://www.cnbc.com/2020/09/29/5-charts-show-how-the-us-and-chinese-economies-depend-on-each-other.html. Last accessed 23/08/2021.
[98] Bloomberg View. (2018). *US Needs China More Than China Needs the US*. Available: https://www.industryweek.com/the-economy/article/22025438/us-needs-china-more-than-china-needs-the-us. Last accessed 23/08/2021.
[99] Darren Winters. (2019). *Dollar Milkshake*. Available: https://www.darrenwinters.com/dollar-milkshake/. Last accessed 23/08/2021.

CHAPTER III

POLITICAL POLARISATION AND TURMOIL

As any average observer of today's riots and orchestrated colour revolution may be aware of, the hardening of political enmities within the society are steadily eroding the moderate middle ground and, what is appearing in its wake, is the normalisation of political extremism – even the state sanctioning and financing, of some forms. Racial divides have also become intertwined with political divides and there is a strong push to divide people along the lines of skin tone; politicising everyone of a specific race and, in essence, this transforms one's skin colour into some kind of political uniform in the eyes of the extremists. This is obviously wrong and the its steady promulgation, especially by the powerful plutocrats of the age, is a sign of impending disaster and civilisational fragmentation. As the old adage goes, a house divided cannot stand[100]. However, have we seen this type of behaviour or societal upheaval before within the historical record, and can these historical precedents inform us on how this situation may develop and thus, inform us on how to best position ourselves to weather the coming storm.

The Achaemenid empire, for example, prior to *Alexander*'s invasion had experienced several internal political issues and differences – these were quelled but left unresolved – so much so that upstarts on the empire's borders, like Macedon, began to plot the conquest of the empire sensing this weakness[101]. When *Alexander* began his conquest across the Hellespont, he faced large contingents of Greek mercenaries in the employ of the Persian Satrapies. These mercenaries had become slowly incorporated into the Persian military structure and, by the time of *Darius II*, their leadership was thoroughly incorporated into Iranian

---

[100] *Proceedings of the Republican state convention*, held at Springfield, Illinois, June 16th, 1858. Springfield, Illinois. 1858.
[101] Dave Roos. (2019). *How Alexander the Great Conquered the Persian Empire*. Available: https://www.history.com/news/alexander-the-great-defeat-persian-empire. Last accessed 30/08/2021.

aristocracy[102]. These troops received approximately a gold Daric per month, in 401 BCE, around seventy years prior to the beginning of *Alexander's* conquests[103]. Debasement was not really witnessed during the Achaemenid period as, typically, there was only partial reliance on currency or money as a form of payment; a lot of payment done by the central state to civil servants, approximately two-thirds, was done in tracts of land or goods[104]. Digressing though, eventually *Darius II* was murdered by one of his own generals and *Alexander* would later take on the mantel of *King of Kings*, in his place. *Alexander* would die shortly after and, from the political and successor disputes, his newly acquired empire would fracture into successor states, ruled by *Diadochi*. Therefore, we can conclude that the internal strife – dissimilar from our own, I may add - was more acutely focused on a monarchical court difference rather than an ideological difference. Facilitated disorder and disunity within the military structure and thus, this led to the dissolution, or supplanting, of the empire.

The Gupta empire, of Northern India, respectively of the periods of 320AD to 550AD, reached its zenith in the year 450AD and from that date onwards it faced continued and intense harassment from the Hephthalite Kingdom to the north, a nomadic Hunnic people[105]. This continued and prolonged military campaign against them sapped the economic capacity of the country and weakened the military[106]. Though, eventually, managing to repel the Hunnic invaders to the north in 528AD, the nearly-century long conflict created instability and political turmoil due to the weakened state of the empire. This resulted in a dissolution of the central authority, and although the Gupta dynasty would still rule a small kingdom within the heartland for a hundred years or so after their

---

[102] Professor A. Sh. Shahbazi. (2021). *Achaemenid Army*. Available: https://www.iranchamber.com/history/achaemenids/achaemenid_army.php. Last accessed 30/08/2021.
[103] Xenophon, *Anabasis* 1.3.21
[104] Kleber, K 2015, *Taxation in the Achaemenid Empire*. in Oxford Handbooks Online. Classical Studies. Oxford University press. https://doi.org/10.1093/oxfordhb/9780199935390.013.34
[105] Kim, Hyun Jin (2016). *The Huns*. Routledge; Milton Park, Abingdon, Oxon.
[106] Grousset, Rene (1970). *The Empire of the Steppes*. Rutgers University Press. Pg. 69.

decline, their ability to maintain their sphere of influence to the outlying regions of their once greater empire was gone[107]. This is similar to the Western Roman empire and their inability, during the twilight years of the empire, to project power and influence on the provinces and *foederati* contingents of the imperial domain; regional fragmentation and political strife soon followed[108]. Furthermore, this is also a cautionary tale of the woes of a nation engaging in near perpetual conflict and the societal issues that can arise from it; one could draw parallels between the Gupta's prolonged conflict and the various protracted conflicts the West has conducted in the last fifty years, and still continues to conduct today in the Middle-Eastern theatre. As *Sun Tzu* famously stated in his masterful work, *The Art of War,* "There is no instance of a nation benefitting from prolonged warfare."[109]

If we look at the waning of the Byzantine empire too, we find that prior to the ultimate conclusion of the empire, through the Ottoman conquest of Constantinople in 1453AD, and subsequent annexation of the Peloponnese, that there was an almost insatiable need for infighting and political squabbling – at crucial times when the empire required a united front to withstand the rising tide of Turkic invasions[110]. This occurred throughout the history of the Eastern Roman empire, but became acutely pronounced during the 14th and 15th centuries shortly before its eventual destruction. Disastrous economic policies, an over-reliance of mercenaries and aristocratic nobles instituting a furthering of economic inequality, for short-term profit-making, all played a part in the lead-up to the periods of massive civil wars and internal political issues that plagued the crippled empire – and would eventually lead to its destruction[111].

---

[107] Pran Nath Chopra (2003). *A Comprehensive History of Ancient India,* Pg. 174.
[108] Rebenich, Stefan (2012). *6 Late Antiquity in Modern Eyes.* In Rousseau, Philip (ed.). *A Companion to Late Antiquity.* John Wiley & Sons. Pg. 78.
[109] Sun-tzu, and Samuel B. Griffith. *The Art of War.* Oxford: Clarendon Press, 1964.
[110] Reinert, Stephen W. (2002), "*Fragmentation (1204–1453)*", in Mango, Cyril (ed.), The Oxford History of Byzantium, Oxford and New York: Oxford University Press, Pg. 248–283.
[111] Procopius, & Dewing, H. B. (1914). *History of the Wars, Book III.* London: W. Heinemann.

Yes, it is true, that social unrest and societal fragmentation can occur for a number of reasons – some I have detailed above – but what is clear today is that the cacophony of issues that presents us is more akin to the fall of the Western Roman empire, rather than any of these other empires. Though, we may share a few similarities with these, too. It is my hypothesis, from my observation of current events, that Human psychology is complex, yes, but it is also repeatable, and such is the Human condition, and our innate nature, that we react similarly to arising situations[112]. With this in mind, the reason I constantly refer to the past is because of this aforementioned hypothesis, that we are bound by our nature to react to similar situations in a similar manner. Is this true? Is it not? One cannot truly say, but it is the only possibility for us in the present to glean the content of the future, and that is of the upmost concern to us living through these troubling and harrowing of times, for our progeny and our very existence as a free humanity.

As we can bear witness to, citizens in the West are being shot for stating "all lives matter" and the ones, who will not bend the knee to the zealots of the new religion, are considered inherently evil and are summarily punished for such infractions[113]. Is this the world that we wish for our legacy to inhabit? Is this the mark of a society that values freedom and equality? No. It is a society that is on the verge of civil strife and anarchy. One that has been hijacked by ideological fanatics and puritans hellbent on reshaping the minds of the citizenry, by means of force, in a vain attempt to remake the world in their own image; utopia, mired in fantasy and impossibilities. They will fail in their revolution, but the damage wrought by such actions is one which will sow the seeds of division and eventual civil war – it is plain to see, for anyone with eyes to see and a mind for basic reason. Mark my words, what we see now is

---

[112] Ward, G. C., & Burns, K. (2017). *The Vietnam War: an intimate history*. Abridged. [New York]: Penguin Random House Audio Publishing

[113] Justin L. Mack. (2020). *Jessica Doty-Whitaker: What we know about the fatal shooting of the Indianapolis mother*. Available: https://eu.indystar.com/story/news/crime/2020/07/23/jessica-doty-whitaker-what-we-know-shooting-along-canal/5486333002/. Last accessed 31/08/2021.

simply a teardrop in a vast ocean, it is nothing compared to what will happen if we fail to resolve these tenuous fires of disunion; just like what happened to greater empires and civilisations than ourselves. If I may be permitted to make this final point upon the subject, we must be aware that special interests, like those active in the downfall of Rome, are at work within our various nations. They stoke fires where previously there were none, they lift up rabid voices of dissent where previously there were just faint murmurs of complaint, and they funnel funds into assemblies of men, to compromise their ethics, and control their actions. Make no qualms about it, there are at present a vast array of special interests whom would wish for nothing more than for Babylon to be made asunder. Some desire to watch the world burn, some have ambitions of power, but whatever the reason their presence is an ominous shadow that lurks over us all, and we would be wise to acknowledge that.

NORMALISATION OF THE RADICAL

The inability for political sides to resolve conflicts in a healthy fashion, without the need for violence, is something that is beginning to be conceived and carried out in the modern political arena, and something that is beginning to be taken to the streets and people, apolitical bystanders most of them, are being forced to choose sides. These political differences are beginning to be entwined with extremist racial ideology, and this is something that is occurring on both sides of the political aisle[114]. What is occurring is an artificially created mass-division of society along the lines of race, gender and political affiliation, and these fires are being fanned by the media through political propaganda, aimed directly at radicalising the foreign contingent within the nation against the natives, and the inverse is true for the right-wing contingent of the media[115]. The media

---

[114] The Economist. (2021). *America is becoming less racist but more divided by racism.* Available: https://www.economist.com/special-report/2021/05/14/what-it-means-to-be-an-american. Last accessed 31/08/2021.
[115] Deggans, E. (2012). *Race-baiter: How the media wields dangerous words to divide a nation.* New York, NY: Palgrave Macmillan.

are complicit in this terrifying push for open conflict on our streets, and they are already beginning to see success with their propaganda campaign – at the time of writing this literary work, there is extreme and radical violence breaking out sporadically across Western nations. Presently, history is being rewritten, an open societal hatred towards the founding peoples is being propagated, and a great divisiveness is occurring along every line of petty difference, and there is a clamour for power by radicals within our nations[116]. I write this not to instil fear in the reader, but in a manner wished to galvanise us few left who adhere to the values of liberty and common-sense; the brave few who are not ready to allow our great civilisation simply to crumble to dust, without so much as a sound of dissention. We cannot run from this any longer, we cannot remain silent while the radicals gain more and more power in the political sphere, and we cannot remain silent in the hopes that it will pass over our doorway – it will not! and it will not stop until it utterly undoes all that we hold dear and sacred. We must stand and resist for if we do not, our children, and their children's children, will curse our very names, to the ending of the world; for leaving them a world wrought with such misery and despair. We are the future and we can write it anyway we wish – so, lest we break all bonds that hold us together as a nation, or lest we hold our manhood cheap, we must persevere and deliver this world from the grip of darkness.

What perturbs me the most however, is the seemingly incessant need for the media to glorify this new form of radicalism. We have seen of late, that instead of the media vilifying such riotous behaviour, they instead praise it and euphemistically exclaim that these are "mostly peaceful protests"[117]. I have long pondered the changing cultural landscape of our

---

[116] Catherine Fieschi. (2021). *Europe's phantom political centre risks fuelling populism.* Available: https://www.ft.com/content/9e8fdde1-c6a6-49e0-90ed-85aa594d2306. Last accessed 31/08/2021.

[117] Joe Concha. (2020). *CNN ridiculed for 'Fiery But Mostly Peaceful' caption with video of burning building in Kenosha.* Available: https://thehill.com/homenews/media/513902-cnn-ridiculed-for-fiery-but-mostly-peaceful-caption-with-video-of-burning. Last accessed 31/08/2021.

great nations, of our civilisation for that matter, and it was not so long ago that I was a young lad and watching movies such as the "The Patriot", for example. I recall being visibly shocked at the scenes in which the British dragoons and regulars locked people inside a church and burned it to the ground. However, as I write this now, there has been the deliberate burning of several historical churches from Washington DC to Nantes, France[118]. In Portland, rioters attempted to barricade the access and egress ways of several Federal buildings and set it alight[119]. Moreover, within that aforementioned movie, I recall after I watched it recently, that I picked up on a great sense of nationalism, naturally, and very much a narrative of racial, national and religious unity, throughout. For example, the black characters were all in the end treated equally and with respect, and there was a real sense from all the white characters that they were creating a nation, where all men were created equal under the light of Providence. Be this historically true or not, it really does capture the more recent sentiments of the early noughties – where this type of race-baiting and hatred did not reign quite as free and ubiquitously. It was quite nostalgic yet saddening to watch; realising that paradigm is long dead and that the common-sense nature that once prevailed, just a short while ago, has now been laid firmly to rest.

POLITICAL IDEOLOGY OR EMERGING RELIGIOUS MOVEMENT?

This new form of ideological fanaticism is nothing new and is rather in-keeping with the nature of Humankind to drift towards a mob mentality; tribalism runs deep within our psyche, of course[120]. However, we are

---

[118] Théophile Larcher. (2020). *Volunteer Confesses to Starting Fire at Nantes Cathedral.* Available: https://www.nytimes.com/2020/07/26/world/europe/fire-nantes-cathedral-arrest.html. Last accessed 31/08/2021.

[119] Portland Police Bureau. (2020). *People attempted to break into Federal Courthouse and lit fires downtown.* Available: https://www.portlandoregon.gov/police/news/read.cfm?id=251013. Last accessed 31/08/2021.

[120] Clark, Cory J. and Liu, Brittany S. and Winegard, BoM. and Ditto, Peter H. (2019) 'Trib-

seeing, I would pontificate, a re-emergence of a brand of intolerance not witnessed since the twilight of the Roman empire; or Western Rome. This brand of novel "woke-ism", as it is termed, bears very striking similarities to the Essene cult, and later the early Christian cult, within the Roman empire[121]. As a preface to this brief section, I will cover this in far more detail in the "Religion and Belief" section, but I think ANTIFA, or "woke-ism", straddles the line between political and religious ideology; so therefore, I have included a brief excerpt of it in this. I wish to say as well, that we are beginning to see a galvanisation of both brands of extremism, on both sides of the political aisle, but it is simply that the left-wing form looks like it is in the ascendancy, and could very well capture the centres of power all over the West in the coming decades.

Therefore, that being said, can we truly conclude that this new brand of extremism that we are beginning to witness is reminiscent of the early forms of Christianity, and the role they played in the Roman empire? Well, we will investigate this postulation to see if it holds water.

In brief, some of the characteristics we can attribute to both cults are: they are viciously intolerant to their perceived enemies; they both have their own form of the devil, or source of evil inherent within the world, "whiteness"; there are certain "purity-tests", for example, kneeling and virtue signalling, and heretics, or "racists" in modern parlance, are summarily dealt with; they have their own shrines and they bend the knee, or give penance, to them (see the recent video of the kneeling crowd venerating the BLM statue in Bristol[122]); they have their own holy books and sacred doctrines, be it Marx, "Rules for Radicals", or white privilege; they wish to create a type of "Kingdom of God" on Earth, so to say, or "utopia", as they call it; their victimised and martyred messianic figure(s) are POC's and other "marginalised" groups; they

---

alism is human nature. ', Current directions in psychological science., 28 (6). Pg.587-592

[121] Michael Vlahos. (2021). *Church of Woke: The Next American Religion?* Available: https://css.cua.edu/humanitas_journal/church-of-woke/. Last accessed 01/09/2021.

[122] Siddique, Haroon (7 June 2020). *"BLM protesters topple statue of Bristol slave trader Edward Colston"*. The Guardian. Archived from the original on 7 June 2020. Retrieved 7 June 2020.

believe themselves morally superior to the non-believers, and in turn the non-believers are automatically dehumanised and vilified for their lack of faith; they have their own places where the priest will give sermon, namely that of colleges and universities, the professor now assuming the mantle of priest, and the sermon has now become synonymous with the lecture; they will even shun their families, if their relatives fail to convert to the new faith (see the video of the girls outing their families and parents for not being BLM supporters[123]); they have begun to engage in literal self-flagellation and self-mortification (see the recent video from the US, in which two white men are seen whipping or flaying themselves, while crying out "I am sorry"[124]); they have established a belief that the authorities wish to suppress them because their beliefs are so good and righteous, and this reinforces their delusions (The fifty straight days of riots in Seattle, for example, and the screams of "oh my god" when they are inevitably arrested or forcibly beaten back, or when they attempt to attack a vehicle and its inhabitants and are inevitably run over, and this buttresses their belief that the opposition are evil and lack Humanity); and, finally, the attempt of this cult to actually take footholds by force and attacking the "idols of evil", as they see them (We can see this via the footage captured of the "woke" mob besieging the Federal courthouse in Portland, and one mob participant attempting to attack a federal agent with a hammer, as he stepped out through the barricade door[125]).

As I have stated, I will detail this further in a future section, but I find it very interesting and comically ironic that an ideology that prides itself

---

[123] Hanna Lustig (2020). *Teens on TikTok are exposing a generational rift between parents and kids over how they treat Black Lives Matter protests*. Available: https://www.insider.com/tiktok-george-floyd-black-lives-matter-teens-parents-racist-views-2020-6. Last accessed 01/09/2021.

[124] Ismaeel Naar. (2020). *Watch: White protesters in Charleston slammed for showing up in chains, whipped backs*. Available: https://english.alarabiya.net/News/world/2020/06/25/Watch-White-protesters-in-Charleston-slammed-for-showing-up-in-chains-whipped-backs. Last accessed 01/09/2021.

[125] Department of Justice. (2020). *18 Arrested, Facing Federal Charges After Weeknight Protests at Federal Courthouse in Portland*. Available: https://www.justice.gov/usao-or/pr/18-arrested-facing-federal-charges-after-weeknight-protests-federal-courthouse-portland. Last accessed 01/09/2021.

on its adherence to secularism, atheism and nihilism can be easily swayed to a type of secular cult or dogmatic religiosity.

The Lack of Resolve to Resolve

Within the decline of an empire, we find that there is a lack of will to resolve internalised disputes and senseless polarisation ensues[126]. Where there might have been a strong and robust society only a decade or so ago, now there is an inexorable sway towards ideologies that ensure an ingrained division is sown within the societal framework. Pluralism truly reigns; there may be several, or hundreds, of various religious or political sects of whom each share a natural inclination towards enmity with the other. The only event we can draw comparisons from is the civil war within the former Yugoslavia – where several groups, who divided themselves along ethnic and religious lines, committed heinous acts against each other – and where there was once peace and unity within the union of those various peoples, that quickly devolved into animosity and irreconcilable hatreds[127]. The aforementioned example of the Byzantine empire shows that in the later stages of a declining civilisation, we find that there is such a drive towards navel-gazing and self-preoccupation, stemming from pomposity, leads the empire to believe that the enemies amassing on their borders are of less importance than the internal rivals. If there were leaders that could see past their own greed for power and their egocentrism, then they may understand that it would be their people and their progeny who would suffer the repercussions of shrinking borders and a collapsing empire. Subsequently, congruent with the spirit of the age, people care for their own needs and society becomes more like a collection of atomised individuals, each pulling in separate directions, each trying to best each other with ungodly wickedness. Rather than, say,

---

[126] Jared Diamond. (2020*). Behind the Lines: When Empires Collapse.* Available: historynet.com/behind-lines-empires-collapse.htm. Last accessed 01/09/2021.
[127] Briney, Amanda. (2021, August 5). *What Is Balkanization?* Retrieved from https://www.thoughtco.com/what-is-balkanization-1435451

a bastion of patriotic peoples, who have a strong in-group preference and an unbreakable fellowship with their common brethren.

Supply Chain Breakdown and Food Shortages

The food supply of an empire is of great import, too. The logistical capabilities that the empire can provide to its citizens is directly proportional to its ability to maintain its sphere of influence, and ensure obedience to its rule. We find that within a declining civilisation, the food supply becomes less and less tenable for the central authority to procure and supply-chain breakdown may be a precursor to civilisational collapse or a cause of it; for obvious reasons[128]. Trade, internally and externally, may also be affected by disaster, climate change or invading forces, and this can be witnessed in several empires of old – most notably the Romans and the Byzantine empires – but is not a causal factor of collapse in and of itself[129]. However, it may be a sign that either the martial forces of the empire, or civilisation, are unable to maintain security within their borders and on the frontier, or it is a sign that there is a breakdown in the economic or monetary order caused by several factors; such as climate change or disaster. This is termed a "Black Swan event", an event that is random and unforeseen[130].

If we take a look at the research produced by researchers from Utrecht University, Wageningen University and Stanford University we find their scholarly study entitled *"A virtual water network of the Roman world"*[131].

---

[128] White, C. (2018). *"The emergence of complex political organisation"*. In. *A HISTORY OF THE GLOBAL ECONOMY*. Cheltenham, UK: Edward Elgar Publishing. doi: https://doi.org/10.4337/9781788971980.00018

[129] Kyle Harper. (2017). *How Climate Change and Plague Helped Bring Down the Roman Empire*. Available: https://www.smithsonianmag.com/science-nature/how-climate-change-and-disease-helped-fall-rome-180967591/. Last accessed 01/09/2021.

[130] Ponkin, Igor. (2019). *"Black Swan" Event as Manifestation of Uncertainties in Public Administration*. Mediterranean Journal of Social Sciences. 10. 9-15. 10.2478/mjss-2019-0018.

[131] Dermody, B. J., van Beek, R. P. H., Meeks, E., Klein Goldewijk, K., Scheidel, W., van der Velde, Y., Bierkens, M. F. P., Wassen, M. J., and Dekker, S. C.: *A virtual water network of the Roman world*, Hydrol. Earth Syst. Sci., 18, 5025–5040, https://doi.org/10.5194/hess-18-5025-2014, 2014.

In which they detail the ways that civilisations of the past dealt with the managing of their food and water supply, and how they combatted climactic changes upon that supply, in hopes that we can glean some wisdom from their experiences. The researchers used reconstructed maps of the Roman landscape and population to approximate the drivers of agricultural production and urbanisation. From this, and from the understanding that to ensure urban and population growth a stable food supply must be ensured, they began to see a complex network of trade, internally and externally, which ensured the most basic of amenities; food and water. Within the Roman empire, on average, 90% of its water supply was utilised within the area of irrigation and since Egypt had the Nile, which ensured natural irrigation effects upon the surrounding farms adjacent it, Rome would eventually conquer it and Egypt would play a pivotal role within the Empire, due to its stable food supply[132]. However, prior to that conquest, Rome's mostly Mediterranean climate was variable year after year and this posed a significant problem for Rome's burgeoning state, as it forced the Romans to adopt a rather unorthodox method of distribution in regard to its food and water[133]. This ensured that areas within the empire with poor crop yield supported the areas with stable or good crop yield. However, if the fragile trade networks were facing issues or, if say, more than 60% of the areas in the empire were in a period of drought the system would collapse precipitously, weakening the empire immensely. This type of distribution network collapsed significantly due to the Western empire's lack of centres of food production and the inefficient centralisation of land-ownership[134] – as the Eastern empire had Egypt, for example – and the repeated incursions of barbarians and growing autonomy of the frontier provinces ensured

---

[132] Erdkamp, Paul, *The Food Supply of the Capital*; in The Cambridge Companion to Ancient Rome, Cambridge: Cambridge University Press, Pg. 270.
[133] European Geosciences Union (EGU). (2014, December 11). *Water's role in the rise and fall of the Roman Empire*. ScienceDaily. Retrieved September 1, 2021 from www.sciencedaily.com/releases/2014/12/141211090608.htm
[134] Huntington, E. (1917). *Climatic Change and Agricultural Exhaustion as Elements in the Fall of Rome*. The Quarterly Journal of Economics, *31*(2), 173-208. doi:10.2307/1883908

the empire could not function optimally[135]. Are we seeing this today in the West? Not yet, but we saw some shortages of certain items due to COVID and also the 2020 riots. Furthermore, we saw at the beginning of this pandemic an almost doubling of the wholesale beef price; with food prices seeing a small up-tick overall, as of 2020. Currently, we are seeing strange activity within the bond market and this foreshadows a higher fear of future inflation by investors (this has come to pass, circa. 2021), and furthermore vegetable and fruit prices are seeing increases in the South-East Asian region; specifically, Australia[136].

As an addendum to this, I posit this brief understanding, in saying, that I may have been quite prophetic in writing this section last year, 2020, and now we are seeing this potentially flare up in the West. Inflation is not just a problem, but logistical breakdown, too. I have noticed this within my locality and I know of others, within the West, of whom are experiencing shortages of specific items. Food is very much always the final straw that breaks the camel's back: a civilisation is characterised by its urban metropolises, the beating heart of the empire, and the beating hearts are sustained by the ecological centres and their supplementary logistical and provisional support. Without the stability of the food supply, civilisation ceases.

INDISPUTABLE CORRUPTION

Corruption is something existent throughout any civilisation, permeating its zenith and its lows. However, as a civilisation begins to run its course we tend to see, an almost, overt display of corruption in mostly every level of society, but especially within bureaucratic or public institutions. This occurs today, in the developed and developing world, and even in

---

[135] Jones, A. H. M. *The Later Roman Empire, 284–602: A Social, Economic, and Administrative Survey* [Paperback, vol. 1] ISBN 0-8018-3353-1 Basil Blackwell Ltd. 1964. Pg. 1027.
[136] Alex Turner-Cohen and Chris Stubbs. (2021). *'Growers are desperate': Fruit prices to rise by 30 per cent, report warns.* Available: https://7news.com.au/lifestyle/food/growers-are-desperate-fruit-prices-to-rise-by-30-per-cent-report-warns-c-2279469. Last accessed 02/09/2021.

historical examples as we may see. As the 12th president of the World Bank, *Jim Yong Kim* said, "let's not mince words: In the developing world, corruption is public enemy number one."[137] Indeed, but it is also a major issue for concern within the developed world too, and we can see that from examples of the *Clinton* crime syndicate, or political family, depending on one's own opinion[138]. However, the *Clintons* are not just the only politically connected family who dabble in corruption, lest we forget the *Bush* family and their previous dealings with Nazi and Nazi sympathisers tied with funding Hitler's regime[139]. Even the *Trump* dynasty has a shady past, too.

If we contrast that to Rome, we find a basket of corruption there too and even more so, one may say. If we look at the case of *Marcus Licinius Crassus*, part of the *Licinia* senatorial clan, he became one of the largest real-estate owners in Rome by a number of means, all shady of course, but one way in which he did this was by employing his own fire-fighter company. How can one make money doing this? Well, when a building was in the midst of burning in Rome, as most of the city was made of wooden dwellings, he would have his fire-fighting company appear at the burning building and negotiate a price with the owner of the blaze-stricken structure to put out the fire. Now, the prices for the service of saving the building were typically steep and most did not or could not pay. After the structure was reduced to a smouldering ruin, *Crassus* would buy the property at a fraction of the cost and then, naturally, develop new stone properties on top of the plot of land. He would rent those out and effectively, after some time, he began setting the rent prices within

---

[137] The World Bank. (2013). *Remarks by World Bank Group President Jim Yong Kim at "Speak Up Against Corruption" Event*. Available: https://www.worldbank.org/en/news/speech/2013/12/19/world-bank-group-president-jim-yong-kim-corruption-event. Last accessed 03/09/2021.

[138] Thompson, L. (1994). *The Clinton Body Count: Coincidence or the Kiss of Death?*

[139] Ben Aris and Duncan Campbell. (2004). *How Bush's grandfather helped Hitler's rise to power*. Available: https://www.theguardian.com/world/2004/sep/25/usa.secondworldwar. Last accessed 03/09/2021.

the city. There is much debate though, concerning the potentiality that *Crassus* ordered all of these fires started in the first place, rather than them being accidental occurrences[140].

Now, let us compare to our modern day and let us take one of the most accomplished criminal dynasties of our day; the *Clintons*. Some of the many and varied exploits of this clan include; the 2012 Benghazi Attack[141], Commerce Department trade mission controversy[142], the Haiti child trafficking controversy[143], Hillary email controversy, Podesta email leak[144], Clinton foundation-state department controversy[145], the sale of uranium to Russia (Uranium One)[146], Seth Rich and the fifty-plus victims suspiciously found dead in relation to nefarious Clinton activities[147], the Arkansas drug ring out of Mena airport[148], Bill Clinton sexual misconduct and rape allegations (Kathy Shelton)[149], and Hillary Rodham Clinton, in her time as a lawyer, defending a child abuser by smearing the fourteen year-old victim and laughingly remarking, after the perpetrator took a polygraph and passed it, "I lost all trust in polygraph

---

[140] Marshall, B. A. (1976). *Crassus: A political biography*. Amsterdam: A.M. Hakkert.
[141] Kevin Jackson. (2020). *New Evidence: Hillary Clinton LIED about Benghazi Attack*. Available: https://theblacksphere.net/2020/06/new-evidence-hillary-clinton-lied-about-benghazi-attack/. Last accessed 03/09/2021.
[142] Susan B. Garland (12th September 1994). *"Clinton Cozies Up to Business"*. Business Week.
[143] Katie Weddington. (2010). *January 29, 2010 – Clinton friend, Laura Silsby, and child trafficking in Haiti*. Available: https://clintonfoundationtimeline.com/january-29-2010-clinton-friend-laura-silsby-and-the-child-trafficking-case-in-haiti/. Last accessed 03/09/2021.
[144] Franceschi-Bicchierai, Lorenzo (October 20, 2016). *"How Hackers Broke into John Podesta and Colin Powell's Gmail Accounts"*. Motherboard. Retrieved: 03/09/2021.
[145] Helderman, Rosalind S.; Hamburger, Tom (February 25, 2015). *"Foreign governments gave millions to foundation while Clinton was at State Dept"*. The Washington Post.
[146] Becker, Jo; McIntire, Mike (April 23, 2015). *"Cash Flowed to Clinton Foundation Amid Russian Uranium Deal"*. Retrieve: 03/09/2021– via NYTimes.com.
[147] Thomas Dishaw. (2013). *Comprehensive Clinton Body Count List*. Available: https://www.governmentslaves.news/comprehensive-clinton-body-count-list/. Last accessed 03/09/2021.
[148] JUDICIAL WATCH. (2019). *Guns, Drugs, CIA at Mena, Arkansas: Judicial Watch Demands Answers*. Available: https://www.judicialwatch.org/investigative-bulletin/guns-drugs-cia-at-mena-arkansas-judicial-watch-demands-answers/. Last accessed 03/09/2021.
[149] Chasmar, Jessica (October 19, 2016). *"Leslie Millwee, former reporter, accused Bill Clinton of sexual assault 'on three occasions' in 1980"*. The Washington Times. Retrieved: 03/09/2021.

tests after that"[150] – but to name a few of the many crimes. One may ask though, well if that is the case, that they have been involved in nefarious activity, how have they eluded the authorities for so long. Simple. Much like the strategy of *Crassus*, they utilise their inordinate wealth, generated from illicit activities, to bribe and lobby government officials to look the other way, or pass legislation supporting their activities. Eventually, they generate enough capital and blackmailable material, on rivals or other political entities, to make a bid for political office. It is disappointing, but it has been occurring for millennia, since the dawn of humankind actually, and it is unlikely it will ever end.

Furthermore, for that matter, if we briefly look at the rise of *Nancy Pelosi* and how she generated $120 Million from a salary, now at the height of her career, of $223 Thousand per annum, then we see what can only be termed resolutely as corruption[151]. It is quite a story; I can assure you. Nancy Patricia D'Alesandro Pelosi, daughter of Thomas Ludwig D'Alesandro, a congressman for five terms and the mayor of Baltimore, of whom had some shady connections with the Baltimore chapter of the Mafia and of whom was investigated by the FBI under instruction by President John F. Kennedy, is highly corrupt; publicly so. Before attaining the position of Speaker of the House, Pelosi managed to divert billions of dollars in subsidies to a light rail project of whom the main benefactor was a company headed by a high-dollar Democratic donor, CEO Marc Benioff, and in which her investment company CEO husband was a major investor in. Moreover, Tech-giant Salesforce sold a large plot of land to the Golden State Warriors, the main facilitator of the profiteering from such a deal was House Minority Leader, at the time, Pelosi; who swelled real-estate prices in the area. From the said light rail project, of

---

[150] Washington Free Beacon. (2014). *AUDIO: Hillary Clinton Speaks of Defence of Child Rapist in Newly Unearthed Tapes.* Available: https://freebeacon.com/politics/audio-hillary-clinton-speaks-of-defense-of-child-rapist-in-newly-unearthed-tapes/. Last accessed 03/09/2021.

[151] Stephanie Asymkos. (2021). *How Rich Is Nancy Pelosi?* Available: https://finance.yahoo.com/news/rich-nancy-pelosi-210041125.html?guccounter=1&guce_referrer=aHR0cHM6Ly93d3cuZ29vZ2xlLmNvbS8&guce_referrer_sig=AQAAAChSvV6XNIZvPN1SI_Zy-wQds1z1moccdKpIlLIkmNSfv848qn5RCvLA. Last accessed 03/09/2021.

which Pelosi lobbied for taxpayer money to be diverted to, in the San Francisco Mission Bay neighbourhood – where the development was occurring – received a massive boost in real-estate prices after the, priorly mentioned, Salesforce built a new campus in the region also. The Pelosi's just so happened to priorly own vast quantities of cheap, dilapidated real-estate in the Mission Bay Area of which then rose in value, due to the mass-transit system being built in the area, netting her stupendously high capital appreciation on such property. Plus, her husband netted some tidy increases in his investments, he may have sold covered calls or simply set aside a portfolio of call options, with optimal leverage backing those calls which would have gave him a vastly higher profit margin, as compared to a simple buy-and-hold position. Options trading, with their assumed net worth, is probably far more likely the strategy of his. Without options, the profit generated from the appreciation in the stock price of Salesforce would have only netted the Pelosi's around $2.4 Million, thus it behoves us to realise that there was something far more complex at play, in terms of trading.[152][153][154][155]

In the modern-day context we find, also, a great deal of wealthy and powerful individuals being able to elude taxes – taxes that the average citizen must pay. However, though it may be unfair, this is nothing new and we find that between the 3rd - 5th centuries AD, the late-era imperial period, we find that Roman officials and politically connected individuals used their financial and political leverage to purchase themselves immunity from taxation[156]. Naturally, being uncaring of the cumulative

---

[152] Unusual Whales. (2020). *Pelosi and a lifetime of trading*. Available: https://unusualwhales.com/i_am_the_senate/pelosi. Last accessed 03/09/2021.

[153] Mr Reagan. (2021). *Pelosi Crime Family*. Available: https://www.youtube.com/watch?v=v-TiaNajmWzc. Last accessed 03/09/2021.

[154] SOPHIE MELLOR. (2021). *House Speaker Nancy Pelosi's husband cashed in on Big Tech just as Congress was set to pounce*. Available: https://fortune.com/2021/07/08/house-speaker-nancy-pelosi-husband-paul-big-tech-stocks/. Last accessed 03/09/2021.

[155] Ed Lin. (2019). *Speaker Nancy Pelosi's Husband Bought Up Salesforce Stock Options*. Available: https://www.barrons.com/articles/speaker-nancy-pelolsis-husband-bought-up-salesforce-com-stock-options-51563274805. Last accessed 03/09/2021.

[156] Neesen, Lutz, *The Revenues of Rome*. The Journal of Roman Studies, Vol. 71 (1981), pp. 170

effects of such impacts that would pose to the empire, but such is the age of decadence and of also decline[157]. Curiously, at that time, when the empire's coffers were starving, we find that many Roman officials were becoming so wealthy that it created massively high disparities between the rich and poor – much akin to what is beginning to occur today with our wealth inequalities[158]. Interestingly too, we find that much of the Roman currency in circulation was to be found in the hands of imperial and local government functionaries, such as the *apparitores, curioso, tabularii, officiales*; and the rest who had come to believe themselves entitled to make as much profit from their official positions as the market and empire could burden. *Ambrose* (340AD-397AD), the respected Bishop of Milan, wrote, "Everything was up for sale for price, and this was what to begin with brought every evil upon Italy, and resulted in universal deterioration."[159]

Furthermore, military officers, higher echelon ones at least, profited a great deal from their own legionnaires, by actively falsifying roster documents and by failing to report the names of men who had vanished or went AWOL, in order to keep the allowances due to them. Skimming small portions of the pay that were rightfully due to working soldiers, and taking money in exchange for easy treatment and extended furloughs, often for several years duration[160]. This would weaken the military and ensure a breakdown of discipline and cohesion. I will detail this to a greater degree in future sections, but this is one of the areas in which sealed the empire's fate and allowed the barbarian hordes an effortless conquest of the imperial dominion.[161]

---

[157] Ralph W. Mathisen (University of South Carolina), "*Julius Valerius Maiorianus (18 February/28 December 457 – 2/7 August 461)*", De Imperatoribus Romanis.
[158] J. Hueston. (2017). *How Social/Income Inequality and the Fall of Rome is Relevant Today.* Available: https://pages.vassar.edu/realarchaeology/2017/11/05/how-socialincome-inequality-and-the-fall-of-rome-is-relevant-today/#:~:text=Before%20the%20collapse%20of%20the,incredibly%20high%200.43%5B1%5D. Last accessed 03/09/2021.
[159] MacMullen, R. (1988). *Corruption and the decline of Rome.* New Haven: Yale University Press. Pg. 153
[160] Procopius & Mihaescu, H. (1972). *Historia Arcana.* Bucharest: Editio Academiae Reipublicae Socialis Romaniae. Ch.24.
[161] Bernardi, Aurelio. "*The Economic Problems of the Roman Empire at the Time of its De-*

Chapter III

Refugee Crises

Coincidentally, at the era of decline of the Roman empire, we begin to see, starting in 375AD, almost a century to the year of the collapse of the Western Roman empire, large swathes of Germanic migratory bands sought asylum, en masse, as refugees fleeing the expansionary Hunnic tribes to the east[162]. The Hunnic tribes were the ISIS of their day, merciless and ruthless, and they drove their vanquished Gothic foes westward and southward towards the Roman border. Reportedly, approximately 200,000 men, women and children fled to the imperial yoke[163]. Interestingly, the Eastern Roman emperor, Valens, gave specific tribes highly favourable terms and, running counter to the traditional way of dealing with the assimilation of barbarian tribes, grouped them into large masses, and did not customarily disperse them; ensuring that cultural and ethnic assimilation into the imperial fabric did not occur[164]. These masses of warlike tribes, filled with hungry refugees, would have sensed the weakness within the imperial system and, as they did, they rebelled in earnest. This resulted in the infamous battle of Adrianople in 410AD, in which the Romans would suffer a crushing defeat and even their emperor would be slain[165].

There are many lessons we may take from this – not least that of lack of border integrity within declining empires – but this situation is almost identical to the refugee crisis that the West now faces; however, we are taking in vastly more people than our comparative Roman predecessors[166].

---

cline," in The Economic Decline of Empires, edited by Carlo M. Cipolla, 16-83. London: Methuen & Co. Ltd., (1970), Pg. 52.
[162] Crabben, J. v. d. (2010, July 15). *Migration Age*. World History Encyclopedia. Retrieved from https://www.worldhistory.org/Migration_Age/
[163] Heather, P. (2005). *The Fall of the Roman Empire*. London: Pan Books. Pg. 182.
[164] Lenski, N. (2002). *Failure of Empire: Valens and the Roman State in the Fourth Century A.D.* University of California Press. Pg. 317s
[165] Kerrigan, M. (2021, August 2). *Battle of Adrianople*. Encyclopedia Britannica. https://www.britannica.com/event/Battle-of-Adrianople-378
[166] Olav Dirkmaat. (2015). *Remarks on the European Refugee Crisis and the Fall of the Roman Empire*. Available: https://www.goldrepublic.com/news/refugee-crisis-roman-empire. Last accessed 05/09/2021.

We house them in hotels at the expense of the treasury and taxpayer, and we insist on allowing them unbridled control and positions of power within our governmental and military hierarchy. For example, we have the capital city of the UK, arguably one of the great nations and cities within the Western conglomerate, now being led by a second-generation immigrant who seems to be sabotaging the entire city. Through rising criminality going unabated, allowing insurrectionists to attempt to tear down historical landmarks in the name of racial supremacy, and further facilitating the ethnic osmosis of the city[167]. We have many other examples throughout Europe, the Americas and Oceania but that is the most poignant by far. Funnily enough, we have very little records of *foederati* or migrants-turned-citizens causing as much calamity within the twilight periods of the empire, barring the eventual conquests. Even *Stilicho*, a half-Vandal, half-Roman, attempted to defend the empire until his eventual execution by his political rivals[168].

Conversely, like the Goths, the African and Middle Eastern migration into Europe right now is unrelenting and is, in theory, caused by a terrible invader in their homeland – though, with some it is simply economic migration[169]. *Ammianus Marcellinus*, a contemporary historian of the period, wrote extensively upon this crisis and stated, regarding the refugees, "Not one was left behind," Marcellinus continues, "not even of those who were stricken with mortal disease." The Goths "crossed the stream day and night, without ceasing, embarking in troops on board ships and rafts, and canoes made of the hollow trunks of trees." Marcellinus recounts that "a great many were drowned, who, because they were too numerous for the vessels, tried to swim across, and in spite

---

[167] James Delingpole. (2020). *Delingpole: London Is Finished – Killed by Boris Johnson, Sadiq Khan and Coronavirus*. Available: https://www.breitbart.com/europe/2020/07/16/boris-johnson-and-sadiq-khan-have-destroyed-london/. Last accessed 05/09/2021.
[168] Hughes, Ian (2010). *Stilicho: The Vandal Who Saved Rome*. Barnsley: Pen & Sword Military.
[169] John Whitaker. (2017). *EU Finally Admits Most "Refugees" Are Economic Migrants—Recommends Mass Deportation*. Available: https://nationaleconomicseditorial.com/2017/06/23/eu-migrants-not-refugees-recommends-deportation/#mh-comments. Last accessed 05/09/2021.

of all their exertions were swept away by the stream."[170] I do not need to mention how similar this is to our current dilemma within the West[171]. However, these refugees began to become agitated through potential Roman corruption, through the officials skimming grain and financial provisions to the migrant Goth camps, and they began rebelling and raiding *en masse* throughout Greece and Thrace[172]. Comparatively, we have seen a number of migrants, in our own period who have went on either killing sprees or sprees of crime, be it organised or unorganised, and some have done this based on their "poor accommodation", according to them. The recent attacks in the British city of Glasgow come to mind; furthermore, the funeral of that attacker had several hundred participants who were sympathetic to the plight of the deceased criminal and resolute in their admonishment to the ruling class for not doing enough[173].

However, Marcellinus writes two years later, "with rage flashing in their eyes, the barbarians pursued our men."[174] They began to raid and sack the cities of the empire and attempted to force Rome to grant them parcels of land in exchange for peace; definable extortion, of course. After the momentum garnered from the Roman defeat of Adrianople, the Goths and other tribal confederacies, accompanying their migratory bands, picked apart the empire, piece by piece, and after the execution

---

[170] Ammianus, M., & Yonge, C. D. (1862). *The Roman history of Ammianus Marcellinus: During the reigns of the emperors Constantius, Julian, Jovianus, Valentinian, and Valens.* Pg. 517.

[171] Diane Taylor. (2020). *Almost 300 asylum seekers have died trying to cross the Channel since 1999.* Available: https://www.theguardian.com/uk-news/2020/oct/29/almost-300-asylum-seekers-have-died-trying-to-cross-the-channel-since-1999. Last accessed 05/09/2021.

[172] Dr. Cheryl Benard. *I've Worked with Refugees for Decades. Europe's Afghan Crime Wave is Mind-Boggling.* Accessed here: https://nationalinterest.org/feature/ive-worked-refugees-decades-europes-afghan-crime-wave-mind-21506?page=0%2C2

[173] Emer Scully. (2020). *Funeral of Sudanese asylum seeker, 28, shot dead by police after stabbing six people in Glasgow knife frenzy is delayed by an hour after more than 100 mourners turn up to ceremony.* Available: https://www.dailymail.co.uk/news/article-8536823/Funeral-Sudanese-asylum-seeker-28-shot-dead-police-Glasgow-delayed-hour.html. Last accessed 05/09/2021.

[174] Ammianus, M., & Yonge, C. D. (1862). *The Roman history of Ammianus Marcellinus: During the reigns of the emperors Constantius, Julian, Jovianus, Valentinian, and Valens.* Pg. 609-618.

of *Stilicho*, and what seems to be a type of ethnic conflict between the *Foederati* and the Roman inhabitants in Italy, 30,000 embittered *foederati* joined Alaric's Gothic invasion force[175]. They sacked Rome shortly after in 410AD.

Is there something similar happening in the modern West, presently? I believe so, and what we must recall is that we have already seen the beginnings of this type of disastrous and mismanaged migrant influx. The rhythm is peculiarly the same as Rome's dilemma in the fifth century AD, and so I suggest looking towards this as a type of cautionary tale against bringing in mass amounts of foreign contingents at once into an empire, or civilisation, with an already weakening sphere of influence and ensuing internal political strife. And, much like the inability for economic and fiscal reform in declining empires, there is a stringent aversion against sensible immigration reform.

Usury

Usury has been misidentified as "the charging of excessive interest", however, this is an easing of the traditional stance on usury, a euphemism, and the original definition being "the charging of interest upon a loan". Though the church has loosened its stance upon usury, as it has on other moral issues, I tackle this issue of usury from an entirely secular position. As I have made abundantly clear prior, I tackle issues from rational and pragmatic premises, not from religious ones and alas I am unfortunately not strictly Christian. Though, one may ask, how can you be against usury or the charging of interest? To be against it, one would need to resign oneself to the fact that without credit the momentum of economic growth would cease to exist, no? This proposition is predicated upon the premise that demonstrable inflation is something that would permeate a system of sound money – gold or silver – and one must therefore charge this interest "fee", and all of its various incarnations, to incentivise and

---

[175] Heather, P. (2005). *The Fall of the Roman Empire*. London: Pan Books. Pg. 224.

facilitate lending; one, also, must facilitate great amounts of lending to just have a shot at growing a fledgling commercial endeavour. Moreover, that a system of sound money and sound economics would require, as our current system seems to require, ungodly quotas of economic growth just to remain solvent. Firstly, gold and silver, or bimetallic standards, had annualised inflation rates of 0.1% on average[176] and to prove this we find many a nation in the 18th and 19th century refinancing their entire debts on perpetual bonds – the British Consol, beginning in 1751, being the most notable example of this[177]. Secondly, it can be argued that in the short-term, national debt can positively affect the growth of an economy, however, the debt incurred, at least on a national level, can lead to the enslavement of an entire nation and the collateralisation of its populace for means of securing of more debt, to maintain the payment of interest. This, in turn, allows the phenomena of private central banks and the instituting of unsound currency to become introduced. In time, this currency by fiat destroys the civilisation and only propels the populace into greater hardship by ensuring, by virtue of the long-term incurrence of inflation via an infinitely increasing money supply, that the holder is disabused of the ability to store any of their long-term accumulated productivity and labour within the contemporary, and fiat, means of exchange. We have seen this most evidently with the British Pound and US Dollar and their behemothic devaluing over the long-term of their lifecycle. This demands the holder of fiat to engage in unquenchable asset acquisition, just as a basic necessity, to resist devaluation of their stored labour.

It is clear to the casual observer, that the Federal Reserve and Bank of England hold the reins of power within the financial system; as they, comprehensively, hold the levers of economic and monetary control. They, by definition, can hold the nation to ransom and control the

---

[176] Michael D. Bordo. (2018). *Gold Standard*. Available: https://www.econlib.org/library/Enc/GoldStandard.html. Last accessed 06/09/2021.
[177] Matthew Yglesias. (2013). *Don't Repay the National Debt*. Available: https://slate.com/business/2013/01/perpetual-bonds-a-clever-way-to-manage-the-national-debt-in-a-time-of-low-interest-rates.html. Last accessed 06/09/2021.

direction of the political destiny of the nation by means of denying or supplying infinite credit to the political-class, to fund promises made to the electorate and for re-election. Thus, by basic reckoning, usury is an unjust system, not just from its premise, but from the inexorable fruits it bears the indebted nation. Thirdly, this fee of interest is utilised not as a fee but as a mechanism for undue profit, when utilised within the framework of compound interest. Hence, it is not a reasonable fee and is a brigand's way of legalised robbery of the vulnerable. Moreover, by the continuum it produces, allowing the charging of interest brings forth major scenarios in which, as we have seen, the very core of the financial system can be captured by external forces wanting for personal gain. A reasonable man would not abrogate his own control over his food supply to others, not consciously anyway, therefore why do so with the medium of exchange required to purchase said food? Fees for the untimely payment of simple interest loans and a business fee, or portion of the profit of the endeavour, for the forgoing of profit, upon the principal lent, and the risk incurred is reasonable to ask. However, charging of interest, by its very principle, implicitly makes serious provision for the almost unavoidable probability of abuse by shrewd schemers. Usury can, ergo, be described as one of the most integral parts in the decline of a civilisation.[178] [179]

One must understand that if money, by definition, is simply a medium of exchange, then how can it justly be pronounced that one unit of exchange may breed others exponentially, as the act of compounding posits? *Aristotle* railed against usury within his writings and understood that "Money is sterile" and is simply a means of exchange rather than a definite article of inherent value or trade.[180]

It is true that simple interest can exist within a society who has adopted a fiat currency, for as long as the currency survives, but the notion of

---

[178] Daniel Lemire. (2011). *Usury and the collapse of empires*. Available: https://lemire.me/blog/2011/08/09/usury-and-the-collapse-of-empires/. Last accessed 06/09/2021.

[179] "Math is enough to explain why usury makes financial collapse inevitable.": Orlov, Dmitry. (2013). *The Five Stages of Collapse: Survivors' Toolkit*. Gabriola, BC, Canada: New Society Publishers. Pg. 21.

[180] Birnie, A. (1958) *The History and Ethics of Interest*, London: William Hodge & Co.

compound interest is preposterous and only serves to unnaturally aggrandise the debtor who has not created anything of value, nor does he lend with the promise of the indebted creating anything of value in return. Otherwise, for business purpose loans, there would be a profit-sharing clause within the contract and interest would thus be rendered obsolete. Thus, most acutely with compound interest, this can become a form of slavery and theft. In a modern context, credit cards charge upwards of 21%-25% interest each year and some free-market economists astonishingly state that the market should be free to set the interest rates itself, without the burden of regulatory boundary. I came to this fantastic snippet of information on a blog entitled "financialreform.com", and I must share it with you as I think the points raised in it salient and it gives an oversight as to why it is not just immoral to charge compound usury, but why it is the mark of a parasite that wishes to prey upon the vulnerable masses to do so.

"More to the point, let us imagine that I had loaned you not £150 but £100 in 1927, a nice round figure. I charge you 3% interest. In the first year, you pay the interest only, £3, so the entire principal is still owed. Let's imagine that the next year, the interest rate rises to 5%, and again you pay only £3 on the loan. Now the total owed is £102.

Now let us imagine that we are not talking about 5% per annum, but 5% per month, and that this interest is compounded monthly; that is very important, we are not talking about simple interest, but compound interest.

Currently, payday loans attract far higher interest rates than that. When people fall behind with payday loan repayments, they can go into enormous debt, and when this is compounded: compound interest on compound interest, they can never break free. It should be clear that this kind of exploitation, which can be used to suck people dry, involves generating a profit for the lender far, far greater than he could ever have made from a regular investment."[181]

---

[181] Alexander Baron. (2014). *The Refutation of Usury*. Available: https://www.financialreform.info/f_r_refute_usury.html. Last accessed 06/09/2021.

It is understood, too, that the national debts of nations compound not just per annum but per decade, consequently the tax-payer, you, are in a state of involuntary service to the usurers in perpetuity. This is an unsustainable state of affairs and is quite frankly unscrupulous, to say the least. As a side note, with a national debt of $28Trillion, if we assume a dollar per second, and subsequently divide that unit of seconds into years, we reach a number of 887,285 per calendar years. Therefore, as you see, the debt is unpayable, nor can it be paid for the system is built on the perpetuating of debt. Thus, the perpetuation of further economic depravity and evermore erratic cycles of "Boom and Bust".[182]

---

[182] Wayne A.M. Visser and Alastair McIntosh. *A Short Review of the Historical Critique of Usury*. Accounting, Business & Financial History, 8:2, Routledge, London, July 1998, pp. 175-189.

Chapter IV

Religion and Belief

Within declining empires, we typically see an exodus of the general population from the once predominant systems of belief or religious institutions. These religious institutions, by consequence, begin losing their traditional remit and become incongruent with the prevailing sentiments or moral compass of the empire[183]. Within this vacuum, as per Human nature, there is usually a desire to adopt a new form of ideals or tenets, and this may be in the form of a new religion – be it secular or divine. Most religions do have some aspect to their ideological framework that is political in nature – just as political ideologies may have aspects of religion intermixed within them, too – and in the early years, or the years preceding the era of revelation, they will take on similar characteristics to attain power and burrow themselves into society; as I have previously mentioned in the last section. However, this adoption of a new religion may not take place and the dominant religion of the empire may wane in membership and cultural dominance for a short time, and following the collapse may see an upsurge of membership again, once the atheistic sentiments in society

---

[183] Altemeyer, Bob. (2004). *PERSPECTIVES: The Decline of Organized Religion in Western Civilization*. The International Journal for the Psychology of Religion. 14. 77-89. 10.1207/s15327582ijpr1402_1.

have diminished or been swept away by a resurgent fundamentalist cohort; we have seen this within the Arab empire, for example[184].

How does this pertain to the contextual landscape of the modern West, though? Well, as I have previously stated, we are beginning to see new forms of religious ideologies, disguised in the thin veneer of social justice movements[185], but I wish to discuss the mass exodus of the populace from the traditional forms of the revealed religion. I say traditional, but naturally our ancestral religions were abandoned in much the same way the Abrahamic one we adopted is now becoming. However, the concern for the decline in religion does not stem from the notion that individual religions, or religion in a broad sense, contain any sort of inherent virtue or lead people to become better; I am sure they do, but that is not the reason for the concern. The reason a decline in the traditional religions and belief is a concern, and a sign of decay, is that in the *age of conquest*, or era of civilisational youth, we find typically that most adhere to the set religion and the early conquests are engaged in the name of that religion, or God(s). This type of self-sacrifice and heroism that is only achieved by men who believe in a higher being or higher spiritual reality, and not by reason or rationalism, unfortunately, is what drives the civilisation onward to new heights, and ensures the citizenry are all pulling in the same direction, so to say. However, if we fast forward to the *age of commerce*, and the beginnings of the merchant class, we find that self-sacrifice turns to and inward preference, one predicated upon financial self-aggrandisement. Fast forward further, to the *age of intellect* and that of *the age of decadence*, you find a society revelling in unbridled cynicism where self-sacrifice, honour and virtue are bygone principles of a less graceful age. However, in the midst of the hubris of their injuriousness against their progenitors, they fail to understand that those virtues are what brought the accord of peace between the warring states,

---

[184] Hillel Ofek, "*Why the Arabic World Turned Away from Science,*" The New Atlantis, Number 30, Winter 2011, Pg. 3-23.
[185] James A. Lindsay and Mike Nayna. (2018). *Postmodern Religion and the Faith of Social Justice*. Available: areomagazine.com. Last accessed 10/09/2021.

that once constituted the area of imperial dominion. Therefore, religion is something that may rouse the population into a nationalistic fervour, or typically dissuade the adherents against selfishness and instruct charity, or even allow the various disparate groups of a civilisation or empire to live and work in harmony. However, that is not to say religion is innocent and uncorruptible; religion is typically a corrupt institution, parsimonious in all it endeavours to do, but it can be terribly useful within the area of warfare and as a bulwark against civilisational entropy.

Rationalism and reason, though I myself are a benefactor of such and I believe in the bettering qualities of such within the individual, do not afford the civilisation the same level of efficiency and useful patriotism, upon their mass-adoption. Yes, I am myself a self-styled sceptic and rational thinker, but it is clear that the democratisation of such tools of inquiry and the mass-inculcation of principles of rationalism and reason, in the masses, have led to disastrous effects. Least of which is the mass-stupefaction of the populace, in terms of how they solidify a graspable understanding of reality, and ultimately the resultant over-scepticism has led to the youth criticising the very founding principles of our Western societies[186]. We must understand that the average citizen will never, nor do they wish, to be a rationalist, an empiricist or engage in the burdensome labour of dialectical, critical thinking[187]. They simply wish to be governed by capable and strong leaders that understand their plight, retain a proudness for their traditions, have a sense of confidence in knowing of their progeny's security, and be left to raise a family, have

---

[186] Habermas, Jürgen. 1987. *"The Entwinement of Myth and Enlightenment: Horkheimer and Adorno."* In *The Philosophical Discourse of Modernity: Twelve Lectures,* translated by F. Lawrence. Cambridge, MA: MIT Press. Pg. 116: "Critical Theory was initially developed in Horkheimer's circle to think through political disappointments at the absence of revolution in the West, the development of Stalinism in Soviet Russia, and the victory of fascism in Germany. It was supposed to explain mistaken Marxist prognoses, but without breaking Marxist intentions."

[187] Sean Illing. (2019). *The myth of rational thinking.* Available: https://www.vox.com/future-perfect/2019/4/25/18291925/human-rationality-science-justin-smith. Last accessed 10/09/2021: "The desire to impose rationality, to make people or society more rational," he writes, "mutates ... into spectacular outbursts of irrationality."

a companion, own a piece of land to call home and work for their own success. Anything surplus to that aforesaid list is simply not a requisite to their happiness. However, with the advent of rationalism and forms of critical thinking, these people, who may have been driven towards a simple life, begin to loath the simplistic nature of such an existence, and begin to critique the fundamental attitudes and ideals of a system that prescribes that aforesaid simplistic existence. Eventually, religion and the fundamental beliefs and values of the civilisation are put into question and critiqued beyond repair, to phrase it comedically. This is where we see the advent of so-called *Critical Theory* and the left-wing revolutionaries of the Frankfurt School, the Fabian Society and even the Illuminati of the Jacobins of Weishaupt. Thus, this lack of adherence to the normative societal virtues and beliefs creates, in and of itself, a paradigm shift in which the normal man, or woman, is unwilling to readily self-sacrifice for the community. Consequently, this spells the eventual destruction for the society, and the momentum of their earlier expansionary tendencies will be subsequently sapped.

LEGAL ARBITRARINESS AND JURIS PRUDENCE

In the state of the modern West, our rights have slowly been withered away to such an extent that what now remains is a scant remnant of what once was[188]. The most egregious of these erosions of liberty is that of freedom of expression. That being, the ability of the citizen, through the dissemination of information and ideas, through deliberation and lively debate with their peers, to provoke positive change and participate within the political process. This erosion of freedom of expression has become ghastlier and ghastlier as the decades roll on, and now in some European nations one can face jail time, and utter banishment by any hopeful employers, for simply criticising the ruling establishment and their

---

[188] Michael J. Abramowitz. (2018). *Democracy in Crisis*. Available: https://freedomhouse.org/report/freedom-world/2018/democracy-crisis. Last accessed 10/09/2021.

CHAPTER IV

various policies. Most notably, that of immigration and demographic and cultural transformation[189]. Why is this? Why are the ruling establishment battening down the hatches and attempting to silence any voice of dissent? It is because they fear the citizenry and the power of an idea sown into the psyche of the populace, springing from its roots and taking form. A state that fears the ideas of its citizens, and actively attempts to curtail the dissemination of said ideas, is not a state that works in the best interests of its citizens, naturally.

I did not know where to include this section and I thought it should be included in the political section, but after much thought and deliberation I decided that a civilisation's legal ideas are directly correlated to the religious ideas and fundamental beliefs borne out of that said civilisation. Therefore, I have included this very important section here and I think it fitting.

The slow decline in liberties, most importantly the freedom of expression, is something witnessable throughout the history of declining empires[190]. That being said, typically when empires rise and conquer new territory, there is a an almost unquenchable urge to centralise power – even if the founding principles or peoples of the nation are hostile towards such a notion[191]. Thus, in this drive for greater degrees of bureaucratisation and centralisation of control, through stringent regulation and declaration of arbitrary maxims, we find that the ruling class desire to control even the behaviour of their own citizenry; their thoughts, their feelings, their actions, etc. We have begun to see this with the new round of draconian acquisitions of power during this COVID pandemic – and there will be more to come, no doubt[192]. During periods

---

[189] Jacob Mchangama. (2016). *Europe's Freedom of Speech Fail*. Available: https://foreignpolicy.com/2016/07/07/europes-freedom-of-speech-fail/. Last accessed 10/09/2021.
[190] Watts, E. J., & Kugler, M. (2018). *Mortal republic: How Rome fell into tyranny*.
[191] Jason Daley. (2018). *Lessons in the Decline of Democracy from the Ruined Roman Republic*. Available: https://www.smithsonianmag.com/history/lessons-decline-democracy-from-ruined-roman-republic-180970711/. Last accessed 10/09/2021.
[192] James Crabtree, Robert D. Kaplan, et al. (2020). *The Future of the State*. Available: https://foreignpolicy.com/2020/05/16/future-government-powers-coronavirus-pandemic/. Last accessed 10/09/2021.

of intense centralisation of power within civilisation, and these periods are usually indefinite in timescale, freedoms are obviously curtailed until the civilisation collapses, and are ergo unable to enforce these freedom-crippling legislations. Rome was similar in this regard and so was Athens; the tragic fable of *Socrates*, for example, where the great thinker was tried and executed, via forced ingestion of hemlock, for the crime of "corrupting the youth of Athens", but all he seemed to be guilty of was displaying inquisitiveness in the realms of politics, and questioning the Athenian government's descent into madness. Now, you are probably rather baffled right now, on the one hand I have stated that critique, or introduction of *critical theory*, and rampant scepticism are despondent ails of society, and something to be fought against, and let me explain my answer and try to provide a greater depth of clarity upon my position therewith. Criticism of government is sought, and criticism of the policies of government is healthy and is something that can affect change in a strikingly positive way. But criticism of a nation, of her people, of their history of things, that cannot be changed without tearing down the very edifice of the civilisation itself, is something that is aberrant and should be guarded against within every facet of society. Thus, these revolutionary soothsayers that espouse such rhetoric care not for the common-good, nor for the betterment of the citizenry and wish only to acquire power by means of demoralisation and ideological subversion. I hope that provides clarity upon my position.

Digressing, as we can see in the contrasting environments of republican Rome and imperial Rome, there were different ideas held concerning the freedom of expression. Though there was never an express right held by the citizen to freedom of expression, there was a growing recognition, legally, within the *Respublica* of the right thereto mentioned; and with the growing idea of *libertas* for the citizenry, which were positive laws or types of civil privileges – not the same God-given liberty held by American citizens, but a precursor of sorts. *Libertas* encapsulated within it a series of rights granted by the act of law; the right to lawful marriage, the right of the offspring of said marriage to be Roman citizens automatically, the right to not pay certain taxes (local taxes and such), the right to uphold the ascendant status of the *paterfamilias*, etc. Some of these rights we still retain and some have been phased out. Interestingly, by the end of the empire, the small percentage of the class of "citizens", predominantly found in the Republican-era, became a ubiquitous class and by the end of the empire the majority of its populace were classed as citizen, and the entire exclusiveness of the term had diminished greatly; caused by the fact the elite used citizenship as a tool for Romanisation. We find furthermore, during the end of the empire, that freedom of expression became a highly contentious issue for the elite and, superseding the genesis of the imperial age, we find that it became recategorised as libel (*injuria*); and in turn, libel became a matter subject to criminal, rather than civil, law.[193]

The *Lex Maiestatis*, which was enacted in the last third of the 2nd century BC, during the *Gracci* Period, became the first law regulating freedom of expression or slanderous material[194] [195]. This law was later expanded during the empire and the main change came in the era of *Augustus*, in which he redesignated criminal status to slanderous writing against "great people"; conviction would result in the author's book burned[196]. From this point onward, this law became open to rampant abuse and a way in which emperors and the elite imposed their arbitrary will upon the populace. *Bauman* writes "The *maiestas* law rapidly attained such a degree of flexibility that it protected the *persona* of the deified predecessor, as well as that of the incumbent ruler, against any diminution of his dignity,

---

[193] Rudich, V. (2006). *Navigating the Uncertain: Literature and Censorship in the Early Roman Empire*. Arion: A Journal of Humanities and the Classics, 14(1), 7-28. Retrieved September 10, 2021, from http://www.jstor.org/stable/29737288

[194] Craies, William Feilden (1911). *"Treason"*. In Chisholm, Hugh (ed.). Encyclopædia Britannica. 27 (11th ed.). Cambridge University Press. Pg. 223–228.

[195] Gentili, A., & Antonius, W. (1607). *Alberici Gentilis Iurisconsulti, Professoris Regii, In titulos codicis si quis imperatori maledixerit, ad legem Iuliam maiestatis, disputationes decem.* Hanouiae: Apud Guilielmum Antonium.

[196] Cramer, F. (1945). *Bookburning and Censorship in Ancient Rome*: A Chapter from the History of Freedom of Speech. Journal of the History of Ideas, 6(2), 157-196. doi:10.2307/2707362.

status or security"[197]. Furthermore, we see an example of the law's use in the period of *Nero*, in which it was applied to "a member of the audience who failed to listen attentively to *Nero*'s 'heavenly voice'", and in the time of *Domitian*, where a woman was convicted for undressing in front of a statue of *Domitian*'s likeness. This is very closely similar to a man in the UK being convicted of a hate crime because he comedically instructed his dog to do a Roman salute to speeches of Hitler, or certain outlandish phrases. This was on the back of a ruling in which, by the court's own admission, the court decides the context of jokes and if it was offensive or if it was intended to offend; let that sink in[198]. Digressing, we find that the Roman citizenry despised the law and wished for its removal, and this was granted during the time of *Severus Alexander*, in the 3rd century AD[199], but we find similar decrees in the periods of 319AD to 406AD, in which it was decreed, "provided for the destruction of defamatory writings and the punishments of the authors"[200]. Like our own society, that began with protections and recognitions of rights, especially that of freedom of expression, that has been slowly eroded to the point that one can be jailed or blacklisted in certain Western nations for simply criticising or jesting about the government, or their policies. In the case of Rome, libellous expression went from a misdemeanour to, legally, a criminal act against certain protected parties.

However, if we look at the idea of freedom, and the legal basis for it within our own Western nations, then we find a man named *John Locke* – who was arguably one of the greatest enlightenment thinkers, in terms of legacy – and influential for the establishment of the founding principles of common law, and modern Western juris prudence. Now, for the purposes of this discussion, if we assume *John Locke*'s definition

---

[197] Bauman, R.A. (1999). *Human Rights in Ancient Rome*. Pg. 107.
[198] Brendan O'Neill. (2018). *Count Dankula and the death of free speech*. Available: https://www.spectator.co.uk/article/count-dankula-and-the-death-of-free-speech. Last accessed 10/09/2021.
[199] Bauman, R.A. (1999). *Human Rights in Ancient Rome*. Pg. 108.
[200] Bauman, R.A. (1999). *Human Rights in Ancient Rome*. Pg. 108.

CHAPTER IV

of freedom correct[201], and I believe mostly in the affirmative that to be true, then I think most readers will be able to understand that the new laws that seek to curtail many of your freedoms – be that of property, life or the freedom of expression – have no basis in the originating principles that founded Western juris prudence. They thus originate from a place of ideological insanity, rather than reasoned postulates. If we briefly look at *John Locke*'s treatises, to discern his idea of freedom, we find detailed in his *Second Treatise of Civil Government* (1690), *John Locke* states, "This freedom from absolute, arbitrary power, is so necessary to, and closely joined with a man's preservation, that he cannot part with it, but by what forfeits his preservation and life together"[202]. Additionally, a supplementary remark by *Locke* provides us his definition of fair government, that being "law and not force, must be the basis of government. A government, which is not based on law, is oppressive", and that government and communities were founded to "preserve their property" and to "moderate the dominance and limit the power of all members of society"[203]. Furthermore, stating "a liberty to follow my own will in all things, where the rule prescribes not; and not to be subject to the inconstant, uncertain, unknown, arbitrary will of another man: as freedom of nature is, to be under no other restraint but the law of nature." And lastly, stating "In the state of nature, liberty consists of being free from any superior power on Earth. People are not under the will or law-making authority of others but have only the law of nature for their rule."[204] *Locke* was one of the main intellectual progenitors of common law and enlightened Republicanism, but in the modern legal landscape

---

[201] Rickless, Samuel, *"Locke on Freedom"*, The Stanford Encyclopaedia of Philosophy (Spring 2020 Edition), Edward N. Zalta (ed.), URL: https://plato.stanford.edu/archives/spr2020/entries/locke-freedom/.
[202] Locke, J. (1980). *Second treatise of government* (C. B. Macpherson, Ed.). Hackett Publishing. Ch. IV, Section 23.
[203] Democracy Pro et Contra. (2020). *Thomas Hobbes and John Locke*. Available: dandebat.dk. Last accessed 10/09/2021.
[204] Locke, J. (1980). *Second treatise of government* (C. B. Macpherson, Ed.). Hackett Publishing. "State of Nature" Chapter.

our legal system and rights have been circumvented by corrupt politicians and ideologically zealous judges.

Therefore, we see that arbitrary legislation or diktats in *Locke*'s view, or ones that defy reasoned law, the general concordat of a government who protects its citizenry's property, are what defines a tyrant or defines a state of tyranny [205]; a government's reliance on force, rather than law. Though a "state of nature", being antithetical to man's rights, too – as brigands and malfeasance would be permitted to persist unabated. What comes to mind from this conclusion are laws that attempt to legislate against and outlaw emotions and, by extension, thoughts and speech. Furthermore, laws in which a citizen is unable to criticise his or her government, for fear of legal reprisal enacted upon them by the panoply of the state. Diktats prescribed, on high, by a dictator who imposes their will or view of the world onto others – the arbitrary and unequal enforcement of laws or laws that are devoid of any basis in the observable natural order or in reason, itself – is what plagues our modern times. As it was in Rome, the republican ideals soon gave way to a massive drive towards centralisation and dictatorial control; with speech against "great people" and the ruling elite being rendered an act worthy of a criminal. By comparison, we bear witness to the phenomena of hate speech, which is simply, in its most generalised form, no pun intended, a legal framework in which arbitrarily selected characteristics – and their championed policies – are deemed worthy of sacred legal protection, from being subjected to slanderous writing, speech and, with current developments, even criticism. Simply put, this so-called progressivism, has interchanged *Augustus*'s legal term of "great people"[206] with "marginalised groups"; if we were so inclined to be reductive about such matters. Lo, how the circle of time turns and subjects us once again to the dilemmas that afflicted the past; with such

---

[205] Locke, J. (1980). *Second treatise of government* (C. B. Macpherson, Ed.). Hackett Publishing. Chapter 18-19.
[206] Rogers, R. (1959). *The Emperor's Displeasure-Amicitiam Renuntiare*. Transactions and Proceedings of the American Philological Association, 90, 224-237. doi:10.2307/283706. Pg. 224: "law of treason, which Augustus had extended to libel and slander."

vicissitudes as these, why would hell terrify anyone with even a crumb of courage.

ATHEISM AND NIHILISM

Atheism is something that is all pervasive now, and not just a nonchalant brand of atheism in which one resigns himself to being a non-theist or non-believer, but now we see it has become a fertile ground for many other roots to take hold and flourish in – nihilism, pessimism, and politically and racially divisive ideologies, for example. Atheism and a breaking away from the traditional belief structure are something that pervades the declining phases of civilisation[207]. This ushers in an era in which the traditional structures of morality are bent and reformed, to accommodate the new heights of debauchery and depravity that the society wishes to partake in. I say this not in a prudish way, but in a strictly rationalistic sense, in which one must understand that if the general societal message that permeates is one which advocates, to the populace, practises that will raise divorce rates, single-parenthood, promiscuous sex, sexual aberrance, drugs, alcohol, boorish habits, etc, then a society will be likewise formed that reflect those messages. Hence, we must understand that the messages being transmitted to society, presently, will result in the utter disintegration of anything remotely resembling a civilised society; the law of the jungle will ensue[208], as we are beginning to see. The family structure is the atom of a functioning civilisation and to knowingly, or inadvertently, attempt to subvert or sabotage that should be met with the strictest of punishments, as the sabotaging of such a structure will lead to the demise of the civilisation, and the subjecting of its populace and children to a perennial state of war and decay[209]. However, we are seeing

---

[207] Glubb, J. (1978). *The Fate of Empires and Search for Survival*. Edinburgh: Blackwood. Pg. 15.
[208] Carcopino, J., In Rowell, H. T., & Lorimer, E. O. (1956). *Daily life in ancient Rome: The people and the city at the height of the empire*. Harmondsworth, Middlesex: Penguin Books. Pg. 78.
[209] Zimmerman, C. C. (1947). *Family and civilization*. New York. Pg. 110

the exact opposite of punishment in the modern context, and such decay is met with roaring applause and ringing endorsements by the political class, on both sides[210].

Atheism today has become something of a symbol for Western progressive thought, the crowning achievement of enlightenment philosophy, one could say, but in actual fact this is nothing new and such patterns are replete throughout the historical timeline; some of which I have already touched upon. Thus, I will not spend much time upon the historical comparatives, but I wish to discuss where this possibly stems from, psychologically speaking, and why atheistic, or religiously divergent, thought is something that proceeds the *age of intellect*, in most civilisations[211]. We understand that entropy is an irreversible force, something that is inexorable and seems to drive civilisations in certain directions, so therefore it is no surprise that postdating the zenith of a civilisation we find that, beginning with the aristocracy, the bubbling scintillas of protestation against the religious hegemony and dogma begin to take hold. This trickles down the hierarchical pyramid of society until even the lower classes are infected by such heresy, for lack of a better word, but this typically occurs during the latter stages of the empire, or civilisation, and signals a weakening disposition of such[212]. Digressing,

---

[210] Sophie Lewis. (2020). *The coronavirus crisis shows it's time to abolish the family*. Available: www.opendemocracy.ne. Last accessed 13/09/2021.

[211] Gibbon, E. (1867). *The History of the Decline and Fall of the Roman Empire* (Volume 1*)*. London: Bell & Daldy. Pg. 51: "Notwithstanding the fashionable irreligion which prevailed in the age of the *Antonines*... they diligently practised the ceremonies of their fathers, devoutly frequented the temples of the Gods and sometimes condescending to act a part on the theatre of superstition, they concealed the sentiments of an atheist under the sacerdotal robes... It was indifferent to them what shape the folly of the multitude might choose to assume and they approached with the same inward contempt, and the same external reverence, the altars of the *Libyan*, the *Olympian*, or the Capitoline *Jupiter*."

[212] Spengler, O. (1932*). The Decline of the West* (Vol. Abridged). (H. Werner, A. Helps, Eds., & C. F. Atkinson, Trans.) New York: Oxford University Press. Pg. 206: "The spiritual in every living culture is religious, has religion, whether it be conscious of it or not. It is not open to a spirituality to be irreligious; at most it can play with the idea of irreligion as Medicean Florentines did. But the megalopolitan is irreligious; this is part of his being, a mark of his historical position...One tolerates something either because it seems to have some relation to what according to one's experience is the divine or else because one is no longer capable of such experience and is indifferent."

Chapter IV

the *age of intellect* heralds with it a great scepticism of everything, some may be typified as good and others as bad, but we find that there is a general consensus amongst the academics, which tends to exude out into the greater society, in the belief that all problems may be solved by the intellect of man alone[213]. Naturally, this is a misguided assumption, and we see generally those problems are solved via the cohesion of the group and the cohesion is borne from the willingness of its members to act in a manner of self-sacrifice to that group. Religions are swept to the side because they look to higher powers and understand the failings and limitations of man. Religions typically promote ideas of in-group preference and unity through sacrifice; sometimes to an extreme dimension though, it has to be said. This is what paves the way for the eradication of religion; that being the proliferation of the hubris of man. You, the reader, may find a pattern in declining empires, while reading this book, and that being that declining empires exhibit a striking level of hubris and conceit, even if it is exhibited in an indirect way, and the mantra of civilisation will be: "it will be different this time". Be that in the adoption of fiat currency or the discarding of religion, it is always the same.

Now, that all being declared, I understand the issues of organised religion and I too look at the history of the Catholic church and see a collection of massacres and oppression. However, with that being said, the concern of irreligiosity, of which I speak of, is one of a spiritual and moral sense; rather than a secular and establishmentarian one. Religions may be used to unify society and encourage family structure, and it may too be used to acquire illicit wealth and power for its Pontiff. However, government and any power structure may be used in such a fashion, but these structures are necessary evils and the inevitable decline of societies are written in stone. But the decline does not have to mean the end of one's nation or people, and such institutions that encourage the nuclear

---

[213] Glubb, J. (1978). *The Fate of Empires and Search for Survival*. Edinburgh: Blackwood. Pg. 12.

family and a strong sense of patriotism can be good sources of resisting the forces of entropy. Though, as I previously stated in regard to Rome's priestly class, the modern institutions of religion have been thoroughly corrupted, but smaller sects may still serve the local community in which they reside; in a traditional way, that can ensure the local populace prosper.

Nihilism is something that has emerged from the same intellectual soup of hubris. It evades all reason and subjects the subscriber to a view of the world, in which it is bereft of any meaning or wonder. A digital-like prison, in which morality has no bearing and no standard is too sacred to profane against. The Nihilist may believe that by accepting nothingness, through nihilism, they can begin to see what is of actual value and uphold it, bypassing the denial and illusion of this age. This is incorrect, and I would argue that if you accept nothingness as an intrinsic quality of your existence and the external dynamic of your reality, then by the virtue of that lens that you discolour your world through, you may not find actual value because what is of value to you is simply a greater form of nothingness, by the virtue of your acceptance of nothingness as a motif of existence. One can discern this as factual by the very fruits that the tree of Nihilism has borne, since its advent with *Nietzsche*, who had some profound insights but some were blemished by a dire sadness, and we find Marxism has filled the void of traditional religion, there are absolutely no boundaries within society and everything from gender to tradition is open to relativistic tinkering. By that token, the modern iteration of art holds no beauty and is unequivocally nightmarish, modern architecture contains little form or reflects none of the characteristics of natural order, and the traditional fabric of society has been so pulled at, that all that truly remains is but a thread.[214]

I would tend to lend credence to the idea that individuals are naturally drawn to religions or to belief systems that incorporate dimensions or

---

[214] Hibbs, T. (2012). *Shows about Nothing: Nihilism in Popular Culture* (2nd ed.). Waco: Baylor University Press.

personas higher than oneself. One can witness truth today, look at even the area of modern science, at least as it is exhibited in the media, or modern politics, each are constructed with aspects of religion inherent within them. For example, modern science, as is displayed by the media, shows a very palatable form of science, in which consensus is a recurrent theme and "experts" announce decrees from on high. However, in reality science contains within it little consensus and for every scholarly article or peer-reviewed study, there is most likely a dozen attempting to refute it. And these so-called experts are mere men, fallible and prone to error, and the other "experts" in the field, that the original "expert" does find himself in, may disagree. However, as a matter for the record, I wholly support the tool scientific inquiry is, but I disavow the way science is hijacked by the government and media for nefarious ends. Nevertheless, the media colours science in such a fashion as to ensure it comes across as divinely inspired, almost; that the expert be the prophet and the consensus be the commandment, but none of these prove, conclusively, the specific media piece in question and leave the fruits of science open to abuse.[215]

Moreover, let us examine modern politics, I have already discussed the modern institutes of higher education being similar to ecclesiastical centres - Meccas of Marxism, if you will – but it is true[216]. Additionally, Marxism holds for itself a rather extensive record of acting like a quasi-religion. Marx, the prophet; Das Kapital and other canonical texts, the holy scriptures; the universities and colleges, the ecclesiastical institutes for the study of that theological doctrine; the professor the priest; the sign of penance or act of confession: to change your gender, dress as the opposite sex, berate capitalism and your nation's history, become queer,

---

[215] Britannica, *The Editors of Encyclopaedia. "Henri de Saint-Simon"*. Encyclopedia Britannica, 15 May. 2021, https://www.britannica.com/biography/Henri-de-Saint-Simon. Accessed 15 September 2021: "A scientist, my friends, is a man who foresees; it is because science provides the means to predict that it is useful, and that scientists are superior to all other men.
[216] Jon Miltimore and Dan Sanchez. (2020). *The New York Times Reported 'the Mainstreaming of Marxism in US Colleges' 30 Years Ago. Today, We See the Results*. Available: https://iea.org.uk/the-new-york-times-reported-the-mainstreaming-of-marxism-in-us-colleges-30-years-ago-today-we-see-the-results/. Last accessed 15/09/2021.

confess your white privilege, attack heretical symbols of white supremacy, kneel before a statue of a black power militant, and arbitrarily kneel before a person of a darker skin tone; the marginalised and historically downtrodden are the messianic figures of the movement; the capitalist, or white male, the personification of evil. One could go on with the similarities ad infinitum, but I think it is clear that at least some part of the human's nature is drawn towards structures that we would tend to define as religions, even if they be secular or non-divine in nature, but why is this? Why do people find the act of listening to the commandments and pronouncements of a faceless, unaccountable entity, of which has the potential to be highly doctored by an external interest, so irresistible? I think it is something that goes to the very core of what it means to be human, that being that we desire answers and we wish to explain observable phenomenon[217]. It is the reason I am writing this book after all and discussing my ideas with you, the reader. We wish for answers and the priestly class, like all pious businessmen, have a solution to exploit the problem; and they write a holy scripture, showcase an expert paper or marginal study on the glittering media, or write drab and boring exhortations upon the nature of dialectical materialism. These figures, or the ones they claim to be divinely inspired by or are channelling, and their doctrines are thus venerated as divine, and become the central point of devotion or belief for the adherents. For some, they act out in violence against non-believers and attack heretical works. For example, the destruction of Western cities in light of these 2020 BLM riots and the vicious attacks upon people who question the media and the government's narrative concerning the pandemic, and this is justified in the mind of the believer because the infidel is a dehumanised entity who lacks the moral righteousness, inscribed in the soul of the said believer. As the old adage goes, "those who can make you believe absurdities, can force you to

---

[217] Maria Konnikova. (2013). *Why We Need Answers*. Available: https://www.newyorker.com/tech/annals-of-technology/why-we-need-answers. Last accessed 15/09/2021: "Individuals' desire for a firm answer to a question and an aversion toward ambiguity," – Arie Kruglanski.

commit atrocities"; this is the problem with religion or religious types of mediums of information. However, used for good, religions can be quite useful to the development and stability of a people.[218]

Finally, I wish to discuss the reason established religions, or at least the mainstream elements, tend towards catering to the societal norms and bending to suit, what should be, divinely delivered doctrines. I think the reason is simple, that humans tend towards the path of least resistance and like all primates we are social creatures, and to go against the external society and maroon ourselves voluntarily, upon an isolated island of loneliness, is not entirely conducive to our own preservation. Therefore, the various comments we are hearing from the Pope, the support for non-traditional forms of matrimony, or the allowing of female priests and bishops is simply a reflection of that psychology; and also, there is a financial aspect to it, obviously.[219] Conversely though, we find that localised sects or even ancestral Heathen sects have a far greater emphasis upon the more traditional customs that were inherent within Western culture, prior to the modern dilution of such customs, and as such they will most likely outlive the collapse of our society. If their demographic trajectory has a positive projection for the future, that is.

An Abundance of Inaction

Within civilisations that are beginning to falter – be they in the *age of intellect, decadence or decline* – we find that there is an over-reliance upon the idea of endless talk and little action. Parliaments and assemblies

---

[218] Cloete, A. (2014). *Social cohesion and social capital: Possible implications for the common good*. Verbum et Ecclesia, 35(3), 6 pages. doi: https://doi.org/10.4102/ve.v35i3.1331: "Although a variety of definitions exist on social capital the core elements seem to be the networks, trust, norms and reciprocity that exist between individuals and groups. Social cohesion could be viewed as the positive outcome of social capital formation for a community that in return could lead to more social capital formation".
[219] University College London. (2017, February 21). *Humans are hard-wired to follow the path of least resistance*. ScienceDaily. Retrieved September 15, 2021 from www.sciencedaily.com/releases/2017/02/170221101016.htm

become hotbeds of babbling rhetoricians; of whose role it seems to be perennially engaged in incessant debate, to disguise the lack of meaningful action that is produced from such dens of interminable monotony and subsidised refreshments. This is true for many other institutions as well, from scientific to even the local townhall – people seldom agree on matters that are largely uncontentious, so they certainly can come to no agreement on controversial subjects. Needless to say, this stems from the verity that individuals are inextricably diverse in their views, and everyone has some sort of unwavering interest in any matter worthy of disagreement. However, I am fully aware, if we may presume the certitude of *Thomas Hobbes* rebuttal of assemblies or Democracies in his magnum opus *Leviathan*[220], that this may be a weakness of Democracies rather than the symptomatic corollary of decline. Though, to play devil's advocate for but a moment, we do see the same type of inaction be produced from interregnums or empowered councils within the court of a weak monarch.

Digressing however, the repercussions from such inaction by the assembled leadership is best put by *Sir John Glubb* himself when he states, "Amid a Babel of talk, the ship drifts on to the rocks." Entertain me for just a moment, do you recall having ever watched debates in a parliament or assembly, witnessed the ineptitude of new legislation, or witnessed the implementation of policies in which you have thought to yourself: "Why are the leadership in these positions? They clearly lack prudence and one could scarcely believe that they could run a 'piss-up' in a brewery, never mind run a developed, first-world nation". The reason for this? Well, the overall reason is nepotism, but what results from this caterwauling of mindlessness is pure, unfiltered compromise. It is a sole problem inherent within assemblies and within debates. To find the middle-ground, one must discount the good points of both and settle on a resolution that imbues within it the mediocrity of both proposals, to ensure the contentedness of the house. This inept form

---

[220] Hobbes, T. (1968 (1651, originally.)). *Leviathan.* Penguin Books: Baltimore.

of problem-solving leads, as *Sir John Glubb* explains, to utter destruction and projects weakness to external foes.[221]

INEQUALITY OF EVERYTHING

I have detailed previously the matter of moral decay, but moral decay produces a tertiary belief within the ruling aristocracy, and that belief is that "what's mine is mine and what's yours is mine, too". This leads to an ensuing of wealth inequality, naturally, and the extraction of wealth from the various subservient classes of society may be done under the benevolent guise of "wealth redistribution" or "affirmative action", but the end is always the same: the elite skim from the top the cream and give a partial amount to the affected[222]. This is connected to the matter of moral decay because once the ruling class have dispensed with the burden of morals, they have free reign to engage in what they wish to without limitations, Thus, what is typically seen is a growing disconnect between the aristocrats and the plebeians, socially and economically, and the middle-class usually dissipates within this socio-economic crucible. In the USA at present, we find that CBO data indicates that the top 1 percent earns 93 times as much as the bottom 20 percent.[223]. Comparatively, in the book *War and Peace and War: The Rise and Fall of Empires* by *Peter Turchin*, we find that:

"The richest 1 percent of the Romans during the early Republic was only 10 to 20 times as wealthy as an average Roman citizen. "Now compare that to the situation in Late Antiquity when "an average Roman noble of senatorial class had property valued in the neighbourhood of 20,000 Roman pounds of gold. There was no "middle class" comparable to the small landholders of

---

[221] Glubb, J. (1978). *The Fate of Empires and Search for Survival*. Edinburgh: Blackwood. Pg. 12.
[222] Rathbone, Dominic. "Earnings and Costs. Part IV, chapter 15", Pg. 299–326. In: *Quantifying the Roman Economy: Methods and Problems*. Alan Bowman and Andrew Wilson eds. Oxford University Press 2009, paperback edition 2013.
[223] Congressional Budget Office. (2020). *The Distribution of Household Income, 2017*. Available: https://www.cbo.gov/publication/56575. Last accessed 20/09/2021.

the third century B.C.; the huge majority of the population was made up of landless peasants working land that belonged to nobles. These peasants had hardly any property at all, but if we estimate it (very generously) at one tenth of a pound of gold, the wealth differential would be 200,000! Inequality grew both as a result of the rich getting richer (late imperial senators were 100 times wealthier than their Republican predecessors) and those of the middling wealth becoming poor."[224]

It is exactly the same situation we find today in the modern West[225]. Furthermore, we find that that the political class begin to be consumed by their own interests, and generally discard the interests of the nation or its citizens. We find this in the area of them enacting policies of currency debasement, therefore affording them the opportunity of building great works and gifting generous welfare to the population in the present, by stealing the prosperity of the future and damning their progeny to debt. By extension we witness exactly the same circumstance in play today. For example, the SNP, the Scottish National Party who are the reigning demagogues within the devolved parliament of Scotland, have recently just been caught in a rather serious scandal. Since we are all in the throes of a pandemic, the pupils of Scottish schools have been unable to undertake their end of year examinations, so therefore their mock tests, or prelims, that they undertook earlier in the year should be used to determine their grades. However, the SNP instructed the SQA, the bureaucracy responsible for the marking and awarding of qualifications, to engineer a formula, or algorithm, in which the students from the most deprived areas were unfairly disadvantaged and their grades lowered from their previous prelim results. Why have they done this? It is simple, really. In Scotland, tuition fees are paid for and generous financial benefits granted to students, but in such a time, as now, where economic activity

---

[224] Turchin, P. (2006). *War and peace and war: the life cycles of imperial nations.* New York: Pi Press. Chapter: Born to Be Wolves.
[225] Berman Y, Ben-Jacob E, Shapira Y (2016) The Dynamics of Wealth Inequality and the Effect of Income Distribution. PLoS ONE 11(4): e0154196. https://doi.org/10.1371/journal.pone.0154196

CHAPTER IV

and the resultant tax revenue from such activity has been stopped there is clearly a lack of budget to afford this costly endeavour. Therefore, instead of cutting the benefit for all, for this year, the SNP have corruptly lowered the pupil's grades, around a quarter of the total, to stop a flood of native university students from attending Scottish universities, and potentially costing the SNP a great deal of economic and fiscal headache. Moreover, there was discussion, because of the lockdowns, that students were studying harder because their parents were home as well and encouraging them – and some prior studies anticipated an increase of 80% on the pass-rate of students this year. Furthermore, as a side-note, a lot of the university faculty and some politicians, more than likely, hold a large portfolio of rentable property in the university districts of Scotland, or have a vested financial interest in the private institutions that are Scottish universities. Therefore, it is well understood that foreign students, who pay their own higher tuition fees and stimulate the local rental market, are of greater importance to these verminous officials. In a society who has a strong moral fibre and cares for their future, one would not witness such abhorrent and blatant corruption.[226]

War and Peace and War: The Rise and Fall of Empires by *Peter Turchin* is a fantastic book and I strongly advise one to read it if they have an interest in the details as to why the various collapses and weak-points of the Roman republic, and empire, began to be. Along with other imperial cycles throughout history. *Turchin* continues in that specific excerpt:

The set of values developed by the early Romans called mos maiorum, was gradually replaced by one of personal greed and pursuit of self-interest.

"Probably the most important value was virtus (virtue), which derived from the word vir (man) and embodied all the qualities of a true man as a member of society,"

---

[226] James McEnaney. (2020). *Revealed: Poorest Scots schools hit four times harder in SQA results scandal.* Available: https://www.thenational.scot/news/18802660.revealed-poorest-scots-schools-hit-four-times-harder-sqa-results-scandal/on-shirley-anne-somerville. Last accessed 20/09/2021.

"Virtus included the ability to distinguish between good and evil and to act in ways that promoted good, and especially the common good. Unlike Greeks, Romans did not stress individual prowess, as exhibited by Homeric heroes or Olympic champions. The ideal of hero was one whose courage, wisdom, and self-sacrifice saved his country in time of peril," Turchin adds.

And *Turchin* goes on to explain:

"Unlike the selfish elites of the later periods, the aristocracy of the early Republic did spare its blood or treasure in the service of the common interest. When 50,000 Romans, a staggering one fifth of Rome's total manpower, perished in the battle of Cannae, as mentioned previously, the senate lost almost one third of its membership. This suggests that the senatorial aristocracy was more likely to be killed in wars than the average citizen....

The wealthy classes were also the first to volunteer extra taxes when they were needed... A graduated scale was used in which the senators paid the most, followed by the knights (equestrians), *and then other citizens. In addition, officers and centurions (but not common soldiers!) served without pay, saving the state 20 percent of the legion's payroll"*[227]

Typically, we find a metamorphosis of the nature of the male of a society through the various ages of an empire's existence. Their natural will for self-sacrifice slowly erodes and morphs into a dishevelled mess, characterised by greed and self-interest. Interestingly, this becomes reflected in the various constructions and environment of a civilisation. Where once there was order, beauty, colour and tidiness; there will be chaos, ugliness, achromatic dullness and unkempt surroundings. I have witnessed this first-hand, for instance in our small town we have a beautifully carved granite drinking fountain that was generously gifted, in the 1880's, by a wealthy philanthropist to the town. It always looked tidy and one could even drink from it until very recently, and there was even a lower fountain for your dog to drink from, too. Now, however, the area surrounding it is covered in weeds, it is overgrown, the fountain's taps

---

[227] Turchin, P. (2006). *War and peace and war: the life cycles of imperial nations.* New York: Pi Press. Chapter: Born to Be Wolves.

have been parted from the original structure, the benches surrounding it gone, the banister to the elevated area in which it sits are rotten, and the fountain's bowls, for the draining of the water, contain used-syringes and used-condom packets. Within less than a decade, that monument, that was integral to our local park, has been carelessly abandoned by our corrupt local council; left to become ruinous. However, our local council is efficient in other aspects, they are famous for being the only council, in the country, that has a chief executive that earns a greater annual salary than the Prime Minister and we have the greatest number of executives that earn six-figures, annually. We have important positions such as the Executive for Cultural Development, which will net an individual a salary of £117,000, per annum. Therefore, it is fully understandable why there is not enough surplus capital available, to the local council, to repair an endearing community monument; we have to pay for the privilege of them creating unimportant and high-paid positions for their cronies. This is the type of corruption and decay that is quintessential to the decline of an empire and is representative of its growing wealth and social inequality.

Radically Superficial

The so-called radicalism we see today is something that is touted as radical, but takes root in an ideology that has been tried and failed hundreds of times within the past and is ingrained within the intellectual and political fabric of mostly every Western nation. The actual radical developments that our society requires are ones in which, at our present predicament, are unobtainable and unfathomable to our political elite's unimaginative minds. Predictably, we find that in declining empires there is a great abundance of power within the status quo, but by the status quo's predictable nature, we find that there is a lack of novel thinking and solutions become very emblematic, rather than being significant reforms that shake the slumbering sloths of the political class from their trees.

Michael Grant described something very similar in his short book entitled, "*The Fall of the Roman Empire*", in which he explains:

"*There was no room at all, in these ways of thinking, for the novel, apocalyptic situation which had now arisen, a situation which needed solutions as radical as itself. (The Status Quo) attitude is a complacent acceptance of things as they are, without a single new idea.*

"*This acceptance was accompanied by greatly excessive optimism about the present and future. Even when the end was only sixty years away, and the Empire was already crumbling fast, Rutilius continued to address the spirit of Rome with the same supreme assurance.*"

This blind adherence to the ideas of the past ranks high among the principal causes of the downfall of Rome. If you were sufficiently lulled by these traditional fictions, there was no call to take any practical first-aid measures at all."[228]

Grant's analysis of the mindset of the late-Roman elite, and also the citizenry of those days, was right on point. We find that there was an optimism of progress or progressivism prior to the collapse – this connects in with the hubris and laughable ideas of sophistication held by late-era imperial citizens – and that the political elite, or the ones that held sway in the halls of power, had entire assurance of the empire's progress and were supremely optimistic. In retrospect, they were deluded ideologues who mistook the bright light of the train hurdling towards them as a sign that they were close to a utopic paradise. We see a similar situation today and our political class seem unwilling to even abandon unpopular positions; rather they will double down, as they assure us, they know best, and will carry on pursuing the deadly but enticing light of progress. The brighter it seems to get, the dimmer the average person's lot in life becomes. Now, that is a definition of progress only a sufficiently cultured creature of modernity may appreciate.

---

[228] Grant, M. (1990). *The Fall of the Roman Empire*. London: Weidenfeld and Nicolson.

Chapter IV

Contrived Beliefs and Manufactured Ideas

A cynical may say that the dealers in ideas, politely named the media, have a disproportionate amount of power to influence elections, by influencing the electorate; of whom we see can be led like sheep and act rather one-dimensionally to situations, unfortunately. Therefore, what strength does the system of Democracy entail if the electorate are bumbling idiots, and even the highly educated among the populace can be subverted and coerced into becoming revolutionary slogan-chanters? The answer is absolutely none; it is a system that is designed to allow the oligarchs to control more effectively and that being said, Democracy can quite rightly be described as an oligarchy in which the populace cannot see the oligarchs. The Prime-Ministers, the Presidents, the Heads of State, all figureheads, puppets if you will, dangled on a string like a carrot while the ventriloquist-like oligarchs instruct them in the rhetoric to spew forth onto the drooling masses of mental invalids. It is a sad analysis, I can concur, but democracies and republics really do lull the populace into a state of utter inaction. It truly renders it futile in attempting to reverse this decline systematically, and I have resigned myself to the belief that if our various cultures, values and nations are to survive this slowly unravelling situation, then it will be in a piecemeal fashion.

Powerful media conglomerates are able to contrive events of such magnitude and scale, even if they be falsehoods inherently, that are able to alter the minds of the masses, that it is truly staggering that they are still permitted to operate, in this manner, unabated. Am I for a free press? No, but the alternative is just as worse, as we have seen now that small media companies may grow and, as all companies wish to do when they own the lion share of the market, they inevitably drift to create monopolies and nullify competition. What consequently happens, is that these media companies become indelibly ingrained within the political apparatus, and begin to lobby governments to work on their behalf or work on behalf of governments. This creates a system in which the government and the media companies work hand-in-hand, bringing us full-circle back to the original alternative proposition to a free-press, that being namely a controlled press. A similar conclusion has occurred with every other sector within the economy; most notably banking and military-industry. However, the astute among you, will understand the above cerebrations as a criticism of both Capitalism and Communism and you are correct, both systems are inherently flawed, and though the adherents of each system critique the other's system in this eternal dualistic struggle, each fail to understand that both systems – in its end phase – resemble the other; namely monopolies, corporations, an intermingling of government and corporate interests, dissolution of liberty, etc. However, that is tangential to this overall discussion, I just wished to list it.

Continuing on, these media monopolies begin to peddle ideas without the fear of the opposition disparaging their carefully woven web of lies – as there is no opposition. They can contrive any event they wish, for example, the government requires the falsity of "weapons of mass destruction" as a pretext for the invasion of a belligerent nation; "absolutely no problem, Sir, we will get on that right away; just ensure you pass that law to further secure our monopoly over our given market" says the media conglomerate. Moreover, the CEO's and other individuals in the high echelons of these companies, become very politically connected and tend to seek public office; we have seen this with large investment banks, such as Goldman Sachs, whose ex-employees have a very bad habit of joining the US government in top positions as soon as they leave Goldman[229]. For example, from Steve Bannon to Mnuchin, Trump like many of his predecessors has an inordinate amount of ex-Goldman executives working in his

---

[229] Dealbook. (2017). *The People From 'Government Sachs'*. Available: https://www.nytimes.com/2017/03/16/business/dealbook/goldman-sachs-goverment-jobs.html. Last accessed 23/09/2021.

administration. Moreover, roughly twenty-six ex-Goldman executives are in high positions of power throughout the Western world, and this obviously poses the question as to how much corruption and nepotism is rampant between just this firm and the US government[230]. As a final quip to the "vampire squid", as it has been called, we must recall this is the same Goldman Sachs who in the midst of the financial crisis of 2008, as proved by the email reproduced above from ten years ago today, Goldman Sachs by their own admission was "toast" and would have gone bankrupt, if it had not been bailed out by the US government by using the future productivity of the tax-payer as collateral.[231]

This is just one financial institution among a myriad of large global players, but we already see the insidious nature of the merging of corporate and government power; definitionally fascism[232]. This type of system is quintessential of the late era of democracies, ironically enough, but we must understand that these corporations, unsurprisingly, can be traced back as being subsidiaries of a handful of larger corporations. For example, greater than 90% of the media in the US is controlled by Bertelsmann, National Amusements (Viacom CBS), Sony Corporation, News Corp, Comcast, The Walt Disney Company, AT&T Inc., Fox Corporation, Hearst Communications, MGM Holdings Inc., Grupo Globo (South America), and Lagardère Group[233]. Every other company, who are not them directly, are subsidiaries and this is termed an oligopoly, a market form in which a market is dominated by a small group of large corporations. This type of market form, and subsequent political order, is most obviously antithetical to the idea of true Democracy.

---

[230] David Floyd. (2019). *26 Goldman Sachs Alumni Who Run the World (GS)*. Available: https://www.investopedia.com/news/26-goldman-sachs-alumni-who-run-world-gs/. Last accessed 23/09/2021.
[231] Better Markets. (2018). *Email Shows Goldman Admitted It Was "Toast"*. Available: https://bettermarkets.com/newsroom/email-shows-goldman-admitted-it-was-toast. Last accessed 23/09/2021.
[232] *Discorsi del 1927*: Milano, Alpes, 1928, p.157.
[233] Ainger, Katharine (April 2001). *"Empires of the Senseless"*. New Internationalist.

Bread and Circuses

The infamous bread and circuses, or the amusing of the poor, by the political-class, as a means of distracting them from politically important developments or events. Rome was infamous for the practise, but we have been quite successful, if not more so, with our own form of such frivolous entertainment. However, we are transfixed within digital colosseums and amphitheatres now, rather than physical ones.[234]

In the period of the Roman empire, we see that sports teams took on an ambience of divinity surrounding them[235]. The stadia events soon channelled all of the nationalistic fervour that once existed for the empire, into trivial and mindless tribalistic rivalries between chariot teams or gladiators. It became a religious-like ritual of blood and death, or mindless entertainment and carousing. We see today the same level of fervour for sports and sports teams, so much so that sports events become of national significance, and are elevated to "breaking news" level whenever a sports event develops. Naturally, we should all understand, I hope, that sports and entertainment is utilised by the oligarchy as a means to control the masses, it is the opiate of the commoners and thus keeps their ire targeted at other things, other than the political class. This is the same reason the policy of "bread and circuses" was instituted within Rome. To keep the plebeian's fat and merry on grain and alcohol, and to captivate their attentions with frivolous amusement.[236]

---

[234] Toner, J. P. (1995). *Leisure and ancient Rome*. Cambridge, England: Polity Press. Pg. 69.
[235] Todd Stankas. (2019). *The Gladiators: Ancient Rome's Celebrity Outcasts*. Available: https://sites.google.com/view/sonoma-state-history-journal/journals/2019-2020-journal/the-gladiators-ancient-romes-celebrity-outcasts. Last accessed 26/09/2021.
[236] Ben Moreell. (1956). *Of Bread and Circuses*. Available: https://fee.org/articles/of-bread-and-circuses/. Last accessed 26/09/2021. "The evil was not in bread and circuses, per se, but in the willingness of the people to sell their rights as free men for full bellies and the excitement of the games which would serve to distract them from the other human hungers which bread and circuses can never appease. The moral decay of the people was not caused by the doles and the games. These merely provided a measure of their degradation. Things that were originally good had become perverted…"

Chapter IV

However, one could state that sports today is much like it was in Rome, a quasi-religion. As I have already alluded to, devotion to one's nation has been supplanted by devotion to one's team, one may go on pilgrimage over hundreds of miles just to witness their team playing away, they venerate the symbols and crests of their team as diligently as a religious adherent would a religious icon, they will sing their praises at the modern day stadia, they will wear these colours and aforementioned symbols like they are divinely blessed, and finally, they will embroil themselves in fights, even amongst their fellow countrymen over petty sport rivalries. It is a religion, an opiate for the masses of lemmings stupid enough to take it seriously. No entertainment, provided at the expense of the public purse, is ever done for solely your entertainment, it is a contrived event, of whose date is specifically selected, to distract the masses attention from a serious political event. If one may call me a "conspiracy theorist" for such an idea, then they most obviously do not understand the game of politics, or the game of leadership, as these are tools adopted by all leaders to maintain and cultivate their power base.[237]

It is not just sports though, other forms of media, plays and theatre for example, have been used for millennia to sow ideas into the minds of the populace, of which imparted some benefit to the political class. For example, in ancient Hellas it was compulsory to attend plays at the amphitheatre; the state would even pay for the poor to attend and, furthermore, prisoners were temporarily let out of jail to view the drama. Why did the ancient Greeks think it so important to view a play? Simply put, because each play imparted some sort of cultural programming into the psyche of the people, and this developed the society in the way the political class saw fit. This can be used to strengthen society or destroy it. Now, if you focus and think back on the various programs, media, plays,

---

[237] Michael Serazio. (2013). *Just How Much is Sports Fandom Like Religion?* Available: https://www.theatlantic.com/entertainment/archive/2013/01/just-how-much-is-sports-fandom-like-religion/272631/. Last accessed 26/09/2021.

etc, you were exposed to as a child, then as an adolescent, and finally as an adult, how much have the cultural and social messages of these "plays" changed? I would harken quite a lot, and one could argue this cultural development was not a positive one, as we are witnessing with the societal and cultural breakdown of late.[238]

---

[238] Paul Kingsnorth. (2021). *The West has lost its virtue*. Available: https://unherd.com/2021/08/why-the-west-will-collapse/. Last accessed 26/09/2021.

CHAPTER V

MILITARY

The military system of an empire, and its efficiency, is the life blood of its engine of momentum and ultimately its functional survival. What we find within declining empires is a military system that was once strong but then slowly drifts into a state of weakness, and this is caused through a slow and systematic lowering of standards spurred on by the admission of diverse tribes within its ranks, an atmosphere of general corruption and growing autonomy of the officer-class, and lowering standards of patriotism amongst the troop which hampers the effectiveness of the various units, legions or battalions in a geo-political sense.[239]

This weakening of the military is typically symptomatic of an assortment of other influencing factors such as economic troubles, over reliance upon slaves or migrants, the rise of a rival empire, overextension and overspending, the loss of traditional values and patriotism, and lack of loyalty to the nation amongst the new migrant populace or foreign contingents within the military. The Roman empire during

---

[239] Lachmann, Richard. (2011). *The Roots of American Decline*. Contexts: 2011;10(1):44-49. doi:10.1177/1536504211399050. "Rather, I have found that consolidation of the defence industry has allowed interlocking elites (defence contractors, military service heads, and bankers) who have financed industry consolidation to resist the reallocation of spending away from highly profitable though strategically worthless weapons systems."

the fifth century experienced every one of these aforementioned issues, simultaneously, and this effectively sealed their fate[240]. Moreover, we may see that once the empire is weak, militarily speaking, the nations of whom still possess masculine vigour and patriotism will, and while amassed upon the frontiers of the empire or within, will descend upon it in its throes of death to divide up the spoils; such is the nature of life. Therefore, to digress, can we truly say with confidence that we are seeing the beginnings of what happened to the Roman military, occurring within our own Western militaries? We will use this chapter to deliberate upon these ideas.

FOREIGN COHORTS

The influx of migrants or foreign elements within the military, or a reliance upon them to fill recruitment quotas, causes great hinderance to the cohesion of the military; as we can bear witness to it causing the same diminishment of cohesion within the social sphere of the civilisation[241] [242]. Historical precedent for this was also set most notably within the Roman empire, in which beginning in proper during the aftermath of the Gothic war (376-382 AD), we see the Roman legions begin to become little more than semi-autonomous units of mercenary barbarians, usually fighting under their own chieftain in their own fighting styles, and with lacklustre discipline contrary to the Roman legions of old[243]. This had begun to creep into the military hierarchy of Rome for several reasons prior to the late era of the empire, of something I will detail below, but it

---

[240] Ferrill, Arther. *The Fall of the Roman Empire: The Military Explanation.* (London: Thames and Hudson, 1986), Pg. 7. "Strictly military considerations must play a large part in any explanation of the fall of the Roman Empire."
[241] Rebecca Wickes, Renee Zahnow, Gentry White & Lorraine Mazerolle (2014) *Ethnic Diversity and Its Impact on Community Social Cohesion and Neighbourly Exchange*, Journal of Urban Affairs, 36:1, 51-78, DOI: 10.1111/juaf.12015
[242] Putnam, Robert D (2000). *Bowling Alone: The Collapse and Revival of American Community.* New York: Simon & Schuster.
[243] P. Southern and K. Dixon, The Late Roman Army (London, 1996). Pg. 53.

became far more pronounced within the fourth and fifth centuries. This reduced the standardisation of the military, in equipment and tactics, and the later army structure became largely disorderly and inflexible, comparable to the military of old.[244]

Therefore, the question remains, why did the Roman political and military classes permit such laxness within the ranks? The reason is political expediency. As we see now, the reason for the admission of mass numbers of migrants into our own borders is to attempt to stabilise the economic and demographic haemorrhaging of our own civilisation. Essentially, akin to Rome, due to constrictive taxes required for the ever-expanding hegemony and inflation, and other economic factors, there is a sharp decline in childbirth in the nation. Within Rome, we find that they had the inverse problem to ours, that their population had a relatively low life expectancy, with diseases such as pulmonary tuberculosis being quite rife, this made long-term economic planning impossible and the potential for the growth in the tax base was hampered. The solution, as with all political classes throughout history, is not to solve the root issues plaguing the society, no pun intended, but to simply import taxpayers, to fund the continuation of welfare schemes and to fiscally support the economically unproductive of society, namely the poor and young. Achieving this either through migration or slavery, and both can be nuancedly synonymous within certain civilisations. However, typically after a hundred or so years the immigrant tax base begins to demographically stabilise and they form productive tax quarters, usually self-segregated, in urban areas. Alas, the issues stem from the cultural osmosis that occurs, the diminishing social cohesion, incompatible interests, and if a welfare system develops then it creates further burdens upon the state by the virtue of the exponential nature of population growth. Slavery poses other problems too, not least to mention the moral abhorrence of such a practise, but the issues surrounding the disincentivising of labour-saving devices which stunts

---

[244] Southern, P. (2014). *The Roman Army: A History 753 BC - AD 476*. London: Amberley Publishing.

growth in production, and the catastrophically lowering wages and thus the default expelling of the native worker from the labour market. Interestingly, this is what fuelled Rome's early conquests, post-political annexation of Greece, and that was namely the acquisition of greater amounts of slaves to financially benefit the patrician and landowner class and their mercantilist pursuits, of which they comprised the bulk of the military as recruits were required to furnish their own military equipment and supplies. Therefore, to conclude, the reason for the admission of immigrants into a nation is typically not to help the incoming migrants, though the political class may feign such moral pomposity to defend their political machination from attacks by the lower classes, but it is to attempt to ensure the political class have a sufficient supply of taxable individuals, or individuals to protect their interests overseas, in far-flung wars of aggression masked as acts of liberation.[245]

In this day and age, we are beginning to see similar signs of military decay, but we are not seeing an entire non-standardisation of equipment, instead we are beginning to see some Western militaries slowly turn towards becoming more defensive-like forces rather than being the once militaristic juggernauts they once were. However, in certain Western countries, such as the UK, the military arms and equipment, even the size and funding of the military, is becoming abysmal and US general, *General Mark Milley*, stated in 2017 that "too small and is nowhere near prepared for a war"[246]. Although, the British military has increased its size and presence in times of war, but it is hard to see with the current pool of fighting-aged men that Britain could, in any way, put up any resistance against a formidable invasion or in a significant conventional

---

[245] Wiedemann, T. (1980). *Greek and Roman Slavery* (1st ed.). Routledge. Pg. 110. "Strabo tells how a massive slave trade sprung out of the collapse of the Seleucid Empire. Large numbers of the slaves eventually found their way to Italy where they were purchased by wealthy landowners who needed huge numbers of slaves to work on their estates." (Moya K. Mason, *"Roman Slavery: Social, Cultural, Political, and Demographic Consequences"*).

[246] Laura Mowat. (2017). *Britain's Army is TOO SMALL and is nowhere near prepared for a war, warns top US official*. Available: https://www.express.co.uk/news/uk/822512/Britain-s-army-too-small-unprepared-war-General-Mark-Milley. Last accessed 27/09/2021.

war. However, the defence budget is increasing ever so slightly, beginning in 2019, so there may be a turnaround and hopefully a more rugged sort of Briton begins to be cultivated within the society, but I would not hold your breath. Although, I wish to stress that I do not pick on Britain for any personal reason and what is occurring there is happening in piecemeal across the Western world, but like the Italian peninsula during the 4th century, we find that a starkly high majority of Western males today subscribe to ideas of pacifism and find the idea of serving in the military, in any capacity, beyond thought[247]. Though, I empathise with the idea that many wars were and are being fought for ulterior political motives and thus, as many see it, fighting for a corrupt political class in far-flung campaigns may be less than attractive. As is duly expected, this likewise situation once led to the policy of utilising costly mercenary barbarian forces and *foederati* within the aging Roman military, and as we are seeing today with such companies as Blackwater, it may occur once again.[248]

TERRORIST, THE NEW BARBARIAN?

Is the word "terrorist" now the modern equivalent of the ancient term "barbarian"? One could conclusively argue it is. For example, the barbarians of old were known to adopt a modus operandi in which they inhabited the fringes of the frontiers of control for the empire, they were the ideological or political opponents of the empire, and they adopted unconventional and asymmetrical methods of warfare to dispel

---

[247] Northedge, F. S., & Edwards, P. (1967). *Peace, War and Philosophy* (Vol. 6). The Encyclopaedia of Philosophy: Collier Macmillan. Pg. 63-67.
[248] Tribble, Joseph M., *"The Mercenary Tradition and Conflict Privatization: A Revolutionary Shift in the Cyclical Nature of Mercenary Use"* (2018). MSU Graduate Theses. 3303. https://bearworks.missouristate.edu/theses/3303. "This extended into the use of foederati by the Romans... served under the Foedus, which was "considered a contract for the service whether the agreement was made by an individual foederatus or by a group of foederati serving under a leader of some sort." And "Blackwater, DynCorp, and Triple Canopy are not the same thing as Qaddafi's mercenaries…they are bound to follow the laws of the countries where they are based and operate and, in theory, are only hired for noncombat operations like guard duty (though that line is often a thin one in war zones)".

the imperial hegemony from their lands. Interestingly, we find that barbarians, in the final push for Western Rome, utilised the infrastructure and siege weaponry of Rome to bring down the ailing empire[249]. In conjunction, we find that terrorists today are engaged in the same type of struggles, and they utilise the infrastructure and technology of the empire against itself; for example, planes were utilised on September 11th, cars and vans utilised for mowing pedestrians down, etc. Moreover, if we look at the current terminology and accepted politically correct vernacular, then we can witness that today they do not call these attacks "terrorist attacks", nor do they refer to the perpetrators as "terrorists", by contrast they will refer to them as "incidents". This speaks volumes and echoes to the cultural and ethnic osmosis that was occurring in Rome, too. Thus, the only explanation one could ascertain by the actions of the authorities calling these heinous crimes and attacks, mere "incidents", is that they establishment is becoming slowly populated by peoples who are less and less Western, and they share a kinship, be it a religious or ethnic one, with the perpetrators. Therefore, in the interests of their own kin, tribe and to abrogate bad optics, so to say, they have chosen new terminology to euphemise these attacks. However, the older terms are utilised for politically right leaning or "white" nationalist attacks, as that group obviously do not hold the power within the Western political or social structure.[250]

Conversely, we saw a similar occurrence in Rome, where the loyalties of the foreign migrants were ultimately with their respective tribes, even if they feigned loyalty to Rome outwardly, and the more barbarians that flooded into the various sectors of society, and the society as a whole, the more these various social institutions began to take on the customs and values of their new barbarian counterparts. Funnily enough, these

---

[249] Peter Heather (2006), *The Fall of the Roman Empire: A New History of Rome and the Barbarians*. Oxford University Press. Pg. 84–100.
[250] Kelly Sadler. (2021). *The pervasive racism against White males*. Available: https://www.washingtontimes.com/news/2021/mar/24/the-pervasive-racism-against-white-males/?utm_source=GOOGLE&utm_medium=cpc&utm_id=chacka&utm_campaign=TWT+-+DSA&g-clid=CjwKCAjw-sqKBhBjEiwAVaQ9az2V1oAAf. Last accessed 28/09/2021.

barbarians most likely held, privately, strong animosities towards Rome for the perceived historical injustices perpetrated on their ancestors; such as slavery, conquest and dissolution of tribes and confederacies. Similar to the modern context, the West but only a few centuries ago was busily conquering these various tribes that now inhabit our lands in staunch numbers, thus we cannot truly believe that these peoples do not still hold onto some nationalistic resentment against us for past injustices. Well, we can bear witness to the growing tide of resentment through the 2020 riots in the USA and the various BLM marches, that openly call for the extirpation of Western history and culture; that the European is somehow inherently evil, by nature. Naturally, adopting these points of rhetoric would spell the end for our civilisation.[251]

As a tangential point, we are beginning to see talk amongst the political class of "white supremacy" being the most egregious threat to the national interests of the West[252]. Naturally, this an entirely different weaponization of the term "terrorist" and is focused innately inwards, towards the civilisation as a whole. That said, "white supremacy" is now deemed as anything remotely European in nature; the very Founding Fathers of America, are seen as symbols of "white supremacy" by far-left extremists. Thus, should the entire nation of America be then deconstructed and rendered to ash, as a form of making good on the sin of "white supremacy"? Well, the extremists, who occupy high government now, would answer in the affirmative and are actively doing just that. Moreover, this current inward search for the barbarian, with such "white supremacist" rhetoric, will lead to a galvanisation of all sides and a mobilisation of hatred amongst the various opposing racial, political and cultural groups; one in which facilitates polarisation and future violence

---

[251] Tom Ames. (2021). *The Western Roman Emperors: from 410 AD until the Fall of the Roman Empire*. Available: https://www.historyhit.com/the-western-roman-emperors-from-the-sack-of-rome-to-the-fall-of-the-western-roman-empire/. Last accessed 28/09/2021.
[252] Harper Neidig and Rebecca Beitsch. (2021). *Biden officials testify that white supremacists are greatest domestic security threat*. Available: https://thehill.com/policy/national-security/553161-biden-officials-testify-that-white-supremacists-are-greatest. Last accessed 28/09/2021.

amongst these groups. Thus, such irresponsibility from the political class can only be intentional; they may feign ineptness, but the overseers of their actions know exactly as to what they do and to what it shall affect.

OFFENCE MAKES WAY FOR DEFENCE

Military strategy and theory within the late Roman empire also changed; moving from less conventional, set-piece engagements to low-intensity guerrilla warfare when challenged, utilising a vast array of unstandardised *Limitanei* border forces that focused on causing attrition to the enemy by way of its labyrinthine network of forts[253]. This military was still effective and if the economy was not so crippled and the bureaucracy not so stifling, it might have been effective at deterring small invasion forces of disunited tribes on the border. However, this was a distinctive difference from the beginnings of the empire, in which its military was mainly utilised by the state for conquest of territory and prized slaves, which would be used to stimulate productivity and the economy; at least for a short-period of time, but this would naturally cause technological stagnation further into the empire's lifecycle; post-conquest of Britannia[254]. As a side note, one should also be aware, that when conquest ceases, we begin to see the rise of the bureaucratic state - oppressive taxation, loss of liberties and centralisation of everything – and this is in part caused by the need for the state to maintain its holdings, firstly, and to find new ways in which to stimulate the economy and thus finance the military which maintained the internal power dynamics within the empire. *Stefan Molyneux* puts it cleverly, in which he states that bureaucracy is like water, in which whilst the empire expands the water will continue to find its level and spread out through the provinces, but once the empire achieves the extent of its limit it will begin to fill and fill, until it drowns the empire whole.

---

[253] Luttwak, Edward (1976). *The grand strategy of the Roman Empire from the first century A.D. to the third*. Baltimore: Johns Hopkins University Press. Pg. 130-145.
[254] Flohr, M. (2016). *Innovation and Society in the Roman World*. Oxford Handbooks Online. doi:10.1093/oxfordhb/9780199935390.013.85.

Chapter V

Is what is occurring with our system the same? No, but it shares some similarities.[255]

Digressing somewhat, we find in our modern times that the Western military strategy is beginning to move towards a more defensive posture in some ways[256]. We see that geopolitical enmities are beginning to form between power blocks – China and the US being the most notable – and longstanding alliances are beginning to wane. NATO, to take a for instance, is becoming fractured and the US is beginning to withdraw its support from the European countries who seem to continually renege upon their obligatory commitments. We can see this with the US withdrawing troops from Germany and beginning to pull funding for several European militaries. This will naturally lead Germany and Europe to diminish their ties with the US sphere and go out on their own, with their own union's army, as has been discussed, or begin to come under the yoke of the emerging sphere; comprised of China and Russia, as the leading figures.

As can be ascertained, the high-point of military prowess for the US was last seen in the Iraq war; since then, the republic's armies have slowly become burdened by politically correct ideas, not taking seriously the war in Afghanistan, and becoming embroiled in failed efforts of subterfuge in Libya, Syria and Iraq which does not serve their long-term interests, but it seems only to serve Israel's. The American military, and their Anglosphere allies, have spread themselves thin and with the staunchly dismal domestic economic situation, a weakening dollar long-term and increasing welfare distribution, we can see that though America is still a force to be reckoned with for many generations to come, its decline

---

[255] Finley, M. I. *"Technical Innovation and Economic Progress in the Ancient World."* Economic History Review 18, no. 1 (1965): 29–45.
[256] Eugene Gholz, Benjamin Friedman & Enea Gjoza (2019) *Defensive Defence: A Better Way to Protect US Allies in Asia*, The Washington Quarterly, 42:4, 171-189, DOI: 10.1080/0163660X.2019.1693103. "US strategy in East Asia is defensive—seeking to maintain the territorial status quo and to preserve open trade and investment. The military component of that strategy largely involves helping allies defend their territories against China as the PRC grows richer and spends more on its military."

has already set in[257]. Have they begun the same defensive strategy as the Roman state? Geopolitically no, with the trade wars and sanctions against any country that crosses them, but in small-scale conflicts such as Afghanistan, we find that they emulate the Romans in the incessant drive towards becoming involved in conflicts that they become bogged down in. The Parthian and Dacian Wars of *Trajan* are a counterpoint example of this. As the military demand for a certain superpower increases – be it from their allies or the politicos that demand more provinces to tax, or more countries to indebt to the IMF – then they must be consistently growing by utilising incentives for services, of which is a form of welfare in and of itself. Although, what we find with the US is that though the demand for the military is increasing with all the geopolitical situations arising around the world, we are beginning to see a decrease in terms of weaponry efficiency and personnel; despite the constant increase in military spending, year after year. In a *Centre for New American Security* report 2017, penned by CNAS Adjunct Senior Fellow Steven Kosiak, he states that "Measured in terms of personnel and major weapons platforms, the size of the U.S. military has been on a generally downward trajectory for decades"[258]. Moreover, we see personnel lay-offs, the largest since the end of the Cold-War and a cutting back on these welfare incentives for service. Meanwhile, in a 2021 military report, we are seeing a reduction in force in the marine corps with 2,000 personnel lay-offs, and the air force losing 6,000 personnel to the newly appointed Space force. Yet, there will be a 3% increase in soldier's pay; which is obviously a political necessity at this point.

---

[257] Eric Edelman, Gary Roughead, et al. (2019). *Providing for the Common Defence*. Available: chrome-extension://oemmndcbldboiebfnladdacbdfmadadm/https://www.usip.org/sites/default/files/2018-11/providing-for-the-common-defense.pdf. Last accessed 29/09/2021. "America's longstanding military advantages have diminished. The country's strategic margin for error has become distressingly small. Doubts about America's ability to deter and, if necessary, defeat opponents and honour its global commitments have proliferated."

[258] Steven Kosiak. (2017). *Is the U.S. Military Getting Smaller and Older?* Available: https://www.cnas.org/publications/reports/is-the-u-s-military-getting-smaller-and-older. Last accessed 29/09/2021.

Chapter V

As a sidenote too, we will see – much like in Rome – an abandonment of the provinces upon the hinterland of the frontier; evacuations from these areas will be seen and a general contraction of the projection of the military hegemony, of the Anglo-American Empire, will become witnessed in short order proceeding such evacuations. Rome evacuated Germania Superior, leaving it embarrassingly to the invading Alemanni who annexed the *Colonia* there. It would then, later on in the Empire, abandon Dacia in a similar fashion. How long shall it be until we see the US abandon the eastern territories, militarily, it has modern-day proxy governments in? It abandoned the Indochina theatre, the Middle-Eastern theatre will be likewise abandoned, then Europe too will be abandoned; how long, like Rome, will it take after that until the heartland is invaded by the barbarians knocking at the gates? Naturally, this will be done under the guise of "refocusing military efforts in a changing geopolitical landscape", but we all know it shall be an easily discernible case of military contraction, due to the lack of resolve in the political class and the weakening of the military machine. Will the same fate befall the Sons and Daughters of Liberty, as it did the Children of the Tiber?

Pax Americana

The era of the *Pax Americana*, as it has been delightfully named, reigning supreme from post-1945, and it still nominally exists today[259]. Unlike the British, *Pax Britannica,* at the turn of the 20th century, it seems that the American empire is unwilling to come to the realisation that the unipolar world order that once existed is dwindling, and a bipolar, even a tripolar, world order is emerging quickly. The British managed to effectively dismantle their empire with minimal issues to their actual national wellbeing, in terms of the loss of their identity or invasion; though some cynics may say our chickens have come home to roost now, belatedly

---

[259] Kirchwey, G. W. (1917). *Pax Americana*. The ANNALS of the American Academy of Political and Social Science, 72(1), 40–48.

so. However, as the British diplomat Lord Salisbury stated "Whatever happens will be for the worse. Therefore, it is our interest that as little should happen as possible."[260] As you can see, the British understood that the elements of decline were setting in and that it was an inevitability that the sun was about to set on the enterprise that had been financially benefitting Britain from as far back as 1700. Though, it was becoming burdensome during those later years. The Americans do not possess the same capacity for the eating of humble pie, unfortunately; and that is not an insult, Britain is beginning to feel that decline and collapse now, along with their European brethren, so therefore the decolonisation of the empire seemed to be for nought, unfortunately. Though, one may argue that to continue holding on to the dream that the American hegemony is still viable in this changing world will inadvertently lead to a war with the emerging powers of the world; namely China and Russia, and their co-belligerents. This cataclysmic war, if it does not become nuclear, will lead to a systematic weakening of all sides and thus a third power that distances themselves from the conflict, shall step in to claim the broken and embattled states' territory. I would nominate a power such as Israel, with the depopulated, war-torn, and food-starved regions surrounding it, will sweep in and annex vast quantities of territory, much like the Rashidun Caliphs of the mid-7th century. Creating for themselves a vast empire that will effectively control the majority of the world. Israel seems in a good location geopolitically, geographically and culturally for this, but it may be a South American nation or even India too, though I air on the side of it more likely being that of Israel because of its dominant position within the Levant; and its very weak neighbours.

If we take a look at the share of GDP per country, as a percentage of world GDP, then we find that, during its ascension to superpower status in 1945, that the US accounted for 40%-50% of the world GDP; this dwarfed the old superpower Britain and the European nations by some

---

[260] Roberts, Andrew. (1999). *Salisbury: Victorian titan*. London: Weidenfeld & Nicolson. Pg. 328.

margin[261]. However, in contrast, we find that the Chinese will overtake the US as the dominant economic power of the world, as per a percentage of world GDP[262]. The US economy, in all honesty, is rapidly shrinking and experiencing one to two percent GDP decline every year on average – with COVID destroying dozens of percentage points from the total[263]. On the other hand, China is estimated to account for roughly half of global GDP share by 2024, while at the same time the US will be at approximately 13.86%[264] [265]. What am I saying? The US as we know, the global dominant military and economic power, is finished. It is being pulled apart right now, and milked by the financial swindlers for every last bit of value and they are fleeing for greener, Eurasian pastures. However, it is a tumultuous time for China as well because the US-China trade, the US trade deficit with China to be more precise, very much mutually benefits both nations, but China seems to wish to be more than just a mere accessory to US trade policy and they are beginning to ratchet up the hostilities against their neighbours; even if they be nuclear powers too; prime example India. Finally, China is also beginning a strong push for homogeneity within their territorial extent, ethnically and ideologically; the Uyghurs of Xinjiang and the ethnic displacement of Tibetans with Han Chinese. Naturally, China is consolidating its land holdings and attempting to bring harmony through pure unity; this is a prerequisite for fledgling empires and is an attempt at creating stability and, as the

---

[261] Mike Patton. (2016). *U.S. Role in Global Economy Declines Nearly 50%*. Available: https://www.forbes.com/sites/mikepatton/2016/02/29/u-s-role-in-global-economy-declines-nearly-50/?sh=3cbdf4185e9e. Last accessed 30/09/2021.

[262] CEBR. (2020). *Macro-Economic Forecasting: World Economic League Table*. Available: https://cebr.com/service/macroeconomic-forecasting/. Last accessed 30/09/2021.

[263] Martin Crutsinger. (2021). *US economy shrank 3.5% in 2020 after growing 4% last quarter*. Available: https://apnews.com/article/us-economy-shrink-in-2020-b59f9be06dcf1da-924f64afde2ce094c. Last accessed 30/09/2021.

[264] John Kemp. (2019). *China has replaced U.S. as locomotive of global economy: Kemp*. Available: https://www.reuters.com/article/us-economy-global-kemp-column-idUSKB-N1XF211. Last accessed 30/09/2021.

[265] Plecher, H. (2020, May 27). *United States - Share of global gross domestic product (GDP) 2024*. Retrieved 30/09/2021, from https://www.statista.com/statistics/270267/united-states-share-of-global-gross-domestic-product-gdp/.

Soviets would call it, to bring normalisation. I do not condemn nor praise the policy of China, I am not Chinese nor Uyghur, so therefore it is not my quarrel and I merely comment upon it as a neutral observer. However, we must understand that, given human nature, if the roles were reversed and the Uyghurs wielded supreme power within the country that, given their Islamic belief system and mostly nationalist sentiment, they would initiate the exact same policy upon the Han Chinese as is being perpetrated upon themselves. We must understand also that the Chinese state has persisted and survived for over three millennia and the reason for this persistent survival is because it holds in high contempt ideologies, nations, and ideas that could bring disharmony and instability upon the nation; and it deals with them ruthlessly.[266]

Is this moral or immoral? Morally, would it be permissible for the Chinese to cease to exist? No, I do not think the Chinese would answer in the affirmative, but the rival nations or opposing ideologies of China may believe it should. Conversely, would it be morally permissible for the rival nations or opposing ideologies of China to cease to exist? No, I do not believe they would answer in the affirmative, but I would presume China would welcome such a fate for them. As you can see, in terms of geopolitics, morality is not considered, nor should it be, and the only moral maxim that should be observed by the nation is that no member of the tribe should endanger the survival of the tribe, nor accept the encroachment of external influences upon their tribe. Morality, especially the modern Western view of it, is untenable and is ruinous to any nation that adopts, as a matter of policy, the hallmarks of such frivolous idiocy. Internally, the ideas of morality, typically the *"golden rule"* is very much required and keeps the tribe, or nation, working in good order; informing the legal code and allowing for social cohesion. The imposition of morality should never endanger the tribe, when it does it should never

---

[266] Mirić, Siniša, *"Social Stability and Promotion in the Communist Party of China"* (2018). All Graduate Theses and Dissertations. 7117. https://digitalcommons.usu.edu/etd/7117. "Like every authoritarian regime, the CCP faces threats from the masses over which the elites rule. Reducing social mobilization is a key component of the CCP's rule."

be applied, nor should it be applied to declared enemies of the nation. This is how our ancestors would have approached such matters; and that can be ascertained from the fact that the more peaceful among us, in the primordial-state of human kind, would have been utterly destroyed, and would have been taken advantage of by the ones who harnessed hatred and violence against them. It is an unfortunate reality, but fortune favours the bold and the ones who lack the will to power typically do not leave a lineage behind. Interestingly, the reason our civilisation is in such a decrepit state at present is because we seem to wish to avoid this aforementioned natural law, and cling to the foolish idea that we can transcend our inborn nature to fight, compete and protect our interests above all others.[267]

Rise of the Upstarts

The West, for the most part, has been in a state of seventy years of peace, or *Pax Americana* as previously stated, in this period we have miraculously transformed into the seeming reincarnation of the long extinct Dodo bird. Where in previous ages we tested our civilisation's mettle, so to say, against other competing global predators and thus maintained our virility and dominance, we now seem to be unable to even exert our own interests domestically without capitulation[268]. For example, if a government wishes to deport illegal migrants, who are defined under European and US law as criminal, they must jump through a minefield of legal obstacles – including UN courts, various federal or union courts,

---

[267] Storr, A. (1971). *Human Aggression*. Penguin Books Ltd. 1970. London: British Journal of Psychiatry, 119(552), 563-563. doi:10.1192/bjp.119.552.563-a. Pg. 20. "That man is an aggressive creature will hardly be denied. With the exception of certain rodents, no other vertebrate habitually destroys members of his own species. No other animal takes positive pleasure in the exercise of cruelty upon another of his own kind." And, "By one estimate, there have been only 292 years of peace in the world over the last 5,600 years, and during that time more than 3,500,000,000 people have died in, or as a result of, more than 14,000 wars."

[268] Ikenberry, G. J. (2008). *The Rise of China and the Future of the West: Can the Liberal System Survive?* Foreign Affairs, Vol. 87(No. 1), Pg. 23–37. Accessed here: http://www.jstor.org/stable/20020265.

massive NGO legal aid, etc – just to attempt to enforce the fair law of the land; do not forget the resounding accusations of racism piled against such attempts, too. The UK has succumbed to it all and has unbelievably began to task their border force with actually aiding and abetting the criminals, traffickers and illegal migrants[269], and housing them at the expense of the UK taxpayer [270]! Naturally, this is not the behaviour of a civilisation that has much of a future left at all; I mean, it is the behaviour of a country who does not even believe in itself, nor tragically do they actually believe the British exist as a distinct ethnic or cultural group. For instance, some MP's have attested to the fact that as soon as a migrant is granted citizenship, through the judicial system, or even lands on British soil, that they miraculously become just as British as an individual who has fought and bled for the nation, or whose ancestors have a strong claim and history within these isles. Whether this is correct or not, is irrelevant, but we see this as a similar motif amongst every great civilisation near the point of its terminus or its *decline* phase[271].

Conversely, our geopolitical rivals seem to be strong and very intolerant towards outside ideas or groups[272]. Ironically, we wish to create unity through division within our societies, while our rivals seem to be inclined in creating unity through actual unity. This divergence in policy will persist and the insane policies of the Western governments will not cease until they are toppled by, most likely, populist uprisings. Unfortunately, these populists will either be left or right-wing totalitarians who will

---

[269] Rob Merrick. (2021). *Home Office launches investigation after migrants picked up in French waters and brought to UK*. Available: https://www.independent.co.uk/news/uk/politics/migrants-channel-illegal-priti-patel-b1860174.html. Last accessed 05/10/2021.

[270] Jonathan Bucks. (2021). *Dozens of migrants are living in a plush hotel close to the Duke and Duchess of Cambridges' home in Kensington Palace - with 55 asylum seekers put up for as long as nine months*. Available: https://www.dailymail.co.uk/news/article-9848203/Dozens-migrants-living-hotel-55-asylum-seekers-long-nine-months.html. Last accessed 05/10/2021.

[271] Glubb, J. (1978). *The Fate of Empires and Search for Survival*. Edinburgh: Blackwood. Pg. 13-14.

[272] Turdush, Rukiye and Fiskesjö, Magnus (2021) *"Dossier: Uyghur Women in China's Genocide,"* Genocide Studies and Prevention: An International Journal: Vol. 15: Iss. 1: 22–43.

emerge from the ashes of national despair, and will ride on the coattails of the universal misery, that will ensue from the culmination of these said failed governmental policies. I will discuss this later on in the next chapter, but keep this in mind. Furthermore, the chaotic situation that emerges will be capitalised upon by our rivals who will expand their respective spheres of influence, while we wallow in economic ruin for a time. If one is familiar with the apparent pattern of the *East to West Cycle*, one may conclude that if the pendulum of power swings every five-hundred years between East and West, determining the politically dominant half of the world at any given time, that we are by virtue overdue for the pendulum to swing in favour of our eastern counterparts[273].

The Chinese have begun to already probe for weaknesses in the Western sphere; with the small skirmishes with Indian troops, to the posturing within the South China sea, and the intimidation of their rival neighbours such as Japan, we are beginning to see a realisation by China that the old-world order is slowly becoming undone.

THUCYDIDES'S TRAP

Thucydides's Trap is a well-established geopolitical theme that seems to have permeated history and politics for millennia. Coined by *Graham T. Allison*, and based on the famous quote from *Thucydides*[274], an Athenian historian and general, who insisted that the Peloponnesian war between Athens and Sparta was inevitable because of the rising dominance of Athens, and Sparta's fear that they would be eclipsed as the dominant power within the Southern Hellenic sphere. It has been used lately in regard to the expanding presence of China and their apparent global

---

[273] Robert A. Nelson. *Prophecy: A History of the Future*. Chapter 9: Cycles, Earth Changes, & Time; Wheeler Weather Cycle. Available: https://cyclesresearchinstitute.org/cycles-research/weather/wheeler/. Last accessed 05/10/2021. "Another 510-year pattern occurs in the rhythm of world dominance, alternating between the East and West."

[274] Thucydides, and Rex Warner (1968). *History of the Peloponnesian War*. Baltimore, Md: Penguin Books. "It was the rise of Athens and the fear that this instilled in Sparta that made war inevitable".

aspirations, and the fear that the US has in being unseated by this upstart.[275]

We can see wars throughout history fought because of this apparent fact. For example, the Entente facing off against the burgeoning German empire and her allies. Rome and Eastern Rome's face-off with the Persian and Parthian empires. Or, today, we see the ramping up of tensions between the Chinese and US spheres of influence. What is interesting, however, about this whole issue is that a team, from Harvard Belfar Centre for Science and International Affairs, found from historical analyses of the last 500 years that 12 out of the 16 cases that could be most probably concluded as an example of *Thucydides's Trap*, ended in bloodshed and ended badly for both nations[276]. However, that being said, four of the examples did not end in conflict so there is a small probability that future war between the superpowers can be averted. Though, the structural shift in the power dynamics of the geopolitical situation between nations most often necessitates the fertile breeding ground for open warfare; and wholly destructive warfare at that.

We find that *Thucydides*, over 2400 years ago, stated, as a response to the crucial reason for the outbreak of war between Sparta and Athens, "It was the rise of Athens, and the fear that this inspired in Sparta, that made war inevitable."[277] Is it inevitable for warfare to rage between China and the US? No, but it is a possibility if the mutually beneficial economic situation between the two powers deteriorates, then it is more than likely to put a strain on relations. The US and China, one must remember, are very fragile economically. China, for instance, has been referred to as the "Paper Dragon", and this is in large part due to their over-reliance upon

---

[275] Graham Allison. (2015). *The Thucydides Trap: Are the U.S. and China Headed for War?* Available: https://www.theatlantic.com/international/archive/2015/09/united-states-china-war-thucydides-trap/406756/. Last accessed 06/10/2021.

[276] Harvard Belfar Centre for Science and International Affairs. (2017). *Thucydides's Trap Case File*. Available: https://www.belfercenter.org/thucydides-trap/case-file. Last accessed 06/10/2021.

[277] Thucydides, and Rex Warner (1968). *History of the Peloponnesian War*. Baltimore, Md: Penguin Books. "It was the rise of Athens and the fear that this instilled in Sparta that made war inevitable".

CHAPTER V

radical *Keynesian* economic and monetary theory; which forces them onto a path of relying upon the injection of greater and greater amounts of credit to prop up their waning sectors, typically following logically on from an economic slump[278]. This inevitably causes market distortions and the facilitation of asset bubbles; the most notable example being the continuing sub-prime automotive and used sub-prime automotive bubble, which is directly attributable to the Federal Reserve bond-buying program following on from the 2008 financial crisis.[279]

Personally, I would air upon the side that war is not an option currently speaking, though the US is stubborn, and the unipolar order that they have created for themselves will be something that they will be unwilling to relinquish without a fight. Though with the COVID economic damage for both countries, it will be interesting to see if this is the proverbial straw that breaks the camel's back, severing economic ties partially or wholly between the two powers. In such a circumstance, war would be more likely, but both parties would still be reluctant to enter into conflict, in even an extreme circumstance, due to the potential it would pose in causing systematic irrevocable weakness in the nations of the two powers. Such a war would leave no victors, just the moribund remnants of a survivor.

BUILD THE WALL

As I previously stated, the late Roman empire had a shift towards a more defensive approach to warfare and frontier protection, the Roman *Limes*

---

[278] International Monetary Fund: Asia and Pacific Dept. (2021). *People's Republic of China: 2020 Article IV Consultation-Press Release; Staff Report; and Statement by the Executive Director for the People's Republic of China.* Available: https://www.imf.org/en/Publications/CR/Issues/2021/01/06/Peoples-Republic-of-China-2020-Article-IV-Consultation-Press-Release-Staff-Report-and-49992. Last accessed 06/10/2021. "China's total government debt stands at approximately CN¥ 46 trillion (US$ 7.0 trillion), equivalent to about 45% of GDP."
[279] Foohey, Pamela. *Bursting the Auto Loan Bubble in the Wake of COVID-19 (November 24, 2020).* 106 Iowa Law Review 2215 (2021), Available at SSRN: https://ssrn.com/abstract=3737513 or http://dx.doi.org/10.2139/ssrn.3737513

and the series of British frontier walls display this[280]. However, we find that this was not a display of inwardness, but a display conveying the empire's reluctance to push any further with its conquests. It was also to control trade within the empire, as bureaucratisation had begun to become implemented within all the provinces, and siphoning of coinage was beginning to be conducted by the various officials.[281]

Funnily enough, we find that today both the left- and right-wing factions of the populace, have had enough of the interventionist policies of the US, as of late, and many demand that the US adopt a more isolationist policy; in terms of military incursions on foreign soil, at least. Moreover, we find that the US citizenry have had enough of foreign migrants streaming into their lands and ethnically and culturally displacing the reigning Anglo-centric nation that is the US. Although the political class seem all too happy to sell off the South-Western states to these incomers, much like Rome did with its frontier provinces[282]. However, it is clear that we are beginning to see a rise in sentiments similar to the Roman sentiment that led to construction of vast defensive structures to control the frontiers and the foreign elements. Naturally, a wall on the Southern border of the US will not control anything, nor will it stem the tide of illegals or migrants. It is an effort born out of desperation.

---

[280] Spring, P. (2015). *Great Walls and Linear Barriers*. Pen and Sword. Ch. 24.

[281] Gibbon, E. (1867). *The History of the Decline and Fall of the Roman Empire*. London: Bell & Daldy. Chapter: Reign of Diocletian; Increase of Taxes. "The number of ministers, of magistrates, of officers, and of servants, who filled the different departments of the state, was multiplied beyond the example of former times; and (if we may borrow the warm expression of a contemporary) 'when the proportion of those who received exceeded the proportion of those who contributed the provinces were oppressed by the weight of tributes.' From this period to the extinction of the empire it would be easy to deduce an uninterrupted series of clamours and complaints. According to his religion and situation, each writer chooses either Diocletian or Constantine or Valens or Theodosius, for the object of his invectives; but they unanimously agree in representing the burden of the public impositions, and particularly the land-tax and capitation, as the intolerable and increasing grievance of their own times."

[282] Sine Nomine. *Notitia Dignitatum*. Chapter: Notitia Occ. XLII & Notitia Occ. XXXIV and XXXV. Note: On the *Laeti* (federated and settled Barbarians) settlements within Italy, Gaul, and the Danubian provinces within the period of the late Empire.

Chapter V

Now, with this being said, we cannot automatically jump to the conclusion that civilisations engaging in a campaign of wall building immediately conveys a sign of their decline. Of course not, but the reasons for the construction of walls and the history, that precedes the construction, does indicate certain shifts in societal sentiment which can be indicative of decline. For example, as mentioned previously, Rome was an empire built on conquest whose citizens and leaders must have understood that their frontiers were in constant flux, changing upon defeat and victory. However, with the advent of pessimism and a unanimous reluctance by the political and lower classes to continue incessant conquests in far-flung regions; especially, post-*Teutoberg*, but more pronouncedly following the ascension of *Hadrian* [283]. Thus, these walls acted as hard, defined borders which brought a close to the imperial tradition of conquest; for the most part. By comparison, the US is in a similar state with their nearly two-hundred years of conquest and warfare, we find that the lower classes, beginning in the 1960's, began to become jaded with the military campaigns for various reasons[284]. This has only intensified with time and the foreign migration, legal and illegal, is beginning to become an annoyance to the lower classes, too. This is why populist leaders are beginning to become, ironically, more popular. The rhetoric espoused by them is one-dimensional, straight-to-the-point and without compromise; Trump is a move in this direction, but I will delve into this issue in more detail within the next section.

However, we see that with this Southern border wall that it is very dissimilar in its function from the imposing structures of the Great Wall or the Roman *Limes*. These aforementioned defensive structures were constructed with the intent of controlling trade and deterring attack. They naturally succumbed to the latter issue, but the main function of

---

[283] Le, R. P. (2003). Le Haut-Empire Romain en Occident: D'Auguste aux Sévères, 31 av. J.-C. - 235 apr. J.-C. Paris: Ed. du Seuil. Pg. 56.
[284] Howlett, Charles F. *"Studying America's Struggle against War: An Historical Perspective."* The History Teacher, vol. 36, no. 3, Society for History Education, 2003, Pg. 297–330, https://doi.org/10.2307/1555689. "A major effort to make peace history a permanent fixture of American histography began in the 1960s."

such imposing border controls was to ensure that the imperial trade, migration and other such matters were more efficiently controlled and accounted for. Though, this is completely unlike the modern US counterpart as those walls lack garrisons every one-and-a-half or two miles to ensure control over the expanse of the border; and it lacks any actual strong deterrence from individuals who would seek to breach or undermine it. Thus, I would state that the southern border wall, and the campaign promise of Trump to "build the wall!", is nothing more than symbolic gesturing and is pathological in nature. Does that mean I am for uncontrolled migration? No, I have made a strong case that endless migration, with little chance of forced integration, undermines the society in the long-term. Though, I am simply inferring from historical precedent, and the contemporary tales, the only logical conclusion one could reach on this matter: that the migratory tide will not be stemmed by a flimsy wall on the border and erecting such flimsy symbolic gestures is rather telling of the growing sentiments of the society. That being, they wish to relinquish the mantle of hegemon of the world and are tired. I do not think this wrong, I am of a non-interventionist mindset myself, for reasons outlined throughout this literary work, but I am simply bringing attention to the visible facts.[285]

Populist Caesars

Caesar. A very interesting character, indeed. A character who heralded the death knell of the republic and ushered in the era of the stern imperator. We have the beginnings of modern parallels, or at least similarities. I hypothesise *Trump* to be a similar character – not the same, but similar

---

[285] Peter Harris. (2019). *When Will the Unipolar World End?* Available: https://nationalinterest.org/feature/when-will-unipolar-world-end-59202. Last accessed 10/10/2021. "The other way is that the United States might simply choose to retrench for its own reasons. In fact, this is how *Charles Krauthammer* predicted that the unipolar world might end: with isolationist forces inside the United States pushing for an end to deep overseas engagement out of a misguided belief that international security no longer depended upon American preponderance abroad."

in vein – and his rise came on the back of a desperate crying out for change within the political landscape of the nation. Has he changed much? Well, the answer received from such a question is dependent upon one's perspective, but he has not brought universal, systematic change as of writing this piece of literature, in 2020. However, he has set a bold precedent which lays the foundations for future populists, of whatever political persuasion, to capitalise upon the troubles of the society and propel themselves to strong political positions. That being acknowledged, the time of the centrist is drawing to an end and citizens are demanding far stronger and more decisive leadership from the political class.[286]

This has been witnessed somewhat with *Erdogan* and *Putin*, more contemporaneously, but with other historical figures such as *Napoleon* and even Hitler. These individuals bring rapid, unbridled and somewhat system-altering change which can either herald a golden-age or an era of intense deprivation and despair. They are typically far more authoritarian than their predecessors, and far more politically charged when motivating and organising movements. Be these good or bad, in politically desperate times when demographic, economic or military catastrophes are facing the nation, there will more than likely be the rise of an opportunist who will and can capitalise upon solving the issue at the expense of one's liberty or freedom. Though, some of these populist figures may do it from a position of patriotism, this will ultimately have no bearing on how they may deal with dissidents, foreign adversaries or matters of state; in fact, it may make them more draconian in the way issues are dealt with in their respective regimes.[287]

---

[286] Julian Coman. (2020). *Michael Sandel: 'The populist backlash has been a revolt against the tyranny of merit'*. Available: https://www.theguardian.com/books/2020/sep/06/michael-sandel-the-populist-backlash-has-been-a-revolt-against-the-tyranny-of-merit. Last accessed 11/10/2021. "By championing an "age of merit" as the solution to the challenges of globalisation, inequality and deindustrialisation, the Democratic party and its European equivalents, Sandel argues, hung the western working-class and its values out to dry – with disastrous consequences for the common good."

[287] de la Torre, C. (Ed.). (2018). *Routledge Handbook of Global Populism* (1st ed.). Routledge. https://doi.org/10.4324/9781315226446. Chapter: Populism and authoritarianism.

Now, for the left-wing individuals reading, I am unfortunately not going to be partisan and say *Trump* is some dictator or Fascist. No, he is a duly elected President, and as such he is acting in accordance with the law and of his office; as of writing this circa 2020. However, there are of course many extreme examples that show where rampant divisive populism may lead to – Fascism and Communism, being the most heinous examples. Though, this will be unlikely to plague the US for some time; for as long as the dollar reigns supreme and the economic hegemony of the US is still partially intact, although this seems to be dwindling by the day. They are cautionary tales, that of Populism went awry, and ones in which we should heed and ensure we thus abide by the virtues of caution and restraint when demanding change. We should steer away from divisiveness of all kinds, and ensure we create a more united society and build bridges with our countrymen, lest ideological division devolve into fratricidal in-fighting; and that will naturally lead the country to a state beyond repair. However, it seems the situation, as of late, is going in such a direction as stated, and these recent BLM riots are an indication of that.[288][289]

Another very interesting matter is that one may conclude that *Trump* may be a safety valve, for the growing ire of the masses against the political class. It does make sense, though we can only speculate on such wild matters, as I can safely assure you that we would never learn conclusively the truth of such political machinations outright. In this time of transformation, into a different system and society, we find that *Trump* has been a safety-valve for the patriots among the Western population and a rallying cry, an encompassing symbol for vilification, for the emerging radical system. He, as a character or symbol, has seemed to serve many purposes and, tin-foil hat aside, has been very useful to

---

[288] Col. (Retired) Robert E. Hamilton, Ph.D. (2018). *Rhetoric, Violence, and Civil War: The Balkanization of America?* Available: https://www.fpri.org/article/2018/11/rhetoric-violence-and-civil-war-the-balkanization-of-america/. Last accessed 11/10/2021.
[289] Seger, Karl A (2001). *Left-Wing Extremism: The Current Threat.* United States. https://doi.org/10.2172/780410.

many entities and groups within society in controlling and entrenching opinions. This, by extension, sows division within society, which is an optimal tool in suppressing dissent and keeping the plebeian majority preoccupied with interclass squabbling. Thus, this allows the political elite to act with relative impunity and without criticism. Although, *Trump* can simply be described as a sign of the changing sentiments within society and the growing irreconcilable divide between the various political groupings; a divide that will only grow ever more unpleasant with the results from this next election (circa. 2020).

INABILITY TO ABSORB DEFEAT

As I have previously alluded to in prior sections, the inability of an empire to absorb defeats is a paramount sign of decline in the cohesion of the nation and state. This is best exhibited in the comparative examples of Cannae and Adrianople, within the context of Rome, but is also exhibited in a more modern sense within the long history of the British empire. A British nationalist would loath to hear it, but the fact is the British empire and its composite nations, prior to the Act of Union, had long series of defeats – some almost totally catastrophic. In reference to the Battle of Medway, 1667, for example, where the Dutch almost came close to capturing London[290]. However, the British spirit was indominable at the time and overcame these setbacks, much like their Roman and later American counterparts, to forge an empire greater than all that came before it. Alas, during the later years of the empire, post-1945, we find that small insurgency groups – Israeli terrorists in Palestine, *Mau Mau* rebellion, and the Indian terrorism and independence movements - brought the military and bureaucratic might of the empire to its knees, and the national spirit to resist these rebellions and independence

---
[290] Patrick Boniface. (2017). *The Royal Navy's Darkest Day: Medway 1667*. Available: https://www.military-history.org/feature/the-royal-navys-darkest-day-medway-1667.htm. Last accessed 12/10/2021.

movements throughout the empire was missing[291]. Thus, we find a parliament and establishment swiftly moving to a policy of decolonisation – and arguably, we are still in midst of decolonisation today with the large swathes of land being granted to foreigners on our own shores. Interestingly too, if we observe the late-era British military we find within the First and Second World Wars a strong hubris and witlessness among the military hierarchy[292]. The inability to adapt to the new and emerging form of warfare, much like Rome and the emergence of cavalry-oriented warfare, and, for example, within the siege of Singapore, by the imperial Japanese, we find an insane belief amongst the political and military leadership that the island fortress was impregnable and that the Japanese would never dare to attack it! They did, and with their superior aircraft and fewer numbers they took the so-called impregnable fortress and took many British prisoner.[293]

This form of hubris is something we have borne witness to within other declining empires[294], so it is unsurprising, but it is nevertheless an annoyance to see such unadulterated mindlessness from leadership that should know to not underestimate the enemy. Though, post-WW2, we find that the imperial decolonisation was actually the correct policy decision, though it seems to have led to a rather long and protracted death of the imperial stock, as opposed to an expeditious decline such as Rome. As I have previously mentioned, Rome was subject to a series of, what should have been, utter defeats that should have debilitated the Roman state beyond repair at Cannae and also the Gallic sack of

---

[291] Imperial War Museums. (2018). *The End of the British Empire After the Second World War*. Available: https://www.iwm.org.uk/history/the-end-of-the-british-empire-after-the-second-world-war. Last accessed 12/10/2021.

[292] Meyer, G. J. (2006). *A World Undone: The story of the Great War, 1914-1918*. New York: Delacorte Press. Pg. 264.

[293] Churchill, Winston S. *The Second World War: The Hinge of Fate* (Vol. 4). New York: Houghton Mifflin Company, 1978. Bloomsbury Collections. Pg. 81. ", "the worst disaster and largest capitulation in British history".

[294] Mir Sadat. (2021). *Confronting the disaster left behind in Afghanistan*. Available: https://www.atlanticcouncil.org/blogs/new-atlanticist/confronting-the-disaster-left-behind-in-afghanistan/. Last accessed 12/10/2021.

Rome. However, this did not dampen their resolve and they went on to subjugate both of those civilisations and utterly eviscerate any memory of them. Though at battles at which, arguably, they lost fewer fighting men, such as Adrianople, we find that the empire, instead of being entrenched in their resolve to right that defeat, succumbed to mass demoralisation and thus Adrianople is seen by historians as the beginning of the end for Roman dominance, within the Mediterranean theatre.[295]

The United States has suffered such defeats, historical and far more contemporary. For example, we may look at the disastrous war of 1812, where Washington DC itself was burnt to the ground by the British and all hope seemed lost, we find that the American resolve tightened and they later managed to eke back an almost status quo peace with Britain – who was largely weakened following the Napoleonic Wars[296]. Moreover, fast forward to today and in far more modern contexts, we find that within the Vietnam war and even the Afghan war that the American desire to become engaged in prolonged conflicts, that have substantial casualties, in the case of Vietnam more acutely so, is not there and the American public are averse to the potential of any defeat. However, that being said, the US is quick to retaliation if any slight is conducted against them or their allies and thus the US, as an empire, is still strong and dangerous to its adversaries – much like Rome, even within its ailing years.

Putting Man Before God

Logos (λόγος) or the idea of the universal reason that orders the cosmos and whose providence, be it in a secular or divine sense, brings order from the complexity and chaos of existence; the natural order being the absolute truth, so to speak. Now, it was and has once again become a

---

[295] Corry Atkinson (n.d.). *Adrianople: Before and After*. Available: https://uncw.edu/csurf/explorations/volume%20xii/adrianople.pdf. Last accessed 12/10/2021. "Not only did political fragmentation result from Valens' downfall, but it also set in motion the events that would help bring about the end of the Western Roman Empire."
[296] Tennessee State Library and Archives. (2014). *The Treaty of Ghent*. Available: https://sharetngov.tnsosfiles.com/tsla/exhibits/1812/no4.htm. Last accessed 12/10/2021.

rather popularised concept within the Christian theological circles and schools of thought, and for the extent of this small discussion upon the inversion of the Logos in recent years, or universal order of nature, I will be utilising it in its more philosophical sense; though, our Christian friends may see it in a divine sense if they wish and it will still be pertinent within the context of this brief discussion.

As the old adage goes, "truth is always the first casualty of war" and this truth is self-evident from the culmination of this long societal drift towards decline. Alas, we can bear witness to the imperceptible war that begun at the turn of the 20th century, fomented and orchestrated by Fabian and orthodox Marxist socialists, that, sensing the observable weaknesses of the West, began the slow and methodical march through the institutions. Steadily growing their power and acquiring prestigious and powerful roles in various commercial, political, military and educational behemoths. Today they own mostly all major conglomerates and have established an oligopoly. In conjunction, we can see the results today that have been born of this unholy union of Marxists and Capitalist institutions – a divided society, of whose corporations incessantly, with perfidious intent, foment revolution and unnatural ideas within the minds of the youth through detectable programming – education, news, etc – and indetectable programming – popular culture, advertisement, etc. These forms of programming are ones that some religiously minded may call "Antichrist", comedically as a secular thinker I tend to agree with my religious counterparts, but many secularists with a scintilla of sense understand that these are the means as to which aids the revolutionary in debasing society to a primordial state, a primitive and barbaric cacophony of violence, of which they can then attain the acquiescence of the terrorised population who will cry out for normalcy once more. The catch being, the normalcy provided is one in which the government, through front organisations and entitled corporations, will control all means of production and, most importantly, food distribution. It is a form of hostage-taking, but on a grand-scale.

Chapter V

Therefore, if God, or the Gods, may be defined as a characterisation of the general order of the world, and our far more closer human world, then we have forsaken all reason, logic, and general principles of civility and what may bring long-term stability for our progeny, and our nation; we have become atheistic. What the Collectivists have instituted is Democracy, funnily enough, of whose electorate is a disparate collection of peoples of whom have been moulded to despise the ethnic majority and normalcy. What do I mean by that? That the higher truths, or universal order, is being bent and distorted to the whimsical diktats of the collective Marxist mobs. This is something that occurs in periods of decline, that being that truth is the first to be sacrificed upon the alter of hysteria. The urge within the mob for rampant self-destruction is so great that one must pay homage to this irrationality or pay the price, of which may be the ultimate one. The intolerance for the ideological opponent is one that is rooted in a distinct mental pathology that is almost a form of cognitive dissonance. That being, the world view has become such a part of them, that if the tenets of which are revealed, by the ideological opponent, to be without merit then the ideological adherent will see that as a direct attack upon their person, "violence" if you will, and will respond in a likewise manner. This is why the duplicitous notion of "speech is violence" has become so prevalent amongst the extreme far-left elements within society.

Thus, Logos, the truth or force of the absolute truth, in end-stage civilisations is substituted in favour of the appeasement of the preponding herd-mentality - even if the system of government is averse to this type of majority rule, it will become apparent, nonetheless. Collectivisation occurs and not just effects negatively rugged individualism, but destroys the idea of truth. In being, that the individual must sacrifice truth on the altar of the group, to appease their emotional well-being, if that truth runs contrary to the stated principles or fleeting sentiments of the group. Thus, Man ascends above God. As *Nietzsche* wrote, "God is Dead", and he was right as man has learned to become God, almost - in so much that man will distort the higher truths of existence upon the arbitrary diktats of the collective.

Without truth and the freedom to pursue it, wherever it may lead, man is little more than a mindless, instinctive animal playing out an existence bereft of dignity. If we must bend the knee to the collective's whims at every moment - prostrating ourselves to the masses of drones - then we resign ourselves to an age of darkness, where the worst of humanity is brought to the fore and a bleak primitivism will thus ensue.

Inward Search for War

Something that typifies the temporal and amoral attitudes of the ages of decline and ruin is a stark shift in attitudes between defeating the external enemies of the empire to searching inwardly for that foe[297]. This can take many forms, ideological difference, political or religious difference, aspirations for power or wealth, wealth disparities, and even sports team rivalries. However, what is striking is the commonality that runs through both opposing sides in these civil showdowns – that being, that they both think the other an enemy and an obstacle to the changing of the system which will undoubtedly, in their own mind, bring them a completeness or a happiness[298]. This is more a representation of the iniquity of the society of which they find themselves in and the toll it takes upon their mental state, rather than a deep-seated admiration for any one given ideology they may subscribe to. For example, in the chaos in Charlottesville, and this chaos still reaches into today's political and civil realm, that both sides thought the other evil, beyond all reproach, and that the only way to achieve a better future, the collective utopic vision that each had at the fore of their thoughts, was to eliminate the

---

[297] Kaegi, Walter Emil (1981). *Byzantine Military Unrest, 471–843: An Interpretation.* Amsterdam: Adolf M. Hakkert.
[298] Lim, Richard. *"Religious Disputation and Social Disorder in Late Antiquity."* Historia: Zeitschrift Für Alte Geschichte, vol. 44, no. 2, Franz Steiner Verlag, 1995. Pg. 204–31.

Chapter V

other side – either physically or through optics[299]. The right-wing side's vision was one of nostalgia for a past that they had not experienced, one for tradition and an ethnic and cultural security within the classical framework of the nation, and one that may wish for a revival of the imperialist doctrines of old, be it jingoism, feudal-like structures and supremacist tenets; though this is not always entirely the case, on the last points. The left-wing side's vision was one that looked beyond into the future and they see the past, the same one venerated by the right, as an age inherently replete with barbarism and despair, slavery and cruelty, and though they are partially correct – both sides having valid criticisms of modernity, albeit – they fail to understand that the future governmental structure, they wish for, will usher in the same despairs that wrought the past. As one can imagine, both of these sides have commonalities in the pursuit of totalitarian and utopian like structures – empowering a small clique at the apex of the hierarchy to impose their diktats, of which they hope will bring wholeness to their lives – but both are irreconcilable. Not on the grounds of the political application of power but in so far, they hold diametrically opposite venerations and vilifications of the respective national future and past. Although, whoever emerges victorious from this complex cultural and metapolitical struggle, it is clear our present will be irrevocably altered beyond repair.

Historically, to provide further detailing of this seemingly intrinsic pathology, we see that the Roman state - Republican, Principate and Byzantine - were mired in sport team infighting and this acted as a front for the extension of political and religious bigotry, too[300]. I have highlighted this within the infamous *Nika* riots previously within this piece of literature, in the section titled "Pessimism and Religious Osmosis", therefore I refer you to that for greater clarity on such phenomena. We see it too in Ancient Hellas (Greece), in which sports rivalries would occur

---
[299] Azmon, G. (2017). *Being in time: A post-political manifesto*. Pg. 49.
[300] Cameron, A. (1976). *Circus factions: Blues and Greens at Rome and Byzantium*. Oxford: Clarendon Press. Chapter VI: "The Religious Sympathies of the Factions".

also [301] and even in the periods begrimed with national weakness, such as in early 15th century France, we find that opposing political sides were engaged in all-out slaughter of each other, even in the midst of external invasion from England, and arguably one of their greatest warrior-kings; *Henry V*. Ironically, one of the gruesome slaughters between the two opposing sides in France – the Burgundians and Armagnacs – occurred during a delegation to deliberate upon how best to handle the matter of the English invasion; whatever occurred at this event led to it transpiring into a grizzly battle between the two sides. This only fractured the political landscape of the country even more so, with the Burgundians entering into an alliance with the English forthwith, following this event[302]. Retrospectively, with the benefit of hindsight, we can understand in our modern day that this was an example of political and military ineptitude, but to the political players of the day, the differences were too much to bridge and the dehumanisation of their rivals was so complete, that they could not stem their unruly hatred for each long enough to defeat a foreign adversary. The atmosphere of infighting that led to such events in 15th century France are eerily reminiscent today, and we all seem to be busily cultivating a likewise home for prolonged civil strife; as we can already glimpse at the initial embers of such a civil war, and mark my words if it is not smothered in swift order, and our course altered, then our entire civilisation, painstakingly built by all who came before, will be consumed by an unquenchable inferno that will leave nothing but destruction in its wake.

However, if I may add, it seems to any conscious individual, who has the ability to critically reason, that this entire debacle and civil strife is being carefully engineered by powers who lurk in shadows and whose influence is unseen to the general, uninformed populace. However, the

---

[301] Jenny Murray. (2004). *Rather than Promoting Peace the Greek Olympics Fuelled Ancient World Rivalry, Says Historian.* Available: https://warwick.ac.uk/newsandevents/pressreleases/ne1000000086426/. Last accessed 18/10/2021.
[302] Sizer, Michael (2007). *"The Calamity of Violence: Reading the Paris Massacres of 1418".* Proceedings of the Western Society for French History (Michigan Publishing), Vol. 35.

duality of, say, the media is so blatantly obvious that it defies belief as to how one cannot see the fascination that the media holds for polarising the populace into two seemingly opposing camps. One may speculate as to what the owners of the media conglomerates have to gain from stoking such flames, but one could conclude that it is the application of what is termed the *Hegelian or Triadic Dialectic* – Thesis, Antithesis and Synthesis – and that it is a means for reshaping the society; bringing it ever closer to the type of digital serfdom, it seems, the oligarchic elite wish for us[303]. Thus, I find it paramount to state this point, that factionalism destroys a nation and divides it along a myriad of lines, until nothing remains but a divided populace that are weak and more easily coerced and controlled, by the real wielders of power. By countrymen fighting countrymen, branding each other as evil doers, and thus engaging each other in attritive battle – mentally or physically – then this grants external foes, or internal at this stage, the golden opportunity to lay claim to the national holdings of the nation more easily and subtly. Diversionary tactics and sowing of chaos within the enemy ranks, so to say. Thus, in this age of encouraged blind fanaticism, be it of whatever political stripe, in our mindless rage against our fellow countryman we have inadvertently sown the seeds of our own future ruin.

THE PLASTIC MAN

This will be a short section, but I wish to bring attention to the way media is utilised as a weapon to reprogram a populace into any mould sought by the ruling regime; whatever form it may take. It may seem strange to include such a topic within this section upon military but, to the informed on such subjects, *"Information Warfare"* and *"Psychological Warfare"* play key roles within understanding the full-spectrum application of efficient techniques of warfare, and we must further understand that

---

[303] Maybee, Julie E (2020). *"Hegel's Dialectics"*. The Stanford Encyclopedia of Philosophy (Winter 2020 Edition), Edward N. Zalta (ed.), URL: https://plato.stanford.edu/archives/win2020/entries/hegel-dialectics/.

any military will also utilise such techniques of informational warfare upon their own domestic population, too. This is as a means of control and moulding of advantageous characteristics to be inculcated within the domestic populace, patriotism can be a typical one for instance, but so can docility.[304]

Digressing however, I have coined the term "Plastic Man" to describe this phenomenon and as such I am referring to the malleability of the human mind; thus, by extension one's world view, too. I have long pondered the liberality of the modern man and woman and how it has come to be; who inculcated these ideas within their minds and who continues to update these, with each new "cultural leap forward", so to say? Was it by their own arduous intellectual deliberations, and long periods of self-reflection upon their ideas that they were simultaneously led, as a collective, to such profound understandings of moralist liberal thought? Or was it a product of their environment and the nexus of propaganda spewed forth by education, media and advertisement instructing them on what to believe and, most importantly, as to what their peers believe? I would hearken to the latter.[305] Thus, we may conclude that these forms of media – entertainment, education, etc – are all a means of producing the desired citizen, or serf, for the system, but this is not inherently malevolent in and of itself; if it benefits the societies survival, and by extension the survival of the individuals who comprise such a society, then it can be argued a necessary evil, so to say. However, we are seeing the cultivation of a type of modern human who is devoid of morality and agency, and who will only express emotion and feign moral righteousness at the behest of his masters; which seem increasingly to be the media, at this point. He will take a knee and raise his fist, broadcasting it on social media to signal his virtue, like a peacock brandishing its feathers. He will clap for the socialised medical system when told to do so at a specific

---

[304] Robert Longley. (2019). *An Introduction to Psychological Warfare*. Available: https://www.thoughtco.com/psychological-warfare-definition-4151867. Last accessed 20/10/2021.
[305] Tversky, A., & Kahneman, D. (1981). *The framing of decisions and the psychology of choice*. Science, 211(4481), 453–458. https://doi.org/10.1126/science.7455683

time, place and day every week if instructed to. He will even attack an individual who deviates from the mandated dress-code, the cultish de rigueur, if he witnesses such profligates. I often ponder if this ostensibly liberal man, this "Plastic Man" if you will, the blank slate devoid of even a slither of autonomy, could be made to goosestep down the street, Roman saluting intermittently, while extolling the supposed virtues of right-wing doctrine if commanded to by the media? Why not, these automatons will engage in anything that seems to be approved and adopted by their peers – of which that false consensus is implanted within their psyche by their masters, at the large media institutes – so therefore we may conclude in the affirmative, yes, this would be feasible.[306]

I hope you, the reader, understand the gravity of this situation. That we are sharing the same societal space with individuals who actively do anything the media command of them on demand, and that if they witness anyone who may diverge from those divine media proclamations then they will be inclined to viciously attack them, dox them, or even kill them; as we have seen in the USA, as of 2020. This type of witch-hunt mentality, a brutal mindset of mob justice, will only lead to perpetual and persistent violence until the mob's orthodoxy is established, and any scintilla of divergent-thought being routed out. That is not the mark of a free society, nor a society that champions freedom. Wherein, we have indoctrinated automatons whom busily scurry about engaging in the rites of thought-policing and of whom demand strict ideological conformity from every individual, lest they brand them as heretical in their own peculiar modern way. It is a regressive form of human organisation and belongs in the dark-ages, not in the modern West where the rights of man are to be championed, nurtured and protected; unpopular speech and opinions are included in that, if not the sole reason we were provided, by Providence, such a right. As *Voltaire* famously stated, "those who

---

[306] Ross, David & Louis, Richard & Sasso, Melissa. (2019). *The Increase of How Mass Media Coverage Manipulates Our Minds*. 10.4018/978-1-5225-7513-9.ch010.

can make you believe absurdities, can make you commit atrocities"[307]. However, maybe that is to the heart of the issue; the new generation of rulers have no need for freedom any longer, as freedom was found to be a prerequisite to higher levels of productivity from the citizen, as it motivated the innate human spirit of yearning for liberty, and now with automation we find more can be produced with less workers – thus, a vast swathe of humanity has been rendered obsolete, in the eyes of the rulers. A large supply and a low demand for the human resource, in the eyes of the rulers, will lead to the transition of a new politico-economic paradigm, a fourth-industrial revolution if you will, and the new world that will be fashioned from this new precept will resemble a hell on earth.[308]

OIKOPHOBIA

The term *Oikophobia*, you may be familiar with it, is in ubiquitous practise today by all manner of radicals; both left and right. The term is used to describe an irrational fear of one's own household or people; this has been colloquially extended to describe the implacable self-hatred the Western youth hold and display for their own people and civilisation presently, in light of real or perceived historical transgressions to currently considered deified groups of people. It is moreover a marker to describe the relationship between the unnaturalistic and unsustainable behaviours exhibited by people who self-style themselves as progressive, in this aforementioned regard. Thus, it allows us to put into focus, through a colourising lens, the truly destructive nature of the wide-spread adherence of such *Oikophobic* beliefs and their further propagation. I will detail the reasons for this modern resurgence of the extreme and insatiable hatred of

---

[307] Voltaire (1765). Torrey, Norman Lewis, translator. *Les Philosophes: The Philosophers of the Enlightenment and Modern Democracy.* Capricorn Books (1961). Pg. 277-8.
[308] Klaus Schwab. (2016). *The Fourth Industrial Revolution: what it means, how to respond.* Available: https://www.weforum.org/agenda/2016/01/the-fourth-industrial-revolution-what-it-means-and-how-to-respond/. Last accessed 20/10/2021.

one's own and why it has come to be. I will further deliberate upon ideas that may solve it, including via electoral reforms, political regionalisation and peaceful divorcement of political classes - of whom hold differences irreconcilable, by all rational measure.[309]

The basis surrounding the resurgence of *Oikophobia* is two-fold. Firstly, I must preface and provide clarity to my reutterances of "resurgence of *Oikophobia*", and one may find themselves perplexed at such a notion; did this afflict ancient peoples, too? Yes, and the most compelling example of such is Late-Rome, but such existed within Athens and related Greeks likewise. Proceeding the first, through to fourth, Macedonian Wars, wherein the latter saw the entire annexation of Greece and much of the Balkans, we begin to find an importation of Greek literature and the popularising of literature first in Greek, and then in Latin; the adoption of the *Dactylic Hexameter* from the Greeks and the heroic retellings of the Punic War from *Gnaeus Naevius*'s epic poem, were examples of the popularisation of literature and the dissemination of nationalistic sentiments within the Latin world. With military superiority, a nation begins to see itself as culturally superior – naturally – and thus they believe themselves to be engaging in a sort of humanitarian crusade in propagating their culture to others, through either force of arms or diplomatic annexations, subsequently then assimilating "barbarian cultures"; such occurrences have replayed themselves within the American, British, Athenian, Arabic and Persian empires, as it did with Rome herself. However, paradigmatically, we find that Rome in its phase of decline turns from this nationalistic zeal and distaste of the "queer and effeminate Greeks", as said *Naevius*, in the earlier years of conquest and imperial development to a period in which literary authors such as *Varro*, *Quintilian* and *Horace* begin to look at Roman religion, customs and Latin culture in a strikingly objective and critical way. Alas, the irony being that this type of naval-gazing of one's own civilisation,

---

[309] Pupo, Spartaco. (2015). *Oikophobic prejudice against nation in the contemporary political thought. the Italian case.* Notizie di Politeia. 31. Pg. 3-22.

through the lens of extreme critical debasement, only arises from the vast quantities of wealth and abundance that has been garnered by the society through its previous conquests, the ones it now contemptuously critiques nonetheless, and from this it has allowed a perennial leisure class to form that has the time and the luxury to pursue such avenues of censorious thought. To put it succinctly, *Oikophobia* reproves that success which it owes its very existence to. Naturally, we find very little dabbling in such self-deprecatory philosophising in the early and more infant stages of a society's development – one may conclude that this is engendered by the overwhelming need for survival and social cohesion. Once, the necessity for social cohesion dwindles – exemplified by little to no threat of predation, enemies, an abundance of wealth, stable dominion, etc – then the populace, most notably among the growing aristocratic or oligarchic classes – indulge in the wondrous enjoyment of self-debasement to express their vain desire to appear outwardly moralistic. Or simply because, like a curious child, it is sometimes fun to play with fire when one feels they are untouchable by the flame; though, the enumerable historical precedents set on this would suggest to the contrary.[310]

One may find similarities within *Seneca the Youngers* ideas regarding cultural and civilisational equality among all nations. For example, in *Seneca's, Epistulae Morales ad Lucilium, XLIV. On Philosophy and Pedigrees*, he states "All men, if traced back to their original source, spring from the gods. You are a Roman knight, and your persistent work promoted you to this class; yet surely there are many to whom the fourteen rows are barred; the senate-chamber is not open to all; the army, too, is scrupulous in choosing those whom it admits to toil and danger."[311] Yes, one may state that this is an example of meritocracy which is admirable, but if we

---

[310] Dr. Benedict Beckeld. (2015). *Oikophobia in Roman Antiquity*. Available: http://www.benedictbeckeld.com/philosophyblog/2015/6/6/oikophobia-in-roman-antiquity. Last accessed 25/10/2021. "As the peak of Roman power comes and goes, a stage of weak decadence – oikophobia – naturally sets in, as it had done among the Athenians and Greeks in general, and as it will continue to do in future societies."

[311] Seneca, L. A., & Campbell, R. (1969). *Letters from a Stoic: Epistulae Morales ad Lucilium*. Penguin Books. Chapter: XLIV On Philosophy and Pedigrees.

CHAPTER V

look at the implied concept sub-textually here, we find a radical idea of equating necessary hierarchy with nepotism; the halls of government and the high echelons of the army cannot be open to everyone, for if that was the case then the society was cease to function. For, it could be said too, if an army is populated by ten thousand generals and no common footmen, then the title general loses its value and the army quickly loses cohesion; as such, these lofty ideals of egalitarianism slowly dissipate under the stress of existential threats to a groups survival. Moreover, if we look at this entire quote in context with his other work, we may find that he favoured the idea that Rome should not call herself the better of others, implied by his criticisms of the developing customs of the time. Though he was correct in these assertions, in retrospect, he seems to see these inequities as ample evidence that Rome was thus unremarkable comparative to the contemporary nations and tribes. This is an unpragmatic view, as he, as a citizen of the Empire, should have championed his nation rather than chip away at the very edifice of it, for his egocentric desire to appear intellectually avant-garde; in hindsight.

We see similar Oikophobic remarks on the Athenian experiment within *Plato*'s thoughts, in which he seems to have informed and inspired *Seneca*'s later teachings, in which is stated "Every king springs from a race of slaves, and every slave has had kings among his ancestors."[312] We can all agree with meritocratic virtues, yes, but it must be understood that these types of intellectual pronouncements lead to a strain of discourse that eventually leads to the societal adoption that, indeed, the nation in which one resides in is unremarkable, and all people are the same. If that is the case, then this logically leads to the idea that, if we are all the same, then what sets us apart as a unique nation and tribe. Thus, continuing on from that, when the erosion of pride in one's own heritage sets in, the historical conquests of these other past tribes, now seen as equals by the modern generation, logically brings about a hypercritical self-contemplation of

---

[312] Lucius Annaeus Seneca (1917) *Ad Lucilium Epistulae Morales*. English Translation by Richard M. Gummere (Haverford College), Volume 1 of 3, Epistle XLIV: On Philosophy and Pedigrees. Pg. 287. William Heinemann, London.

the very traditions, social edifice and customs of the nation that made these past transgressions possible. Then, introspectively and existentially, one is then inclined, by acting from virtue of principle, and the moral credence derived from it, to slowly dismantle their history and societal framework in an effort to stave off future transgressions against these, now, equals. To thence make policies that afford greater privileges to these "historically marginalised peoples" - even if the perceived historical marginalisation may be debatable - and enact legislation depriving rights and privileges from the natives, who are busily embroiled in this cult of self-hatred. To "balance the imbalances", so to say, though as to what metric the balance is measured and thus corrected by is questionable. The scales of society do not seem to be visible unfortunately and, by the pedigree of human fallibility, the continual need to rectify social injustice, real or sought, is a difficult addiction to break, for a society searching for purpose in the void of vacuous consumerism. "The road to Hell is paved with good intentions".

This is simply one line of potential development. Accordingly, we see such a conclusion from earlier principles of equality manifesting today in a similar approach, as outlined above – and I call this a *Theoretical Continuum*, that being that a political, economic or social principle or ideology's fruits cannot be theorised in a mere one-dimensional visualisation from the virtues of the principle remaining unaltered into perpetuity, and one must give careful consideration as to the other potential branches of thought that will mutate and derive from these principles or ideology. As I have demonstrated above, this continuum of development, as we see in all human endeavours, within the school of thought will change and mutate the idea to such a degree that it may have the opposite effect as to its progenitor's intentions; based upon the adherents inhabited societal environment and the societies level of civilisational decline or incline. We can see the disastrous effects of an ideology or principle being subjected to no *Theoretical Continuum* prior to dissemination, or stress-testing based upon extreme external conditions, within the Marxist ideology of *Karl Marx*, which has spawned countless ineffective dictatorships and crippling economic systems since its inception. Though Capitalism has fared better, it still is ineffectual during extreme societal circumstances and periods of decline.[313]

As a tangential point, we find that today a great deal of those who self-style as "woke", or the Oikophobes, are usually rather hypocritical. We have seen time and again the distinct incongruencies between their publicly espoused principles and private actions. Where they preach equality but live lavishly; much of this proven by the liberal Hollywood crowd, who seem to have a penchant for instructing the peasants on how to live and exercise their moral agency. However, *Seneca* was afflicted by such hypocrisy funnily enough. Though, he espoused Stoicism he was rumoured to be nicknamed *Seneca Praedives* (Seneca the very wealthy) by his friends and, being of equestrian class, a nobleman of sorts, in service to mad emperor Nero, he accumulated approximately three-hundred-million *Sestertii* (other Roman Senators only being worth roughly five-million, comparatively). Furthermore, he found himself involved in sex scandals several times[314]. Do I say this to belittle or demean the teachings of *Seneca* or Stoicism? No, I actually find great merit in both, but it shows the hypocrisy that we all possess a small share of. Thus, by the derived logic, in declining societies what may be moral is not what may be right, and that it would seem it is mercy, generosity and moralistic gestures that forces declining societies to prostrate themselves, to what should be their subordinates – in a civilisational sense. Hence, these are the hallmarks of a civilisation in decline; not in progress. I just wish to add briefly, we see similar sentiments expressed by *Tacitus*, in which he extolls the virtues of the Germanic tribesmen who fought and slaughtered

---

[313] Batra, Ravi (1978). *The Downfall of Capitalism and Communism: A New Study of History.* London: McMillan. Pg. 238.
[314] Motto, Anna Lydia. *"Seneca on Trial: The Case of the Opulent Stoic."* The Classical Journal, vol. 61, no. 6, The Classical Association of the Middle West and South, 1966. Pg. 254–58. "That Seneca amassed an enormous for- tune is attested by several ancient sources. l Juvenal (Sat. 10.16) refers to him as Praedives, "very rich," and the philosopher himself in his writings is not reticent about his own great wealth."

his countrymen on many an occasion[315]. Thus, this is a similar example of this zeal of equality beginning to form within the psyche of, at the very least, the aristocrats and academia – of which similar antinational sentiments have their genesis from in today's society. The endgame of this dabbling, within the dangerous game of *Oikophobia*, was the societal revolution of militant Christianity and the assimilation and eclipsing of Roman culture itself, with proto-Catholicism.

Oikophobia seems to be being promulgated by the intellectual classes, and this is to be expected in a civilisation's post-*age of intellect*, however we must understand that this type of rhetoric is ripping the heart from the very body of the nation; it will result in deterioration and subordination to either a foreign adversary, or a totalitarian government as seen post-Weimar Germany. If we wish to avoid this then we must understand and bring awareness to the act of engaging in hypercritical debasement of one's own nation – but this does not equate to criticism of the government, as this, contrary to the political classes reigning belief, does not form the nucleus of a nation, the people do. Thus, we must come to shine a light upon the educational institutions that promote the perversion of one's own patriotism, steering it into the jagged cliffs of self-hatred, and we must expose who is funding this quickening of decline. If we fail in this endeavour, we subject all of our descendants to a grave existence, in which nothing will exist but a soulless and dust-laden husk of where once dwelt a great civilisation. Where they will bewallow in misery and strife, poverty and despair; whilst holding in high-contempt their forefathers for forsaking their future, for the fleeting pleasures of the present.

Therefore, this begs the question, how can this be somewhat reversed or even delayed; this prevailing self-loathsome proposition? I think the extreme nature of this type of *Oikophobia*, that we bear witness to everyday, stems from the overall cacophony of circumstances that besets us. That being we are nominally democratic, have a multiplicity of

---

[315] Tacitus, Cornelius, and Rodney P. Robinson (1935). *The Germania of Tacitus*. Middletown, Conn: American Philological Association.

various incompatible tribes and ideologies cohabiting, and that we have a general feeling amongst working individuals that they pay their taxes and work and receive no more, or perhaps less, than their either inherently wealthy counterparts or the welfare recipients. These types of alienations create social tension and it has boiled to a point now that we are on the precipice of the imposition of social strife – and this is beneficial for the elite class in remaining in power, but not for the working classes. Thus, if we are to remain nominally democratic, it would be a prudent reformation to institute a tiered voting system, in this way if one is a landowner or owns his own house, pays taxes, has a job, contributes to society either through employment or voluntary charity work, is a member of the emergency services, a veteran, or works for the betterment of society in some way, they may have a higher number of votes than those who do not possess these accolades, nor wish to play their part; this would make valuable the voices of those who selflessly help their family or tribe, thus encouraging this positive behaviour. Consequently, we may retain Democracy, if wished for by the prevailing sentiment, and retain a degree of democratisation to appease the electorate.

As *Plato* relayed an analogy *Socrates* once stated to another, which has come to be regarded as the "ship of fools" analogy, in which he states, paraphrasing, "imagine you were on a ship and set for a journey across the Aegean. Who would you wish deciding upon the captain? Anyone at all? Or just people educated upon the principles of navigation and seafaring?". "The latter of course", exclaimed the man. "So", said *Socrates*, "why do we think it logical for anyone to just decide who should be the ruler of a country then?"[316] The moral of this story is that *Socrates* is stating that voting is a responsibility rather than a freedom, that can be used and abused by a clumsy electorate. Not just anyone is capable and knowledgeable enough to decide upon the political destiny of the nation, so then we should have with this a set of standards guiding us

---

[316] Plato, Lane, M., & Desmond, L. (2007). *The Republic*. London: Penguin Classics. Book VI: 488a–489d.

on who are the capable individuals to vote and who are not; we have similar standards for captains and even sailors, so why not likewise with the ship of the state, then? To digress, moreover, a tiered voting system will disincentivise some welfare recipients, who really should not be in receipt of government welfare in the first place, to hopefully discontinue with their wastefulness or thus be disallowed the responsibility to vote. Furthermore, it should breed a more well-informed and sentient citizenry, who are well attuned to the political on-goings of the nation and who will be more dutiful in their vigilance of the monopolists, thus limiting the said monopolist's power acquisition hopefully. As a side note, a reduction in welfare recipients will most likely have to coincide with a greater loosening of regulation upon small businesses, thus we may incentivise businesses to form and reciprocally provide gainful employment for these citizens returning to work, though, charitable welfare is permissible to disabled individuals. However, government should reduce taxation and fund this small allowance via tariff allocations on select imports, thus reducing government size and the meddling in a private citizen's affairs.

Another solution may be decentralisation, though this is unlikely to come in one fell swoop. With the irreconcilable differences I have already previously stated, the only remedy in the long-run to maintain minimal peace and stability against all of these competing parties is through a policy of gradual decentralisation and regionalisation. This may be achieved by encouraging, firstly, a greater size of families which will bring demographic stability, and reciprocally cultural and long-term economic stability. This could be achieved, at present, by diverting welfare finances to productive and pro-reproductive members of society, championing a degree of *Agorism*, in which self-sufficiency can be cultivated so to speak, and through the disintermediation of government involvement within the schooling system. Hence, ensuring a decentralised curriculum and syllabus is instituted, guaranteeing it is far more difficult for agents of radicalism, or just the natural degeneration of culture, to infect the minds of the youth; of whom is invested our precious future and our legacy.

Though, I do understand these are unachievable through political means as government is unlikely, if historical precedent is an unbreakable pattern, which I believe to the affirmative, to relinquish any power illicitly gained unless said government, as an entity in and of itself, is routed out and vanquished as a legitimised institution in the minds of the citizenry. Therefore, something that is achievable right now is to engage in *Agorism* and the ideas of creating secondary-markets and utilising counter-economics, in a community setting, to slowly starve the institutions of the power of your productivity, and of your labour. Creating community cooperatives, farmer's markets, self-sufficient land on which you own and grow your own food, accept gold, silver or cryptocurrency for various business transactions, source your own water, create your own power and fuel, etc. Endeavour in any way you can to detach yourself from the vampiric parasite that is the government; that has attached to you and will continue to suck the lifeforce from you, depriving you of your liberty, property and love of your community, nation and culture until there is absolutely nothing left but a pile of dust, where once stood a free man.

If you wish to know more of *Agorism*, then please read a book by *Karl Hess* entitled *Community Technology*, in which he states many practical ways to implement self-sufficiency into your life and thus deprive your productivity and labour input into an unjust government's coffers. To conclude, once government reaches a threshold of power it tends to rip away the entirety of our freedoms, as is being seen now, thus it behoves us to act in self-defence and peacefully retract our labour and productivity from such a monstrous enterprise.[317]

Ideological Subversion

Yuri Bezmenov, in the early and late 1980's, was famously interviewed by G. Edward Griffin, the American Journalist, and he furthermore gave some very elucidating talks upon the Soviet technique known as

---

[317] Hess, K. (1995). *Community technology*. Port Townsend, WA: Loompanics Unlimited.

"*Ideological Subversion*"; a blueprint to destroy the nation of your enemy from within and without firing a shot to do so. Now, I must preface this by stating that I include this within the military section because demoralisation of the enemy is a valid tactic within warfare. Moreover, it seems that this type of "*Ideological Subversion*" becomes more apparent at the end of civilisational cycles – either it is the primary causal factor of the decline into the end, or it is a symptom of weakness and such weakness is exploited by internal antagonists within the nation.[318]

"Supreme excellence consists of breaking the enemy's resistance without fighting. If the mind is willing, the flesh could go on and on without many things. Victorious warriors win first and then go to war, while defeated warriors go to war first and then seek to win. To know your Enemy, you must become your Enemy."[319] As said the great military theorist *Sun Tzu*. The idea that demoralisation, through acquisition and subsequent subversion of an enemy's national institutions and sapping of their fighting spirit, is one that has seen great success in the many centuries of Human warfare[320]. Concurrently with that theme, one may say that the Communist and Marxist revolutions of the 20th, and minorly of the 19th century, are ones that utilised principles derived from *Sun Tzu's* teaching, in a primitive way mind you, to wrest power from the ruling regime, be whatever it may. We are seeing neo-Marxist revolutions today within the US, UK and the entire West, and one could argue that this is simply the next logical phase of an attempt made by Marxist revolutionaries to capture the reins of world power. The preceding phase being the long march through the institutions and consequential assimilation of the old customs, into the new cultural and political paradigm, which we term "political correctness" today. *Yuri Bezmenov*,

---

[318] Porlando. (2020). *Bezmenov's Steps (Ideological Subversion)*. Available: https://unintendedconsequenc.es/bezmenovs-steps/. Last accessed 28/10/2021.
[319] Sun-tzu, & Griffith, a. S. (1964). *The Art of War*. Oxford: Clarendon Press. Chapter III: Attack by Stratagem.
[320] Rushdie, S. (2005). *Shalimar the clown: A novel*. London: Jonathan Cape. Pg. 179. "Power does its work by stealth, and the powerful can subsequently deny that their strength was ever used at all."

the Soviet defector and whistle-blower, stated that within his time at the Soviet intelligence service – infiltrating various countries, to facilitate the cultivation of suitable conditions, in which Marxists may subvert and ultimately control these aforementioned target countries – that there were four main phases, of *Ideological Subversion* (also named active measures (активные мероприятия)):

- *Demoralisation*: The act of facilitating the education of an entire generation into the ideology of revolutionary Marxism.
- *Destabilisation:* Subversion and sabotaging of integral sectors of the nation; such as economy, foreign relations, defence, etc.
- *Crisis:* A planned insurrection or sporadic chaos; ultimately leading to a violent change of power structure or economic order.
- *Normalisation*: The period in which stability is restored, until the next cycle has reached crisis point.

Such forms of military subversion have been utilised even by the CIA and other Western intelligence agencies within Ukraine, in which they euphemise the term *Ideological Subversion* by adopting the novel phraseology of "Colour Revolution"[321]. However, each system is similar in scope and function. One could conclude that what *Yuri Bezmenov* wrote and talked about in the early and late 1980's has come to fruition today and some may say we are at that *Crisis* point, of which was aforementioned. It is speculation, but one may glean one kernel of truth from all of this chaos; that there is a merciless and relentless drive, by a powerful shadowy cabal to slowly and methodically chip away at the very edifice of Western civilisation, and everything it holds dear and values. Is it Marxist in its ideological framework? Yes, on the surface, but the real

---

[321] Sreeram Chaulia. (2006). *Democratisation, NGOs and "colour revolutions"*. Available: https://www.opendemocracy.net/en/colour_revolutions_3196jsp/. Last accessed 28/10/2021. "These three revolutions the "rose revolution" in Georgia (November 2003-January 2004), the "orange revolution" in Ukraine (January 2005) and the "tulip revolution" in Kyrgyzstan (April 2005) each followed a near-identical trajectory; all were spearheaded by the American democratisation Ingos working at the behest of the US foreign policy establishment."

string-pullers do not desire an ostensibly titled Marxist utopia, no, they wish for a type of system that one could aptly describe as a Technocratic Feudalist Serfdom. In which these oligarchs utilise novel technologies to more efficiently manage and control the vast swarm of peasants they wish to lord over. This system will be a utopia, but unfortunately not for the vast majority of the world's population; of whom will be subject to brutal taxation, a diminishing of basic rights, loss of all social mobility, extreme wealth disparity and managed culls from time to time. We can glean these facts from various institutes and renowned think-tanks; The Club of Rome's documents and discussions[322], the UN's Agenda 21 and sub-goal Agenda 2030[323] [324], The Bill and Melinda Gate's Foundation's push for eugenics policies under the guise of reproductive health and vaccination schemes[325] [326], The Fabian Society and the Frankfurt School's underpinning advice on revolutionary infiltration of the fabric of Western society[327], The Georgia Guidestones[328], etc.

---

[322] Meadows, D. H., Meadows, D. L., Randers, J., Behrens, W., & Club of Rome. (1972). *The Limits to growth: A report for the Club of Rome's project on the predicament of mankind*. New York: Universe Books.

[323] Robinson, N. A., & International Union for Conservation of Nature and Natural Resources. (1993). *Agenda 21: Earth's action plan annotated*. New York: Oceana Publications.

[324] Watson, R. T., & United Nations Environment Programme. (1996). *Global biodiversity assessment: Summary for policy-makers*. New York: Cambridge University Press.

[325] Akshay Tarfe. (2021). *Why Are Indians So Angry at Bill Gates?* Available: https://thediplomat.com/2021/06/why-are-indians-so-angry-at-bill-gates/. Last accessed 28/10/2021.

[326] TEAM, E. (2016). *Deaths in a trial of the HPV vaccine*. Indian Journal of Medical Ethics, 7 (3), 143. Retrieved from https://ijme.in/articles/deaths-in-a-trial-of-the-hpv-vaccine/. "The trial was being conducted in Andhra Pradesh and Gujarat by the NGO PATH with support from the Indian Council of Medical Research and local health authorities. They were funded by the Bill and Melinda Gates Foundation. The vaccine is supplied by two companies, Merck Sharpe & Dohme and Glaxo Smith Kline."

[327] Habermas, Jürgen. 1987. "The Entwinement of Myth and Enlightenment: Horkheimer and Adorno." *In The Philosophical Discourse of Modernity: Twelve Lectures*, translated by F. Lawrence. Cambridge, MA: MIT Press. Pg. 116: "Critical Theory was initially developed in Horkheimer's circle to think through political disappointments at the absence of revolution in the West, the development of Stalinism in Soviet Russia, and the victory of fascism in Germany. It was supposed to explain mistaken Marxist prognoses, but without breaking Marxist intentions."

[328] Rose Eveleth. (2013). *Nobody Knows How to Interpret This Doomsday Stonehenge in Georgia*. Available: https://www.smithsonianmag.com/smart-news/nobody-knows-how-to-interpret-this-doomsday-stonehenge-in-georgia-5592082/. Last accessed 28/10/2021.

Chapter V

I would hope that the perfidiousness of the creatures who hold political and high office is apparent to all those reading, and it is becoming more so by the day. The inability for individuals to grasp the gravity of the current situation, that being, that we are not going back to "normal" and that the freedoms we have relinquished will not be returned to us in any swift order; alas, such is the nature of government. The war the radicals have been imperceptibly waging against us and our kin for, irrefutably so, over a century has been relentless in its drive and it seeks to eradicate the very fundamental expressions of truth and naturalness; it seeks to make normal the abnormal; to render truth a relative construct decreed by an irrational precursor society; to diminish the agency of man in the pursuance of his own happiness and the evaporation of his spirit of resistance in the face of tyranny; that age-old adversary that seeks the trampling of man's divinely endowed rights. Thus, the environment for the production of this technocratic dystopia has been set, it will be merciless in its administration of regulation, it will lack moral constraint in its purging of dissidents and it will be unconstrained in its implementation of a purely collectivised society, in which freedom is abolished by order of the crack of the whip, or the stomping of the jackboot on the face.

I wished to keep this description brief and within context to our current situation; that is why I have intentionally omitted much information concerning *Yuri Bezmenov*'s insights into this military strategy, but you are free to peruse this information for yourself on any social media or video sharing platform while it is still available. Moreover, I wished to provide you, the reader, with this short excerpt on the modus operandi of *Ideological Subversion* because I think it rather paramount, to one's understanding of the present global and domestic situations that affect us all. I too think it very much, as previously stated, an either intentional quickening of the pace of natural civilisational decline or a purposeful fabrication of a decline, through miseducation and misguiding of the youth into forms of radicalism and extremism. In conjunction too, I wish to make clear to any detractors of such information above, that may insinuate that it is simply the ramblings of a "far-right conspiracy theorist", or false propositions to that affect, then I must make it bluntly clear that I am certainly not right-wing, nor do I care for theories; which is why I probably have an aversion to established political ideologies of any stripe, much like organised religion for that matter.

Certainly, everything I write about is meticulously researched and is the culmination of approximately a decade of intellectual discernment of academic and reputable non-academic sources. For example, if a powerful player such as the UN, releases a three-hundred-page report, informing of a universalist agenda for the 21st century, in which they wish to abolish property rights, inventory manage all natural and human assets, create habitable mega-cities, and institute a strict command-and-control economy and society, then that is not a conspiracy theory, naturally. That is just a plain fact straight from the horse's mouth, unfortunately so. I will delve into this transformation and blatant drifting away from Democracy in the next chapters.

Chapter VI

Plato's Five Regimes

P*lato*'s five regime's is an astoundingly astute observation of the cyclical nature of government types and how societal breakdown, under certain conditions, leads to the fertile grounds for specific new types of political orders to establish their dominion, over the old order's ashes. I will discuss and list the various political regimes as outlined by *Plato* and how each one specifically feeds into the other; then, I will discuss the implications of these observations by *Plato*, on our contemporary state. Moreover, I wish to discuss the fatal flaws in the Platonic theory of aristocracy, or the system advocated by *Plato*, and how this seems to be informing the overall change in the political and social landscapes we see as of late.

This idea is entitled the *Kyklos* (κύκλος), or cycle, in which the political evolution of civilisations or nations may be understood through cycles. I find a great framing of this concept within the work of *Polybius*, who details extensively the three major forms of government and their respective three negative sub-forms, that they inexorably devolve into. However, for the uninitiated on the concept, the form in which *Plato* frames this idea of *Kyklos*, or anacyclosis in modern academic parlance, is far more palatable and some may regard as vastly more interesting. However, I wish to provide this preamble to inform you, the reader, that

I may discuss this idea in more breadth as I am familiar with many other authors' postulations upon the subject of *Kyklos*.

Oligarchy

I begin at Oligarchy and you may wonder why, but I would pontificate that even though most of the world has, by this stage, adopted even a marginal form of Democracy it is honestly Democracy in name alone. The main power, even to any individual with the affliction of circumscribed thinking, is held by a small, wealthy cabal who would presuppose their intellectual, moral and potentially genetic superiority over the vast conglomerate of peasants below them. Why do I say that? Simply put, because the states we witness throughout history are an extension of the nature of the men who comprised them. Thus, extrapolating out that logic, if the men who comprised the central yoke of the system were truly moral individuals, they would then wish to enact reformations that would create a more equitable environment for us all, as compared to the distinct inequalities of wealth and power we are beginning to see manifest within society today. Naturally, there are other reasons that would point to their inherently immoral nature, such as needless wars and the series of contrived pretexts designed to foment casus bellis; for asset and influence acquisition and for the engineering of the social environment, domestically (*The Republic*, Loeb, 550c–555b).

That being stated, *Plato* described Oligarchies as a system in which the value of a citizen, in terms of the permissibility of the general society and political system, in allowing them to gain power or position, is derived from the capital or property wealth of that said citizen.[329] Thus, the rich have power and the poor have not. This system also fosters a class divide, in a strictly neutral political sense, that being said it creates an environment that eventually fosters the disintegration of personal

---

[329] Sikkenga, J. *"PLATO'S EXAMINATION OF THE OLIGARCHIC SOUL IN BOOK VIII OF THE 'REPUBLIC.'"* History of Political Thought, vol. 23, no. 3, 2002, pg. 377–400. JSTOR, www.jstor.org/stable/26219874. Accessed 24 Mar. 2021.

freedoms and the middle-class. This unequips the lower-classes of the financial and political means of deposing these Oligarchs, and thus the Oligarchs, in their desperation to maintain hegemony, will rework the constitution or *Juris Prudence* to restrict political power and office to the wealthy, or landed nobility by this time, solely. We are seeing this today with the administrative class that has arose within the West, and their use of the pretext of pandemic, to delay and distort elections and broaden their traditional powers and mandates. Moreover, the political system has slowly been infiltrated by lobbyists who seek to undermine any semblance of the equal application of the law, and access to public office, by means of legalised bribery of political candidates, political office holders, large media conglomerates and captains of economy and industry.

Interestingly as well, one may have seen the slow erosion of traditional markers of morality, or traditional, secular legal verities. Homosexuality, abortion, etc, have all been slowly decriminalised and subsequently championed by our media and political establishment. Let us not debate the moral decorousness of such positions, but alas let us look at why this seemingly surreal and rapid shift of culture has occurred from the top, and trickled down the pyramidal hierarchy of society. *Plato's* rationalisation of this phenomena, within the contextual framework of his ideas on Oligarchy, may provide insight. As *Plato* states, an Oligarchy naturally evolves from the initial tendencies of the preceding Timocracy[330] - I will discuss Timocracy in a later sub-section - and thus contrary to a Timocracies initial love of pride or glory, the Oligarchy changes its love of the immaterial concept of honour, to the material concept of capital; and this is similar to *Sir John Glubb's* beliefs upon this subject, also. Hence, this avariciousness cultivates within the classes of citizens a pursuit of endless wealth, rather than virtue. Thereby, from this accumulation of capital comes with it the material pleasures and lusts that innumerable wealth besets onto its holder. Thus, with the denigration of moral virtue, the laws and constitutions of the nation are amended to facilitate this

---

[330] Thornburg, T. (2001). *CliffsNotes: Republic*. New York, N.Y: Wiley Publishing. Chapter: Book VIII.

frivolous pursuit of material gain and carnal pleasure. We see the same amendments of law and culture today.

In respect to the lower-classes within an Oligarchy, *Plato* states that the increase of vagrants and criminals becomes prodigious in measure. *Plato*, in his raconteur ways, analogises the situation to the class of drones that exist in a beehive; that being, some contain stingers, and some do not.[331] Therefore, of the stingless class exist the vagrants and peasants who have tacitly accepted their lot in life or, though disgruntled by the reality, will inevitably end their life as paupers. In contrast, we have the criminal class who may possess a modicum of will to power, and may well could act as predatory as the ruling class. *Plato* states that wherever paupers dwell so do malefactors, and the reason for this state of malevolence of the criminal is a matter directly attributable to the wicked fettle of the state, ill guidance and want for education.[332]

Though the ruling class within an Oligarchic society may well be as morally bankrupt and pursuant of pleasure as the lower-classes, *Plato* states that they hold one virtue: temperance (*The Republic*, Loeb, 560D). Thus, in strict contrast to the anarchic tendencies of their plebeian counterparts, we find that the ruling class manages to establish a "fragile order within his soul" and thus temper his passions and desires. This may establish the internalised delusion, or project unto the populace the illusion, of superiority in comparison to the lower orders. This is woefully incorrect, but this type of delusionary mentality becomes more pronounced, I suggest, within the latter stages of Oligarchy. As can be alluded to as evident, by the current situation of the pandemic and the policies and comments made by, not just politicians, but the puppeteers in the back, including Gates and such; comments pertaining to knowing

---

[331] *The Arousal of Emotion in Plato's Dialogues*, Author(s): David L. The Classical Quarterly, New Series, Vol. 43, No. 2, (1993), pg. 428-439, Published by: Cambridge University Press on behalf of The Classical Association, Stable URL: http://www.jstor.org/stable/639181, Accessed: 10/08/2008 13:36

[332] Johnson, Lennox. (2017). *The Nature and Defects of Oligarchy – a short reading from Plato's Republic*. Available: https://thedailyidea.org/nature-defects-oligarchy-short-reading-platos-republic/. Last accessed 24/03/2021.

better than the lower classes, and in kind treating them like they are no better than children.

Democracy

Democracy is the consequential evolution of Oligarchy, though it may exist in parallel for a time; in my personal observations. It is a rule and cultural imposition dictated by the whims of the mob, where the idea of freedom, however devoid of meaning or abstract the concept may be dressed up to be, in the prevailing circumstances, is championed but is also, in due time, a mechanism of enslavement. Thusly rationalised, by acknowledgment of the maxim that with the excessive increases of anything, that it usually bores the opposite outcome; from the bosom of the most radical bastions of liberty can be produced the most egregious of tyrannies. The freedoms afforded to the citizen, by divine endowment or legal decree, may in time be utilised in different ways, and the craftier and shrewder citizen may find themselves unshackled from the burdens of regulation in a way that could facilitate their immeasurable rise to prominence, both in power and in wealth, and subsequently they may attempt to seize the reins of power; either by means of subterfuge and beguilement or through direct force of arms. Thus, and I may state that *Plato* does not make this distinction from my interpretation of his work, that Oligarchy and Democracy work in tandem, and they exist in symbiotic parallel, breathing life into each other; until the former expires (*The Republic*, Loeb, 555b–562a).

Much like Oligarchy the lower-class populace who become embroiled in frivolous pursuits, who have untampered passions and short-term thinking, slowly become the normative standard of not just the lower orders but of the society as a whole; even the ruling class become complacent and exhibit only reverence for degenerate pastimes. There is little order and the hierarchy breaks down, the young become equal in status as the elders, the teacher both fears and showers praise upon his students, "the father descends to the level of his sons and learns to fear them", and in turn the children having little respect and approbation for their parents, begin to rebel against the natural hierarchy (*The Republic*, Loeb, 563A-563B). The citizens become very sensitive, at the very notion of any overt sign of authority ruling over them, and they cease to care for charters of law or standards, formal or informal, and they will recognise no higher authority than themselves, no matter the misgivings of their nature. Thus, is the essence of the "Democratic man" and this is how democracy cascades downwards into a self-destructive, infernal firepit of despair and tyranny.

Typically, *Plato* enunciated that Democracies would, or could, be ushered in via the employment of violent revolution[333]. When the chasm of class becomes so apparent and disparate, when the injustice becomes too much to bear for the plebeians, they will "hate and conspire against those who have got their property, and against everybody else, and are eager for revolution. On the other hand, the men of business pretend to not even see those they have ruined". We see this type of civil friction today, though we do not see the outright dismantling of the Oligarchy, as to the contrary the strengthening of it, and the cynical may say these militant revolutionaries and radicals are somewhat funded by this same Oligarchy for ulterior motives and agendas. *Plato* goes on to continue, "Democracy comes into being after the poor have conquered their opponents, slaughtering some and banishing some, while to the remainder they give an equal share of freedom and power".[334]

TYRANNY

Tyranny follows sequentially from Oligarchy and Democracy, and we see such proofs of this from history; most notably the rise of national

---

[333] Van Bryen. (2013). *Plato and the Disaster of Democracy*. Available: https://classicalwisdom.com/philosophy/socrates-plato/plato-and-the-disaster-of-democracy/. Last accessed 24/03/2021.

[334] thelatinlibrary. *Plato's Republic*. Available: http://www.thelatinlibrary.com/legacy/plato/democracy.html. Last accessed 24/03/2021.

socialism, from the smouldering remains of the Weimar Republic. Tyranny, as per *Plato*'s literary documentation of what *Socrates* stated, is rule by one who wields absolute power. It may take the form of an absolute monarch, a fascist demagogue, a warrior-king, an emperor or a God-king. However, these demagogues and firebrands arise from the ashes of a Democracy when they may exploit the fears of the citizenry in regard to an Oligarchy. The tyrant may state that he wishes to redistribute land and property evenly amongst the citizenry, as a ruse to gain power, this was seen within the rise of the Soviet empire, or society will be classless, enjoy the abundancies of life, or have national or ethnic security. However, these promises are empty and are only employed as to facilitate the tyrant's acquisition of the populations obedience for purposes of requisitioning all power, centrally. Once established, a reign of terror will ensue and all political rivals, or counter-revolutionaries, will be rounded up and expunged from the new paradigm; this was seen within many Marxist and Fascist revolutions and also the proto-Marxist revolution, that was the French Revolution. These dissidents, as described above, are majority comprised of intellectuals and charismatic leaders of communities, these individuals are targeted because they may become flashpoints to rouse and muster support for a counter-insurgency against the new regime. As evident, Tyrannies, and the Tyrants who control them with an iron-rod, are inherently desperate enterprises and care only for the clinging on to power; though this is evident in most governmental types, it is acutely evident within Tyrannies. Do recall, if a state is attempting to silence its opposition, enforce a national belief system by force or by the force of law, show no limit to their exercising of greater degrees of power, enforce unnatural mandatory commands, and instil fear in their populace via demoralisation and examples of brutality, then one is living in a Tyranny (*The Republic*, Loeb, 562a–576b).

The irony of Tyranny is that though the Tyrant may offer to the citizenry the order sought, his regime in time becomes a nest of anarchy and arbitrariness; as a Tyrant seeks to destroy all potential intellectuals or other opponents that conclusively see the transparency of the lie that he seeks to perpetuate, so he robs the nation of its source of creativity and genius. This state of affairs leads to chaos in time, and the Tyrant will rapidly become hated by the same people who may have championed and sanctioned his rise to power, and in time they will conspire to overthrow him and his regime. Moreover, we must recall that the Tyrant and the regime become imprisoned by power, that they swiftly become locked in a cycle of imposing more increasingly draconian diktats to desperately maintain control; though this has the opposite effect and only further alienates the populace and thus, in time, the Tyrant may become trapped within their abode, fearful of fraternising with the very people who would have showered them with praise and adulation at the genesis of their rise, to the apex of power.

The Tyranny will eventually falter and be dismantled, typically internally, as the Tyrant will find it increasingly difficult to maintain power and control over all of his subordinates. The populace will also become exceedingly fed up with the state of affairs, and eventually the Tyrant will be overthrown in a coup d'état or via open rebellion. As we can see from historical analyses, Tyrannies tend to last only a short time, in comparison to other governmental types, this is due to a number of factors, both general and localised, but the main factor is the unnaturalness of the diktats imposed by the Tyrant. If the Tyranny attempts to subdue natural instincts through mandate, or disabuse individuals of basic rights or necessities then the relationship-dynamic between the authorities and citizenry will always inevitably breakdown, eventually. What do I mean by this? The citizenry will cease to acquiesce to the authority of the regime and will be unwilling to bend the knee, to any further suppressions of their natural rights. This will end in open rebellion if the citizenry can be formed into a cohesive fighting force by a capable leader, or powerful elements within the regime, sensing the winds of change, will pre-emptively initiate a coup in an attempt to maintain and potentially bolster their political position.

Chapter VI

I would wager, in light of recent circumstance, that we are on the cusp of a dictatorship forming. However, I feel that we are sometime away from the overt display of it; it is being quietly crafted currently, and these crises, we see, are being implemented in an attempt as to utilise the *Hegelian* or *Triadic dialectic* as a means of acquiring a world dictatorship, with plans to asset-manage and inventorise every resource and human-being. A Technocracy of sorts, which is a euphemistic term used in place of despotism.

Aristocracy

Plato is enamoured by the idea of aristocracy and the "philosopher-king", which he states is the most desirable form of government. Though I may disagree with him on principle, he does paint a rather utopian vision of this type of benevolent dictatorship, which has some very intriguing points that could yield merit under specific conditions, but has many major flaws inherent within it, even as a theoretical abstraction. Aristocracy proceeds from Tyranny. (*The Republic*, 369b - 541b).

Like *Plato*, I too find issues with the idea of Democracy and its past and present applications, but I too understand that *Plato*'s idea of the aristocratic state, more akin to a proto-Technocracy rather than the historical applications of aristocratic systems, is a system which we are heading into unfortunately; with some major caveats, of course. The first major caveat being that in *Plato's system* the rulers may not own property, they are forbidden to, and must be sustained by the lower-classes; thus, they cannot be tainted by the interests of personal greed and ambition. This is a commendable policy; however, the ruling class is termed the ruling class for one optimal reason; they rule and thus, in any system, will find ways to circumvent the established regulations. Secondly, they must be trained to understand the true "Good", capitalised to encapsulate a concept, and the Platonic idea of "Good", as vicariously stated through *Socrates*, is one in which is defined by an object or being's measure of value. Value to whom? Well, as we see from the famous dialogue between *Glaucon* and *Socrates*, within the *Republic*, the idea of "Good" is analogised with the Sun. The Sun provides light and therefore allows us sight; the sun is not sight, but sight exists as a cause of what the Sun provides. Therefore, the idea of "Good" seems to be something that provides the most benefit or happiness to the most amount of people; this is a eudemonistic idea of ethics and philosophy. However, who determines this? Who determines of what is of value and what is not? Well, in the Platonic ideal we find that it is the philosopher-kings, or ruling class, who hold the sway on such decisions and as such what they deem as "Good" is cultivated; though, this may offend the minority who deem this "Good" as an afront to themselves or their own ideals. Furthermore, a striking criticism one may lodge against this ostensibly perfect system is that the qualities of such a system, like all utopias, are a hodgepodge of generalities and utter authoritarianism. They promise much and deliver little, though exceptional they are in the application of destruction and death. However, this is the general overview of *Plato's* system:

Plato envisages a system in which there are three classes of whom comprise it, respectively. The first two classes are comprised of the guardian-classes, these are the "Philosopher-King" class, or the ruling caste, of whom have a soul made of gold, the auxiliary class, or the soldiers and enforcers of the will of the ruling class, of whom have a soul forged of silver, and finally there is the class of free-serfs of whom have a soul comprised of bronze. The first two classes are the guardian-classes and are comprised of meritocratically chosen, from the compulsory education system, individuals gifted in the areas of philosophy, gymnastics and having the innate desire for true knowledge; what is "true knowledge" remains unclear. Moreover, the ones who abided by the convictions instilled in them and did not rebel against the polis' belief system would be a candidate. This is peculiar, as through his dialogues, *Plato* argues, by proxy albeit, incessantly against the general belief and state of governance of Athens, of which was the polis in which he resided; namely that of

Chapter VI

Democracy, or rule by the "Demos" or the mob of the unfit, as he and *Socrates* saw it and I too would lodge such a criticism against Democracy, but the remedy is not a benevolent totalitarian dictatorship, however.

Digressing, the first two classes, or the guardian classes, would be unable to hold property and thus this would preclude them from being besmudged by these conflicts of interest when engaged in decision-making. Moreover, the auxiliary class would live in communal barracks and share everything – including wives (449a–471c). The proletariat, to steal a term from that dear prophet himself, or the lower-class of bronze, would be able to hold property and produce goods for themselves, but would be required by legal obligation to sustain the "Philosopher-Kings" and the auxiliary class; of whom did not produce or participate in the economy directly. Additionally, this type of "Kallipolis" (Καλλίπολις), or beautiful city, stems from the issue *Plato* held against the general state of being within the Hellenic world, and Athens in particular, at the time and that was, he felt, that the "wise" of society's – he contended philosophers – wisdom was not being utilised to its maximum effectiveness. Philosophers were nonetheless striving to create the theoretical framework for this Kallipolis and as such, as *Plato* insisted, should be given greater powers within the ruling class; subsequently, he believed knowledge should be the defining characteristic of governance, not power.

Furthermore, he held strong contempt, on intellectual and probably personal grounds, for the system of Democracy, as I have previously outlined. He asserts his major criticism of Democracy, namely that the unskilled and unqualified mob are left to decide upon matters of political governance and he utilises the allegory of the ship and the captain, vicariously spoken through *Socrates*, within the *Republic,* and it goes as follows: "don't you understand that a true captain must pay attention to the seasons of the year, the sky, the stars, the winds, and all that pertains to his craft, if he's really to be the ruler of a ship. And they don't believe that there is any craft that would enable him to determine how he should steer the ship, whether the others want him to or not, or any possibility of mastering this alleged craft or of practicing it at the same time as the craft of navigation. Don't you think that the true captain will be called a real stargazer, a babbler, and a good-for-nothing by those who sail in ships governed in that way?" (*Plato*; *The Republic*, Pg. 204).

In addition, another poignant infraction spawned by Democracy was, as he argued, the lack of justice inherent in such a system. Justice can be an abstract concept, even today in this societally transitory state we find ourselves in, but to the Greeks of antiquity there were several attempts at conclusively defining it[335]. The definition *Plato* subscribed to was encapsulated by the use of the Greek word δἴκαιοσὔ´νη – which is similar to the English word "righteous" or the fulfilment of the whole of man's lawful and moral duties.[336] *Plato* stated that justice is the abstaining of desire to partake in every pleasure and satisfaction, and contenting oneself with the exercising of a specific function for the betterment of the collective or general benefit.[337] This is consistent with a view of morality, in which the moral agent conducts moral actions based on the amount of good or benefit it brings to the collective. Conversely, observing of this principle may actually yield immoral actions and like other utilitarian philosophies, is ironically relativistic in its application of the concept of morality (*The Republic*, Loeb, 2nd edition, 351d); if we assume morality is absolute in principle, thus for example murder, or killing not out of self-defence, would be naturally always wrong, which it is because one is not only destroying another's property and existence, but one is engaged in the sowing of an atmosphere of fear and chaos within the tribe or society; this may lower other citizen's productivity and property value, thus it has economic and social repercussions that ripple throughout the society; secondary-effects. However, in *Plato*'s view, which seems utilitarian from

---

[335] D.R. Bhandari, J.N.V. University. (Unknown Date). *Plato's Concept of Justice: An Analysis*. Available: https://www.bu.edu/wcp/Papers/Anci/AnciBhan.htm. Last accessed 23/03/2021.
[336] Satyagraha. *Righteousness (Δικαιοσύνη)*. Available: https://satyagraha.wordpress.com/2017/02/15/righteousness/. Last accessed 23/03/2021.
[337] Homiak, Marcia, "Moral Character", *The Stanford Encyclopedia of Philosophy (Summer 2019 Edition)*, Edward N. Zalta (ed.), URL = <https://plato.stanford.edu/archives/sum2019/entries/moral-character/>.

its outset[338], the murder of a publicly despised individual - a rabble-rouser, a divergent thinker, a man who holds beliefs contrary to the majority – could be, per definition, justly murdered without prior provocation, simply because it would be advantageous to the general benefit. Hence, we see the general problem with platonic philosophy, namely being that it is broad and inexact in the detailing of its principles. However, *Plato* asserted that one of the main remedies provided by his utopia was the reintroduction of his concept of justice, which he seemed to believe was bereft or bastardised within the Athenian system of Democracy.

In conclusion, there are other ideas contained within *Plato*'s writings concerning a primitive form of gender equality, compulsory education, a banning of frivolous or decadent arts and poetry, a banning of particular modes of music, resource-based economic theory, etc, but I will deal with them individually below as points of order in and of themselves. However, *Plato* conclusively argues that to alleviate the unjust conditions brought forth by Democracy, or the Athenian-style of which, that a sort of proto-Technocracy must be instituted.

Thus, it could be argued, this aristocratic paradise, described by *Plato*, is simply a more ordered form of tyranny; or would become such. In which, we find what would occur would be a system that would begin adhering to the fundamental regulations set forth within the founding charters of law, or a constitution, but in time, like all systems, the ruling class would grow fat, greedy and imperious. They would find ways to circumvent the fundamental charters and documents of the nation, seeking more power by bureaucratic or NGO proxy, and in time transitioning the lower-classes from free citizens who sustain them, to landless serfs with little rights; such is the nature of governments and ruling classes, they seek total dominion and a more docile and efficient slave-class. This axiom, that has been aforementioned, is the way of predation, thusly that the predator will always seek to enfeeble his prey; this increases their efficiency in exploiting the prey and provides them

---

[338] Barrow, R. (2009). *Plato utilitarianism and education.* 10.4324/9780203861219.

with more security, in the knowledge that they will have no predicament arising from the prey resisting. This issue I have just discussed in-depth is solved within a system of absolute monarchy - in the Hoppeian (*Hans Hoppe*) sense, or the Hobbian (*Thomas Hobbes*) sense. In such a system of monarchy, the estate of the crowned monarch, and their heirs, is tied to the well-being and bettering situation, economically, of the peasantry; though costs of wars or a monarch's ill-governance can produce economic despondency, of course, but the principal of the matter still remains. The royal estate's health, financially and otherwise, is bound to the proper productivity of the peasantry. Productivity is typically enhanced via a laisses-faire attitude - this diminishes burdensome regulatory oversight and mitigates the rise of bureaucracy. However, absolute monarchy has attached its own set of impediments that makes it problematic; least of all being the problem with interbreeding in monarchical lines and the unpredictability of getting a virtuous and strong monarch. Moreover, monarchical lines tend to produce fewer and fewer great leaders with each ensuing generation.

Furthermore, by virtue of Human nature, we find that individuals who are educated, in a theoretical rather than practical sense, often exhibit extreme pomposity; especially if they have not been accustomed to the rigours of hard, manual labour and thus the plight of the lower orders will always seem far more distant within their thoughts, which will blind their decisions. We see a similar distancing, or inability for the ruling class to understand the predicaments of the lower-classes today and thus we find an inherent hatred and distrust for government found within these societal castes; hence why governments have availed themselves of bread and circuses with the lower orders, to alleviate the potential for civil unrest. These "Philosopher-kings", would in turn, become the antithesis of "Good" and would view the 95% of the lower-class, or third class, as simply a source of financial sustenance of luxury and they would, within their cognition, render them as mere drones or workers for the exalted ones who would excel and rule over the rest of the herd. Therefore, though this system would be meritocratic in its   stage, we find that with individuals with any scintilla of sense, that once they have attained power within the ruling class, they seek to induct their relatives into the ruling circle or, in this case, would simply indirectly own property through their relatives, who would act as proxy. Ultimately, this type of utopian system would devolve into a nepotistic bureaucracy with court plots and intrigue being rife; at its apotheosis, I envision a warrior-like demagogue, most likely one who has amassed fortunes in an underhanded fashion, from amongst either the auxiliary class or the ruling "Philosopher-Kings", to capitalise upon the lower-classes maltreated and tyrannised state, to create a military uprising and overthrow the dictatorship. He would galvanise the lower orders into action by making promises relating to the betterment of their situation such as wealth redistribution, more freedoms and better social mobility; take your pick. I have already iterated this type of political and social development of ideologies and principles in the term I coined *Theoretical Continuum*; in which, political ideologies and theoretical concepts, widely adopted, are by the mutagen of human meddling and tampering of their members through reform, revolution and general moral decline, are highly volatile in form. This is why all systems, including absolute monarchy, eventually devolve into centralised authoritarianism; it is always the path of least resistance, even though it may yield less of the fruit of productivity.

Interestingly, as I have stated *Plato*'s system was created upon the idea that the auxiliary class, or second-class, would be the military class of whom protected the philosopher kings and imposed their will on the lower classes. Funnily enough, both of these classes could not own property, however the "Philosopher-Kings" could not create a family either, and the auxiliary class had to share communal barracks, food and even wives with each other. *Plato* wished for them to share wives, I think, as a flawed form of eugenics - if the genes of the soldiers were all competing, then a better generation of soldiers was thus born. A similar eugenics program was designed for the ruling-class. However, we see no eugenics program designed for the lower orders. Therefore, if the goal was to create a more efficient society by means of gene selection and competition, then why omit the lower orders from such a policy? Simply put, *Plato* required a slave caste in such a system, and it would negate the stability of the system to augment this caste in the aforementioned fashion. We have to recall as well that both *Plato* and *Socrates* owned slaves and not only condoned slavery but advocated for it, as they stated that slaves created the leisure time required for them to philosophise. As a side note, we can see that having such a strong emphasis upon making the military entirely subservient to the ruling class, and dispensing with the imposition of their will, sets about creating the environment for infringement upon the lower classes and abuse of power. Who limits the power of both of these higher classes? No one and as such this will create the opportune conditions for a tyranny to ensue.

Moreover, *Plato* stated that a mythos had to be implanted within the minds of the populace that they were all "earthbound brothers" and that each had either souls of gold (ruling class), souls of silver (auxiliary class), or souls of bronze (lower classes) and thus each had their own station within this existence.[339] As you can see, this bears strong parallels to *Aldous Huxley's* "*Brave New World*" and the class system existent within that literary and theoretical work. Moreover, we find that *Plato* wished to alter the idea of the Gods and the religion to better inspire the various classes, he wished to ban poetry on the grounds of utilitarianism and imitation (Loeb, 595a–608b). *Plato* writes "the tragic poet is an imitator, and therefore, like all other imitators, he is thrice removed from the king and from the truth." Additionally, he wished for compulsory education in music and gymnastics for youth and their progress and adaptability would be watched and tested throughout their development. Those who resolutely held onto the convictions instilled in them by education would be chosen as guardians and those who rebelled against the city's ideology

---

[339] Plato. (January 1, 1930). Book 3. In: Paul Shorey, *The Republic*. 2nd ed. Unknown Place: Loeb. 416e.

Chapter VI

would be rejected (Loeb, 413d-414a). He also advocated gender equality, quite radically even for modern standards, too. Along with *Plato*'s "Cave" allegory (Loeb, 449a–471c), I think we can glimpse into the mind of *Plato*, in the fact that he knew genuinely of the power of propaganda and the advantage of inculcating of the specific standard of the society - in terms of ideals, world view and compliance - into the youth, as early as possible. Thus, a more compliant and conformed automaton may be produced; the basis of social engineering, if you will. Moreover, it is quite ironic that *Plato* sees one who rebels against the polis' ideology as not worthy of being a "Philosopher-King", let us put the blatant disregard for freedom of speech and individualism aside, and let us instead understand that *Plato* obviously did not see philosophy as a mode of critical-thinking or thinking outside traditional paradigms. Therefore, that bodes the question, what did he see it as? From his writings I cannot say conclusively, so I leave interpretations of such matters up to you, the reader.

As a tangential point, it is interesting to see this slow incline towards this type of utopian vision of human society proceeding *Plato*'s work - one whose modern theoretical proponents are still here with us today and in positions of high influence. For example, we see the work of *Thomas More* and, most notably, *Tommaso Campanella* who discusses this mythological utopian society within the Indian ocean named Ceylon (Modern-day Sri Lanka, presumably); each have their own version of this mythical, holy-grail realm. *More*'s is fairly liberal in comparison to *Campanella*'s; under modern standards of political scrutiny. *Campanella*'s view of this society, of whom is the most intriguing, delves into the governmental structure of this mythical Ceylon. He states that the government is elected by the people and then given ascension by the Senate. The government is comprised of four main elements; the supreme-ruler entitled Metaphysics, he is an absolute ruler in the religious and political sense; then there are three princes entitled Power, of whom is in control of the military, Wisdom, of whom is in charge of the arts, science philosophy, architecture and all academia, and Love, whom is in charge of breeding, education, food, housing and clothing. These princes then appoint all magistrates, of whom form the juris prudence or legal system of the realm. This is a command-and-control system, in which power is tightly controlled and administered by a selective group of peoples of whom are presumably elected from the educated and wealthier classes of society; much like our democratic and republican campaigns today, that being that only the wealthy have the means to run an effective campaign for election. In regard to the economy, *Campanella* states that the working day shall be four hours, in contrast *More* stated that there was a six-hour workday. *Campanella* states "Everything is in common, though placed in the hands of officials for dispensation". This is an early reference to a resource-based, proto-Communist economic structure. The family and gender policies of this realm, as described by *Campanella*, is also rather bizarre and idiosyncratic for the time period (late 16th century, Italy). For example, gender equality in terms of education, military service and communal living is apparent; no one has a private abode, quite literally. Moreover, the nuclear family, or the natural building block of society, is abolished; and children are separated from their mothers, two years after their birth, and raised by the ministry or princely power of Love. *Campanella* writes "They deny what we hold, that it is natural for man to recognise his offspring and recognise them, and to use his wife, his house and children as his own. Since individuals, for the most part, bring forth children wrongly and educate them wrongly they consider that they remove destruction from the state and therefore, they commit their education of the children to the care of magistrates". As we have now; the publicly controlled and compulsory schooling system.

Therefore, we have a system that is almost truly Communist as it proposes, or at least discusses as a radical novelty, to disseminate the ideas, in the underhanded fashion of dialogues, much like *Plato*, a system in which the majority of the tenets of Communism are met. For the late 16th century, and *More* being that of the early 16th century, this is naturally unparalleled and baffling for the period. This begs the question, is the modern-day push for a similar type of draconian system, through the "Great Reset" and such, simply intellectually and ideologically inspired by this many, varied cast of thinkers? Or, has this been some sort of conspiracy for world dictatorship that has existed for millennia, and is only now coming to fruition because the ideological adherents of such a dictatorship have amassed enough power collectively to enact it?

In conclusion, I thought this salient information thus I wished to include it and show the unquestionable link between these many utopian visions through history and through our own troubled present; of which all seem to be woven together by the same thread of thinking. Though, I think the cycles of government, or the *Kyklos*, as posited by *Plato* holds a great deal of merit, I nevertheless do not subscribe to his pontifications upon this utopia; as can be inferred from my above critiques.

Timocracy

The phase of Timocracy, as outlined by *Plato*, is one in which a devolvement of the aristocratic paradise has occurred. A Timocracy comes from two Greek words, the first being τιμή, price or worth, and secondly κρατία which is a widely used political suffix which denotes the meaning "rule by". *Plato* stated that Timocracy occurs when the ruling, or guardian, classes who comprise the governing caste begin to decline in nature and moral fibre. Instead of benevolent dictators who understand the true extent of the "Good", these new generations begin to become far more interested in producing wealth. Eventually, as I have previously stated within the prior section, the growing affluent classes distort the original premises contained within the constitution, or law, to permit themselves to own property and the education system is also amended to focus more solely on the pursuit of individual interests rather than the national, or polis' interests in this case (*The Republic*, Loeb, 543a–550c).

Incidentally, *Plato* remarks that Timocracies, when choosing their leaders, tend to choose the candidate who exhibits a simple nature of whom would be well-suited to war and the waging of it. *Plato* also added that the idea of Timocracy could be precisely characterised by the contemporary Spartan state of his day; however, there is some notable exceptions to the Spartan system which would contradict this assertion. Additionally, the leadership within a Timocracy is largely comprised of individuals who wish to acquire power through the acquisition of national prestige and through right of conquest; this being the most efficient and rational way of imposing ones will and acquiring possessions, both material and political in nature, within most of human history, arguably this is still the case in certain aspects of the modern world too. Timocratical leaders or officials would seek to hide their illicit wealth in perfidious ways, and would loathe thinkers acquiring office – thus seeking to bar them from such stations. They will exude a frugal attitude and will display the virtue of courage, but also hedonism in its purest sense. They crave power and though they may be averse to gaining affluence through mercantilist practises, they may still hoard wealth or engage in mercantilism.

Moreover, as a tangential point, I wish to state that mapping out a *Theoretical Continuum* to *Plato's* ideal system, one could see that by instilling virtues into people and choosing the most meritocratic of peoples ultimately would lead to such a divergence within the system; combined with the innate factors of the human condition too, I may add. Conjunctively, we see that this system would provide the conducive environment for demagogues, with ideas of self-importance and of superior intellect or ability, to come to the conclusion that, yes, they may be better than all of their contemporaries and as such should utilise the most rational solution to centralise all power within their own hands, as to better govern the people; as they know how to reform the system to better the societal condition and bring the society into a state more aligned with *Plato's* form of "Good" or the virtuous way; of which is a vague concept

Chapter VI

in and of itself and is subjective to the subscriber. As *Aristotle* called into question its "lack of relation to anything within the visible or existing realm, so therefore human-beings cannot comprehend or fathom, and as such is irrelevant to human ethics". Digressing, as we know, from recent historical examples, that an idea or ideology tends to produce contrasting and polarising divides upon issues that are meant to be clear and concise; although, it is human nature to find or even create division where there really should be none. However, because of the generalised manner of the form of "Good", outlined in the *Republic* and other works of *Plato*, we can infer that this idea would have a varying spectrum of interpretations amongst the ruling-class of what it pertains to intrinsically. Conversely, the implementation of policies derived from it would become difficult to formulate because of the subjective interpretations of it; this would undoubtedly create power struggles or political bickering amongst upper echelons. This would lead to a Timocratical demagogue arising, of whom seeks power through means of force.

Over and above, a leadership characterised by philosophers would be akin to a balkanised assembly of contemptuously snivelling intellectual narcissists, of whom spend their time engaging in the fruitless endeavour of circular debates about the fantastical principles of their pet theoretical constructs, of which exist in their mind and nowhere else; all variables existent within reality, that could inhibit the implementation of their ideal construct, are typically not properly conceived of, and thus this is how flawed ideas can infect reality. There are notable exceptions, *Marcus Aurelius* being foremost among them. Though one may see my above quote as an insult to the majority of philosophers, which it perceivably is, but consequently the vast majority of philosophers utilise the wisdom derived from the study of philosophy or philosophising for pointless ends; typically to impress or to inflate their self-worth, through the displaying of their understanding of abstract concepts of ethics or principled reason. In addition, philosophy and ethics, by its very essence, are fields of study that help propel one's own individual understanding of life and death, societal interactions and complex concepts that are taken for granted - such as justice – and as such is apropos of developing one's own soul and virtue. However, without practical usage and practise one cannot truly use the gifts philosophy grants and as such most philosophers indelibly resign themselves to the position of theoretician; engaging busily in the idealising and development of laughable theoretical constructs thereof; *Plato, Karl Marx, Jeremy Bentham, George Berkley, Hegel* come to mind, etc. That does not necessarily mean though that these philosophers and political theorists had nothing interesting to relay, but the crux of their theories was rooted in a type of immaterial idealism, some material in aspect such as *Marx*, of which they believed that the human mind and rationalism alone could solve the problems of the world and usher in the ideal state; this has been attempted for aeons with very little success, however. Correspondingly, we find that *Plato* discusses this idea too, that knowledge will supplant power as the dominant force within the ruling-class and as such this is a precursory belief to the more modern hypotheses produced by contemporary idealism. However, pragmatism is superior in most aspects to a theory based upon idealism; idealism may be novel in its concluded premises, but power is not derived from the exercising of knowledge, but by the exercising of the universalist language of violence; unfortunately, in our world, this is still the case.

Therefore, I would succinctly conclude that *Plato*'s "beautiful city" would unquestionably always devolve into what could be deemed a Timocracy, as a demonstrable fact; and it is interesting to hear *Plato* understand and acknowledge this fact, that his system, like all human constructs, is flawed by its members; of whom it seeks to better and make of a more temperate and virtuous nature. Therefore, *Plato* acknowledges that idealism is incorrect in its fundamentally implied assertion - that human nature is benevolent - and as a consequence we cannot develop a political or ethical system based upon a false premise which falsely assumes the inherent benevolence of human nature. This is noted within *Thomas Hobbes* literary work *Leviathan*. As a final point, *Plato* inadvertently concedes that the educational system contained within his system cannot, over a long-period of time, maintain a selfless and just status quo and as such dismantles the required expectation of his own idealistic system; thus, concluding it to be a system that would be wrought with decay, like all other systems before and after it.

Polybius's Anacyclosis

Polybius discusses the triad of general forms of government and at length the sub-divisions, or degenerate forms of these governments, of which order is primarily the most desired force within society, naturally. *Polybius* states that societies within their infancy will find themselves in a general state of ochlocracy, or mob rule, in which from this will be produced a monarchy, by a strong and charismatic leader that can organise and provide. Fast-forwarding, this monarchy will devolve when the monarch's descendants become lacking of virtue and the principles that the progenitor of the dynasty displayed, and because of the plentiful power they hold will wield it in a despotic way and will become de facto tyrants; the nation will suffer from weak leadership and a leader who will resort to draconian measures to desperately cling to power.[340]

However, this tyranny will quickly be overthrown by the leading nobility or wealthy denizens of the capital. They will institute some form of plutocracy or outright aristocracy, of which they may grant some modicum of privileges to the citizenry or land-holders. This too will become retrogressive and will devolve into an oligarchy, because of the lack of virtues exhibited by the leadership or by the citizenry alike. This oligarchy will be typified in its differentiation to aristocracy or plutocracy in that centralisation of power will occur more blatantly and the oligopoly, or market monopolies in specific economic sectors, will become more pronounced and lobbying, or legalised bribery of officials, will become the norm to maintain said monopolies. The oligarchy may

---

[340] Polybius (1889). *The Histories*. Translated by Shuckburgh, Evelyn. Macmillan. Book VI.

exhibit at this regressive state a leadership comprised of fewer and fewer individuals, of which many may be unrelated to royal bloodlines or nobility as it had in the past, but most forthrightly there will be a lack of care for the citizenry and strange ideas of this special class's supremacy may take hold, or peculiar religious ideals.

The oligarchy is then deposed, typically in a violent fashion, by a mob or, what we would deem, a paramilitary or revolutionary movement[341]. Thus, a democracy will be instated to divert the nation away from the trappings of the monarchical and centralised systems of the past, of which by this point would be despised with great zeal. Democracies are quick to become decadent and lacking any clear national path; this allows distinctive forms of corruption to leech onto the governing body, be them a simple assembly or a *Trias Politica* model of which is observable within the American system, and in earnest they will slowly diminish the power of the electorate or citizenry and implant their own agents, whom will push their personal agenda ahead of the national one. This type of system becomes disreputable swiftly, but even in a debased form it can exist for a considerable length of time and thus can reap great destruction upon the national constitution. Although, I disagree with *Polybius* in his hypothesis that democracies will always degenerate back into ochlocracy, though if ochlocracy be a strict synonym for chaos, then I would tend to agree, but it would seem that democracies can devolve into a number of various governmental types all with likewise similarities concerning one ruler and a centralisation of power.

Machiavelli, the Renaissance political-theorist, remarked much upon *Polybius*' work and upon the idea of anacyclosis he states within Book I, Chapter II, of his fabled work *Discourses Upon Livy*, that these cycles or political evolutions are not linear in their progression and maintain a circular structure, of which they may alternate freely depending on specific

---

[341] Hermans, M. 1991. *Polybius' theory of the anacyclosis of constitutions*. University of Cape Town. "This is also one difference between the transition from good to corrupt constitutions, and that from tyranny to aristocracy, and oligarchy to democracy: while the former is gradual and hardly discernible, the latter are brought about by violent revolutions."

social and political conditions being prevalent for such a transition. I tend to agree with this[342]. However, I still do believe that with the innate nature of human psychology, being what it is, that there is a certain degree of linearity apparent throughout history due to human-beings reacting in a similar manner, to similar prevailing social and political stimuli. Though, it can be argued, that every circumstance will present itself differently and thus we cannot predict outcomes conclusively, this is thusly true, but historical patterns can lend the spectator of the present a glimpse of the potential future; thus, informing his immediate actions.

If I may add too, that if we may conclude that humans tend to act behaviourally similar when encountering similar environmental stimuli, then let us extrapolate this conclusion out and thus tackle the idea of the seeming political reversals we see throughout history. What do I mean by "political reversals", I hear you say? For example, the Weimar republic hastily and with thunderous applause transitioned to the dictatorial Third-Reich. Another example would be the French revolution, where the inverse occurred, an absolute monarchy transitioned to one of the most liberal republics ever seen in human history. The Ottoman Empire's transition into the liberal Turkish democracy of *Atatürk* is another example – though that looks like it may revert back to its old ways rather soon. Why does this maxim of reversal occur? Is it a hallmark of human psychology when one is faced with insurmountable troubles caused, or perceived to be caused, by a certain system that one adopts the extreme opposite, as an assuagement to the vexations of the present system? Why not choose the less radical approach, the middle ground, the system that in time would most likely produce a far more stable form of government? This is sadly seldom the case and hence a far more terrifying system takes hold, imposing its corrupt diktats upon a tired citizenry.

Digressing, I would conclude that it is typically human nature to wish to attempt the extreme opposite of a system before finding the middle-

---

[342] Machiavelli, N., Mansfield, H. C., & Tarcov, N. (1996). *Discourses on Livy*. Chicago: University of Chicago Press. Introduction: Pg. XXXVIII.

ground. Case in point France, which is now a fairly stable republic, for the time being, though it reverted back to an imperial system after the revolution, and once again finally returning to a more stable form of republicanism post-1870 and post-Commune of Paris. Therefore, we may understand that human nature can be fallible and easily led to disastrous ends by the pursuit of the extreme opposite of any given political system.

Chapter VII

The Trappings of Democracy

Democracy, nominally the system that still somewhat reigns within the modern West, though that seems to be less and less so with every subsequent year. Throughout history we see that a great deal of zealous proponents of Democracy have understood and alluded to, even within their respective literary *magnum opuses*, that Democracy is a system with many flaws – some that can lead to inexorable disaster for the nation[343]. I will take this chapter to detail the various opponents of Democracy's literary works and arguments against the said system. These will span quite some period of history, as they are numerous, but will include *Hans Herman Hoppe* and *Thomas Hobbes'* work primarily. Though, I will touch upon some of *Rousseau's* comments, who was an early major supporter of the implementation of a direct Democratic system.

Moreover, I will touch upon the idea of Caesarism, which can be a product of Democratic systems, but can exist in other types of systems

---

[343] Constitutional Rights Foundation. (2004). *BRIA 20 2 c Hobbes, Locke, Montesquieu, and Rousseau on Government*. Available: https://www.crf-usa.org/bill-of-rights-in-action/bria-20-2-c-hobbes-locke-montesquieu-and-rousseau-on-government.html. Last accessed 1/11/2021. "He believed in a direct democracy in which everyone voted to express the general will and to make the laws of the land. Rousseau had in mind a democracy on a small scale, a city-state like his native Geneva."

as well. *Oswald Spengler* discusses this idea of Caesarism and has some very in-depth, though abstract, ideas on the subject of Caesarism and Liberalism – of which I think it of merit to mention and discuss, respectively.

Ancient Examples of Flaws in Democracy

The flaws of Democracy are numerous and one could not discuss them in any brief manner, but these flaws have been understood since the times of the first recorded Democracies and, due to the nature of humanity, we find they repeat whenever the system of governance is implemented in any great sense[344]. The issue with Democracies inherently, and unabashedly, is that they can be captured by domestic or foreign special interests for nefarious purposes; this is done through bribery, either directly to both electoral candidates or through the counters and organisers of the ballots. It is rather an easy affair, and all one really needs is amoral individuals predisposed to accept your bribe and a deep-pocket as to which to procure these large bribes from. This was prevalent within the Roman Republic, *Ambitus* or literally to "illegally canvas support", was the word utilised to describe what we deem today as bribery[345]. *Julius Caesar* famously bribed *Curio* to support his bid for senate, the mighty and of high-repute *Cicero* fell to the temptations of bribery a few times[346], and the political class seemed intent on bribing citizens with bread and circus to maintain

---

[344] Lintott, A. (1990). *Electoral Bribery in The Roman Republic*. Journal of Roman Studies, 80, pg. 1-16. doi:10.2307/300277

[345] Lintott, A. *ambitus*. Oxford Classical Dictionary. Retrieved 3 Nov. 2021, from https://oxfordre.com/classics/view/10.1093/acrefore/9780199381135.001.0001/acrefore-9780199381135-e-346.

[346] Rauh, Nicholas K. "*Cicero's Business Friendships: Economic and Politics Within the Late Roman Republic.*" Aevum, vol. 60, no. 1, Vita e Pensiero – Pubblicazioni dell'Università Cattolica del Sacro Cuore, 1986. Pg. 3–30. "Even before arriving in the province, he was torn between his desire to behave as an exemplary provincial governor and his eagerness to please his friends who were pressing him to bend the law with regard to their interest in the province."

obedience[347]. Athens, of which was a direct Democracy, and of which held some elections for officials, some of the grander positions being left to the drawing of lots funnily enough, but it too had instances of vote purchasing and other such marks of corruption; though it seems they may have attempted to resist these, on a societal level and a legal level too.[348]

The failings of Democracy, as with all systems, seems to begin with the increase of affluence and commercialisation within the imperial or national boundaries. This inevitably leads to merchant classes rising which have an insatiable desire for wealth and power. This ultimately leads them to put to use their inordinate capital in the pursuit of political power, for themselves or for an agent that will legislate on their behalf. Professions began to take root around this financial exchange with promising political arrivistes, of which these newly established professions acted as the financial mediators for such arrangements – we call them today "lobbyists", but the name they adorned in the age of the ancient Republic of Rome was *Divisores*[349]. This became of such an issue, that in the year of 55AD, *Crassus* championed a legislation entitled *lex Licinia de sodaliciis*, that sought to established regulated bribery organisations and provided legal credence to convict members of such organisations for practises that deviated from the regulation; though *Crassus* may have simply been acting to protect his own power-base from competing powerbrokers with such a piece of legislation[350]. *Q. Aurelius Symmachus*, in 376AD, wrote in consolation that "the hideous voting tablet, the crooked distribution of the seating places within the theatre among the clients, the venal run, all of these are no more! The elections are transacted between the Senate

---

[347] Holland, T. (2003). *Rubicon: The last years of the Roman Republic*. New York: Doubleday. Pg. 301; Cicero, To Friends, 8.7.
[348] Staveley, E. S. (1972). *Greek and Roman voting and elections*. London: Thames and Hudson. Pg. 271
[349] Cicero, M. T., & Centre Traditio Litterarum Occidentalium. *Epistulae ad Atticum*. Turnhout: Brepols Publishers.
[350] Cicero, M. T., In Kerin, R. C. B., & In Allcroft, A. H. (1890). Cicero: Pro Plancio. London: W.B. Clive. Chapter: 16.

and the Emperors: equals elect equals, and the final decision rests with the superiors"[351]. This was in hopes of the demise of the final vestiges of the Senate, even though by that stage in the Principate it was little more than a symbolic spectacle. Lo, of how many people now, our contemporaries, wish for a similar demise or total reformation of our systems of governance within the West? The majority I would suspect, but this reflects the overall lack of trust and hope for our Democratic or Republican systems and with the recent elections in the USA, and the potentially dubious swing-state results that are either highly miraculous or fraught with fraud, I speak politically neutrally mind you, then one has to wonder how can a Democracy persist without the majority trust within the institution of elections? Never mind the issue of a balkanised populace.

In the end, most Republics succumb to political infighting, populist power-plays and a general disintegration of traditional taboos against corruption and political violence. Most prior to this date engage in the same, tired old Machiavellian tricks of holding unfair elections or withholding elections, lack of meaningful reform and growing oligarchy, abuse of the successive terms doctrine (*lex annalis*, in the case of Rome*)*, abuse of the auspices of power, violence and political gang warfare, bribery and electioneering, cabals and conspiracies, predetermining of results, usurpation of constitutional roles, and procedural abuses[352]. It seems that the longest running Republic, the Most Serene Republic of San Marino, in existence since 301AD and constitutional since 1600AD, is as such because it is so infinitesimally minute that it can maintain social cohesion and shake off the potential disintegration that occurs with larger, more varied societies that have a plethora of competing interests, which are exacerbated by the myriad of diverse styles of Republicanism.

---

[351] Hill, Lisa. (2013). *Conceptions of political corruption in ancient Athens and Rome*. History of Political Thought. 34.
[352] Troxler, Howard, "*Electoral Abuse in the Late Roman Republic*" (2008). Graduate Theses and Dissertations. Accessed here: https://scholarcommons.usf.edu/etd/537. Retrieved: 03/11/2021.

CHAPTER VII

THOMAS HOBBES AND DEMOCRACY

Thomas Hobbes's magnum opus, *Leviathan,* is a deep and, one could say, realist's view upon the nature of Democracy and the human condition itself. Like *Machiavelli, Hobbes* understood that any system of government that is to function optimally, for any perceived length of time, must have at its core of fundamental principles the sincere acknowledgement that the human creature acts in self-interest; it cares not for morality, unless it is required to be feigned for social approval, generally speaking[353]. *Hobbes,* a pro-royalist living at the time of the English Civil war, discusses controversially, still presently so, the idea of absolute Monarchy being more effective a system comparative to, what *Hobbes* defined as, "Assemblies". Of which we can name Democratic systems of governance, but both terms are synonymous. Of the three generalised systems of government outlined by *Hobbes* in *Leviathan* - that of Democracy, Aristocracy and absolute Monarchy - he argues that the latter is superior to the prior two. Ultimately, he describes Democracy as an "aristocracy of rhetoricians"[354], which I would assert to be a clever way to summarise such a system. However, within this section I will outline some of *Hobbes'* points of scrutiny against the sacred relic of Democracy and briefly explain why I feel, in my humble opinion, them to be not only true but incontestably prophetic. A reason as to why Democracy is not only ineffective, but a monumental regression in human development.

Hobbes propounded, in his landmark literary work, the prototypical idea of the social contract[355]. Arguing that individuals act in a spirit pursuant to greed and power, and that their natural predisposition is

---

[353] Hobbes, T. (1651). *Leviathan*. Penguin Books: Baltimore. Chapter 13: Of the Natural Condition of Mankind as Concerning their Felicity and Misery. "The life of man, solitary, poor, nasty, brutish, and short."
[354] Hoekstra, K. (2006). *A lion in the house: Hobbes and democracy*. DOI: 10.1017/CBO9780511618376.012. "An aristocracy of orators, interrupted sometimes with the temporary monarchy of one orator".
[355] Hobbes, T. (1651). *Leviathan*. Penguin Books: Baltimore. Chapter 19: Of the Several Kinds of Commonwealth by Institution, and of Succession to the Sovereign Power.

not inclined in forming cohesive societies; or large-scale civilisation, more rightly. However, they can be brought to reason by the informal understanding that it is of everyone's, of whom share a commonality and common interests, mutual benefit to stray from the free state of nature and form cohesive social units. Alas, in the natural state, where freedom is so replete it invites chaos, that the mass of people would assuredly destroy each other in an embittered struggle for wealth, power and honour; *bellum omnium contra omnes*. He postulated that in a state reflecting true nature of being, men were only capable of holding that which they could maintain by force of arms[356]. As there was no unity, there was not common law, and as *Hobbes* believed "property rights" is only granted by the observance and the power of law[357]. Of which I disagree, I believe that, as we are seeing currently, and have seen historically, rights are bestowed naturally and inherently and maintained by the fear that the government holds for the citizenry. Common sensibilities can be distorted rather effortlessly and where one generation can be ardent defenders of liberty, the next can be poisoned by the notion that exploitation of the masses derives from private ownership of property; as we have borne witness to. However, law, once written, must be dutifully maintained against encroachment by government or co-conspirator alike, of whom may seek to rein in that power for their own treacherous ends.

However, though I may resoundingly approve of *Hobbes* on a whole, I do hold to some expostulations of his various ideas; as is normal for any ideas I approach. Continuing on, *Hobbes* insistently did not endorse the idea of inalienable and divinely-gifted rights; that which does not predate the formation of the common legal sensibilities of a community[358]. I

---

[356] Hobbes, T. (1651). *Leviathan*. Penguin Books: Baltimore. Chapter 14: Of the First and Second Natural Laws, and of Contracts. "For as long as every man holdeth this right, of doing anything he liketh; so long are all men in the condition of war."

[357] Hobbes, T. (1651). *Leviathan*. Penguin Books: Baltimore. Chapter 13: Of the Natural Condition of Mankind as Concerning Their Felicity and Misery. "It is consequent also to the same condition that there be no propriety, no dominion, no mine and thine distinct; but only that to be every man's that he can get, and for so long as he can keep it."

[358] Hobbes, T. (1651). *Leviathan*. Penguin Books: Baltimore. Chapter 26: Of Civil Laws. "And first it is manifest that law in general is not counsel, but command".

understand his cognition upon such a matter, it is true that these ideas cannot take full legal root prior to the formation of the community, and the formation of the canon of law. However, one would have to concede that rights, as per the actions they produce, do exist within a natural state also. For instance, a right to property, or the maintaining of *de jure* control over your own territory, is granted, therein, from your own will to power through the exercising of force of arms, or through maintenance of the delicate balance of civility; through conferring fear and respect unto neighbours, and neighbours unto you. This is absolutely akin to "rights" that are expressed formally within law; by the actions produced therefrom. Subsequently I would argue, the idea that law solely grants these rights is a misnomer. Thusly, these rights were only listed formally, within legal charter, as an appeasement to a swelling of anger within the people towards the government; most likely. Hence, the government merely rescinded their regulation of these basic instincts, by the fear they held at the time for the people. By this token, government did not miraculously craft one these rights at the time of drafting, implanting these instincts within oneself by legislative decree, but they merely reduced their oversight over the regulation of one's already innate instincts; of which, they abbreviated as "rights". For it is instinctual for man to bear arms to defend his family and nation; it is natural for man to demarcate the land required to sustain himself and respect the territory of another equal, without due cause to act on the contrary; and it is natural for man to speak freely that which is of importance to him. When these rights are not practised freely by the populace, then they are simply only practised by the government. As consequence, if the government enjoys privileges which place them upon a higher station than oneself, then one ceases to stand an equal to the government and is, by all rationale, held underfoot to the whimsical nature of that said infernal institution. Pray, is this not so?

Though *Hobbes* plainly gives merit to the postulant that rights are derived from the community, he bases his "social contract theory", however, not upon Democratic principles, but upon the notion that citizens should unite under the rule of a strong and autocratic king[359]. Contending that the only check to stem the greed and lust for power, inherent within Man, and ensure law and fair order, was the imposition of such a rule. I agree with *Hobbes* on account that greed and the lust for power is what drives Man, and as such having short-term leaders who can exercise power and authority, with relative impunity, will consequently produce a governing class who are opportunistic short-term predators, rather than dutiful guardians of their estate, of in which their interests are inextricably bound. One may be perplexed at the notion that absolute, hereditary monarchy - the centralisation of all power and authority into the hands of one man – would be anything other than antithetical to the idea of freedom, but let me explain the case, of the genius of such a system in the safeguarding of said freedoms. In our current system, the short-term periods of leaders and officials leads to the creation of a sort of magnetism that draws together the most amoral, megalomaniacal and parsimonious individuals within society – most are lawyers, businessman and bankers for example – and most are not, say, military-men, workers or, by this state of being, even family men. Thus, these leaders we have are easily corruptible, have little invested in the future and are driven by the accumulation of capital for material gain and pursuit of pleasure. Moreover, the leadership, as corrupt as I have attested to, is also plagued by the predicament of short-term periods producing a desire within these individuals to pilfer the national coffers as quickly as possible, for if they do not endeavour to at present, then they will be unable to in the future. Finally, it creates a leadership hinged upon a lack of foresight and prudence when engaging in decision-making; the repercussions of their actions, that may be felt a generation from now, will be of no consequence

---

[359] Hobbes, T. (1651). *Leviathan*. Penguin Books: Baltimore. Chapter 19: Of the Several Kinds of Commonwealth by Institution, and of Succession to the Sovereign Power. "The difference between these three kinds of Commonwealth consisteth, not in the difference of power, but in the difference of convenience or aptitude to produce the peace and security of the people".

Chapter VII

to them, but to their inheritors; and as such, they have the luxury of kicking the can down the road. Likewise, in such a system a culture that hinges upon a lack of foresight and responsibility for consequences of future actions is cultivated and engendered; and with the combination of a gravely weak leadership only aggravates decline.

Additionally, *Hobbes* stated that systems that indelibly advocate assemblies, such as Democracy, could be said to be perpetual interregnums; replete with the trappings that such a period brings forth[360]. Interregnums, or periods in which there is a lack of heir or a contest of the throne, is typically led by council of regents *pro tempore*. Of which, as *Hobbes*, describes there is, with the multiplicity of competing interests, an inability of the regents to accomplish anything meaningful and they may clamour to increase their station and wealth, even at the expense of the nation. *Hobbes* likens this to assemblies, but states that the situation is amplified as there are even greater amounts of competing interests – or interests that can be exploited for corrupt intent, by a third-party. On the other hand, to this, monarchies, as many modern proponents of monarchical systems and as *Hobbes* suggests, act differently in their fundamental approach to the welfare of the nation and people[361]. As Democratic leaders act in a fashion that betters them, as their interests are not tied to the betterment of the populace, the monarch, whose

---

[360] Hobbes, T. (1651). *Leviathan*. Penguin Books: Baltimore. Chapter 19: Of the Several Kinds of Commonwealth by Institution, and of Succession to the Sovereign Power. "And as a child has need of a tutor, or protector, to preserve his person and authority; so also in great Commonwealths the sovereign assembly, in all great dangers and troubles, have need of custodes libertatis; that is, of dictators, or protectors of their authority; which are as much as temporary monarchs to whom for a time they may commit the entire exercise of their power; and have, at the end of that time, been oftener deprived thereof than infant kings by their protectors, regents, or any other tutors.".

[361] Hobbes, T. (1651). *Leviathan*. Penguin Books: Baltimore. Chapter 19: Of the Several Kinds of Commonwealth by Institution, and of Succession to the Sovereign Power. "The riches, power, and honour of a monarch arise only from the riches, strength, and reputation of his subjects. For no king can be rich, nor glorious, nor secure, whose subjects are either poor, or contemptible, or too weak through want, or dissension, to maintain a war against their enemies; whereas in a democracy, or aristocracy, the public prosperity confers not so much to the private fortune of one that is corrupt, or ambitious, as doth many times a perfidious advice, a treacherous action, or a civil war."

interests are bound within his estate, which is constituted by his subjects, is behoved to act in a manner that enriches the populace; or face the mutual-destitution of aforesaid parties. In addition, a monarch bears the mantel of leadership for life, which extricates him from an ability that his Democratic counterpart enjoys, which is to avoid a higher likelihood of forcible removal and potentially capital punishment, for wrongs carried out against the citizenry. Democratic leaders may be elected out after their term is up, or relinquish it prematurely an office, thus this provides an illusion to the populace that the problem has been routed out and thus no further action is required. However, in contrast, the monarch can only be removed via voluntary abdication or forcible removal by the populace. Thus, he should be prevented from drawing the ire, too much, from his subjects lest he be extirpated by an angry peasantry or nobility. However, monarchies have their own complications entangled within their doctrinal vines, but one can make a strong case that monarchy, whatever form, is far more efficient and stable a system than Democracies historically, and contemporaneously, speaking.

Hobbes wrote about human nature, thusly: "The desire for power, wealth, knowledge and honour. All this can be reduced to the first, that is the desire for power. For wealth, knowledge and honour are just different forms of power."[362] This is true, that power is the holy grail to which all men seek, even if they do not know it directly. Power, that is in this context, to hold dominion over your fellow man and utilise his labours to financially better yourself; such is the way history has played out, with notable exceptions here and there. However, there is an unorthodox way of looking at power and authority, and how it plays into the monarchical and Democratic system, of which I will illustrate later in this section. Digressing, as we see with the advent of the growth of governments, of any type really, but notably of an assembly and with bureaucratic leanings, this type of innate desire in-built within the human psyche comes forth

---

[362] Hobbes, T. (1651). *Leviathan*. Penguin Books: Baltimore. Chapter 11: Of the Difference of Manners. "I put for a general inclination of all mankind, a perpetual and restless desire of power after power, that ceaseth only in death".

Chapter VII

and begins to run amok throughout society; with the ultimate goal being to develop or refine a system of total and uncompromising slavery of a controllable, docile slave-class; that is the goal of all government and individuals who aspire to positions therein, be under no illusion. Therefore, this in-built desire, in *Hobbes'* belief, can be diverted to be used for the betterment of society; for in a world of competing monarchs, be it military or economically, a society that champions personal freedom and voluntarism will emerge the more efficient as compared to its neighbours. In essence, it befits the monarch to implement and defend such rights and supplementary policy.

How so? Well, a man who chooses his own profession and trade, working at it tirelessly and with commitment, yields greater productivity than a slave who is forced to toil a specific labour. Why? Simply put, man enjoys freedom and a taxed serf who thinks himself free, taking pride in his profession, will wear that like a badge of honour and the pride and freedom he feels in completing his work – keeping the majority of the profits yielded from his labour for himself and his family – will feel he has accomplished and achieved something for the time invested in his toil. A slave, on the other hand, has no such luxuries and keeps nothing of his labour, nor does he take pride in it as it was not his initial choice to end up in such a line of work[363]. Naturally, he may actually attempt to produce less, if no quota is set by his master, for with the disdain he feels for his master in subjecting him to such toil, he may seek to lower his master's profits through yielding less production for him. There are multiple other reasons, but naturally this is a pattern witnessed in economics and society for millennia – that said, men tend to work more

---

[363] Hobbes, T. (1651). *Leviathan*. Penguin Books: Baltimore. Chapter 19: Of the Several Kinds of Commonwealth by Institution, and of Succession to the Sovereign Power. "Now in monarchy the private interest is the same with the public. The riches, power, and honour of a monarch arise only from the riches, strength, and reputation of his subjects. For no king can be rich, nor glorious, nor secure, whose subjects are either poor, or contemptible, or too weak through want, or dissension, to maintain a war against their enemies; whereas in a democracy, or aristocracy, the public prosperity confers not so much to the private fortune of one that is corrupt, or ambitious, as doth many times a perfidious advice, a treacherous action, or a civil war."

vigorously and with greater zeal if they are giving the illusion of choice or freedom. Similar tendencies seem to make themselves apparent within the military and political fields, too. For example, on the whole, volunteer militaries tend to outperform militaries comprised of conscripts; with notable exceptions, such as Emperor *Napoleon Bonaparte*'s military, but *Napoleon* has always been an exception as was his military aptitude exceptional. Apropos that previous thought, the military conflict over the Falklands Islands, fought between the Argentinian and British militaries in the early 1980's - over a territorial dispute surrounding a disparate and overly unimportant small cluster of Islands in the South Atlantic - showed the British military besting the land forces of the Argentinians, who were largely young conscripts, with relative ease. However, in contrast, from the information I have digested, it seems as though, despite the imbalance of military air assets, that the Argentinian air force, of whom were all volunteers, distinguished themselves on the field and gave a good account, as stated by their foe and friend alike.[364]

Finally, as one could well imagine, within the political sphere the illusion of choice is of grave importance to the ruling-class. It provides them a smoke-screen to maintain power and the veneer of freedom for the masses below. Democracies, ironically, were and have been adopted for this sole reason by rulers; the irony being that they are not a rule by the people, but a rule of the people by the mass-delusion of self-rule; a fools' paradise, if you will. One can be provided with a plethora of candidates but with each changing of the mask, the face wearing it remains unaltered. This is why Democracies are demonstrably always either plutocracies, oligarchies or aristocracies when the true source of power is ascertained, in the focus of the astute observer. A masquerade of political theatre, a shallow musing for the unenlightened, a coarse pill to swallow for the aware – the political sphere was remade in the image

---

[364] Corbacho, Alejandro (September 2004). *Reassessing the Fighting Performance of Conscript Soldiers During the Malvinas/Falklands War (1982)*. Documento de Trabajo, No. 271. Available at SSRN: https://ssrn.com/abstract=1013423 or http://dx.doi.org/10.2139/ssrn.1013423.

of the Democratic ideal because Democracy is like a key to the door of the future for governments; and that future is perpetual enslavement and a strict ordering of the masses, for the benefit of the elite and their subordinates. The unapologetic Platonic paradise. However, as you can see, the illusion of choice and voluntarism is something implemented by rulers as a means of maintaining an economic, military and socially cohesive edge over their opponents. Although, such freedoms for the lower-orders, I can predict, would be far more fervently safeguarded by the monarch as he does not have the luxury of being switched out after a short-term, as our present collection of rulers and their various puppets do. In this regard, monarchy is superior I would argue.

In conjunction, if we look at *Locke's* ideals regarding his advised system and *Hobbes'* view, then we find very profound questions come forth from the various contrasting defined articles, present within their respective systems. For example, *Hobbes* wishes to implement unconstrained monarchy. Of which, if the monarch deems fit that property and liberties traditionally regarded as sacrosanct be abolished for the good of his estate, unlikely but albeit possible, then there is little to oppose his will – this is a grievous flaw. However, *Locke* underestimates the potential for Democratic abuses, too – that an "elected legislature can trample a man's rights as easily as a king can", to quote a line from Hollywood. For example, as we can see presently, it seems to be more beneficial for external corrupting elements – of which tend to subvert the rights of man for the benefit of themselves – to operate within a Democratic system, as parliamentarians or representatives can be easily compromised through blackmail and bribery and each has short term limits. Thus, a fugaciously short-term time horizon emerges which leads to high time preference decisions; kick the proverbial can down the road, so to speak. Though, advisors to the King and external money-lenders could just as easily control a King through the same means as to which they would control an elected official. Therefore, both are of course fallible, but which one is less so? I would argue monarchy, but that is because I have witnessed first-hand the abuses of Democracy, so I am rather biased in this regard.

That said, I would argue that there will always be abuses within any government type because individuals have an aversion to organise militarily, with swiftness, to respond to the threat of rising tyranny – from whatever political host it emerges from. The reason tyranny prevails and always manages to hatch from its cocoon is because extra-governmental forces acquire vastly disproportionate resources, and power within their own hands. They then use this to tip the balance of power in their favour, by the purchasing of inordinate amounts of military assets, political assets and ultimately, they, like a parasite, turn the apparatus of the state on those that it was created to serve. The citizenry, within these scenarios of growing tyranny, unfortunately only wish to be left alone and to hold on to their small island, their remaining small piece of paradise, and thus incessantly ignore the metastasising problem of encroaching tyranny, until it comes to a chronic and irreversible state. This is why revolutionary states that have enshrined in law something akin to a second amendment and a legal duty prescribed to citizens, to overthrow governments that attempt to oppress the people, is crucial to the preservation of the fragile flower that is human liberty. Oppressive governments may rear their ugly head in the form of arbitrary deprivation of property or rights, and utilising the colour of the law or the shock of an event to cultivate legislation, or a state of being, that is or could be used to dispossess the people of their life, labour and inherent right to be unmolested by governmental powers. Government is a necessary evil to provide a semblance of order, this is useful in times of war for instance, but in peacetime it is simply a gluttonous pest that can be done without.

Conversely, *Locke* stated that, before the formation of governments and societies, humans had basic "rights" that were derived from "Natural Laws" bestowed by providence itself[365]. These were the "right to life, health, liberty and property." However, these were only laws secured by

---

[365] Locke, J. (1663). *Essays on the Law of Nature*. Pg. 82-83.

the individual's application of force to ensure them; as is all rights and laws, as I have previously alluded to. *Hobbes* believes contrary to this and states, as I have previously mentioned, that laws derive from the community's common sensibilities and as such rights exist not without law, which is force to obligate[366]. I disagree, as I have prior argued, and it is not because I discount his argument that force provides security to law and rights – I do not, he is correct. However, I disagree with the overall distinction between rights and laws, that being that if laws are to be expressed as the common sensibilities of a group, their innate nature if you will, then what makes it dissimilar from "natural rights" then? Other than its scope, that being rights benefit the individual and canonised law benefits the group. It seems the differentiation is merely a round-about way to sophistically use the word "rights", but rather mean "privileges" granted by law or one's inherent nature constricted by law. If law is defined as the collective realisation of the natural group instinct, then why, in the same breath, are rights deemed duly requiring restriction, merely because it empowers the individual? Moreover, by *Hobbes'* own dictation on this matter, he states that "The right of nature, which writers commonly call *jus naturale*, is the liberty each man hath to use his own power as he will himself for the preservation of his own nature; that is to say, of his own life; and consequently, of doing anything which, in his own judgement and reason, he shall conceive to be the aptest means thereunto."[367] Thus, we understand that for law to be established – that being the common sensibilities to be canonised and understood through

---

[366] Hobbes, T. (1651). *Leviathan*. Penguin Books: Baltimore. Chapter 14: Of the First and Second Natural Laws, and of Contracts. "For though they that speak of this subject use to confound jus and lex, right and law, yet they ought to be distinguished, because right consisteth in liberty to do, or to forbear; whereas law determineth and bindeth to one of them: so that law and right differ as much as obligation and liberty, which in one and the same matter are inconsistent."

[367] Hobbes, T. (1651). *Leviathan*. Penguin Books: Baltimore. Chapter 14: Of the First and Second Natural Laws, and of Contracts. "The right of nature, which writers commonly call jus naturale, is the liberty each man hath to use his own power as he will himself for the preservation of his own nature; that is to say, of his own life; and consequently, of doing anything which, in his own judgement and reason, he shall conceive to be the aptest means thereunto."

legislation – a monopoly on the use of force or the exercising of this "right of nature" must be established. This is what we call government or the state, but we must fully be cognisant of the truth that just like *Hobbes* seeks to restrict the "natural rights", contrary to canonised rights or privileges, more aptly put, then law must be used as the primary means to obligate and regulate the nature of man to curtailment of his instincts. The contradiction arises from this, that by obligating a citizen to curtail his right of nature – that which provides him liberty to use his power to preserve his nature or interests, really – then you must enforce that curtailment by the usage of the right of nature. Thus, by *Hobbes'* account, *lex* is very much a contradiction in terms and inevitably will fail in its objective because, as I may have previously stated, that you ultimately do not mitigate the "right of nature" or the abundance of will and power, you merely centralise those instincts towards self-interest and the power to defend and pursue it into the hands of a small clique, the government or the state, through their principal weapon: legislation or *lex*. This is why governments that begin as benign and laissez-faire Republics grow to become corrupt and despicable tyrannies; it stems from the inequal distribution of power within society and the establishing of, in essence, a political pyramid-scheme that recruits more citizens by conquest or by having them born into an ensnaring legislative web called "citizenship".

Locke, too, subscribes to ideas that are without natural counterpoints – meaning they exist not within nature and are thus abstract to human understanding. For example, the idea of "Tabula Rassa", or the idea that every human is born a blank slate with an empty mind, devoid of instinct[368]. This also follows on from the misguided idea that "all men are created equal"; a proposition *Locke* was fond of, and so too

---

[368] Locke, J., & Nidditch, P. H. (1979). *An essay concerning human understanding*. Oxford: Clarendon Press. Book II, Chap: I. "Let us then suppose the mind to be, as we say, white paper void of all characters, without any ideas. How comes it to be furnished? Whence comes it by that vast store which the busy and boundless fancy of man has painted on it with an almost endless variety? Whence has it all the materials of reason and knowledge? To this I answer, in one word, from experience."

Chapter VII

all Democratic advocates likewise, as it underpins their advocation of Democracy, utterly; I will discuss this in detail in a later section. *Locke* argues that all man is born with the freedom to either love their fellow man or act in aggression towards him. Naturally, *Locke* was living at a time prior to the advent of the Theory of Evolution, therefore was unaware that our ancestors who survived to pass on their genetics to the future generation were most assuredly brutal, violent, intolerant of others, and averse to showing of fellowship to strangers; unless our ancestor was seeking a tribe of his own. This was due to the harsh and unforgiving environment in which they inhabited, that if a person clung to abstract concepts of love, acceptance or pacifism then they would not survive long enough to transmit their genes to offspring, because they would have been either gored by predators, human or otherwise, or would have been seen by potential mates as unworthy of protecting and providing for their offspring; thus, they would have been deemed as sexually unattractive to these potential mates. Unfortunately, might equals right and that is the intrinsic law nature seems to abide by; the natural law, if you will. By extension, humans maintain their rights, or basic instincts conducive to civility within their group, when government fears angering and bringing to bear the wrath of the populace down upon them. That said, the old adage of dispersing political power as to keep it unconcentrated, and thus keep tyrants at bay, fails to identify the true vector of power; that being military might. Military power is what must be dispersed if the people are to retain their rights; this is why the second amendment was such a landmark course chartered by a political system, up to that point in human development. That being, it understood that the concentration of political power is nothing without a standing army willing to back its wielder. Therefore, to safeguard liberty, it is necessary to disperse military armaments and organisation to the people, as to negate the threat a standing army would pose to the domestic populace's interests. Succinctly, "*Vivere militare est*", or "to live is to fight", so said *Seneca the Younger*[369]*;* where peace is to be rendered an aberration, in a world whose existence is contingent upon the irrepressible competition of all life.

As an abridged rebuttal of *Locke's* and the Democratic side's chief presupposition of "all men are born equal", we must understand that all are not born equal – some have the potential, genetic or otherwise, to be intelligent, brawny or amoral and as such genetically transmitted traits alone prove this to be incorrect. Moreover, the idea of ethnicity and inter-ethnic, or cultural, conflict plays a rather overarching role within this dispute. That said, it has been witnessed throughout history wherever Democracy has succeeded, most notably within the *Althing* or *Thing* in Germanic, Norse and Icelandic societies, has been in small, manageable, ethnically and culturally homogenous groups. Multicultural societies of whom practise Democracy, to speak nothing of the other governmental forms, have a difficult time surviving without fracturing – be it formal separation or protracted civil disunity[370]. The dissolution of Czechoslovakia and Yugoslavia are recent examples of such failures of ethnically heterogenous experiments within nominally democratic systems.

Tangentially, if we look at genetically diverse populations and view their social cohesion (as I have previously alluded to), relative to the proportion of their genetic diversity, we find that genetically diverse groups have less social cohesion and tend to fracture and engage in infighting more often; this may be multifactorial, or may be a result of either the level of selective pressures, or lack of, within their environment or their predominant genetic diversity[371]. For example, we may look at

---

[369] Lavery, Gerard B (1980). *"Metaphors of War and Travel in Seneca's Prose Works."* Greece & Rome, vol. 27, no. 2, Cambridge University Press. Pg. 147–57. Accessed here: http://www.jstor.org/stable/642536.

[370] Cochran, D. C. (1995). *Ethnic Diversity and Democratic Stability: The Case of Irish Americans*. Political Science Quarterly, 110(4), 587–604. https://doi.org/10.2307/2151885

[371] Putnam, R.D. (2007). *E Pluribus Unum: Diversity and Community in the Twenty-first Century The 2006 Johan Skytte Prize Lecture*. Scandinavian Political Studies, 30: 137-174. https://doi.org/10.1111/j.1467-9477.2007.00176.x. "In the short run, however, immigration and ethnic diversity tend to reduce social solidarity and social capital."

the Yanomami, a relatively small indigenous tribe of South America, and inspect their social cohesion as it equates to their genetic diversity and we see a tribe that is highly genetically diverse and very non-cohesive. Their genetic diversity is a result of their wonderfully abundant environment, with little climactic and harsh conditions, compared to northern climes, consequentially there is a severe lack of individual and group selection materialising, and highly hierarchical mating culture. Thus, we find that the environment reflects a specific gene-pool, that in turn, reflects a culture that is primarily focused upon sex, frivolity and lax social bonding due to the lack of need to cooperate, as survival is achieved easily[372]. This culture produces a high level of children per female, but low instances of high-investment rearing and as such mothers tend to engage in infanticide if they have too many children or children have malformation; the Brazilian government has sought to pass laws forbidding this practise among indigenous tribes[373]. This produces low-value offspring.[374]

Moreover, due to the high centralisation of mate selection, it is typically observed that the small number of alpha-males get a disproportionate number of females. As a result of this bottle-neck effect of the available females, there are vast amounts of inter-male conflict at the subordinate levels and, thus, social cohesion is diminished greatly from this occurrent dysfunctionality. In consequence, due to this state of affairs, there is little in the way of marriage rites, socio-sexual ethics or civil development. This recipe for genetic dysfunctionality causes a chain-reaction wherein

---

[372] Sister M. Noel Menezes, RSM; *Individual and Society in Guiana Tales of the Yanomami. Daily Life in the Venezuelan Forest.* Hispanic American Historical Review 1 November 1986; 66 (4): 806–808. doi: https://doi.org/10.1215/00182168-66.4.806. "Adultery, incest, homosexuality, heterosexuality, and polygamy seem to fill the work, implying that the Yanomami lead a very sex-conscious life."

[373] Marcelo Toledo. (2016). *In Brazil, Activists Defend Infanticide Among Indigenous Tribes.* Available: https://worldcrunch.com/culture-society/in-brazil-activists-defend-infanticide-among-indigenous-tribes. Last accessed 11/11/2021.

[374] Varano S, Scorrano G, Martínez-Labarga C, Finocchio A, Rapone C, Berti A, Rickards O. *Exploring the mitochondrial DNA variability of the Amazonian Yanomami.* Am J Hum Biol. 2016 Nov;28(6):846-856. doi: 10.1002/ajhb.22877. Epub 2016 Jun 1. PMID: 27245361. "Among the Yanomami samples studied to date, the Santa Isabel Yanomami show a higher genetic heterogeneity."

genetic diversity is greatly amplified; this leads, as is seen in some parts of Africa, the most genetically diverse continent on Earth in terms of human diversity, to sporadic bouts of civil war and a perpetual cascade of fracturing nations.

Furthermore, interestingly, from these societies is produced little in the way of development – be it technological or ethical – and as such we find these societies to be replete with primitive tools rather than wondrous artifices, and lower IQ averages are prevalent amongst these groups[375]; though there are outliers, naturally. This leads to a less self-critical, and less analytical population; they do not examine the world around them in great detail, nor do they wish to cultivate novel solutions to complex problems that face them. Consequently, leading to a less technologically aspiring peoples. Within harsher environments, where there is a requirement for seasonal understanding and development of the means to survive the testing winters, in East Asia and Europe for example, we find that these peoples of higher IQ's on average; more genetically linear or homogenous, too[376]. We know environment plays a key role in the development of man, as the diasporas of these more genetically diverse populations tend to gain higher average IQ markers after successive generations have lived and thrived in these said harsher environments[377]. These groups may have intermixed with these higher IQ native peoples somewhat, but that does not explain the entirety of the cause, nor does it explain the individuals, belonging to the aforesaid

---

[375] Eppig Christopher, Fincher Corey L. and Thornhill Randy (2010). *Parasite prevalence and the worldwide distribution of cognitive ability.* Proc. R. Soc. B.2773801–3808. Accessed here: http://doi.org/10.1098/rspb.2010.0973.
[376] Kanazawa S. *General intelligence as a domain-specific adaptation.* Psychol Rev. 2004 Apr;111(2):512-23. doi: 10.1037/0033-295X.111.2.512. PMID: 15065920.
[377] Christopher Jencks and Meredith Phillips. (1998). *The Black-White Test Score Gap: Why It Persists and What Can Be Done.* Available: https://www.brookings.edu/articles/the-black-white-test-score-gap-why-it-persists-and-what-can-be-done/. Last accessed 16/11/2021. "Second, even IQ scores clearly respond to changes in the environment. IQ scores, for example, have risen dramatically throughout the world since the 1930s. In America, 82 percent of those who took the Stanford-Binet test in 1978 scored above the 1932 average for individuals of the same age. The average black did about as well on the Stanford-Binet test in 1978 as the average white did in 1932."

diasporas, being more positively inclined to exhibit behaviour in contrast to their ethnic kin who did not migrate. That said, diasporas of these groups to Europe, as we have seen, tend to display a greater degree of in-group preference and seem to vote similarly as a unified Democratic bloc[378]. Although this is not unique, most immigrants tend to gravitate towards their groups for many generations until eventual assimilation or conquest of the new land, as a means of survival. As a closing thought, one may sum this up as less pressure leads to more diversity, and more diversity leads to less quality control over beneficial mutations becoming expressed, within the ethnic lineage. Apropos to that preceding statement, one may conclude, that quality is far more advantageous than equality, in a long-term genetic outlook.

As we have seen, for the most part Democracy has only existed within the West, and the world for that matter, since the onset of the industrial revolution – three-and-a-half-centuries at the maximum. The USA and Europe - the USA with its unexploited virgin land especially - have had unparalleled access to a great abundance of resources and they have too had a great amount of technological clout and progress, coupling this. Thus, with these unprecedented boons, we have seen that Democracy, like the Republic of Rome, has been able to fortuitously transition and exist within this rare paradigm of pluralism; for the time being. This is due to the fact that industrial paternalism and similar policies, hitherto unachievable in past centuries, have been enacted and afforded relative prosperity for all; at the expense of the welfare of future generations mind you. Once this economic, technological and subsequent military hegemony ceases to maintain dominance, then too these Democracies of the West will likewise cease. Even *Rousseau*, a rather radical thinker of the 18th century, and a staunch proponent of, at that time, radical direct Democracy, enunciated that Democracy was rightly only efficacious on a small-scale, such as a city-state, and would succumb to larger nation-

---

[378] Vermeulen F, Kranendonk M, Michon L. *Immigrant concentration at the neighbourhood level and bloc voting: The case of Amsterdam.* Urban Studies. 2020;57(4):766-788. doi:10.1177/0042098019859490.

states given enough time[379]. Therefore, rendering its application largely irrelevant. The reason for *Rousseau* believing this to be the case was, most likely, because Democracy relies on one thing being ubiquitous within society; trust and unity. This is why pluralistic societies, but most assuredly pluralistic democracies, last only a short while in the grand-scheme of things. Although, Federalism can assuage ethnic and social divisions within a country for a short-time, as stated within the 1998 study entitled *"Why Democracies Collapse: The Reasons for Democratic Failure and Success"*, however federalist governments are far more prone to collapse than unitary ones, found the study; hence, there is a trade-off.[380]

Moreover, it takes only basic skills within discernment to understand that if many cultures, each with their own loyalties, history and traditions, are brought into close proximity with one another and each are, with the exponential nature of population growth in mind, vying for land and resources, then one only has to question as to how long before conflict ensues; be it violent or political. It is the nature of the tapestry of human history, unfortunately. Though the pluralist may declaim abstract virtues of peace and love, we who reason are left bewildered and slightly befuddled at the notion that, in their mind, they seem to rob every one of their identities and see us all as *"Tabla Rassa"*, blank-slates, devoid of our own intricate and beautifully ornate cultures and traditions. These people deride basic common-sense and reduce us all to mere sterile, biological machines devoid of uniqueness, awaiting to be injected with the truth of enlightened modern liberalism; this is incorrect and highly insulting to us all.

---

[379] Constitutional Rights Foundation. (2004). *BRIA 20 2 c Hobbes, Locke, Montesquieu, and Rousseau on Government*. Available: https://www.crf-usa.org/bill-of-rights-in-action/bria-20-2-c-hobbes-locke-montesquieu-and-rousseau-on-government.html. Last accessed 1/11/2021. "He believed in a direct democracy in which everyone voted to express the general will and to make the laws of the land. Rousseau had in mind a democracy on a small scale, a city-state like his native Geneva."

[380] Diskin, A., Diskin, H., & Hazan, R.Y. (2005). *Why Democracies Collapse: The Reasons for Democratic Failure and Success*. International Political Science Review/ Revue internationale de science politique, 26, 291 - 309.

Chapter VII

Concluding this thought thusly, Democracy is a fragile system, fraught with the potential for instability, and it hinges upon the notion of trust and uniformity of cultural sensibilities and universal commonality. As a result, one must understand that one cannot bring foreign contingents *en masse*, like interchangeable spare-parts, and expect them to honour, respect and understand the long-standing traditions, history and common-threads that brought us to the conclusions on issues we share today; nor can it be certain they will champion our form of Democracy, though it is certain they will partake in the fruits borne from it. We see a general attempt at cultural convolution originating from the political class, in which this pluralism is to give way to integration and assimilation of the native and foreign cultures into one amorphous, novel entity. Where both cultures and people must relinquish, by necessity, the true image of their rich cultures and customs for the expediency it will grant for the political-class's pet-project of globalism. I do not think this moral, nor do I think it desirable as it seeks to diminish the wide and colourful tapestry of human expression, communicated through the medium of different culture and through the deep roots of history and tradition. Life is meaningless without beauty and true belonging, and ultimately difference; even if difference is a direct source of conflict, I would rather the risk of conflict shadow mankind forevermore than bow to the clinically-dead and devoid culture globalism offers. Any man, of any creed or colour worth his salt, would be inclined to agree with me.

Digressing, *Hobbes* makes another poignant remark upon the possible superior nature of monarchy, as compared to assemblies; or Democracies. He states "The resolutions of a monarch, are subject to no other inconsistency, than that of human nature; but in assemblies, besides that of nature, there ariseth an inconsistency from the number. For the absence of a few, that would have the resolution once taken, continue firm, (which may happen by security, negligence, or private impediments,) or the diligent appearance of a few of the contrary opinion, undoes today, all that was concluded yesterday"[381]. What *Hobbes* is drawing attention to is the lack of firmness in staying the course of a particular decision, once the decision be taken, within Democratic systems; we can see the truth of this point from the shambolic response that has constituted the government's handling of the 2020 viral pandemic. Monarchs would appear to be more, from virtue of their unquestionable authority, able to stay the course with decisions and thus ascertain their true merit and plan future decisions, accordingly, having been more well-informed on the success or failure of said particular approach. Moreover, *Hobbes* eloquently articulates this other profound point, it goes, "A monarch cannot disagree with himself out of envy, or interest; but an assembly may; and that to such a height, as may produce a civil war"[382]. This is true, as we can see ideology and difference can draw men to ire and regrettable action; it can be said, decisions are rarely settled unanimously and on good accord. Therefore, as such, we see in most of the West the increased volatility stemming from political bickering, a lack of will to concede an election is one of many recent developments, be the election results dubious or not, it leads to avenues of instability. Can monarchy not devolve into civil in-fighting? Yes, but long-term monarchy uninterrupted by dynastic dispute, such as Capetian France, showed fairly strong periods of stability; though absolute rule was not as dominant within the nascent stages of the Capetian reign, in fact it was non-existent. Though, no system is impervious to the boiling-up of competing interests set on a course for war, but it would be obvious that Democracy seeks to amplify the quickening of this inevitability by ensuring, in theory, there are a whole country's competing interests brought to the fore.

As and additional tangential point, I wish to draw attention to the rather unorthodox way of viewing the concepts of power and authority – of which bears significance to the question of monarchy and assembly.

---

[381] Hobbes, T. (1651). *Leviathan*. Penguin Books: Baltimore. Chapter 19: Of the Several Kinds of Commonwealth by Institution, and of Succession to the Sovereign Power.
[382] Hobbes, T. (1651). *Leviathan*. Penguin Books: Baltimore. Chapter 19: Of the Several Kinds of Commonwealth by Institution, and of Succession to the Sovereign Power.

Chapter VII

I cannot quite recall where I heard this from, therefore I cannot provide reference but by happen chance if the author of this statement reads this book, then please do contact me and, in future revisions of this work, I will cite you as the author of this idea. The idea goes, that we in the modern day have falsely conflated the concepts of power and authority. Power being the implicit ability to get something done, and authority is the right to command as to what should be done. Thus, in a monarchy (the author draws emphasis to a distinctly Catholic-oriented one), authority is concentrated in the hands of a few and power is widely diffused within the society as a whole. In Democracy (more accurately termed an Oligarchy, as there is no such enterprise as Democracy, says the author, and I agree), by staunch contrast, it is the inverse with power being highly concentrated, and authority being so distributed so as to render it meaningless. I thought this such a substantial postulation, or view of the matter, that I had to include it here and I am sorry to the original author that I could not track down the reference; do contact me at your earliest convenience if you come to read this and wish to be cited.

In a concluding thought, *Hobbes* sought to advocate a system that, in its principle, redirected the inborn, fallible nature of man, of which he stated was an unquenchable desire for power and pursuit of self-interest, to ensure the ruler would work in the best interest of the nation and the citizen. I have discussed many tangential concepts too and provided a broad set of arguments from many thinkers upon the lack of merits of Democracy, primarily utilising *Hobbes* as the benchmark source. Though what could be called superior, Democracy or Monarchy? I cannot truly say, and I leave such speculation up to you, the reader. Although, I can state that whichever system may be decidedly more profuse with supporting evidence, one must recall that with whatever system should be chosen, in your mind, we would find that both would just as easily collapse as the other would, given enough time. As *Sir John Glubb* asserted within his work *"Fate of Empires: and Search for Survival"*: "It is, therefore, interesting to note that the life-expectation of a great nation does not appear to be in any way affected by the nature of its institutions. Past empires show almost every possible variation of political system, but all go through the same procedure from the *Age of Pioneers* through to *Conquest, Commerce, Affluence,* and to *Decline* and *Collapse.*"[383] As a student of history, I tend to agree with this contention, but it is desirable to decide upon a system in which general freedoms are maintained and observed for the longest possible period.

THE GOD THAT FAILED

Hans Hermann Hoppe has numerous, very salient refutations of Democracy within his literary work, *"Democracy: The God that Failed"*[384]. He attempts within the book, generally, to compare traditional monarchies with Democracy, as practised in the West. He does this not to show the favourability of a monarchy as compared to contemporary Democracy, but he simply means to show the general regression that has occurred by the adoption of a system of governance that was previously considered archaic in practise, ironically enough. *Hoppe* makes some poignant predictions, for a literary work published in 2001, on the growing "secessionist regions" and economic bankruptcy that would hit the West, much like the eastern socialist republics ten years prior from that publishing.[385]

A salient point touched upon too, within the work, is on the need for the capital-city focused government (judicial monopoly, as is said) to force internal integration of ethnic, tribal and class groups through the expansion of the road and transportation networks; bridging the gap between the rural and cosmopolitan and thus ensuring a greater degree

---

[383] Glubb, J. (1978). *The Fate of Empires and Search for Survival.* Edinburgh: Blackwood. Pg. 16.
[384] Hoppe, H.-H. (2001). *Democracy - The God That Failed: The Economics and Politics of Monarchy, Democracy and Natural Order.* Routledge.
[385] Hoppe, H.-H. (2001). *Democracy - The God That Failed: The Economics and Politics of Monarchy, Democracy and Natural Order.* Routledge. Pg. 290.

of integration with the capital's policies[386]. We see this in the UK with the incessant need to shorten travel time to London and expand road networks, even if the data purporting to its economic and job creating effectualness be rather vague[387]. He also expounds upon the idea of the egalitarian ideals, a hallmark of Democratic systems, and of which a mass-belief surrounding its inherent truthfulness is a prerequisite for the acceptance of a system of Democracy[388]. This is primarily utilised to drum up slogans and support for whatever candidate needs the political kudos. Equally, that the acceptance of higher rates of taxation and expropriation of productivity, something that would have been regarded as vile by people of old, is widely exhibited as there is a universal illusion held that because anyone can work their way into government that it is now permissible, besides it redistributes wealth from the "haves" to the "have-nots"[389]. Moreover, he provides for the reader a collection of well thought-out, tremendously articulated arguments, or points of interest, against Democracy and in-favour of monarchy. Conversely, it must be understood that this book is decidedly criticised, not because it lacks intellectual merit, but because it is very much a thorough rebuttal to the sacred object of secular divinity; Democracy. I will lay out some of his arguments against Democracy, using monarchy as a sort of contrastable benchmark, and recommend that you read *Hoppe*'s work; it should be a catalyst that will make you second-guess the ostensibly preconceived superiority of Democracy and its widely acknowledged synonymity with freedom.

---

[386] Hoppe, H.-H. (2001). *Democracy - The God That Failed: The Economics and Politics of Monarchy, Democracy and Natural Order*. Routledge. Pg. 141.
[387] George Torr. (2021). *Decision to axe HS2 through Yorkshire 'sickening' for those forced out of their homes*. Available: https://www.yorkshirepost.co.uk/news/politics/decision-to-axe-hs2-through-yorkshire-sickening-for-those-forced-out-of-their-homes-3459052. Last accessed 18/11/2021.
[388] Hoppe, H.-H. (2001). *Democracy - The God That Failed: The Economics and Politics of Monarchy, Democracy and Natural Order*. Routledge. Pg. 218.
[389] Hoppe, H.-H. (2001). *Democracy - The God That Failed: The Economics and Politics of Monarchy, Democracy and Natural Order*. Routledge. Pg. 234.

Within the matter of time preference – as I have stated previously – *Hoppe* states, that since most physical agents within this world wish to substitute a mundane state of affairs with a better one then we must conclude, logically, that governments seek to do likewise. Inevitably, when one seeks to better their condition, they will ponder upon the current situation and on what will better their condition. They will then ascertain when their goals can or could be approximately reached, how long will it take to succeed in this endeavour, how much will it cost, the perishability of the object if it be that, etc. Thus, individuals, most individuals anyway, shall naturally gravitate towards gaining their goals now rather than later – even if it is potentially better to wait – as said *Hoppe*. This is his definition of time preference. Furthermore, he argues, apropos to the definition, that Democratic leaders can be likened to temporary caretakers or renters rather than the monarchical ruler being that of a hereditary owner, that may sell or pass the house on to posterity. As such, a temporary caretaker or renter, who cannot sell the house nor partake in the profit derived therefrom, would not wish to engage in capital consumption to improve the house as the profits derived from such an endeavour would not be enjoyed by the caretaker, naturally. Therefore, it is in the renter's interest to keep the status quo as intact as possible for the duration of his term of stay, and if possible, to squeeze as much rental profit out from the abode, even at the expense of ruining the property; as they be only a caretaker. Moreover, their time preference rate is higher as their term is short and the asset, they have been lent, yields no direct value to them or their posterity. In parallel to our Democratic leaders, of whom many are childless women or bachelor men peculiarly, have thus nothing invested in the future of the country – in terms of genetic investment – nor do they care terribly as to the long-term repercussions of their various decisions, upon the stability of the realm. In short, *Hoppe* rightfully argues that the path of least resistance for Democratic leaders is to pilfer the coffers, placate special interest groups for bribes and favours, and through importation of equality-dependant voters; generally seeking self-interest first before the interests of the nation, as a whole.[390]

Continuing on with our discussion, *Hoppe* states, not within his *magnum opus* but within seminars upon the book, that "most political history would have regarded Democracy as nothing more than some moderate form of Communism". Naturally, a brandying about of the term equality, even in an abstract and meaningless fashion, is replete and as I previously stated egalitarian ideals, though they may be insincerely expressed by the leaders, are nevertheless utilised to meet political agendas, for the sake of self-interests. Thus, *Hoppe* gives a plethora of various political scenarios or machinations – abundantly within the chapter entitled "Free Immigration and Forced Integration" – that may spawn forth from the bosom of egalitarian tenets, and are used in a manner detrimental to the interests of the wider populace; or such is my interpretation of these writings. Moreover, as another point inherent within the matter of egalitarianism, we find that with the naturally inclined drift to egalitarian doctrine, that seems to be an inextricable part of Democratic systems, also comes with it the "collectivisation of individual responsibility"[391] and the proliferation of "public charity", through welfare spending, as *Hoppe* puts it[392]. I have made this point abundantly clear, but I merely mention it now as a clarification of *Hoppe*'s position of critique in regard to Democracy. However, *Hoppe* highlights to the reader that, in a more antiquated time, we find that the majority of government spending – "50% or more" – was allocated to military expenditure. Conversely, we find as Democratic forces began in the nineteenth century to democratise society that welfare expenditure became the most prevalent expenditure. Additionally, to support this

---

[390] Hoppe, H.-H. (2001). *Democracy - The God That Failed: The Economics and Politics of Monarchy, Democracy and Natural Order*. Routledge. Pg. 48.
[391] Hoppe, H.-H. (2001). *Democracy - The God That Failed: The Economics and Politics of Monarchy, Democracy and Natural Order*. Routledge. Pg. 65.
[392] Hoppe, H.-H. (2001). *Democracy - The God That Failed: The Economics and Politics of Monarchy, Democracy and Natural Order*. Routledge. Pg. 65.

claim, public expenditure has risen to approximately fifty percent of the national product in our contemporary period; of which welfare is fifty percent of this total and twenty-five percent of the national product, so says *Hoppe* and the reference for which he cites[393]. Thus, the conclusion may be drawn that, in theory, monarchy emphasizes the foundational concept and sovereignty of private property, while democracy emphasizes the collective power of the majority over the individual and their private property. This is why tax is incessantly going higher, even in unprecedented periods of long-term peace, as we reside in right now, and for what? Simply to increase centralisation through growth of bureaucracy and the pervasiveness of the tentacles of government. This is the irony of Democracy, that it displays itself as a system that conducts its affairs by and for the people, but it seems that Democracy, from its inception, starts the long march to greater and greater control over the citizen's life. Alas, look where we are now, in certain Western Democracies a citizen requires permission and a valid reason to leave their abode. Oh, Western man, lo how you have forgot the gifts your ancestors fought and suffered to bestow upon you; alas, it seems history is taking its demonstrably predictable course.

Following on, we find that *Hoppe* detailed that, primarily, monarchs resemble an owner or parent – they wish to make better the asset or property, leave it in better shape for their progeny than they received it in and aid the facilitation of capital appreciation of the asset[394]. Moreover, in light of the previous economic tone of these points, *Hoppe* states that if we look at the issue of debt through war and peace time then we find startling contrast, on the whole, between the two systems in question. Monarchies tend to lower their debt within times of peace and increase it in times of war, but war is a much costlier endeavour under a monarchy, as traditionally it was seen as the monarch's responsibility

---

[393] Hoppe, H.-H. (2001). *Democracy - The God That Failed: The Economics and Politics of Monarchy, Democracy and Natural Order*. Routledge. Pg. 26.
[394] Hoppe, H.-H. (2001). *Democracy - The God That Failed: The Economics and Politics of Monarchy, Democracy and Natural Order*. Routledge. Pg. 17-19.

to pay for his territorial acquisitions – be it through legal or military means – and as such he was liable for the debt incurred[395]. This equates to an environment in which it is costly for a monarch to wage incessant military war and as such the system is predisposed to acquiring land through legal and contractual means, rather than military struggle; therefore, warfare should be less prevalent with traditional monarchy, in the Western context at least.

By strict contrast, we find that Democracies have an insatiable accruing of debt, be it in times of peace or war, because of the many multifaceted promises made by politicians and the inefficient squandering of the bureaucratic regimes that seem to, like a fire in an oxygen-rich environment, burn more brightly in such a system; a chronic battle over the pilfering of the coffers is an observable problem[396]. In wars too, we find that special contractual agreements and special treatment are seen between crony and politician, and a general way of things is created in which war cannot just be lucrative but can also be necessary to the fulfilment of certain economic and political agendas[397]. We can see this within the American context, constant and unwavering wars and a whole slew of various companies that await and push for new wars for more profit; an entire system built off the back of war, where politicians of whatever political stripe have become sales-representatives for large arms-manufacturers and other war-dependent companies[398]. Democracies are inherently violent systems and it is because no one is really liable for the debt, when it comes to the bottom-line, and as such they are predisposed to incur greater and greater amounts of debt during their tenure; they also have to be seen as making good on the issues caused by their political

---

[395] Hoppe, H.-H. (2001). *Democracy - The God That Failed: The Economics and Politics of Monarchy, Democracy and Natural Order*. Routledge. Pg. 55.
[396] Hoppe, H.-H. (2001). *Democracy - The God That Failed: The Economics and Politics of Monarchy, Democracy and Natural Order*. Routledge. Pg. 27.
[397] Hoppe, H.-H. (2001). *Democracy - The God That Failed: The Economics and Politics of Monarchy, Democracy and Natural Order*. Routledge. Pg. 27.
[398] William Astore. (2012). *America, arms-dealer to the world*. Available: https://www.salon.com/2012/01/24/america_arms_dealer_to_the_world/. Last accessed 19/11/2021.

predecessors. As such all of these issues stem from the lack of liability, as compared to the system of monarchy, as *Hoppe* pointed out.

Although, *Hoppe* does not wish to incite the notion that monarchy is perfect beyond repute, but the structural differences between the two systems will, theoretically, produce two different environments in which will be produced certain paths of least resistance. Democracy incentivises its leadership to fleece as much yield from the golden goose as humanly possible, at the expense of the goose as they have a high time preference rate; as this is the path of least resistance or the logical route. By the contrary, monarchy seeks to nurture and increase the yield the golden goose produces long-term, without bringing it to ruin, and though he may be inclined to loot from it from time to time, he acts as a better steward of it as there are so many factors influencing him to act stalwartly.

Hoppe makes other great points in his deconstruction of liberal Democracy, but he furthermore makes a more overarching assertion regarding the corruptibility of Democratic institutions as compared to monarchical ones[399]. It is true, Democracies are far more predetermined to become corruptible sooner in its lifecycle, but monarchies are just as fallible; naturally because both stem from the same genesis point, that of the human mind. There are many salient arguments against Democracy, but I have covered the vast swathe of them in my previous section upon *Hobbe*'s work, which resolutely conveyed the various structural improprieties inherent within these types of "rule by the people" system. I wish to discuss briefly as well *Hoppe*'s ideas and where they stem from. He is a member of the Mises Institute and as such holds to the fundamental Misean maxim that the principle of private property is fundamental to a sustainable society. As such, people are more inclined to care for their own property than the property of others - or communal property. Thus, if everything is owned by somebody, everything will be maximally cared for. I agree with this tenet and as such it would be informative to a

---

[399] Hoppe, H.-H. (2001). *Democracy - The God That Failed: The Economics and Politics of Monarchy, Democracy and Natural Order*. Routledge. Pg. 86.

generation of whom believe heartily in the villainy of private property to internalise such a tenet.

INCONSEQUENTIAL CONSTITUTIONS

Though I find great value in constitutional forms of government, I do understand the failings derived therefrom. We have seen how the legal charter that breathed life into the USA has slowly been diminished to such an extent, that the teachings it whispers now does fall on deaf ears; followed by none, and the usurpation of which we have borne witness to in the last century or so. The issues posed by Constitutions and their role as a safeguard of the fundamental principles of a society, a guiding light in a sea of darkness so to speak, is predicated upon the false belief that words cannot be altered, nor can the morality and convictions of the populace be altered or change, naturally or unnaturally, along with it. As we have seen, the American people have certainly deviated in culture since the founding of their monumental republic and it can hardly be argued for the better; apart from maybe the abolishment of slavery, but it seems soon after the abolishment of chattel slavery it was reinstituted through means of slavery to inflation and central banks; now to be followed by the defacto slavery through mandates that strip away bodily autonomy.

To quote Adams: "Our Constitution was made only for a moral and religious people. It is wholly inadequate to the government of any other."[400] As you may well be aware of already, the America that the Constitution was designed for has been long eroded away by folly and carefully orchestrated cultural recreation. The universities no longer instil religious principles in the student body as a prerequisite, nor do they instil the virtues of self-reflection of one's own ideas and critical thinking. Thus, the constitution is not just a document that outlines fundamental principles, nor a list of your divinely endowed rights, it is

---

[400] *"From John Adams to Massachusetts Militia, 11 October 1798,"* Founders Online, National Archives, accessed 21st November 2021. Available here: https://founders.archives.gov/documents/Adams/99-02-02-3102.

a barometer as to the intact character of the nation. The vast majority of the youthful generation, and I am sorry to say this, have been captured by radical doctrines of abolishment of private property and they have been inculcated with ideals, within supposed institutes of learning, that the entire crux of Western civilisation and the USA was built on a criminal enterprise of which it likewise is, from its inception, a system predisposed to criminality. Thus, the constitution within a generation or two will likely not even be heeded, even in a symbolic fashion it has already been demoted to this status. Alas, you may say though, "I am a patriot and I am a firm defender of the constitution" or "I took the oath to defend the constitution against all enemies foreign and domestic". If that is so, and with all due respect, then pray do tell why no one seems to be heeding the call and dismantling the Federal Reserve? It is plainly written in Article 1, Section 8, Clause 6, that Congress is tasked "To provide for the Punishment of counterfeiting the Securities and current Coin of the United States;". In reference to the previous clause, Clause 5, it does empower only Congress "To coin Money, regulate the Value thereof, and of foreign Coin, and fix the Standard of Weights and Measures;". Therefore, the Federal Reserve is an illegal institution that is not only engaged in a felony crime of counterfeiting, but is engaged in robbing the entire American populace and their posterity of their liberty and their property. Congress has the ability in Section 1, Article 8, Clause 15, to "provide for calling forth the Militia to execute the Laws of the Union, suppress Insurrections and repel Invasions;". Therefore, the congress has reneged upon their oath too and as such have committed, in some effect, a form of treason if they are aware of this. Thus, as you can see the Constitution is very much a symbolic document that may inform as to the framework of future legislation, but it is actively being circumvented gradually and insidiously by every facet of society because they lack any moral compass.

Moreover, my favourite irony is thus: Section 1, Article 8, Clause 12, it states that "To raise and support Armies, but no Appropriation of

Chapter VII

Money to that Use shall be for a longer Term than two Years;". Two years as a measure of time must have changed as a unit since the writing of this, as it would seem two years is now equal in value to two-and-a-half centuries of a constant, uninterrupted war-footing. Ironically, we find that many patriots support the US military and army quite resolutely, as is only natural for any proud patriot, but unfortunately it has run counter to its constitutional mandate and as such is an unconstitutional standing army conducting domestic and foreign operations, with general impunity. Moreover, we may find that many Presidents, Obama being the most notable, have conducted war without the approval of congress or the authorisation of such action within Iraq, Libya, etc. Many Presidents since 1973 have also flagrantly defied the War Powers Resolution and maintained military troops within target nations for more than 60-days without authorisation by congress[401]. Reagan invaded Grenada, George H.W. Bush invaded Somalia and Panama, Bill Clinton invaded Bosnia, Iraq and Haiti, Afghanistan, Kosovo and Sudan, etc. This type of abuse of power goes back to President Polk and the onset of the Mexican-American War of 1842; in which Polk ordered US troops to annex part of what Mexico considered sovereign territory after some small skirmishes and tensions along the Rio Grande[402]. This led to a de facto state of war and was not authorised by congress, or even sanctioned prior to or after the event. This issue stems from the wording within the Constitution that states, "Congress shall have power to declare war", however this was changed by James Madison from "power to make war". Thus, as the Commander-in-Chief, the various presidents throughout history have certainly taken great liberties in asserting their military power in global issues that really have very little to do with the USA; with some notable exceptions.

---

[401] John Yoo (2011). *Obama is flouting the War Powers Resolution.* Available: https://www.aei.org/op-eds/obama-is-flouting-the-war-powers-resolution/. Last accessed 21/11/2021.
[402] James M. Lindsay. (2011). *TWE Remembers: A War "Unnecessarily and Unconstitutionally" Begun.* Available: https://www.cfr.org/blog/twe-remembers-war-unnecessarily-and-unconstitutionally-begun. Last accessed 21/11/2021.

As you can see, as soon as a rulebook is placed before the eyes of children – read and understood – the shrewd and mischievous among them begin to find ways to dodge the rules, as to suit themselves. It is natural to do so, as no one terribly enjoys being constrained by the demands of others. As such, this is why Constitutions eventually become null and void, starting in the eyes of the political class and cascading down throughout society, that is a populace tends to, after each successive generation, degenerate into the base form of all life; chaos. Thus, no embellished 18th century document, replete with ornately eloquent statements regarding liberty and just governance will ever repress man's inherent nature towards his primal mean reversion; that being power for powers sake, might is right and the shadowy flipside of the creature of man that we have all borne witness to throughout history. One cannot rest on the fanciful laurel that there will be some miraculous adherence to a document distantly written by forebears, that resemble not our own degenerate times. Thus, adherence is only guaranteed if the people are generally righteous, decent, moral and arguably religious. In a long-term outlook, this unquestionably will be doomed because words on a piece of paper cannot guarantee the very condition that makes those words effective; the decency of the majority. It's a circular paradox and as such bears a dilemma for say a Minarchist or a Libertarian.

Alas, the only sure-fire, though however unlikely, way to remedy the ever-concerning issue of government overreach is to first reduce and then entirely eliminate the power of government for all posterity. In this regard, we may paraphrase a quote attributed to Washington, where it was proclaimed, government is like fire[403]. Ergo, you can theoretically control a fire by throttling its fuel supply, in this case money, but as Jefferson ostensibly said, a government only tends to grow larger given the passage of enough time. Thus, it is the height of hubris to believe

---

[403] Forbes Quotes. (2020). *Thoughts On the Business of Life*. Available: https://www.forbes.com/quotes/3611/. Last accessed 21/11/2021. "Government is not reason, it is not eloquence-it is force! Like fire it is a dangerous servant and a fearful master; never for a moment should it be left to irresponsible action."

that we can control such growth for an indeterminate period. History has always proven this idealism unsound. Thus, it may be concluded that the fire must be extinguished completely and we must desist from the delusion that we may be able to control it by a series of checks and balances; we must utterly extricate from our minds the belief of the legitimacy of political power and crush where it seeks to spawn. Though, the problem with this is though some individuals may come to this belief through careful deliberation and deduction, through learning and self-education on history and politics, it can never be universally accepted by the blithering masses as it is utterly antithetical to the default instinct of humanity. That being, for all of recorded history we have had a system of hierarchical structures, where we gravitate towards higher powers than ourselves – a relinquishing of our own agency and responsibility – and this typically comes to rest in a combination of secular and divine hands. Therefore, the only way to live in a state of freedom and equity, free of the trappings of government, would be for everyone to go against their base instincts, simultaneously, and not wish to accumulate any power for themselves; and for people to take responsibility solely for their lives and their immediate needs and amenities. This is an impossible state of affairs and, as such, is why anarchy will never truly see long-term success. As can be seen, no system is perfect, nor does it properly function for very long either.

Anomalies in the Democratic Machine

Democracy, as I have pointed out, has a preponderance of flaws that are always existent within any iteration; no matter how well planned the system seems to have been constructed. Thus, it is always open to abuse and the proliferation of corruption; an oligarchy will always arise within such a system, as it seems predetermined to facilitate such circumstance. I did point out some of the examples of flaws that were present within Democracies of antiquity first, as I am an antiquarian at heart it would seem, but I do not single Democracy out to berate it for mere spinning of controversy or for a matter of spectacle, I single it out because it is the system we just so happen to inhabit right now. Consequently, we all risk succumbing to the inevitability of a tyranny arising out of the ashes from our said flawed system, if we do not insist verily on reform. For example, we see the allegations of election fraud in the present Trump-Biden presidential race – some of the statistical anomalies are very convincing to say the least – and this is something that permeates in every Democratic system. Now, I am no fan of Trump and, for that matter, I am no fan of any candidate that runs for democratic office and all have ulterior motives for power that they attempt to camouflage with flowery rhetoric, designed to appeal to the slavering horde of congenital invalid voters. Thus, I discuss what I am about to in a politically neutral tone; I really dislike both sides of the aisle equally and as such I am a true egalitarian at heart. However, digressing from the light-hearted comedy, we can see this year has produced a myriad of examples, globally, of statistically anomalous and questionable election results. I will briefly detail some of these various cases and some of the anomalies and finally provide my two-cents on the most logical and pragmatic reason for this. As stated, this is just an example of one major flaw in Democracy, the integrity of its main medium for the allocation of leadership that is, but there are so many flaws, some I have noted ad nauseum within the book. However; I would be required to write an almost endless tome to list all of the incongruencies inherent within the Democratic process.

If we take a look, firstly, at arguably the most important election this year, the US presidential election, then we find serious allegations and video evidence of tampering and election doctoring. For example, within the affidavit that Trump's legal team are filing in Michigan, we find allegations and evidence pertaining to election workers and counters assigning ballots to random names on the certified voter files, to people who did not vote and furthermore these ballots were entered into the

Chapter VII

system after the legal deadline[404]. That is just one example. Moreover, we see false information was utilised when filling these ballots out and election workers were alleged to not be checking the authenticity of signatures[405]. For instance, too, it has been witnessed in several states at this point that a multiplicity of voters that were born in the early years of the 20th century – before 1916 – registered to vote via mail-in ballots, even though some of these people have been dead for almost four decades now[406]. It is either there is now a brand-new voter demographic – the deceased – or there is some form of transparent meddling. Moreover, we find that the Dominion voting system, and Smartmatic system, who are corporately tied, was utilised in the same suspicious way in Venezuela to bring Chavez win after win. Smartmatic was founded by two Venezuelans and provided election technology to them after all[407]. Peculiarly, we find that the Clinton Foundation, in 2014, had Dominion donate technology to "emerging democracies"[408]; again, this can be

---

[404] John Droz, jr. (2020). *Michigan 2020 Voter Analysis Report*. Available: https://www.scribd.com/document/487615684/Michigan-2020-Voter-Analysis-Report. Last accessed 23/11/2021.

[405] Rev.com. (2020). *Peter Navarro 'The Immaculate Deception' Report News Conference Transcript*. Available: https://www.rev.com/blog/transcripts/peter-navarro-the-immaculate-deception-report-news-conference-transcript. Last accessed 23/11/2021. "There's the naked ballot problem, which I mean, that was huge because there was just a lot of ballots that came in without outer envelopes. So, there's no way you can do the signature match, yet a lot of these were entered into the tabulation. Pennsylvania kind of jumps out at you at that. Ballots accepted without postmarks and so on."

[406] Senate Homeland Security and Governmental Affairs Committee. (2020). *Witness Statement of Jesse Binnall December 16, 2020*. Available: www.hsgac.senate.gov/imo/media/doc/Testimony-Binnall-2020-12-16.pdf. Last accessed 23/11/2021. "At least 1,500 dead people are recorded as voting, as shown by comparing the list of mail voters with the social security death records."

[407] Reuters Staff. (2017). *Venezuelan election turnout figures manipulated by one million votes: election company*. Available: https://www.reuters.com/article/us-venezuela-politics-vote-smartmatic-idUSKBN1AI1KZ. Last accessed 24/11/2021.

[408] Clinton Foundation. (2014). *The Delian Project: Democracy Through Technology*. Available: https://www.clintonfoundation.org/commitment/clinton-global-initiative/the-delian-project-democracy-through-technology/. Last accessed 24/11/2021. "Dominion Voting, through its philanthropic support to the DELIAN Project, commits to supporting 1 to 5 local election technology pilots with donated Automated Voting Machines (AVM) in emerging and post-conflict democracies every 12 to18 months over the next three years…"

interpreted as the Clinton Foundation wishing to affect the outcome of important elections, in developing nations, for strategic access to their resources for commercial gain, through digital technology, but we must withhold such judgements without further proof. Soros, a change-agent billionaire and an important donor to the Democrat party, also has ties to Smartmatic as he had appointed the chairman of Smartmatic's parent company to the Soros Open Society Foundation, as the new President of the Foundation[409]. This may all be circumstantial links, but it shows the sinister web of, what seems, like interconnected corruption at the heart of the electoral system of not just America, but of the world.

Moreover, Dominion and Smartmatic systems were used in over two dozen states, some swing-states[410], and they were alleged to have switched votes algorithmically from Biden to Trump. As was seen in many states, but most overtly in Michigan where in the early hours of 4th of November, approximately 5AM, Data Firm Decision Desk HQ updated the vote count for Michigan, allocating 138,339 to Biden, but zero to Trump[411]. This is a statistical impossibility and was fortuitously the exact figure required to put Biden in an incontestable lead for the rest of the race within that state. Moreover, there are at least two clips captured that show on live news broadcasts that, in a momentary flash, Trump is deducted a few thousand votes here and that is then reattributed to Biden's total. Obviously, it would seem if true that, as supplementary video evidence suggests, that false ballots were being injected into the

---

[409] Joel B. Pollak. (2020). *George Soros Appoints Chair of Smartmatic Parent Company to Lead Open Society Foundations*. Available: https://www.breitbart.com/politics/2020/12/06/george-soros-appoints-chair-of-smartmatic-parent-company-to-lead-open-society-foundations/. Last accessed 24/11/2021.

[410] Kori Williams. (2020). *Which States Use Dominion Voting Machines?* Available: https://greatamericanpolitics.com/2020/11/study-353-u-s-counties-have-millions-more-registered-voters-than-people-eligible-to-vote/. Last accessed 24/11/2021. "According to its website, Dominion Voting Machines serves more than 40 percent of the U.S. population. Its products are used in 28 states including New York, California, Nevada, Georgia, and Puerto Rico."

[411] Petr Svab. (2020). *Statistical Anomalies in Biden Votes, Analyses Indicate*. Available: https://epochtimes.today/statistical-anomalies-in-biden-votes-analyses-indicate/. Last accessed 24/11/2021.

total either manually or through an automated algorithm; however, that is for a senate or congressional hearing to verify, of course. Naturally, this is suspicious, and these very shrewd techniques were something utilised in the early years of the new millennia in Serbia, Venezuela and every other would-be tin-pot dictatorship around the world; we also have the suspicious election results of Bush in Florida, in 2000, too. However, these are, again, all allegations that must be given the chance to be substantiated in a court of law as to ascertain their veracity. Although, the polarisation surrounding this is primarily why I draw attention to it, as it shows the West and, especially, the USA are very much fractured socially and politically at this point. Furthermore, accounts and admissions in several counties and states have admitted that there were "clerical errors" and, strangely, "glitches within the computing software" that misallocated Trump votes to Biden[412]. Some of these instances are insignificant, but it is troubling to think that this can occur in a nation that for the last two decades, or more, has made it their mission to police the world and set up proxy governments under the guise of protecting and nurturing Democracy, globally. Assuredly, mail-in ballots have been banned in most of the European Democracies for a long time; for example, in France, it has been banned for the most part since the 1970's because of a massive scheme of voter fraud in Corsica, in 1975; essentially, they were casting absentee ballots for dead people, a similar situation that is alleged in the USA[413]. There are many more instances, but it would become very tiresome reading to list all the alleged electoral infractions that seem to have occurred during the 2020 presidential race.

The second contemporary example of election anomalies is the recent New Zealand election, which was a landslide for Labour – the left-

---

[412] Paul Egan. (2020). *Antrim vote glitch: Expert shares how county mistakenly flipped from red to blue*. Available: https://eu.freep.com/story/news/politics/elections/2020/11/06/antrim-county-vote-glitch-software-update/6194745002/. Last accessed 24/11/2021.
[413] Lott, John R., *Why Do Most Countries Ban Mail-In Ballots?: They Have Seen Massive Vote Fraud Problems* (August 3, 2020). Available at SSRN: https://ssrn.com/abstract=3666259 or http://dx.doi.org/10.2139/ssrn.3666259

wing party. The first glaring anomaly is the massive majority victory; an unprecedented and statistically improbable majority victory. Why is it improbable? Well, New Zealand has adopted an MMP system since the turn of the millennia, or Mixed-Member Proportional Representation system, which is designed in theory, among other things, to inhibit any party from attaining an outright majority – it is possible but highly improbable[414]. Labour achieved 64 out of 120 seats. Another anomalous happening was the fact that parties tend to not get over 50% of the vote, the last time that occurred was in 1951, almost seven decades ago and with no MMP system, yet Labour achieved just over 50%[415]. Labour achieved a whopping half of all seats, with COVID-19 making poll-taking difficult and thus polls were few and far between in 2020, therefore it is hard to truly say if the country was that resoundingly behind Adern that she achieved a 13.1% increase upon last elections total vote swing[416]. Suspicious, in light of the contentious issues of lockdowns and freedom shattering parliamentary enactments. Moreover, the suspiciously round percentage of 50% is not a statistical impossibility, but it is a rather nonpareil figure to achieve.

Additionally, we may look at the advanced vote difference where typically parties get the same share, give or take, of the advanced votes and election day votes, however Labour achieved a resounding 9% lead upon these votes which has never occurred before and raises many questions[417]. In conjunction, we also have the issue of votes appearing out of nowhere or votes that had been stricken from the totals on the election

---

[414] Eleanor Ainge Roy. (2020). *Why are coalition governments so common in New Zealand?* Available: https://www.theguardian.com/world/2020/oct/14/why-are-coalition-governments-common-new-zealand-election. Last accessed 24/11/2021.
[415] Al-Jazeera. (2020). *Jacinda Ardern wins New Zealand election by landslide*. Available: https://www.aljazeera.com/news/2020/10/17/breaking-arderns-labour-party-wins-new-zealand-election. Last accessed 24/11/2021.
[416] govt.nz. (2020). *2020 General Election and Referendums - Official Result*. Available: https://electionresults.govt.nz/electionresults_2020/. Last accessed 24/11/2021.
[417] David Farrar. (2020). *Statistical anomalies in the 2020 New Zealand Election*. Available: https://www.kiwiblog.co.nz/2020/11/statistical_anomalies_in_the_2020_new_zealand_election.html. Last accessed 24/11/2021.

Chapter VII

night and then appeared, as if by magic, within the totals post-election night. As in the case of the US, magical updates just appear and change the totals for candidates, dramatically – in the case of the US, this was far more perfidious in nature, it seemed. Digressing, we find that the Electoral Commission a fortnight later announces a new set of totals and Labour wins another three electoral seats. Finally, in the 2002 election, we find that the National Party – the second largest party in New Zealand and equivalent to the Republican or Conservative Party, respectively – suffered a devastatingly low vote percentage than they suffered in 2001, but still held onto the stronghold seats of Northland, Whangarei, Ilam and Nelson. However, in 2020 they achieve a higher voter percentage, but lose these and as such this is anomalous to say the least[418]. As such the statistical incongruencies are apparent and, as we can imagine, the Electoral Commission did nothing to investigate this – in fact, it appears as though they were entirely complicit with whatever was afoot.

If I was a betting man, I would wager that all of these stupendous and simultaneously achieved landslide victories and unprecedented results of late in the US, UK and New Zealand are potentially a result of the current need to expedite the UN Agenda 21 and 2030 goals, in light of this grand opportunity of COVID. It is quite a fortuitous development knowing that the UN requires these types of consolidated and controllable stranglehold majorities to pass all of this draconian legislation, to fulfil the various SDGs (Sustainable Development Goals), of which comprise the "Agenda 21" and sub-goal Agenda 2030, respectively. Of the ones that cannot be controlled outright, we find a state of emergency is called to override the constitutional or legal boundaries; such as in Canada, where Trudeau lost his majority in the 2019 election. Though, it may all just be one big coincidence, and we do not want to be labelled a "conspiracy theorist", do we now? That being the favourite go-to dismissive term for

---

[418] David Farrar. (2020). *Statistical anomalies in the 2020 New Zealand Election.* Available: https://www.kiwiblog.co.nz/2020/11/statistical_anomalies_in_the_2020_new_zealand_election.html. Last accessed 24/11/2021.

the ruling-class when they hear something affrontive to their sensibilities, or their illusory good reputation.

CROSSING THE RUBICON

America seems to have crossed the Rubicon, so to say. One half of the country loathes the other half, if the voting percentages are to be believed and the political caricatures of Biden and Trump are to be trusted in their polarised outlooks; which both are thoroughly suspicious, let us be honest. However, it is truly about what this all symbolises to the average man and woman on the street; these figures and elections are nothing more than talismanic charades and the divisions drummed up is a mere metapolitical strategy. Though, people sense the growing inevitability that we must all choose a side and it seems the ruling-class would rather those sides be the citizenry pitted against each other, rather than the citizenry pitted against their real tormentors. The USA is finished economically and, soon, militarily. All that is left now is to determine if the ruling-class who carried out the artificial dismantling, in pursuit of their agenda, will be able to secret themselves away to their new oriental abode or will they stand trial. I would wager the former, but that is only because this pattern seems to have occurred throughout history in the same vein. In the collapse of any system, where does the nobility suffer? Most scurry away into exile with their belongings or are ransomed off into the court of another monarch, but it seems the lower orders face the brunt of the harsh treatment and it is them alone that experience the consequences of their ruler's actions. Thus, it seems it shall always remain so.

We have seen the systematic dismantling from the bottom and top. Soros funded BLM swooping in to finally destroy small businesses after the government imposed harsh closure orders on them, destroying their revenue streams and starving them of the fiscal nourishment that supports their very existence. Racial, political and historical differences are being bolstered and stoked by the media, the riotous behaviour galvanised,

Chapter VII

and the ostracised ethnic groups targeted for vilification and beaten and abused. All the while, we see the resurgence of the right-wing reflections of these various groups that persist on the left – as the strategy seems to be synergistically entwined with that age-old maxim "let us control both sides". They fight and brawl with the other side, all the while the lower castes choose their team and bring themselves, gradually, to cheer on violence and hate the other; not knowing ultimately why, as it would seem not many cogitate that deeply about it, but only simply knowing that it is a question of them and us, my life over theirs and that they oppose my side and thus must be vanquished. Tribalism at its finest, naturally. Besides this collection of irrationality, we find the *pièce de résistance* of these obscene transgressions is the transgression against liberty herself, being perpetrated by the Western governments upon their own people. They join in with the rioters, not just by instructing their hired thugs to not enforce the peace while the contrived chaos reigns, but by using oppressive legislation as the torch to set the whole nation ablaze; salting the earth and making asunder all that was once good and wholesome. All social and economic structure that held normalcy in place is being undermined and obliterated by the manufactured fear of a pandemic, that has a recovery rate of between 97% and 99.75%, officially[419][420][421]. These cretinous demon-spawn have renounced all fellowship to sanity and good reason, they are an independent cultish clique who act in a self-interest contrary to the nation's stability, and they have made it their duty to renege upon all oaths, spoken and unspoken. Thus, by all sacred laws written, in common, by all free and well-reasoned minds, these

---

[419] Giovanni Scerra. (2021). *The Math of the Pandemic: COVID-19 Mortality Rate*. Available: https://www.linkedin.com/pulse/math-pandemic-covid-19-mortality-rate-giovanni-scerra-. Last accessed 25/11/2021.
[420] Hannah Ritchie, Edouard Mathieu, Lucas Rodés-Guirao, Cameron Appel, Charlie Giattino, Esteban Ortiz-Ospina, Joe Hasell, Bobbie Macdonald, Diana Beltekian and Max Roser (2020) - *"Coronavirus Pandemic (COVID-19)"*. Published online at OurWorldInData.org. Retrieved from: 'https://ourworldindata.org/coronavirus' [Online Resource].
[421] CDC (2021). *COVID-19 Pandemic Planning Scenarios*. Available: https://www.cdc.gov/coronavirus/2019-ncov/hcp/planning-scenarios.html. Last accessed 25/11/2021.

individuals are unforgivable traitors and wish for us only undue harm; for no reason bar that we exist in a world that they desire for themselves. Thus, the irony emerges from this smorgasbord of iniquitous animalism; that in these societies that are the ostensible champions of openness and tolerance, we find beyond the hypocritical veneer, a dictatorship so monstrous in its aims and methods that all murder-machines and genocidal regimes in history, combined, pale in honest comparison. This is coming into view for people with the ability to reason and eyes to see.

Digressing, we find that after the election, and the announced Biden victory, that the left-wing, like berserkers in a blood frenzy, began to run amok attacking even their own. BLM began fighting Antifa, and elderly voters were not immune from the ire of the ravenous mob. One pleaded "there is my Biden sign…please be peaceful!", only to be met with a hurl of racial abuse, ranging from "asking for peaceful protest is white supremacy!" to "Nobody cares about your white-ass opinions!", following it up with "who do you think you are telling black people how to protest? You (expletive) white-ass privilege old man". Naturally, this type of abuse is all too common and is very much encouraged by the political and academic establishment; co-opted by Marxists, of course. However, the entire political debacle in the USA will lead, if it hasn't already, to civil war where chaos will be the dominant force above all others. The baying mobs on both sides will be without mercy for one another and their blood lust will only be sated when the other side is destroyed entirely. We have seen such calls, with many Democrats demanding lists be drafted up containing all the endorsers and supporters of the Trump presidency; where one left-wing pundit on CNN remarked "if we leave survivors… they will do it again". This type of inflammatory language, firstly, will not end well for left-wing revolutionaries as one of two scenarios will occur. The right-wing will either become galvanised by these attacks and will close ranks, engaging in their own type of retributive action which will likely involve violence of some sort, as they are the demographic with the highest gun-ownership and veteran membership, scarred by and

Chapter VII

accustomed to the darkness exuded by war. Or, the government, whom have fabricated this entire state of affairs, will capitalise upon the division sown and the chaos in place to declare martial law or provide themselves with another *Hegelian*-derived reason to increase their mandate, and thus their overall control over the lives of the populace. Funnily enough, in an indirect sort of way, the type of system the real string-pullers desire is one based upon principles derived from Technocracy, not Communism, and eugenics will most likely be fundamental to such a system – as we are seeing from the likes of *Gates* and *Schwab* – and as such the funded Marxist revolutionaries and the funded right-wing nationalists and jingoists will never see their dream of their desired utopias play out. However, they will be integral in the establishment of this Technocracy, as we see in the embryonic stages of the system, these two groups are wiping each other out and providing the chaotic pretext for the formation of the Technocratic global future. Ironically, we may find the ambitious Technocrats become, likewise, restless with just some of the power; individuals such as *Gates* will want it all. Digressing, I am sure if Soros and the entire ilk had any hint of generosity within their devilish hearts, they would have absolutely no reservations as to providing the funded dialectical tribes a raise in pay; they have certainly played both their parts exceedingly well in all of this, albeit unaware of the larger agenda at play of course. As a final postulation on all of this, these riots and chaos are furthermore designed to implement an atmosphere non-conducive to commercial activity and enterprise; this is required to rip the heart out of the private (SME) business sector and thus centralise all commercial, political and economic power within the apparatus of the state. They will control all food, medium of exchange and means to life; by result, they will have vested within themselves all possible sources of power and will be literal Gods, deciding life and death over the mere mortals below; like the Olympian Gods of old, sitting atop the fabled Mount Olympus, abreast of all developments in the mortal world as they see all and know all, by virtue of their apotheosised status. Therefore, you will be required to justify your existence to the coming Technocrats and if you cannot, you will cease to exist within their world.

Alas, it seems the only way to bring equanimity back to this troubled world is for governments to renounce their loyalty to this cultish agenda for global dominion, and for them to trumpet an exeunt to the various actors on this chaotic stage, locked in vicious turmoil. If these various actors fail to pay heed to peaceful words, made in hopes of renewed fellowship with their fellow countryman, then logically they must be addressed in the universal language that even animals understand; that being the discharge of force. However, the government will never do this; it seems they have been all but totally infiltrated and captured by these various forces and act only as such in their favour, by reflection. It would seem that these ruling elite that wish to reimagine society must understand the historical structure of civilisation, and thus the intractability of decay. Hence, I beg the question, why do they seem so resolute in attempting to undo the hands of time? Accordingly, venturing to distort the ineludible sequence of all life, including that of the civilisational variety, but it seems they are emboldened by determinacy to see this merry chase to its foredoomed conclusion.

Caesarism

Caesarism, something I have touched upon prior, but I feel I should have added more and in the section upon Democracy what better location as to make abundant more of the postulations upon such a subject. I will discuss such a subject in the light of *Oswald Spengler*'s literary work *Decline of the West*; this topic happens to be discussed in Vol. 2 of that specific work[422]. Now, as a preamble to what I am about to embark on, in terms of this brief discourse, I am overall not a fan of reading *Oswald Spengler*, generally. You may find this odd and wonder why I am then

---

[422] Spengler, O. (2021). *The Decline of the West: Perspectives of World-History*. La Vergne: Arktos Media Ltd.

Chapter VII

discussing his work and exalting it as one of the books of reference and, in essence, partly an erudite inspiration for this literary work I write. Well, in truth, I dislike his level of pessimism, or harsh realism, but I fear it to be true beyond reproach that the decline, *ad occidentem*, is a bygone conclusion much like the universally shared predestined fate of us all; some of this pessimism unfortunately seems to have seen way to seep into my work, too, I fear. For example, *Spengler* remarks "*Liewer düd aß Slaawe*": That's an old Frisian farmer's saying. The reverse is the motto of every late civilization, and everyone has had to learn how much it costs." "*Liewer düd aß Slaawe*"[423] meaning better "better dead than a slave" – or the German, "Lieber tot als sklave". Essentially, "better to die than live a slave" and he is correct that this becomes the inverse mantra of declining civilisation.

It was only the other day did I overhear something extraordinary, heart-sung approval to this new vaccine news and this ostensible "freedom pass" unveiling - a new pass in the UK to allow one to partake in "normal life" without COVID restrictions, if one allows authorities to test them twice weekly. Back on point, anyway I overheard this man being so assuredly elated at the prospect of doing anything asked of him, just so he may be afforded the chance to return to copious alcohol consumption at the local publican and go to the stadia, once again, to watch his prized diversion of football. Football, in the European sense, is a mindless game in which two teams of eleven kick a bag of wind around a park for an hour-and-a-half, in hopes of shooting the ball into the others net and thus scoring a goal; of which the senseless crowd will, on cue, slaver profusely over themselves in loud cheer; as if they have achieved a moment of victory within their lives, all vicariously of course. *Panem et Circensus*, a formula for pacifism once remarked *Spengler*[424]. However, the point being that this man did not understand clearly enough that the government are

---

[423] Spengler, O. (2021). *The Decline of the West: Perspectives of World-History*. La Vergne: Arktos Media Ltd. Chapter: Cities and Peoples (C), V.

[424] Spengler, O. (2021). *The Decline of the West: Perspectives of World-History*. La Vergne: Arktos Media Ltd. Chapter: The Form-World of Economic Life (A), I.

attempting to steal away his liberty, giving it back piecemeal once their demands were met, the proverbial carrot on a stick, as a way of coercing him into something he would naturally have an aversion in doing. Or, the government believe he would because the government know intimately that whatever they are selling is not in this man's best interests, naturally, and thus it seems only logical to foist it on him; even in an indirect way, as so to give him the illusion of choice in the matter.

Although, you can see as to the tenor of *Spengler*'s publications; they are cold, unforgiving and sharp enough to cut through the milieu of not just his contemporary epoch but of ours, too. Nevertheless, we will steer this ship of discussion away from the wide-open waters of all that *Spengler* discussed, and into the gentler, or maybe not so gentler, inlets of his work on Caesarism. *Spengler*, as I have stated in the beginning of my introductory remarks within the book, believes that there are strong demarcation points that differentiate a civilisation's birth, youth, maturity, and death and as such we can study these, and though there are deviated differences between their story arcs, so to say, all share this major common thread. This is likened to life itself, as to the way nature's children all grow and then wither with the entropic effects of time. That being, these cultures, *Spengler* discussed, differentiate from the notion of civilisation, and though I cannot go into the entire breadth as to why in this brief dissertation upon a mere point in his work, I will say that he saw these epochs or cultures as living organisms that, like a blooming bud, go through the same lifecycle in the fashion of its metaphorical counterpart. Interestingly too, *Spengler* believed that all of these cultures – and their substratum layers or constituent parts – are born out of a fear of death[425]; and the talismanic symbols and ingrained cultural precepts used to overcome this fear, sets the tenor of the civilisation's journey throughout its existence. The beliefs, the tenets, expressed in the form of the culture are unique to that culture, and only hold meaning to them

---

[425] Spengler, O. (2021). *The Decline of the West: Perspectives of World-History*. La Vergne: Arktos Media Ltd. Chapter: Origin and Landscape (A), IV.

and them alone however they all developed that common working. This thesis was in part borrowed from *Goethe*'s "Metamorphosis of Plants"[426] and accordingly *Spengler* called this common working, of all cultures and civilisations (*Spengler* stated that there was a stark difference between culture and civilisation, though for the time being I will use the two terms interchangeably for ease of expression), the "prime-symbol (ur-symbol)"[427]. In this understanding, each culture develops singularly unique metaphysical phenomena to express the areas of youthful vigour, refined maturity and eventually the waning years of life. It is to be understood that when a culture becomes more Faustian – in its later years and such – it shows symptoms of a longing for the unobtainable and a yearning for the infinite. In our culture, the Celtic-Germanic culture that proceeded the Hellenic culture, we witness that we have reached such a tipping point. Additionally, we find that *Spengler* discussed this osmosis in some regard, he discusses around the conceptual framework of the culture and the civilisation. For example, he describes cultures as "virile," "intense," and "marvellous in its ease and self-confidence."[428] Conversely, he regards a civilisation as "death following life, rigidity following expansion."[429] I would not have used such terms, but as to what terms can one use, and he makes very valid points regarding the differentiation between the two diametrical concepts. It is true as to what *Spengler* speaks of, that civilisation is just that, a state in which the golden years of the people are but a distant memory, a vanishment within the vast ocean of time, and as such they continue on in a bewildered state that would be unbeknownst to the previous enterprising generations; a state of tired progress and mass lethargy; the awaiting of the clutches of

---

[426] Goethe, J. W., & Miller, G. L. (2009). *The metamorphosis of plants*. Cambridge, Mass: MIT Press.

[427] Spengler, O. (2021). *The Decline of the West: Perspectives of World-History*. La Vergne: Arktos Media Ltd. Chapter: The State (A), V.

[428] Spengler, O. (2021). *The Decline of the West: Form and Actuality*. La Vergne: Arktos Media Ltd. Chapter: The Problem of World-History (I), VII.

[429] Spengler, O. (2021). *The Decline of the West: Form and Actuality*. La Vergne: Arktos Media Ltd. Chapter: Introduction, XII.

death, to come mercifully comfort them in shadowy embrace. Therefore, this is a poignant point made.

Caesarism is a late mutation within the overall civilisational arc, and is something that symbolises a civilisational environment teeming with a sense of vexing decay, as perceived by an exasperated populous crying out for a saviour. From this well-spring of doom emerges forth an opportunistic demagogue, of whom with a sort of cavalier curtness, attempts to restore the greatness back to the heart of the civilisation. This may be through a promise to rewind back to a romanticised past, or through a disentangling of the wheels of progress, in a vain attempt to burn a path forward to progress; though most are devout conquerors, without question. However, whatever form or methodology this *Restitutor Orbis* takes, all institutions from thereon out are mere shadows of themselves and are symbolic, in truth; the power lies alone with the lone figure. As an additional piece of information, *Spengler* did illustrate the various ages of a civilisation, much like that of the four seasons we experience[430]. For example, spring would be characterised as an age of industriousness and religiosity – this can be seen in the large-scale temple construction of the burgeoning Hellenic civilisation, the grandiose conquests of the Republic of Rome and the industriousness of its citizens, or the pervasive building of Christian cathedrals, in the early middle-ages; as a timeless testament to the inescapable adoration held by the adherents, for their creator and the gift bestowed of his only begotten son; and the work ethic the dedicants of such a religion were prized for, universally. Therefore, as you are aware, we have come a long way since those far simpler times, and we have been catapulted into an age of irreligiosity and political, ethnic and religious division – thusly, the times we inhabit are characteristic of a rather late season within this stylised anacyclosis.

Spengler states "By the term "Caesarism" I mean that kind of government which, irrespective of any constitutional formulation that

---

[430] Spengler, O. (2021). *The Decline of the West: Form and Actuality*. La Vergne: Arktos Media Ltd. Chapter: The Problem of World-History (II), I.

Chapter VII

it may have, is in its inward self a return to thorough formlessness. It does not matter that *Augustus* in Rome, and *Huang Ti* in China, *Amasis* in Egypt and *Alp Arslan* in Baghdad disguised their position under antique forms. the spirit of these forms was dead, and so all institutions, however carefully maintained, were thenceforth destitute of all meaning and weight. Real importance centred in the wholly personal power exercised by the Caesar, or by anyone else capable of exercising it in his place..."[431]. The quote goes on, but I would take up the entire half of the page, so please feel free to purchase *Spengler*'s work and use it as reference when reading this. Digressing, in lew of Democracy, we see that, even *Spengler* alludes to similar notions, that it is the true vehicle of Caesarism; along with the press and money, of which money's chief weapon is Democracy. This is encapsulated within the quote from *Spengler*, "the coming of Caesarism breaks the dictature of money and its political weapon, democracy."[432] Thus, in Spenglerian thinking, we find that the Caesars take over from the money power as the civilisation drifts from an interest in metaphysics, higher truths and higher pursuits beyond the material realm, to a civilisation thoroughly rotten by materialism and perpetual cupidity, without any perceivable terminus. Caesarism is the one who steps in to take the reins of power once the populace has grown intolerant of this established racket. Conjunctively, if we assume this transition occurred within the civilisation we currently inhabit at the turn of the latter state of the enlightenment, circa late 18th century to be precise, then what we see come into view is an observable trajectory of dissolution in our wonderment of the immaterial. Additionally, it is the brazen ideologies and dogmas that grow forth from this pull towards materialism that sets a course for Caesarism, as the spiritual force prevalent within the civilisation begins to be sapped and all that remains is a husk in its wake. It is Faustian in nature, for *Spengler* articulated, "The

---

[431] Spengler, O. (2021). *The Decline of the West: Perspectives of World-History*. La Vergne: Arktos Media Ltd. Chapter: The State (B), IX.
[432] Spengler, O. (2021). *The Decline of the West: Perspectives of World-History*. La Vergne: Arktos Media Ltd. Chapter: The Form-World of Economic Life (B), III.

very word "discovery" has something bluntly un-Classical in it. Classical man took good care not to take the cover, the material wrapping, off anything cosmic, but to do just this is the most characteristic impulse of a Faustian nature."[433] Likewise, we can see the auspicious stride of progress, into this alluring bright future, as a flirtation with self-destruction; a descent embroidered in a well-worn but fine, golden hubris, of which man believes he can supress and surpass his own intrinsic nature. To tear open the vestments of the cosmos and know of the secrets of providence itself; to deify his soul, with discovery of secret knowledge, is the greatest of all material gain in the Faustian mind. Naturally, this will never come to fruition and will always, as menial as reversion may be, come back to the genesis state of primitivism and violence; a state of civilisational purgatory, if you will.

The Caesar capitalises upon this entire manner of existence, with a number of other factors considered of course, some I will touch upon further on, to utterly reconceptualise the world that was, to the world that will now be. It becomes a mean reversion, a reverting to a primitive way where ideas were exchanged by the clash of steel, rather than by gilded oration. This is the world in which the Caesar thrives and carves for himself an empire. However, it is a reconquest of the old nation not in identity, but simply in territory and as such little in the way of the old nation will permeate into the bold, new horizon charted by the Caesar. As *Spengler* writes, and I paraphrase, that power can only be overthrown by another power, and not by principle. Duly then, we see that the power of money can only be "overthrown by blood." This Caesarism invigorates such a spur to action in the common man and society, weary from the past transgression met at the hands of the bustling cosmopolises. The cities, who like a vampire has sucked the country dry and disposed of its victims, like one disposes of meagre refuse, and the Caesar emerges, only too happy to oblige the retributive spirit. To provide reference for

---

[433] Spengler, O. (2021). *The Decline of the West: Form and Actuality*. La Vergne: Arktos Media Ltd. Chapter: Music and Plastic (II), IV.

that prior expatiation, *Spengler* writes "All political, all economic history can only be understood if one recognizes the city, which is more and more separated from the country and ultimately completely devalued the country, as the structure which determines the course and meaning of higher history in general. World history is city history."[434] Moreover, he states "Long ago the country bore the country-town and nourished it with her best blood. Now the giant city sucks the country dry, insatiably and incessantly demanding and devouring fresh streams of men, till it wearies and dies in the midst of an almost uninhabited waste of country."[435] Subsequently, it must be further understood that the Caesar will not be driven by any sort of ideology, though he may espouse such trivial matters to mask his true intent, he is driven above all else in a manner akin to a pure and unadulterated will-to-power; nothing more.

The Caesars are the culminating private politics of men determined to rule at any cost, made manifest. We are now comfortably, no pun intended, in the age of the transition from Democracy to Imperium – an era of contending states will now make way for the *Imperium Mundi*, the "global empire" – and as such we are still to await our chosen leader for such an auspicious occasion; I am sure fate and other interested parties, are busily working behind the scenes to deliberate upon such an important choice. *Spengler* writes "Once the imperial age has arrived there are no more political problems, people manage with the situation as it is and the powers that be. In the period of contending states, back in the period of civilisation, torrents of blood had reddened the pavements of old-world cities, so that the great truths of Democracy might be turned into actualities; and for the winning of rights where without life seemed not much for living. Now these rights are won but the grandchildren cannot be moved, even by punishment, to make use of them. A hundred years more and even the historians will no longer understand all the

---

[434] Spengler, O. (2021). *The Decline of the West: Perspectives of World-History*. La Vergne: Arktos Media Ltd. Chapter: Cities and Peoples (A), III.
[435] Spengler, O. (2021). *The Decline of the West: Perspectives of World-History*. La Vergne: Arktos Media Ltd. Chapter: Cities and Peoples (A), V.

controversies."[436] We see this type of apathetic nature present in the citizenry of today. Where a minority only begin to cherish their abstractly defined rights once they are gone, and the others cannot be bothered to enforce their claim upon such rights in opposition to governmental overreach. In time, it will be generally looked upon by historians as a rather odd and perturbing affair - all of this malarkey regarding rights.

Spengler continues, "Already by the Caesar's time, reputable people have almost ceased to take part in the elections; it embittered the life of the great Tiberius, that the most capable men of his time held aloof from politics and Nero could not, even by threats, to compel the equites to come to Rome to exercise their rights. This is the end of the great politics, the conflict of intelligences, that had served as substitute of war, must give place to war itself in its most primitive form. It is therefore a complete misunderstanding of the meaning of the period to presume, as Monson did, a deep design of sub-division in the diarchy fashioned by Augustus; with its partition of powers between princeps and senate. A century earlier, this constitution would have been a real thing but that would in and of itself suffice to make it impossible for such an idea to have entered the heads of the current force-men. Now it only meant the attempt of a weak personality to deceive itself as to inexorable facts by mantling them in empty forms; Caesar saw things as they were and was guided in the exercise of his rulership by definite and unsentimental, practical considerations. The legislation of the last months was concerned wholly with transitional provisions, none of which were intended to be permanent; this is precisely what has generally been overlooked. He was far too deep a judge of things to anticipate the development, or to settle its definitive forms at this moment, with a Parthian war impending"[437]. Therefore, we may extract from this a meaning pertaining to the Caesar being a

---

[436] Spengler, O. (2021). *The Decline of the West: Perspectives of World-History*. La Vergne: Arktos Media Ltd. Chapter: The State (B), IX.

[437] Spengler, O. (2021). *The Decline of the West: Perspectives of World-History*. La Vergne: Arktos Media Ltd. Chapter: The State (B), IX.

Chapter VII

man solely dedicated to a will-to-power and not the empty form that now resides as politics. He cares not for the frivolities of ideology.

As was seen in the Hunger Games, if the reader be familiar with such fortuitously realistic fiction, the President Snow character is a typical Caesar; he rises to power through acts of beguilement and assassination and opposes all with ruthless intent that dare question his office; though this is not exactly in-keeping with Spenglerian ideas of Caesar, or even the historical character. However, as we see in that same series, the "Capital" only exists from engorging parasitically upon the distrained productivity of the impoverished, yet hardworking, lower-order Districts. As to understand, these lower-orders exist in a place materially impoverished, but their inward self is one forged in a fire of resilience and has been beset by the extreme conditions that would lead lesser man to ruin; Darwinian selection, in other words. The "Capital", by stark contrast, is a place abundantly lavished with splendour and all manner of shiny trinket, where the populace is bedecked in perpetual exuberance and they do develop strange and shamelessly pompous attire. They exist in a state far beyond the natural spectrum of the human experience, with their basic needs sated, they become enthralled on the path of moreish self-actualisation. Where they become increasingly disarmed of all mental faculties, the inability to see, in true form, that which is directly in front of them is acute and without relent; their minds become little more than jellified deposits of fat, where everything is dark and there is not even a scintilla of activity to bear witness to. Thus, they are the affluent slave-class, who faithfully believe the universe persists to maintain solely them; pertinacious narcissists beyond repute. Obviously, this is a hyperbolic fictional detail of how the lower classes actually view the cosmopolitan city-dwellers, in late-era civilisation, according to *Spengler* and many a thinker on this subject, too. Resentment grows within the rustic underbelly and the dispossessed yokel who, by necessity, dwells within the city confines, attempting to survive and make for his progeniture better conditions than himself does currently occupy, eventually hits boiling point. Spurred on by a chaotic event, or several – wherein the wrathfulness of this class cannot be occluded any longer and sporadic rebellions arise therefrom. Moreover, the constant intrusion and encroachment into the lives of the individual by the monied powers, and of the intellegencia, becomes ever more invasive; to such a point that people self-censor and general discussion is rendered meaningless, as to have an opinion contrary to the prevailing, or politically correct, one becomes an act worthy of intense hatred, vituperation and legal consequence. When the massive intrusion of the state on the individual reaches such magnitude as to warrant an instinctive response of fight or flight, then we see the breakdown and cessation of the civilisation.

Ressentiment, a state of having supressed feelings of envy and jealousy that cannot be quelled, is further spurred on in the pre-Caesarean era by the Democratic politicos. Through means of class warfare and derisory division, this ressentiment is not only sown but exploited for self-gain. While these politicians and other respectable reprobates use this to gain power, they spin new ways, like a spider spinning a web, to entrap and encourage more victim groups to add to their burgeoning base of dedicated electorates. With this wish for the proliferation of victim classes, to be electorally prostituted out to political blocs and candidates alike, of whom pine for their attention when the urge to campaign comes and soon chuck them aside, like a used rag, when the campaign season is concluded - we find that a parallel policy of enfeeblement of the proletariat comes to the fore. Through the figure of *Nietzsche's* Philistine "world improver", we find that there is a substantial and exponential increase of regulation, a labyrinth of law if you will, where a stifling of creativity and individual thought occurs; reciprocally creating a nation of infants beholden to an almighty state. While the evaporation of traditional campaigns waged on party platforms ensues, we find that these said campaigns refocus their energies to shining a spotlight, and attentively encouraging their base to venerate the political character and personality of the candidate; this becomes the focal point of all elections

Chapter VII

from thereon out. This then becomes the fertile ground from which will spawn forth the Caesar. As the system begins to age, wavering in its global position, we find that a free-for-all struggle ensues spurred on by the pervasiveness of class-warfare and this ensures that the Democratic process becomes untenable. Short-sighted solutions become utilised to stem the tide of chaos and keep the system from collapsing from its own weight of problems. All the whilst, the executive exercises unprecedented powers, out with the traditional remit, and with impunity, because the congress, or assembly, becomes paralysed by incessant bickering. The gradual paving of the way to the spontaneous rise of a political strongman can take a while, maybe two or three generations, but with every spark of crisis, it threatens to ignite the societal powder-keg. The once sacred institutions of the government become universally reviled and seen as irreparably broken in the minds of the populace; to such an extent, that self-radicalisation occurs *en masse*. Moreover, we must understand that crises in late-era Democracies become endemic to the system, they happen with greater ferocity and tempo, and as long as the system of Democracy exists, in such a dishevelled state, it leads to an ungovernable move towards greater centralisation of power into fewer and fewer hands. Inevitably, by the law of nature, this power in the hands of a few eventually becomes power in the hands of only one; the Caesar. The terminal stage is characterised by the incorrigible shift in allegiances of military assets, from state to political figures. This is the beginning of the imperial age and one could argue that we are just encountering the precipice of this transition right now, and will further see the development of the Caesar in the near to very near future; an age of demanded obedience, an age of human despondency, an age where none shall taste of the fruits of freedom, nor hear the songbirds of liberty sing their sweet, sweet song a moment more; an unknowing slavery, where one will voluntarily slide on the shackles of their own enslavement, by the trust they place into the saviour, of whom will deliver them from the jaws of chaos.

I would implore the reader to read both volumes of *Spengler's* work as it is fascinating and very much a far more compelling theory of history than any, I have read prior. I would air on the side of caution when reading it heavily though, as it can be very discouraging in its pessimism, but it is nonetheless entirely on point with everything; I cannot pick fault. I have covered several points and quotes above and expanded upon it with my own interpretations of predications, or analyses, as one would expect. However, this is included in the "Democracy" section because of the integral part Democracy plays in the rise of the Caesar, in Spenglerian thinking, thus I think it rational to include it here.

E Pluribus Unum

The increasing drive towards a centralised, collectivised world empire - the New World Order as it is affectionately titled by many a world leader - is not a new development within the spectrum of politics and academia; it is something that can trace its long and nebulous roots back to ancient times, as I have previously touched upon in my section upon *Plato's* work. Though this idea of using "revolution" as a means to do it, to actually encourage the fallible masses to fight to overthrow their defenders and construct the bars of their own enslavement, is a strategy that has been utilised since the time of the Protestant reformation. Potentially even stretching back into proto-Protestantism, with sects such as the Waldensians, Cathars, Hussites and Rosicrucianism. Now, this is not to say Catholicism is some bastion of piety and benevolence, worthy of defence, and singularly defending the world of light against that of darkness. No, of course not, to say so is infantile and without merit, but the system that wishes to usurp the nucleus of power, globally, sees all other contenders in its path as trivial obstacles that must be overcome and crushed; if infiltration and subversion is not an option.

We find that most of the religious institutions of recent development in the West, recent meaning post-nativist-religions, have all been compromised by the long march through the institutions; most espousing parables from the handbook of the neo-enlightenment, rather than the handbook of God. Though, the irony being that, the Christian religion was the most logical step forward towards collectivisation and the communal property ideal, at the terminus of Rome; we can see this replete within the New Testament passages, but not really within the Old, strangely. Digressing however, we find that this cult of collectivisation, I do not how to alternatively describe it, has been loyal to the same tenets and goals from the time of *Plato* and we find that the Anabaptist revolutionary *Thomas Münzer*, who has been heralded as a proto-Socialist revolutionary by Marxists and Socialists alike[438][439], wished to implement the same system we find in the works and dialogues published by *Plato*, *Thomas More* and *Tommaso Campanella*, but to name a few. Universal brotherhood and ideals of dismantling property rights for the lower classes, and fantastical utopianism is something that well-connected leaders in all areas of the economy, industry and media champion publicly, or if not publicly under bated breath. More so, we are beginning to see a revamping of the old utopian ideals of collectivism into the formation of the post-modern global order that has been described, by dedicants, as the "Fourth Industrial Revolution"[440]. This may simply be an attempt to stave off the inevitable decline of the hegemonic Anglo-American world order – to rebrand and reformulate it – or an age-old dream of the esoteric founders of secretive organisations to implement a global system of dictatorship, under the guise of some abstract utilitarian justification

---

[438] Blickle, Peter (1981). *The Revolution of 1525: The German Peasants' War from a New Perspective*. Baltimore, Maryland: Johns Hopkins University Press. Pg. 148.
[439] Müntzer, Thomas (1988). Matheson, Peter (ed.). *The Collected Works of Thomas Müntzer*. Edinburgh: T&T Clark. Pg. 437. "*Omnia sunt Communia*" - "all things are to be held in common and distribution should be to each according to his need".
[440] Schwab, K. (2017). *The fourth industrial revolution*. Pg. 12. "The fourth industrial revolution, however, is not only about smart and connected machines and systems. Its scope is much wider. Occurring simultaneously are waves of further breakthroughs in areas ranging from gene sequencing to nanotechnology, from renewables to quantum computing. It is the fusion of these technologies and their interaction across the physical, digital and biological domains that make the fourth industrial revolution fundamentally different from previous revolutions."

of the "greater good". I do not know conclusively, as if I was privy to such fundamentally important information, I would not be writing this book in an attempt to draw attention to it.

    I would argue that in the early ages of a civilisation, empire or culture that secretive orders that held beliefs and agendas, contrary to the prevailing paradigm, maintained a shroud of secrecy around them and their work. However, in the later stages, we find that with the disintegration of the prevailing order that increasingly more political leaders, even academic or commercial leaders, flock to a banner promising something perceivably new and dynamic. That with the fading of the old, comes a renewed vigour for what is perceived as new. Moreover, these leaders are far more susceptible to corruption and bribery within the later periods, due to a slipping of the morals and that extremely crucial sense of duty. Thus, they become little more than pliable pawns, moved around a chequered board at the behest of their masters. Is this simply a conspiracy of likeminded erudite scholars and radical reformers, of which have remained patient, provoking carefully contrived schemes of chaos and dissension; imparting onto the chief target, the nation-states of the globe, a protracted death by a thousand cuts? Or, is this simply a pattern of human psychology, of which it seems given enough time and development, within civilisations, that we find the same tired, old pattern playing itself out? In which, individuals distinguished in the integral sectors of society, wealthy and commanding in their own right, enter into an unholy alliance as to shed themselves of the burden of potential upstart, rival competition. The engineering of the future formulation of an oligopoly, not just in the markets, but in society itself; of which, by extension, the market is a participator in. I cannot fathom a set-in-stone conclusion of what they wholly intend and, I beg pardon to say, that I doubt anyone else will be able to either, unless the proper documentation survives some baneful event, of which classified is thence rendered unclassified, by virtue of a lack of government. Therefore, as for now, set-in-stone conclusions are an impossible luxury out of our grasp.

Chapter VII

Though, you, the reader, may wonder as to why I discuss this subject of conspiracy and the conspiring of coalescing, monied interests in bringing into being a world, in which, the entire panorama of available matter is inventoried and collectively appropriated? The reason is because it is a very real and apparent matter of fact, and the more fragmented civilisations become in the final conclusionary decades of their existence, the far greater the likelihood of monied interests preying upon the wounded creature like a vulture. They may wish to formulate a plan to elevate themselves to a position of political as well as financial status, create for themselves a hereditary title with lands and subjects included, or they may be ideologically driven and wish to create a grandiose utopia, of which they believe is sufficiently perfect enough to solve the ails of humanity. In the end, whatever drives them, all power wishes to maintain its power, and these monied interests understand that a civilisation cannot last forever, and thus a conspiracy hatched to extend the lifespan of their position, be it of a market or political position, is ultimately necessitated. Therefore, this is why they will opt to either artificially collapse civilisation with aid from an allied external foe, of whom after the collapse, or conquest in this case, will ensure the continuity of the monied interest's powerful position, or the monied interests may use radical forces and agendas to induce a "reset"; the latter we are seeing at play right now. This is, from my logical analysis of current and historical circumstance, seems to be the modus operandi of these monied interests; these powers within powers, societies within societies; or secret alliances concerned with monopoly, that seek to thwart rising competitors.

I would argue that the revolutions we saw in the 18th, 19th and 20th centuries, from the American revolution, to the French revolution, and finally to the Marxist revolutions throughout the 19th and 20th centuries, respectively, that we find a concerted effort by interests of Capitalists and radical nobility in the formulation of democratic regimes, and the consequential deposing of monarchy. For example, *Jacob Schiff* was head of the New York investment firm Kuhn, Loeb and Co. He was one of the principal backers of the Bolshevik revolution and personally financed Trotsky's trip from New York to Russia[441]. He was a major contributor to Woodrow Wilson's presidential campaign and an advocate for passage of the Federal Reserve Act [442]. Furthermore, we find characters such as *Haym Salomon*, of whom was a financial broker in New York, was one of the principal funders of the American revolution of whom on the creation of the Bank of North America, found purchasers for government bills to fund the Yorktown campaign of Washington and Rochambeau[443]. Now, why do you think Capitalists, of whom derive their capital from the principle of the buying and selling of goods and services, would wish to encourage the overthrow of the status quo and the ushering in of a state of chaos; which would make their commercial endeavours all the more difficult? Simply put, because war is profitable and the allure of creating a monopoly, in these cases a banking monopoly, provides a key to harnessing great power and an efficacious position. Moreover, Democracy is implemented over monarchy for the reasons stated within the analyses of *Hoppe* and *Hobbe's* work, that being that monarchs are not as easily captured as compared to "here today, gone tomorrow" politicians. Democracy also offers the illusion of freedom, while with passage of every new piece of legislation passed brings forth an imperceptible whittling of greater degrees of freedom. As evidenced by this quote from Montagu Norman, Governor of the Bank of England, while addressing the United States Bankers' Association, 26th August 1924, he stated "Capital must protect itself in every possible way, both by combination and legislation. Debts must be collected, mortgages foreclosed as rapidly as possible. When, through process of law, the common people lose their homes, they will become more docile and more easily governed through the

---

[441] Henry Wickham Steed, *"Through Thirty Years 1892–1922 A personal narrative,"* The Peace Conference, The Bullitt Mission, Vol. II. (New York: Doubleday Page and Co., 1924), Pg. 301.
[442] Griffin, G. E. (1995). *The creature from Jekyll Island: a second look at the Federal Reserve*. Appleton, Wisc: American Opinion.
[443] The Editors of Encyclopaedia Britannica. (2021). *Haym Salomon*. Available: https://www.britannica.com/biography/Haym-Salomon. Last accessed 05/12/2021.

CHAPTER VII

strong arm of the government applied by a central power of wealth under leading financiers. These truths are well known among our principal men, who are now engaged in forming an imperialism to govern the world. By dividing the voters through the political party system, we can get them to expend their energies in fighting for questions of no importance. It is thus, by discrete action, we can ensure for ourselves that which has been so well planned and so successfully accomplished"[444]. As you can see, powerful individuals – especially that of high financiers and monied interests – are truly drawn to the investment opportunity that is dictatorship; this may be achieved under a Democratic guise, too.

That said, the question is posed, if my ascertaining of the coming governmental structure be true, as I have outlined previously while alluding to Agenda 21 and such[445], then as to what mind conjures up a world where humans are transmogrified into soulless digital creatures, where the landscape of nature is made grey and godless, of whom what trickster what dream of a world where profit is extracted at the expense of the evisceration of the colourful medley that is life's experience. What is the use of profit when, as *Klaus Schwab* states, our "physical, biological and digital identities will be merged"?[446] What type of sane individual would wish to inhabit such a sordidly baron realm? Maybe within the question is contained the answer. They lack sanity and are driven by forces beyond our comprehension, forces that drive them mad with power, and blinded by the visions of Elysian fields, that will never come to be, they foolishly charge on. In a paradoxical sense, though unfortunately it must be enunciated, that from the imperfect mind of man, cannot

---

[444] Kirchubel, M. A. (2010). *Vile acts of evil: Banking in America*. Charleston, SC. Pg. 163.
[445] United Nations Conference on Environment and Development. (1993). *Agenda 21: programme of action for sustainable development; Rio Declaration on Environment and Development; Statement of Forest Principles: The final text of agreements negotiated by governments at the United Nations Conference on Environment and Development (UNCED)*, 3-14 June 1992, Rio de Janeiro, Brazil. New York, NY: United Nations Dept. of Public Information.
[446] Il Teatro della Politica. (2020). *KLAUS SCHWAB: Revolution will lead to a fusion of our physical, digital and biological identity*. Available: https://www.youtube.com/watch?v=t1Sp-C3B1KyM. Last accessed 05/12/2021.

be born a plan to perfect the world; the world, from its genesis, was already in a state perfected by dualistic equilibrium, and that life and death, happiness and despair, pain and pleasure, be all experiences that breathe a reciprocity of context. As you may see, we as children of this world carry that dualism with us everywhere; that humanity can be at one moment saintly and altruistic, but at the next monstrously evil and selfish. We cannot eradicate all these bittersweet tastes of life; it simply is an immovable fact as to the manner of our existence. *Ergo, sic vita est hominum.*

Chapter VIII

Opinions upon the Contemporary

This chapter will contain my concluding remarks upon the various subjects I have discussed throughout the book and to where, based on the conclusions expressed within this literature, I think the world will go from here. I have already detailed this thus far, but I wish to create a *vade mecum* that encapsulates the essence of my conclusionary thoughts. Civilisation and decline are synergistically linked to one another, one cannot exist without the other and what I see as decline, others may conclude to be progress. Though I have historical precedent on my side that seems to affirm my conclusion, I am nonetheless in a minority in concluding so and anyone else that agrees with me. Will we be ushered into a new world utopia, as our dear leaders promise? I very well hope so, but all of the signs point to the likelihood that we will not and a future without the freedom to experience life in its entirety, minus forced or coerced inoculation, is no future at all; it is a measly and miserable exchange, actually.

Therefore, what is to be done about all of this? As I stated, *Agorism* is very much a solution and resistance through any available channel of circumvention must be ventured by the individual; if they wish to retain their dignity and freedom from tyranny. Thus, you, the reader, can look at those ideas. Self-sufficiency and a rugged personality can be cultivated and must be cultivated by you, if you wish to survive the next great epoch in this decline of civilisation, but ultimately it is up to you. As you see, I wrote this book not only to explain to you, the reader, the theoretical, historical and observable underpinnings of decline, but I was necessitated to write it to provide explanation to myself; as this era in which we inhabit is rather perplexing, even to one who prides themselves on being a student of history and contemporary political trends. For it is of the upmost importance for the individual to first understand the gravity and overall scope of the problem before they can attempt to plan in a proactive way. In this regard, I very much hope I have provided certain information that you may not have been familiar with before, or opened your eyes entirely to the truly cyclical nature of civilisation and where it dangerously seems to be heading. I do this in hopes that I may provide sufficient impetus to enough people to plan accordingly to protect their family and loved ones from these apocalyptic changes, that seem to be ensuing. "*Si Vis Pacem, Para Bellum*" or "if you wish for peace, prepare for war", said the famous Latin writer *Publius Flavius Vegetius Renatus*, in his work *De Re Militari*[447].

Now, in regards to the aforementioned, that does not extend literally to the idea of storing armaments illegally – please do not believe I am wishing for my readers to go out and purchase arms of war, of course not – but I do believe that every person should have the means and knowledge to survive at least seventy-two hours without direct access to modern amenities, as an act of preparedness for any eventuality. It is as prudent an act as buying insurance, in fact it may be likened in part to a type of insurance. This will provide you confidence in the knowledge that you will survive any eventuality in this every-changing and rapidly deteriorating state of affairs, in the West. Other skills that you can develop too, such as bush-craft, archery, forging, wood-carving, fletching and

---

[447] Valturio, R. (1472). *De re militari*. Uerona: Johannes ex Uerona.

Chapter VIII

bow-making, woodworking, construction and the fundamentals thereof, first-aid, or knowledge of electrics and the generating of it can not only provide you with confidence through self-determination and self-reliance, but can open up new economic and employment pathways to you. It does bear utility; I have to say. You may transmit this information to others too, in the skills you develop and also this book, and help them in their journey to more self-reliance. Above all, this circumvents tyranny as you are acting out with in a secondary market and thus negating their control over your life; nullifying their ability to arbitrarily withdraw access to amenities and luxuries that you, hopefully by now, once relied on, as a means of controlling and forcing you to submit to whatever diktat they deem a requisite to their overall agenda. However, if individuals are not receptive to such information, then do not fret and certainly do not impose it on them, as it was once said "do not cast pearls before the swine". Therefore, with that prelude out of the way, I will lead on with the conclusionary thoughts and other miscellaneous postulations that I felt did not fit neatly into any section thus far.

The Modus Operandi of Capital and the State

> *"The few who understand the system will either be so interested in its profits or be so dependent upon its favours that there will be no opposition from that class, while on the other hand, the great body of people, mentally incapable of comprehending the tremendous advantage that capital derives from the system, will bear its burdens without complaint, and perhaps without even suspecting that the system is inimical to their interests."*
> *— Mayer Amschel Rothschild*

The love affair that always exists between the main holders of capital and the state is a perfidious one and is pronouncedly observable in Democratic nations; it must be said. Why does this occur? Several reasons are available to the rationalists among us, that firstly once an entity controls the means of capital, thereby in large controls the means of production; the human-being, still in the current era. This is done through the ability to produce capital, once the public mints are privatised it creates a seemingly endless opportunity to bribe, control and force politicians and, the cascading degrees of power below them, to implement the policies which will ensure the continued monopolistic stranglehold on the nation's coffers. In full, they grant the privilege, to a nation, of possessing an economy as without the liquidity, or capital, the economic machine ceases to function entirely because exchange can no longer be facilitated, and general fear would ensue. Once that is secured, through the machinations that led to the initial acquisition of the monetary system, through acquiring of compromising images and blackmailable material on political figures and authority, or through mutually-beneficial agreements, one can then begin the long-march through the institutions and slowly – but surely – begin to acquire every single institution and centralise the coordination of these. This is done in order to create what all capital (monopolists) wish for; a system of top-down control, where the oligopoly is maintained by strict government intervention and individuals are resigned to a state of perpetual wage-slavery and impoverishment, as a way to ensure they never rise above their station and endanger the reigning monopoly. These institutions that are to be controlled are to firstly be education and media institutions. They are to be acquired, bought and amalgamated into large conglomerates until only one company rule them all; even if it is through front-organisations, or subsidiaries, to maintain the illusion of a vast landscape of differing business and commercial interests.

We can see this with the passing of the *Telecommunications Act of 1996*, passed by Bill Clinton, which outwardly sought to inhibit the growth of monopolies and promote competition, but invariably accomplished the exact opposite[448]. To the citizens who attempt to raise the alarm and alert

---
[448] Brian Caterino. (2020). *Federal Communications Commission*. Available: mtsu.edu/

Chapter VIII

their fellow citizens to the dangers of the new and emergent monopoly they are either bought-off and recruited to work for the monopoly, lavished with frivolous material gifts and inconsequential positions of supposed power and status, or if they are not receptive to these offers then they are to be silenced in any way deemed necessary. To facilitate the silencing and management of dissenting voices, new law enforcement agencies will be created by utilising circumstances, contrived or apparent, of high-crime and the new paradigm of evolving threats to freedom, to instate a secret-police that answers to powers above the illusory veneer of government; they will be utilised to in information collection, election meddling, media and tabloid management, fomentation of casus bellis and the targeted silencing or threatening of opponents to the monopoly. This will create a system in which the oligarchy becomes hereditary, with lower-orders of puppets that bear the brunt of the populace's abuse and dissatisfaction and, if all fails, will be the ones responsible for the ire of the revolutionary mob.

Alas, once new means of technology become available as to "upgrade" the means of production into a more efficiently controllable, programmable and docile resource then that will be utilised, in earnest. A phasing out or a merging with automation for the outdated means of production will commence and control of reproduction of the inferior means of production will ensue to ensure that a carefully controlled transition to automation occurs. The predecessor means of production, inexorably, by basic regard to logic, will be phased out completely as they will be surplus to requirement once the superiorly efficient automated means of production becomes fully realised within the system. The humans that remain after the great diminishing – the ruling elite and a

---

first-amendment/article/804/federal-communications-commission. Last accessed 06/12/2021. "The Telecommunications Act of 1996 raised the limits on station ownership and in several amendments since increased the limits and loosened the rules on media cross-ownership. However, these developments have not been without controversy. Consumer and other interest groups have protested that the increasing corporate concentration of power violates the public interest and excludes minorities from ownership."

few subordinate classes – will inhabit localised "habitable zones", as per Agenda 21, where this new automated means of production will work and serve them, and the majority of the Earth will be designated as non-human habitation and will be large-scale "sanctuaries" for nature, but will more accurately be cordoned off areas permissible only to the elite for luxury retreats and for exploitation of the resources contained therein.[449]

By what means will the elite ensure the predecessor means of production are expediently discarded of? There are several, the method that would arouse the least suspicion and be as effectual as possible would be a chemical concoction, administered on the back of fear of an overly-inflated pandemic, that would render greater than eighty percent of the planet sterile and the effects of this sterility would last for three to four generations. Thus, ensuring that the world population be reduced by an order of magnitude, in the ensuing generations, by approximately ninety percent of its current total. With the addition of contrived cultural change and reproductive norms – financially inflating the cost of living thus by consequence limiting the numbers of children per family to two or less, inculcating sex education within all schools to sexualise the prepubescent student body, introducing them to contraception, non-monogamous sexual habits, and pornography, in which they will then grow to adulthood to have a multitude of partners which has been shown to have a detrimental effect upon settling down with one person and raising a family, and ensuring a state in which diversions and trivial pastimes, that require one not to leave their house, is proliferated and easily accessible to all. In the midst of the pandemic furthermore, the state may decree sex and relationships be outlawed or heavily regulated under strict guidelines, if they be so dictatorially inclined; thus, the peddling of sex-dolls and other deviant sexual devices will be encouraged

---

[449] Robinson, N. A. (1993). *Agenda 21: Earth's action plan annotated.* New York: Oceana Publications. Chapter 7: "Population programmes should be implemented along with natural resource management and development programmes at the local level that will ensure sustainable use of natural resources, improve the quality of life of the people and enhance environmental quality."

by media and such likewise ilk as an alternative to lack of freedom to engage in normal relationship forming.

Once conducted, the operation of sterilisation, or whatever means applied by the monopolists to discard of the predecessor means of production, will be swift and either forced or strongly coerced. The ones who take it will then force the others who are wary to take it – through peer pressure and violent threats towards them – for they will say "if I have to take it, then they too shall be taking it!" Such critical-thinkers who oppose the establishment dogma will be branded modern heretics and will be mocked, ridiculed, disabused of their reputation, beaten, barred from society and ultimately taken to "isolation facilities", or "hubs", for a brief period under the excuse of "quarantining of the non-vaccinated to safeguard the public health" and there they will be assessed as to their potential to be re-educated. If they are assessed to be able to be re-educated then a long process will occur as to re-educate the dissident through chemical, surgical or psychological means and subsequently they will then receive the vaccine and re-enter society; cleansed of their sins. If they are assessed to be unfit for re-education, they will most likely be summarily executed or starved; execution by means of beheading has already been touted in the US as a far more humane means of execution than that of lethal injection. Additionally, there has been a suspicious procurement in Canada of "Hydraulic Programmable Guillotines", similar reports have surfaced in the US, and with ICD9E978[450], Georgia General Assembly HB1274[451] and the NDAA they are prescribed to do so in law and to "indefinitely detain". As an update too, this Canadian government procurement contract was

---

[450] ICD-10. (2010). *International Statistical Classification of Diseases and Related Health Problems 10th Revision (ICD-10) Version for 2010.* Available: https://icd.who.int/browse10/2010/en?fbclid=IwAR0tDQY5c04SmVSCSCZ6-iqmSMSxHKVY1aG73p2WY-IXpe__FGAb8GoZTRnU#/Y35.5. Last accessed 06/12/2021. Section: Y35.5.

[451] Georgia House of Representatives. (1996). *HB 1274 - Guillotine Death Penalty Provisions.* Available: http://www.legis.ga.gov/.../19951996/leg/fulltext/hb1274.html. Last accessed 01/06/2021. Alternatively archived here: https://web.archive.org/web/20130624015359/http://www.legis.ga.gov/legislation/archives/19951996/leg/fulltext/hb1274.htm

amended to "Hydraulic Paper Cutter", a most fortuitous amendment, is it not?

In the end, through various means we will find that society will be rid of dissidents following on from the modern reign of terror, and this terror will only cease until such times the population is stemmed via the effect of the sterilant properties existent within the vaccine. All the while the sacred "public health" excuse will be used as justification, the same public whose health is put in jeopardy every year when the government proudly opt to provide pensioners with the choice of "heat or eat" because of low pension payments. This is a textbook, quintessential example of the *Hegelian or Triadic Dialectic* in political practise; it's all quite infuriating to see so many fellow citizens fall for such hogwash because it is so incontestably transparent.

Rebellions: Threat or a Tool?

The potentiality of rebellion must be an ever-present danger for our rulers and for all rulers throughout antiquity, for that matter. However, it would seem that this is less so a danger to them in our contemporary period, it would rather seem a tool that may be utilised as some devious pretext for greater acquisition of power and the justification to wield it overtly. This could well be the case, the transition tactically of this methodology is becoming apparent, and with the intentional arbitrariness of the diktats of government during this COVID crisis one has to wonder if they are directly attempting to foment civil strife as to justify the imposition of military force unto the general public. If this sounds absolutely preposterous to you, then do recall that the new rule changes were unveiled around five days away from Christmas – the welcome respite the entire country was promised and was wishing for – and it was unquestionably stolen from them by fear and the threat of force. This is a stark and wildly contrasting divergence from the typical, historical and near-historical, tactics of governments of which they seek to imprison and pacify the populace within a myriad of entertainment and frivolity. Thus, in such a system, one may wish to leave but one has become so anaesthetised by the dazzling allure of the materiality, lobotomised by the splendid pleasure of the entertainment, and enfeebled by the cheap and abundant access of food to engorge oneself on, that they become dependent upon the system; and through this dependency a self-perpetuating system of slavery is fashioned, the chief architect of which is the aforementioned apathetic prisoner; thus, this is how all rulers maintain power, through means of pacification rather than antagonisation. However, the governments of the world – essentially, a federated world empire in its infancy, at this point – are acting in lockstep and are actively seeking, it would seem to the astute observer, to be wilfully fomenting civil disorder and economic and social devastation; a war without bullets they do wage against their own populace, a war where the herd pathology and psychology are altered through chemical and social pressures is the mainstay modus operandi. Hence, one may draw the comparison between a general of old, who possesses an army fewer in number, seeking to draw his opponent in to a setting of his choosing where their innumerability confers no advantage and that they may be more easily vanquished; as such, it would seem that is what is occurring now. Thusly, the propaganda is becoming far more transparent, the brutality of the regime is on display at every anti-lockdown protest, and the psychopathology of the political class is being directly rendered into policies so draconian and independent of the fundamental codes of law that it is setting in motion a chain reaction where the slumbering masses will sleep no more. Is this the intended outcome?

The traditional sense of mode on the maintenance of power was that power was derived from the inability of the masses to perceive with any great clarity the crux of a ruler's criminality and total lack of care of the citizenry's well-being; citizenry are means to an end, in truth. To atomise them as a means to circumvent the majority joining as one collective, one that could unite and tear down the chains of their oppression.

Furthermore, to utterly isolate the ones who are not swayed by cheap materialism and dazzling shows. For example, if one wishes to engage their fellow citizen in discourse of a higher political nature, important to each's interest, that the fellow citizen will be so infantilised by his vapid consumption of trivial sport or entertainment, that he would wish to discuss the score of the game or next week's show rather than lead himself down a path of true intellectual discovery. That path is one in which he will be forced to question the reasoning behind why this entertainment has been made so easily accessible to him, a mere paeon. It would seem though, that all diversions are being made now inaccessible to the citizenry as a way of psychology depriving them of a familiar and reliant opioid. Why is this? Well, a number of reasons are apparent to us. The first is that it truly is a terrible pandemic that is occurring, and the transmissibility is attempting to be curbed by the glorious and omnipotent government. This seems unlikely as the places that are being shut to public usage by government are places that bring a certain joy to people and make them forget of their various worries; families are even being restricted and isolated from each other.

However, conversely, schools, a place where one would believe that the majority of asymptomatic, even though no pandemic in history has possessed a vector of transmissibility through asymptomatic means though I digress, are taking place would be one of the first places to shut in an actual deadly, unpredictable pandemic. This is not the case here however, as it would seem during this intensive vaccine roll-out that the indoctrination of the de rigueur mask culture and veneration of the vaccine must be instilled in the masses of youth, that the connection between the state and the parent, through the impressionable and gullible child, must be maintained for purposes of informing on disobedient and dissident parents, and hence for the control of the parents behaviour through the child. That being, the parent must conform their behaviour to the mainstream or thus they risk imparting to their children dissident ideas, of which will be identified by state educators. As you see,

Chapter VIII

compulsory education is a fantastically brilliant idea from the standpoint of the political elite. They seemingly grant, in a projected spirit of altruism, "free" education to the underprivileged classes of children, that they may achieve just as much as the children from privileged backgrounds. All the while. the parents of these underprivileged children applaud implementation of such a policy as it affords greater social and job mobility to their offspring.

However, what they fail to see in foresight, is that the state now has entire custody of their children and may inculcate in them any cultural or social changes they wish to see within the world; they may implement a cult, if they have not already. Where once children from the working-classes would have worked in factories, mines or farms, a terrible situation albeit, but they would have grown to be educated, if you will, in the stories and culture of their ancestors, that the culture would have remained the same through multiple generations without interruption. Now, in our contemporary timeline what do we see? Well, since the advent of compulsory education in around the 1880's in the UK and 1920's in the USA, with further revisionary acts strengthening the legal compulsory nature, we have seen a dramatic deterioration of culture and we now stand on the precipice of tyranny and utter ruination. This is due to the ability of state education to be captured by extremist fringes, much like the apparatus of government, and skewed to disseminate to the unsuspecting youth subversive messages and radical notions; of which, will first incapacitate and then destroy the national character and the perpetuation of the uniqueness of its spirit. This entire education system has its origins in the military Prussian model[452], and seeks to use a scientific approach to change Man from a noble being endowed with individuality to an animalistic being whose capacity stretches only to the behavioural confines of a one-dimensional bestial reaction pattern;

---

[452] Geitz, H., Heideking, J., Herbst, J., & German Historical Institute (Washington, D.C.). (2006). *German influences on education in the United States to 1917*. Washington, D.C: German Historical Institute. Pg. 21-41.

in such a state, one is like mere putty in the hands of the psychological sculptors[453]. However, that is a tale for another day, or another book, as they say.

However, digressing entirely, the other more likely reason that the mass closure of centres of entertainment and joy is being conducted, I would assert, is due to a carefully orchestrated plan to psychology torment the public; so that they will react in three ways, respectively. The first way is that a certain stratum will react in a way analogous to a child bereft of their favourite toy, or an animal without a supply of their favourite treats, that is that compliance can be cultivated by the dangling of these frivolous luxuries in the face of the despondent masses within this stratum. Like a carrot on a stick, they will prostrate themselves before the cleverly twisted agenda of government, they will inform upon their fellow citizens who resist vaccinations, and the overall propaganda, in hopes to maintain the status quo that provide them the privilege of the luxury and entertainment they are so accustomed to; and they will willingly roll-up their pristine sleeves to the intrusive and suspicious experimental mRNA vaccine. This stratum could be entitled the "Sedated Materialists". They only know the status quo and as such, even if they believe the government evil and inimical to their interests, they will act to protect the accessibility of their frivolous luxuries and lobotomy-inducing entertainment above all else; as this form of escapism is a coping mechanism for them and they would rather maintain the lie because they fear the ramifications of outwardly acknowledging the truth. The second way is the strata which will react with impulsive hostility, they will seek the path of wrathfulness against the authority. In the state of cold-turkey, from entertainment and the various pastimes that made modern society bearable, they will become resentful against the government and may become openly and, potentially, unwarily violent against further provocations by the authority. They will resist the rules, the imposition of tyranny, the arbitrary

---

[453] Foucault, M. (1979). *The History of Sexuality* (Vol. I). London: Allen Lane. Pg. 141. "Biopower": "An explosion of numerous and diverse techniques for achieving the subjugations of bodies and the control of populations".

commerce-banning orders and seek to protest, open their business, and even engage in force against the oppressors. These strata are the consequential result the government desires, as they can then utilise this as justification for further tyranny and the mobilisation of military assets against the populace – to brutalise dissenters and administer vaccines forcibly. If the government do not acquire an authentic reprisal from the populace from this psychological torment, then they will fabricate a contrived one in the form of a false-flag; this will be the justification required to intern dissenters and force vaccinations upon the masses, as the dissenter's narrative will be thoroughly vilified in the media and in the political-correct consciousness. I call this stratum the "Revolutionaries"; as they wish to "revolve" or keep the system intact, but reform it with new blood within the political class. The third way in which people will react is with preparatory action, they will be acquiring goods, knowledge and the means to escape the centres of dense population. They will be preparing to "bug-out", so to say, and will be acting as if they are already present within a state of pure tyranny, a Gestapo-state, and as such they will attempt to remain as politically-correct as possible, outwardly, and within the privacy of their own home will be busily preparing for the encroaching tyranny that is about to ensue. Potentially, for years they may have suspected that such a systemic change was coming, but were always referred to as a "conspiracy-theorist" by their close friends and relatives – vindication is now theirs, however. This stratum I call the "Preppers" or "Conspiracists".

These individuals are the most dangerous to the government as they are typically the most intelligent, well-read and possess the ability to articulate, with reason as well as rhetoric, to their fellow citizens the plan that is about to unfold. Thus, I can imagine these individuals are priority targets when arises the time to tighten the noose around the neck of the various dissenter-classes. In "A Synthesis of a Russian Textbook on Mass Mind-Control (Psychopolitics)", Revised and Edited by Lt. Col. Gordon "Jack" Mohr, U.S. Army, Retired, it states that, "the enslavement of a population can fail only if the rebellious individuals are left to exert their individual influence upon their fellow citizens, sparking them into rebellion by calling into account their past nobility and ideals of freedom. Unless these restless individuals are stamped out and given into the hands of psychopolitical operatives, early in the game, there will be nothing but trouble as the conquest continues."[454] Thus, this is why the intellectuals, especially in Communist rises to power, are always liquidated and purged upon the ascension of the totalitarian regime. It would seem with these types of psychological perturbations that the government wish to draw these individuals out from the woodwork, along with the potential foot-soldiers of any future resistance, thus all that will remain are the compliant individuals who seek not conflict, but will castrate any truculence of spirit they may have possessed just to cling onto some intangible hope of normalcy.

THE MILGRAM EXPERIMENTS

The *Milgram* experiments were a collection of multiple experiments conducted by Yale University Psychology professor Stanley Milgram. The experiments were conducted as to assess a subject's willing obedience to authority in light of visible conflict with one's own personal conscience. In a brief overview of the methodology of the experiment, the experimenter (*Milgram*) ordered the teacher (the subject) to administer what they would believe would be harmful electric shocks to a learner, who was actual an actor and associate of *Milgram*, on the answering of an incorrect question. The electric shocks would be administered in an ascending sequential pattern, all the way to a fatal voltage of four-hundred-and-fifty volts. The subject, the teacher, was led to believe that the learner was actually receiving live electric shocks after answering incorrectly, though in reality it was a ruse as to assess the subject's level of obedience in lew of

---

[454] Mohr, G., & Lord's Covenant Church (Phoenix, Ariz.). (1982). *Brain-washing (mind-changing): A synthesis of a Russian textbook on mass mind-control (psychopolitics)*. Phoenix, Arizona: Distributed by Lord's Covenant Church, America's Promise Broadcasts.

their visible conflict of morality. Within the shock generator was a pre-recorded sound player in which, for each shock, it would play increasingly violent protestation from the learner and eventually the learner would cease to make a sound – which would be presumptive of their demise.

The results produced from this experiment were startling as the vast majority of the participants continued on to the cessation of the experiment, 65%, and all administered voltages of at least three-hundred volts; thus, all followed the experimenter, the lab-coat wearing authority figure, even when his orders were in opposition with their own moral principles. It was found also in subsequent experiments, that when the participant does not have distance, as in this experiment, with the learner and they can visibly witness their pain then it was found that there was a greater degree of refusal to carry out the orders of authority. However, the question of culpability comes into question also. I have found many clips and excerpts of the video recordings of this experiment online and many of the participants I have seen seem to ask the question of the experimenter, "will you take responsibility for this man?", in light of the higher voltages and greater number of screams from the learner, and when the experimenter replies sternly "I am responsible for this man, please continue", they almost always continue on, almost unabashedly so and with greater determination. This is, I believe, because the personal culpability of the individual has been exported to the higher authority figure, thus they believe they act with impunity. For example, there was one man, from these excerpts, that insisted that he was not responsible and when asked "why did you not stop?", replied that "he [the experimenter] would not let me stop. I tried to stop". Thus, we see that the majority of individuals, if we are to extrapolate these findings out, act like automatons awaiting a programmer to instruct them as to what to do; they have little agency and little will; they are powerless to say "no", when they believe themselves inferior to the authority in command.[455]

---

[455] Milgram, S. (1963). *Behavioural Study of obedience*. The Journal of Abnormal and Social Psychology, 67(4), 371–378. https://doi.org/10.1037/h0040525.

Interestingly, this experiment was conducted just proceeding the trial of Adolf Eichmann, a National-Socialist war-criminal, in Jerusalem. Moreover, the findings of such an experiment really are quite relevant today and informs us as to why the entire edifice of government and law enforcement are wilfully engaging in, for example in the USA, unconstitutional or outright unlawful commands; beating people up (London), strangling women (Australia), attacking individuals for playing ice-hockey (Canada) and brutalising bystanders for being out after curfew (California). For example, in the context of the UK, we find that the new "Tier 4" rules were never passed by parliament; the tyrants simply waited until parliament was in a state of recess and, under the guise of urgency, of a rising emergency situation, attempted to utilise the colour of law to provide legal legitimacy to their corrupt undertaking. Therefore, as we do find ourselves in an upside-down world, like some Orwellian dystopia, we can now conclude that, in the UK, we pass statutory regulation into law simply on the approval of the executive and ruling cabinet and we forego all of that superfluous rigmarole of actually debating it within the House of Commons and the House of Lords, respectively voting in favour or against after the culmination of debates, and then providing it with the final required royal ascension. No, that is far too costly in time, we might as well simply employ the same process as a dictatorship does when it writes into law new legislation; that being the ruler decrees and that is the law. We see as well, to bring the discussion full-circle, that the law enforcement branch of the government, as it seems now, are all too happy to enforce "rules" that are not even prescribed law but are corruptly giving such categorisation under the colour of law; all under the guise of a life-threatening pandemic of course. Corruption throughout the ages is truly incorrigible, is it not?

Even in a state, the contemporary modern Man would think, is incontestably Democratic and without a slither of despotism there seems to be the most undemocratic of behaviour. Well, as for the Democracy, that fairy-tale reverie has entirely been rendered asunder now, has it not? You will find that the capacity for tyranny to inflict misery upon

Chapter VIII

Man is not even close to becoming exhausted, even with the brutality of the 20th century's tyrants, some of whom were ostensibly Democratic. As such we should have been dutifully vigilant for the rise of another tyranny; so that we may safeguard our freedoms and our nations for the enjoyment of future generations of our kin. However, it seems that while we were busy playing with our smartphones and anaesthetising ourselves within the brain-rot of modern frivolities, there was a power so insidious and diabolical, busily weaving their web of control throughout the institutions of government, media and academia. What do we see today? The final unfolding of their plan for world dominion and the eradication of the "useless eaters", for the sake of power and for the cause of holding sway for all time over a world of their own; free from the masses of the unnecessary, depleting their resources and crowding their urban areas and their country retreats. They seek a world without the threat of populist uprisings, of whatever stripe, and without the potential for overthrow; with current technology, this dream, of many a despot of old, can now be realised and it is. As Georgetown professor *Carol Quigley* remarked in his work, entitled "Tragedy and Hope", "The powers of financial capitalism had another far-reaching aim, nothing less than to create a world system of financial control in private hands able to dominate the political system of each country and the economy of the world as a whole. This system was to be controlled in a feudalist fashion by the central banks of the world acting in concert, by secret agreements arrived at in frequent meetings and conferences. The apex of the systems was to be the Bank for International Settlements in Basel, Switzerland, a private bank owned and controlled by the world's central banks which were themselves private corporations. Each central bank...sought to dominate its government by its ability to control Treasury loans, to manipulate foreign exchanges, to influence the level of economic activity in the country, and to influence cooperative politicians by subsequent economic rewards in the business world."[456]

---

[456] Quigley, C. (2010). *Tragedy and hope: A history of the world in our time.* Cheyenne, WY: Dauphin Publications Inc. Pg. 324.

The Problematic Condition of Man

Human nature has long been regarded as an inherent problem to the fulfilment of the stated goals of most, if not all, political ideologies; simply take your pick of which one. Thus, in this dawning of a Technocratic age, we begin to see an open disdain for the fundamental psychological and behavioural instincts that underpins what it truly means to be human. Where once the disdain was historically held by the preeminent tiers of society, this misanthropic idea is now slowly percolating downwards and this aberrant idea now resides firmly in the minds of most educated individuals, be them of whatever socio-economic class. What is being sought, by the general trajectory of technological advancement and inquiry, is the creation of a distinct bifurcation of the image of the old and, of what will be, the new human. The new human is that of a facsimile, a simulacrum if you will, clad in the vestiture of bio-digital imitation and merged with unfathomable technology; more machine than man.

This technology will solve the age-old issue held by the multitudinous legion of has-been dictators throughout our species history; the problem of free-will and subjugating a species of, mostly, sentient creatures yearning for freedom and the absence of annoyance from the state. Simply put, the integrated technology that will "lead to a fusion of our physical, digital and biological identity," as stated by *Klaus Schwab*, will nullify our free-will or will track it constantly that we will be required, for sake of survival, to amend it accordingly. *Klaus Schwab*, intellectual Godfather of "The Great Reset" and the author of "The Fourth Industrial Revolution", of the World Economic Forum, states that this may be achieved via implantable microchips or, more futuristically, will most likely be achieved via what is being termed, nano-bioelectronics; this type of technology will eventually lead to the surveillance of your emotions and eventual merging with a type of interwoven network; "the internet of things", as it is fashionably entitled. Thus, they may hold total control over you as if, for example, you watch a propaganda piece on the great leader, president, or whatever the executive title may be in future eras, and you begin to surface emotions of anger, resentment or general suspicion then this will be logged at the central node, or via a sub-node, of the network and you will be visited by law enforcement and your political correctness, or adherence to the collective mindset, will be evaluated. If you are deemed a threat to the reigning order then you, a "human resource", will be forced into a re-education camp or summarily liquidated as defective. What type of technology will track these emotional changes; I hear you ask? Do you wear the perceivably vogue novelty "Apple Watch"? This prototype device is an example of the technology I speak of, though in a form of predictive familiarisation or accustoming for the general public; for you to ultimately enjoy and even yearn for your servitude. For instance, it tracks your vital signs, location, communications, etc, so how far away is the advent of technology that tracks anomalous emotional fluctuations in its users, be it of anger or wrath? This technology is most likely already developed, if the current charted political course is anything to go by, and is simply awaiting supply to the public at a most advantageous time, of course. This technology will herald the rise of what is termed in dystopian "science-fiction" as "Pre-crime"; you will be sentenced and duly punished for thoughts and of actions that may, in likelihood, spring forth from said thoughts.

We can see this growing push for establishing a sterile and clinical world with the growing number of restrictions with COVID. What must we not do? Have joy, be with family, celebrate together as one collective, discuss matters, or be merry in a publican and we must certainly not celebrate Yule, and all of the beauty that goes along with that. What we are seeing is the next intrepid stage in this, what seems at this stage from my prior evidence cited, is at least a five-hundred-year conspiracy – for which the last one-hundred years it has become largely centrally organised and relentless in its singular ambition, to realise the benefits afforded to an elite in the implementation of pure collectivist ideals upon world society. A federated world empire is beginning to be birthed by an unholy union of the morbidly unsound minds of academia and the ardently power-drunk political-class. We are beginning to see the shrugging off of the typical historical vestiges of diversion through bread and circus, now we see that whatever technology is held by the elite above us, the mere paeons, is one in which antiquated notions of "appeasing the mob" is not a requisite to the maintaining of power; however, it would seem that the technology possessed or developed would simply allow one to centrally control and bring into order vast swathes of humans with little ease. COVID has shown us what the elite truly think of the peasantry below, the enfeebled masses that hold little value to these cretinous monsters other than a paltry resource to be exploited and abused, and that the system they crave is near their grasp; a system where the anacyclosis that has governed the rise and fall of human civilisation matters not, a system unassailable to the trappings that befalls all great systems of power and empire; a system of global dominion for as long as the sun does shine and the earth remains nominally habitable, that is. Additionally, it may be said that the elite may, in their vain hubris, decidedly reason that they are above the mere mortals who dwell below at the bottom of the rungs, but they suffer from a distinctly human trait in their desire to craft the most efficient and automated system of governance; that is humans seek, from what seems instinct, to bend nature and our environment to our will and to create the most efficient tools imaginable, so that we may engage in as little work as possible to achieve our respective task. What is simply being constructed is the solution to the problem for systems of the past, the refinement of past principles and the distorting of the environment itself as to accommodate the system that is wished for. That is why we see the radical changes existent within our contemporary period and that is why the "new normal" is being urgently crafted by those who seek the dissolution of the old and the edification of the new; our very innate nature is being changed, firstly through means of psychological reprogramming and secondly, through chemical and finally digital augmentation. If this is not the case and you, the reader, believe me mad, then pray, do tell, why would nominally democratic governments all around the world seek to alienate, torment and imprison the electorate over a virus that has a recovery rate of more than ninety-nine percent? Why the drastic measures? Simply put, because the ploy of the virus was just that, a ploy. A pretext, a justification, for the ramping up of a series of fundamental cultural and societal changes – systemic in their magnitude – that would have otherwise been rejected outright by the public, under normal circumstances. However, in the midst of emergency anything goes, and people are easily manipulatable by a government that seeks to engorge themselves on power.

We may say too that the Human drive to seek community amongst peers is furthermore a great dilemma for the powers that be. That put, the ideas of rebellions are typically hatched in the quiet and dusty publican houses, in the private abodes of dissidents and amongst the congregational masses within church. Thus, this community, or nucleus that may bear ideas contrary and threatening to the power structure, must be extinguished and like a "circuit breaker", the potential wildfire effect of the fomenting of an idea or a rebellious spirit must be implemented within the chain as to smother it before it has chance to breathe life. How may this be achieved? By utilising a medical emergency to craft a mythology surrounding a virus that may be more readily spread amongst people congregating, speaking or being in close proximity as to give ample justification for the state to shutdown forcibly all centres of congregation where exchanges of ideas may take place; publicans, bars, churches, private citizens visiting other houses, travel restrictions between shires, counties or regions, etc. This type of control over the public discourse occurred with the advent and dissemination of the novel technology of the television. Of which, for example in the UK, we would have found prior to this technology local gatherings of the community in townhalls, town squares, town greens, publicans and this would be a place where local issues and politics were discussed; where ideas were formulated, and potentially radical political discourse held. Thus, people acted as one and were homogenous in thought and feeling, they were not atomised nor easy to pick-off by the government; and in the event of unlawful actions by law enforcement or tax collectors, you would find a greater degree of resistance than say the atomised populations that we have now. Hence, when the television arrived, we found that where once the town hall or the public square was heaving with vigorous talk about all manner of things, it changed dramatically into an eery lifelessness. Where one would hear deafening silence and see only the faint flicker of hypnotic light, on one's passing of the houses in the once lively, united town.

In conclusion of thought, it would seem Human nature is fighting against itself with the arrival of these COVID restrictions; the restrictions seek to curtail basic human instinct and interaction. However, this is a pattern consistent with elites throughout history where their entire premise, the presupposition of their belief in their superiority, in comparison to the lower orders, is contingent on viewing Humans as the threat, and of Human nature as the antithesis of efficiency. To be controlled, like some unquenchable inferno. This misanthropic belief system guides their decisions and ultimately leads them into states of delusional hubris which is the prerequisite for the arising of tyranny.

ON COERCION

Coercion; the mainstay weapon employed by all tyrants throughout history and one of the first weapons utilised in the instituting of any "reign of terror" or drastic alteration of society. This "reign of terror" may be anything from dramatic and seismic economic or social alterations, or a military campaign against existential or internal opposition. Secondly, the next weapon utilised is mobilising the majority against the minority, typically a minority whom opposes the reigning regime - this may be a

Chapter VIII

political, religious or ethnic minority, or simply a movement of objectors to the prevailing regime's narrative. Thirdly, and finally, the final weapon utilised by all regimes throughout history - once total control is imposed and the populace, for the most part, are assimilated into the newly formed collective hive-mind - the final remaining dissidents on the hinterland, or fringes of the society, are met with extreme force by the regime's lackeys and totally expunged from said society.

This may be utilised as part of the political stratagem referred to as the *Hegelian or Triadic Dialectic* (*Hegelian* is used as a colloquial term, *Hegel's* does not use this *Triadic dialectic* in a political sense and expounds upon its principles); the dialectic is simple but rather effective in bringing about the formation of new social paradigms within society; paradigms that suit the employer of said stratagem. I have detailed the dialectic previously in this piece of literature and as such I refer you to that for a brevity of definition upon this.

The greater the amount of power, and broadening of the mandate of government, acquired by any state - even one so benevolent as our own, of course - will only lead to totalitarianism. The small nugget of hope is, within this process of political transformation, the dialectic, there is provided always a small window of opportunity to reverse, or at least hold back, the transferring of unwarranted power to the state. All you need do is speak your mind and speak aloud; if you fail to, the world your progeny inherit will be one of darkness and despair. The ones who would attempt to pontificate themselves rulers of us all, will continue unabated in their consolidation of newly found powers, unless the consolidation of those newly found powers are challenged and their feet are forced back down to the flames.

Though, who well knows and our governments may be entirely benevolent, simply afflicted with well-intent but lacking in any perceivable aptitude or intelligence; such affliction and lacking is seemingly pervasive throughout modern society too, does it not seem so?

On Corruption

The complete abolition of corruption is utterly impossible. I take a more long-term perspective upon such matters; it is the cycle of civilisations, anacyclosis in academic circles. The irony is, the higher the living standards, or the expedient accessibility of the general populace to luxuries in abundance is corollary, if not a causal factor, to the proliferation of corruption within any given society. Thus, this creates a far more domesticated populace dependent upon the state to maintain its frivolous pastimes - entertainment, luxuries or even daily welfare, be it currency (prospective UBI or welfare) or grain in the Graeco-Roman civilisation - and hence it becomes exceedingly malleable to this mercantilist class. *Panem et Circenses*, as Virgil stated in response to the Roman's antiquated form of this aforementioned domestication, and this stems from what may be termed the Age of Affluence; which is detailed within *Sir John Glubbs'* work "*Fate of Empires: And the Search for Survival*"; in which he details the seven stages of the growth, youth, maturity and decline of civilisations. As a concluding thought, the foremost prerequisite to freedom is self-reliance; once dependency has been administered the state will almost always grow into an uncontrollable and tyrannical behemoth; then it is only a matter of time before you get the would-be benevolent dictators arising from the merchant classes attempting to institute a 'Brave New World', for us all.

Trump seems to be being used as a scapegoat, a diversion of sorts too. It seems that like the ancient example of the transformation of the Roman Republic to the Roman Empire, we too are currently entering the same state of political osmosis as befell the previous great Empire of old; Trump, if not at present will retrospectively, be determined as the herald of this political change. The change I talk of is naturally a corporatist one, and is not something that is most likely sought by the general populace, at large. We do seem to be being desensitised to increasing instances of political corruption, all the while the media and the general populace,

Chapter VIII

influenced by their media overlords, put this entirely down to chronic ineptitude of the political class; all the while the true wielders of political power, the captains of industry and finance, simply prepare a new puppet to take the last puppets place. It is a system predisposed towards a cycle of perfidious corruption and systemic malfeasance.

I must preface in this current era, I am entirely politically neutral, political theatre is simply a smokescreen for the elite class to covertly enact agendas that, in usual stead, would be abhorred by the general populace at large. However, that said, I think it is clear that Biden will probably be the death knell of the American Empire and the Anglo-American sphere of influence, at least overtly. These, I think forty-plus executive orders, are actively designed to cause sabotage to the American economy and social landscape; it is even more so mad than Trump's facile Southern border wall, which could not even be considered a band-aid on a gaping wound, but most Presidents are as mad as their Roman counterparts of old, be them Emperors or Pro Consuls respectively. The Mainstream-media criticism of corporatocracy is nowhere to be seen of course, they are entirely complicit in this political osmosis, or usurpation, choice of semantics albeit, and their propaganda - which is what it increasingly seems to be - is so transparent and devoid of even a slither of impartiality.

Of course, the system in which we inhabit is a one-party state in all but name, it is misidentified as a system of political dualism for the sake of buttressing the illusion foisted upon the unsuspecting public, that they possess a voice. However, the politically perspicacious among us know differently. Deeply polarising characters, such as Trump, are utilised as a means of divide and conquer - keeping the plebeians squabbling amongst each other, so that they are disarmed of the ability to unite in the face of the growing tide of tyranny. This may be along various lines; political, racial, class or even sports team rivalries. Anything to keep social cohesion minimal and interclass squabbling high.

It is infuriating. To watch the real injustices, go unpunished - all the while seeing a constant hamster-wheel of 'same old, different bogeyman'.

Yes, it is truly annoying – but we should rejoice in our luck to have the honour of bearing witness to the era of "progress"; comically, the irony is tangible enough to be tasted. Unfortunately, "progress" in this context seems to imply the complete dissolution of the economic and long-term stability of the old-world order, that we regrettably seem to be geographically a part of. Conversely though, it is not like any brand of "progress", from the ostensibly populist right or left, is any alternative. It just seems to be radical for the sake of radicalism, in the sense that the ostensible reforms are simply a testament to the foreknowledge of the inexorability of the outcome of the prevailing geo-political and domestic situation befalling us.

ON CRITICAL THOUGHT

The general population do not engage in self-reflection of one's own preconceived notions or critical thinking - they are almost naturally inclined to have an aversion to it and will recoil in horror to the few peers who display even a hint of it. This is because the majority will choose the path of least resistance, psychologists know this and government capitalises upon this seemingly undiscussed fact. This was witnessed within the *Milgram* experiments in the early 1960's, as I have previously discussed.

That being, the individual will act in accordance with the widely perceived societal consensus relayed to them by a touted authority figure; even if the consensus be one that is patently untrue and a fabrication from its premise. This is the entire modus operandi of media, or the reason for media's existence, to contrive consensus - to literally fabricate the supposed will of the majority and broadcast it to the slumbering masses. Thus, the individual will be pressured, by social conformity, to realign his views and opinions in accordance with the majority (path of least resistance) or suffer the consequentially derived social ostracising from said majority. Subsequently, as we are socially dependent creatures - and these lockdowns have quite rightly highlighted that in our minds - we will prostrate ourselves intellectually to the propagated social hierarchy and messaging.

Thus, it has to be cultivated in the minds of the populace that critical-thinking should be considered a virtue and that social conformity, especially in terms of it mitigating ideas and rigorous intellectual discourse, is typically unhealthy in the long-term for a society; positive reformers should be championed rather than admonished, etc. Then we may see positive change, on a macrolevel.

Merchants of the Revolution

The irony of the concept of revolution is that most revolutions and rebellions that have been outrightly successful, throughout history, are the ones that, from their point of genesis, were fomented or funded by the merchant class or aristocracy. Thereto, the reasons as to the fomenting of said successful rebellions are typically tied up in reasons concerned with the protection of the merchant's tax exempt, or reduced tax, privileges or their shrewd tendencies in seeking opportunity to elevate their position at a time of perceivable meekness within the sovereign. For we can see throughout the revolutions of history – and current ones, be them social or military – a distinctive delineation between the reality and as to what the mythology constructed, postdate, the events state; this underlying delineation seems subtly intermixed in the halls of academia, especially if that academia be of a French or American disposition, of whose states were founded by their tradition of revolution. However, digressing, the mythology I speak of is one that paints a generalised picture, a fanciful tale, of recalcitrant patriotism unwilling to bend the knee to tyranny and oppression. Such mythology is politically advantageous to spin and certainly everyone likes an underdog character within a fight, especially if the underdog be your own kin or your extended kin - in the form of your nation and ancestors. The story is the same platitudinous and clichéd trite, the age-old David and Goliath story, an unlikely nation of hot-blooded patriots and men of true-grit and determination, typically paupers, best the superpower of the day, or the all-powerful overlord, and establish a benevolent republic; based on ideals of liberty and justice for all. However, the truth alas speaks contrary to the myth – as it always has.

Axiomatically, history shows that, for instance, the American revolution seems to have been headed by the colonial merchant class and eventually leadership extended to the preeminent military men and academics of the day, too. For example, the economically strangulating and intolerable taxes and Acts designed at further monopolisation of key industries, namely tea and British imports, by the Crown, led to the fomenting of revolutionary acts of protest famously encapsulated by the Boston Tea Party incident and the subsequent Boston Massacre[457]. Stemming primarily from Boston, this ardent anger at importation duties levied against the colonists soon spread to boycotts being administered under Colonial law within New York and Philadelphia[458]. As the revolutionary motto went; "No taxation, without representation" and how peculiar it is to see a revolution – of whom ostensibly championed metapolitical and moralist ideas of the enlightenment – concern themselves so heavily with the economic wrangling of taxation. Indeed, many merchants did lose money during the revolution and the USA was looming on bankruptcy before the turn of the ensuing century[459], but it does seem to me that there was a strong current of wealthy and influential individuals positioning themselves at the head of this idiosyncratic movement; namely *Benjamin Franklin, George Washington,*

---

[457] The American Revolution Reconsidered Author(s): Arthur Meier Schlesinger Source: *Political Science Quarterly*, Vol. 34, No. 1 (Mar., 1919), pp. 72 Published by: *The Academy of Political Science* Stable URL: https://www.jstor.org/stable/2141520 Accessed: 25/02/2021 19:07 UTC

[458] The Boston Post-Boy & Advertiser, John Rowe, The Boston-Gazette, & Country Journal, The Essex Gazette, The Boston Chronicle, Thomas Robie, et al. *Non-consumption and Non-importation* (2019). Available: https://www.masshist.org/revolution/non_importation.php. Last accessed 25/02/2021 19:50 UTC.

[459] Office of the Historian. (Unknown Date). U.S. Debt and Foreign Loans, 1775–1795. Available: https://history.state.gov/milestones/1784-1800/loans. Last accessed 05/03/2021.

Chapter VIII

Alexander Hamilton, to name but a very select few, of whom all had, to some degree, ties with the Colonial establishment and to London; some more than others, arguably. Most notably Franklin who seemed to hold membership of the London Hellfire Club[460], a cult that held debauched orgies and other carnal events for the pleasure of their members, and he furthermore owned property in London[461]; *George Washington*, on the other hand, was an esteemed British Commander, coming to prominence as a Lieutenant in the French-Indian War of 1754-1763; and *Alexander Hamilton* being the only individual whom had very little to do with the British establishment directly, bar being raised partially in Nevis, Leeward Islands, and he would later go onto found the Bank of New York and implement the first National Bank of the United States, under Washington; even though it was bitterly opposed and for good cause so. Many of the Founding Fathers were, as such, very much tied to the old mother country and or, had ulterior personal gains from the positive outcome of the revolution; most notably, Hamilton did exceedingly well in establishing himself as a banking and legal mogul within New York, with further political accolades to boot. Funnily enough too, most were lawyers, plantation owners, bankers, military men or had esteemed positions in their various fields – as I stated, they were the bourgeoise, the merchant class, or the upper-middle class respectively.

This history of protestation against the Crown actually goes far back to the "*Sons of Liberty*" movement, galvanised by the passage of the Stamp Act 1765; this would later culminate in the Boston Tea Party, as mentioned, but with other notable acts of insurrection such as The Gaspee Affair and the attack on John Malcolm, a loyalist customs official of Boston. The organisation, or movement was headed primarily by Samuel Adams and John Hancock, the former being a failed businessman and tax collector and aspiring politician and the latter being a businessman, respectively.

---

[460] Geoffrey Ashe (28-03-2000*). The Hell-Fire Clubs.* Cheltenham, Gloucestershire: The History Press. 121-123.
[461] Benjamin Franklin House. (Unknown Date). *Franklin & the House.* Available: https://benjaminfranklinhouse.org/the-house-benjamin-franklin/. Last accessed 05/03/2021.

Conversely, we have other rebellions post and pre formation of the United States in the, arguably pre-catalyst, event that was the War of Regulation in the Carolinas and the Whiskey Rebellion, during the presidency of George Washington. However, interestingly, these revolutions fizzled out swiftly and were ineffectual – actually they were little more than a peasant rabble roused by indignancy towards contemporary economic realities, to be frank. They were easily dispelled and the pattern consistent between them is this, that they lacked backing by any significant number of merchants, or other men of capital and wealth, and thus they failed to depose their overlords. Whereas, the American War of Independence was entirely a different beast, it had strong backing from members of the legal, merchant and academic professions; snowballing into support from foreign financiers in the form of Dutch lenders and France, which supported the revolution militarily and financially; to their eventual detriment.

If we consider the validity of this concept of merchants being the prime mover of revolution, to be true - and when the fiscal and tax policies of the overarching sovereign or government becomes too intolerable for this class, then that is the pivot point as to where revolutions have historically found their inception. Thus, with that in mind, let us look briefly at the complex circumstances of the French revolution and see if we cannot glean anything from this bloodied stain upon modern history. It has been said of the French revolution that it was largely a series of misidentified resentments and of conspiracy – both of the merchant and lower orders and of the nobility itself, against its Capetian king. Let us briefly look, beginning with the nobility, at the general funders of the revolution. *Duc- d'Orléans* and *Honoré Gabriel Riqueti, comte de Mirabeau*, were both members of the nobility, the former being a cousin to the reigning king, *Louis XVI*, and both played pivotal roles in not only bankrolling the revolution but also leading political sects of it[462]. It seems

---

[462] Mounier, Jean Joseph, *On the Influence Attributed to Philosophers, Free-Masons, and to the Illuminati on the Revolution of France* (Original Publishing 1801), facsimile reproduction with an introduction by Theodore A. DiPadove. Delmar, New York, Scholars' Facsimiles & Reprints, 1974, p.91 – p.155.

CHAPTER VIII

that the revolution was used as a form of power acquisition and a means of achieving a higher station, especially by *Duc- d'Orléans*, who renamed himself *Phillipe Egalite*, and we can glean this fact by the chants heard at the women's march of Versailles: "Long live our father, long live King d'Orléans!"[463]. He furthermore was accused of funding the riots, as well as calling the rioters his "friends", and this accusal came from the *Grand Châtelet*, a high-court within the Paris, additionally accusing him of acting in consort with *de Mirabeau* to conspire to kill the King, *Louis*, and his Queen, *Marie Antionette*[464]. It can be argued that this political debacle began largely as a palace revolution, rather than a spontaneous peasant rebellion. If we briefly look at the character of the *Marquis de Lafayette*, we find a previous revolutionary war-fighter – under the patronage and direct order of the French Monarch – in the American Revolutionary war; in fact, he would name his son *George Washington* and fought in mostly every major land engagement during the conflict. Moreover, he was from a family of extreme wealth hailing from Chavaniac, a province of Auvergne, and again, through his actions, seemed to seek a higher position of power in a constitutional monarchy. However, unlike some of the other members of the constitutional monarchist clique, he did not support *Phillipe Égalité* for this position – actually seeing him as largely weak and having very unworthy characteristics, not well-suited towards kingship. He would actually, to *Phillipe*'s later detriment, persuade *Phillipe* to flee France and seek the head-of-state position within Brabant (modern Belgium), which was in a revolutionary state at the time, the Brabantian revolution, and with much hesitation at first eventually agreed and left France. This, retrospectively, seems to me to be a carefully calculated move by *Lafayette* to take a greater share of power in controlling the direction of the revolution; as he controlled the *Garde Nationale*. However, *Jacobin* revolutionaries, mainly academic, *petit*

---

[463] Elder, Richard W. *The Duc d'Orleans, Patriot Prince or Revolutionary? an Investigation into the Chatelet Inquiry of 1789-1790*, Central Michigan University, Ann Arbor, 1994.
[464] Elder, Richard W. *The Duc d'Orleans, Patriot Prince or Revolutionary? an Investigation into the Chatelet Inquiry of 1789-1790*, Central Michigan University, Ann Arbor, 1994.

bourgeoise and journalists in status, managed to sway the country into adopting republicanism after the *Champ de Mars* massacre – of which *Lafayette* was the leading commander in. This led to the overwhelming vote in favour of convicting and executing the King and Queen and eventually instituting the aptly named "Reign of Terror". Personally, and this is just an opinion of mine, of which I most assuredly cannot back with concrete evidence, but I would surmise that this revolution was simply a ploy by leading nobles and the Second- and Third-Estates to rebirth the French nation into a British-style constitutional monarchy, however with their political mismanagement of the situation – and with the influence of external powers in subverting the mob, such as the *Jacobins* – we find the situation quickly escalated and devolved into chaos. This conglomerate of men, of whom were outwardly a remanent of the *Ancien Régime*, were referred to as the Society of 1789, or the Patriotic Society of 1789, of which split from the more radical *Jacobin Club* early on; and of whom, in time the *Jacobins* would come to loathe as a past vestige of the monarchical regime.[465]

France at the beginning of the revolutionary period was a state of the precipice of ruin. The royal and state expenditure on ill-conceived and costly wars and on personal displays of exuberant wealth was hampering the national coffers. The room provided to the *Controller-General of Finances* and *Finance Minister*, under *Jacque Necker* for implementation of increased taxation to afford all of these prior and current wasteful policies was not present, due to a multitude of unfortunate compounding economic factors that left the nobility and *bourgeoise* classes unwilling to pay higher taxes and the peasantry incapable of even doing so. Largely, these compounding factors can be boiled down to the disastrous harvest in 1788, of which left the price of grain and thus bread at an unfeasibly high level. After the deregulation of the grain market, suspiciously

---

[465] FROM THE LECTURE SERIES: THE REAL HISTORY OF SECRET SOCIETIES. (2020). *Benjamin Franklin's Masonic Connection and Jacobin Reign of Terror*. Available: https://www.thegreatcoursesdaily.com/benjamin-franklins-masonic-connection-and-jacobin-reign-of-terror/. Last accessed 05-03-2021.

by the Constituent Assembly, two days proceeding the passage of the *Declaration of the Rights of Man and of the Citizen*, thus naturally leading to fears of exportation, hoarding and artificial price manipulation – of which, it seems that there is some proof of. However, this led to the infamous declaration within the radical revolutionary media, as faux as our media today, that the hated Austrian *Marie Antionette* stated in response to a question that the peasants have not even a crumb of bread to eat, of which she is alleged to have responded "Well, let them eat cake then". This has been largely concluded, in today's scholarly circles, as mere propaganda designed to whip up hatred for the monarchy amongst the lower orders[466]. Moreover, the artificial shortage of bread being a fact, seems to hold merit in the fact that within the *Plot drawn up a Passy*, in 1789, the alleged second article states "do everything in our power to ensure that the lack of bread is total, so that the bourgeoisie are forced to take up arms." Shortly thereafter the storming of the Bastille commenced[467]. The radicals, who formulated this rebellious plan, were obviously acutely aware of the fact revolutions require the backing of the middle or entrepreneurial classes.

Therefore, one may ask, what was the conditions that led to the outbreak of the revolution? Unlike in the American context of revolution, France was, to demonstrable magnitude, undoubtedly a fertile ground for the ensuing of internal strife. It had suffered a mismanaged economy, was on the brink of bankruptcy due to generations of costly wars and funding of frivolous public works, was suffering logistical issues and food shortages, and the political landscape was fracturing immensely due to internal friction between the many competing powers. Thus, one may conclude that the French revolution was an inevitability during May,

---

[466] Una McIlvenna. (2018). *How Marie Antoinette's Legacy Was Sullied by Vicious Songs About Her Death*. Available: https://www.history.com/news/marie-antoinette-death-myths-execution-ballads. Last accessed 05-03-2021.
[467] Montjoie, Christophe Flix Louis Ventre de la Touloubre, called Galart de. (republished 1833 (Original 1796)). *Conjuration de Louis-Philippe-Joseph d'Orléans, surnomme Egalité*. Paris: Chez G.-A. Dentu, Impremeur Libraire. p.12-p.13.

1789[468]; due to compounding insurmountable factors not in the control of the state, but some may argue to the contrary. However, one may wonder as to where these aforesaid impoverished masses managed to accrue the fiscal and logistical means to supply their burgeoning revolution? The answer is quite a multivariable one, it has to be said. I have detailed the above Third- and Second-Estate figures who still possessed the means to fund such a growing revolution, but proceeding on from the "Reign of Terror", approximately 1793 to 1794, most of these individuals had duly departed their once unassailable political positions – and their funding and participation alone could not have mobilised the means as to overthrow even a weakened Capetian monarchy, even if they had wanted to. Thus, this must lead us naturally to understand who funded the radical *Jacobin* movement, then? The fathers of the Terror and of whom had a heterogenous membership of half-a-million at the turn of the revolution. It could not have been the constitutional monarchists, as they were largely opposed ideologically to the republican ideals of the *Jacobins* and splintered from them early on. Thus, we must find our answer in the other cryptic powers who drove a population mad and sullied the image of the monarchy, as to fuel hatred amongst the First-Estate. The *Jacobin Club* had its origins in a secret association of politicians within Brittany, of whom held their various memberships of quasi-secret societies, including freemasonry, and this would later spread and become very influential amongst not just the nobility but the peasantry too[469]. Many *Jacobins* were Freemasons; the *Duc- d'Orléans, Camille Desmoulins, Mirabeau*, and *Jean-Paul Marat* to name a few; even *Dr. Joseph-Ignace Guillotin*, inventor of the symbol of the revolution, was a freemason, a member of the Nine Sisters Lodge, and *Jacobin* too[470]. This *Jacobin* club goes back to the Bavarian Illuminati and *Weisshaupt*[471], of whose plans were exposed and

---

[468] F.A Mignet (2012). *Histoire de la Révolution Française: depuis 1796 jusqu'en 1814 (Ed. 1824)*. Paris: HACH.LIVRE-BNF.
[469] Kennedy, Michael L., "The Foundation of the Jacobin Clubs and the Development of the Jacobin Club Network, 1789-1791," Journal of Modern History, 51 (Dec., 1979) p.703.
[470] Jasper Ridley, *The Freemasons*, London: Constable, 1999, pp. 136-137.
[471] O.A. Platonov, Терновый Венец России (*Russia's Crown of Thorns*), Moscow: Rodnik,

Chapter VIII

punished duly in Austria in 1788, but it is unclear as to say the origins of their funding – as they kept the membership fee very low, only one *livre* per annum, of which was hardly enough to fund a revolution the likes of which Europe had never borne witness too. I would speculate, if I may be afforded the luxury too, that Swiss bankers and the wealthy freemasons – enlightenment revolutionaries - throughout Europe, which seemed to wish for a de-Christianised Europe in this period and an advent of an age of enlightened reason and utopianism – of which I have detailed as to the history and tradition of earlier in the book – and we can see this within *Maximillien Robespierre*'s push for the implementation of the Cult of Reason and then eventually, the Cult of the Supreme Being; of which was later proscribed by *Napoleon Bonaparte*, Emperor of the French.

Moreover, I simply wish to conclude this with a brief look at the splintering of the *Jacobin Club*, which is something that will lead you, the reader, to understand the panoramic story of the revolution from a better vantage point. The *Girondin*, the relative moderates, and the *Montagnards*, the more radical element, and this has a comparative example in the Mensheviks and the Bolsheviks some one-hundred-and-fifty years later in the Russian revolution of 1917. *Robespierre* was a *Montagnards* and as such the "Reign of Terror" was largely a purge of the political opposition of *Girondin* associates and other pro-constitutional-monarchists[472]. As a tangential but also comparative side point, the English Civil War steered sagaciously by *Cromwell* and of the October Revolution of 1917, of which was financed in large part by "Wallstreet" Western Capitalists[473], we find in no small part that the general inflaming of pre-existing conditions was financed and directed by either external enemies, or the academic or entrepreneurial classes. Predominantly, it may be pronounced, that all of these monarchical depositions were devised by utopian idealists, of whom

---

1998, Pg. 195
[472] Jones, Peter. 2003. *The French Revolution 1787–1804*. Pearson Education. p. 57.
[473] *Wall Street and the Bolshevik Revolution: The Remarkable True Story of the American Capitalists Who Financed the Russian Communists (2012)*. Antony C. Sutton. West Hoathly, West Sussex: Clairview Books. p.16, p.173-174.

were vastly to be found within the entrepreneurial and academic classes, of whom held in their hearts, for ideological and temporal reasons, the desire to engage in the despoilation of the old-order; to fashion from the chaos, an order made anew.

ON DOMESTICATION

The prison is not around you; it is within you. We enslave ourselves due to our inability to think rationally when ordered to become hysterical with fear, by large media conglomerates and governments; who have all been captured by large corporations with ulterior and insidious motives. Induced fear, into the masses that is, is what perpetuates and furthers the stranglehold on power the government seeks to maintain. Without fear, of them and existential threats, contrived or otherwise, how could they possibly maintain the profitable protection racket they have created for themselves? They could not, the citizenry would become less shackled to the government; as the populace clings to them as a frightened child clings to a parent, in times of trouble, again contrived or otherwise.

Have you noticed in the modern-era that education, intellectual aptitude, and general attention-spans have greatly diminished, on average? That is, with the various mind-numbing social media trawling (TikTok, Snapchat, etc) and the quotidian consumerist culture (various sociological studies purport to the negative effects news-feed and social-media binging has on cognition and memory), that it was designed to create a population of narcissistic, self-obsessed, braindead and dependent individuals; of whom think not too deeply about issues, but accept them at face value, as reported by the media (authority figure).

This is why the government encouraged this avenue of technological adaptation - that is, the internet was envisioned to be by its founders, at least universally anyway, a means of elevating the population through the democratisation of knowledge, and education; now look at it.

Although, we may look at it this way conversely, cattle-farmers since the dawn of civilisation have been selectively-breeding the prey we once upon a time hunted, extensively. What trait did they specifically selectively-breed for, at least at the genesis stages? Docility. They selected for docility. Why? Simply put, the ultimate aim of predation is the utter enfeeblement of the prey; to facilitate domestication, they must have no outward defence-mechanism against the aforesaid predation. Hence, this is the same reason governments throughout history have sought policies of inducing docility or domestication en masse, it ensures that a more efficient slave-class is brought into existence. That is, they do not wish for critical-thinkers, they wish for obedient automatons. Just smart enough to run the machines (until universal automation), and dumb enough to tacitly accept every infringement and dismantling of their rights.

Thus, we can say it is not the population's fault for acting like medieval zealots on the hunt for witches, or those wicked souls in league with devils, they have been conditioned for obedience to orders. "Spreader" or "Denier" is tantamount to "Witch" or "heretic"; same tone, different vernacular. Thus, the media command one thing, and the obedient populace seeks the enforcement of conformity, to the said command.

Comically, sheep are far more astute than us; at least they require to be herded by a shepherd or a dog, we simply herd ourselves.

On Hate Crime Legislation

The hubris of the state believing it can legislate away specific emotions. Simply by the act of criminalising it, evermore strictly ad infinitum, does not end divisiveness and hate within society. That being, it does not change the mind of the individual who may hold prejudicial views, it simply isolates them even further from society, and thus, this reinvigorates their misguided prejudice even further; "if they are censoring me, then what I say must be true"; this is how you breed insane militants, not how you rehabilitate their derangement. Accordingly, if these types of individuals were engaged in rational debate, in a public forum, and the marketplace of ideas was allowed to act freely, then I dare say that prejudice would be entirely routed out from society, on all sides. The right to robust and rigorous dialogue upon sensitive issues is the mark of a Democracy; if that is disallowed, we should then dispose of the verbiage of referring to ourselves as a Democracy.

Digressing, similar debates in public forums occurred during the push for the abolishment of slavery, thus it ensured by the end of the 19th century a majority of the public were opposed to slavery; on moral, ethical, and even economically pragmatic grounds.

Though, the government are fully aware of all of this and certainly do not want to be rid of divisiveness within society; divide and conquer is their lifeblood; it would be akin to a Human demanding the abolishment of air, it would be utterly counter-intuitive to the acknowledged maxim of self-preservation. However, it is clear that this is not some moralist stance by the government, but an avenue in which the state can begin encroaching upon the right to freedom of expression. Much in the same way they have disabused you of the right to freedom of assembly, through the guise of mitigating a pandemic, so too shall they disabuse you of the right to freedom of expression under the guise of protecting you from hate (or [insert some other terrible bogeyman that will get you, if you do not acquiesce to state control]).

Thusly, it can be said, they pose these pretences to the public in the form of inarguable premises or irrefutable generalisations - other fallacious argumentation they utilise is Appeal to Authority and argumentum ad populum (argument from the majority). That being, arguments the normal person cannot refute because to do so would be to commit social-suicide and become ostracised; due to the premises being of a distinctly "controversial" nature.

As a quick side-note, if one looks at the *Lex Maiestatis*, the Roman Empire had similar encroachments upon freedom of speech at its terminus; its initial legal passage was conducted under the guise of stopping libel and slander.

CHAPTER VIII

A Thousand Points of Light

"A Thousand Points of Light", a predictive piece of imagery spoken within the famous speech of President George H.W. Bush on the coming "New World Order"; spoken fortuitously on September 11th 1990, a coincidence, I am sure. For what this "New World Order" entailed was rather unclear at the time and I suspect it was made intentionally so. For reasons pertaining to treason, that being for a sitting President to openly espouse loyalty to the long-term objectives of a higher temporal power other than the US can be resolutely determined as treason, of the highest order. However, what does this poetically cryptic phrase mean – it is the centrepiece of the speech nonetheless – and why does he espouse such an assured spirit in the achievement of the New World Order; for he bluntly remarked "And when we are successful, and we will be". We will discuss this topic and furthermore the supranational power that exists above governments, corralling them into lockstep policies; national constitutions being no obstacle to their unbridled agenda for the establishment of total, world dominion.

The phraseology "the illumination of a Thousand Points of Light", evokes the image of the merchant-class's hubris, in that they believe they illuminate these "a thousand points of light". Or the countries, organisations and society itself, will be illuminated, or brought to heel, by them; the capstone of supranational organisations who wield unseen power above governments; the collectivists who for centuries have been busily putting into place the perfect conditions to implement a planned society. I have detailed this previously with the historical works of *Plato, Thomas Mores, Tommaso Campanella*. However, *Aldous Huxley*'s work "Brave New World" and *H.G. Wells* "Shape of Things to Come", the 1939 motion-picture entitled "Things to Come" based off the same *Wells* novel, and we also may include the famous book "1984", by *Orwell*. These well-connected authors all discussed the world to come under the disguise of "science-fiction", much akin to *Plato, Mores* and *Campanella*'s discussions of likewise collectivist utopias; under the antiquated disguise of dialogues.

This foretold planned society, as portrayed by these authors, paints an image of a future where the human spirit will be broken and in its place a transhumanist construct would exist, that would be bereft of soul and the ability to contemplate the world in any great depth. A mere simple machine to be uploaded with a program through chemical or bio-digital means, if you will. As we can bear witness to, this world is gradually coming into view and the technology is there now to implement such a perfect slave-system (see the advent and rapidly developing field of *Nanobioelectronics*, of which will be implantable, injectable, and some will be mesh-implants which will attached to musculature and organic tissue). Parallels may be drawn to this modern-day axiom, or adage, "build back better"; and all governments have started enunciating this catchphrase and most have worn or wear the small pin emblazoned with the symbol of the UN's Agenda 2030, of which is another one of these stepping-stones to world dominion. These governments work in lockstep with each other, it would seem, and this is obviously emblematic of some higher power orchestrating them.

What do these higher powers wish for? They wish to extend their oligopoly, or market monopoly in colloquial speech, to a societal-wide monopoly. They will monopolise life, so to say. They will guide reproduction, ensure that a rigid class structure is maintained, eventually they will assign the digitally-infused automatons jobs as per the merchant-classes needs, and they will ensure that no divergent thought, any small budding flower of liberty, be allowed room to thrive. This will be accomplished via the digitisation of society, "The internet of things" as it is called and this is the ability for them to track your thoughts, feelings, purchases etc. *Edward Snowden* talked about this and described it as "the architecture of oppression", of which your entire life will be spent within a panopticon, a prison. The lockdowns are the gradual phasing in of this type of draconian policy; along with the "Contact Tracing" and the proliferation of Social-media, they are conditioning you to relinquish the last vestiges of privacy you have left.

How can this be, I hear you say? Well, imagine if you will, for a moment, what direction would you say the pathway of technological progression is going to take? Will it become a vehicle for the strengthening of free-thought and individualism under the current regime? Or, will it become an agent of further centralisation and stamping out of those who are "seekers of truth"; seekers of the knowledge that allows one to transcend this world system, this prison without visible bars. Such individuals, who contemplate the breadth of truth, care not for social stigmatisation or ostracisation, they go beyond that and as such, if they possess aptitudes in leadership and oration, can pose a danger to the regime. Additionally, we can see that technology is becoming steadily ingrained in our very existence, technology has become a part of us, specifically digital technology and devices – we are dependent on them – and this has been entirely by design. They are becoming closer and closer to us, closer to our minds and eventually they will be implanted sub-dermally and then, attached to our brains and inevitably will comprise the various limbs and organs of our body. We will become machines, with machine souls and machine minds. More animated construct rather than man in the flesh. Our body and mind envisioned by the cold inventiveness of digital-artificers; imbued with a clinical disposition on life. Our humanity, flaws and all, will be lost to the ravages of "progress"; we will bear the eternal mantel of drone.

Though, we may miraculously overturn this state of affairs, it looks increasingly likely that it will be a small minority that emerges from the other side unaltered, but mentally scathed. The majority are lemmings, they will tread the path of least resistance, all the way over the cliff and to the sudden-stop at the bottom. The reason for this is that the ingestion of mindless propaganda has left the lemming consequentially stolen of mind, a mere husk of where once dwelt a man, they lack foresight and the adeptness to reason laterally. They are the living, breathing embodiment of fear and apathy; they want for little, but endless consumerism and vacuous gestures of goodwill. Thus, they have become bloated on indoctrination and it has rotted their cognition; they are the similitude of the medieval fanatic and mark my words, as per the cabalistic pattern of history, you will find that before the dust settles the ones hesitant to prostrate themselves, to the superstitions peddled by the state – vaccine, progress, tolerance, diversity, socialism, etc – will find themselves dragged out of their homes beaten, humiliated, tried in a kangaroo-court, and executed as a heretic of the state. Thus, this will be the culmination of the "illumination of a thousand points of light", the total victory of the collectivised machine state over the Human spirit yearning for freedom. "A jackboot stomping on a Human face forever".

These coming atrocities against the minority, will be carried out by everyday people because they will be whipped up into a frenzy by the media, they will become hysterical with anger; because if you do not follow the orthodoxy, if you do not take that vaccine, then "you are putting everyone's life in danger; my life, my children's life, because society is an interdependent collective. If you do not take the shot then you may be a spreader; if you do not champion progressive values, then you may be a racist!". As you can see, we are dealing with a societal-wide cult, and social stigmitisation and abuse of the minority are typical tactics utilised in war and instances of social engineering.

As *H.G. Wells* nonchalantly remarked "Countless people will hate the New World Order and will die protesting against it…we have to bear in mind the distress of a generation or so of malcontents".[474]

The Strange Light of Hope

"Paráxeno phos elpídas" (παράξενο φως ελπίδας), Greek for the "strange light of hope", is a phrase I would like to utilise in regards to what I

---
[474] Wells, H. G. (1940). *The new world order: Whether it is attainable, how it can be attained, and what sort of world a world at peace will have to be.* London: Secker & Warburg. Pg. 111.

am about to say regarding our future, and to the solutions one may contemplate. I will not lie to you, the world that lies before us is one which will try men's souls, which will break us down and rebirth us anew; the very synthesis of the meaning of "trial-by-fire". Though, one may be dismayed at this inexorable prospect, I would argue that this is the opportunity of a lifetime – of several for that matter – that though the walls may feel like they are closing in, within that constriction is a falsity of circumstance. That being, we are actually being tacitly granted freedom within this labyrinthian-like scheme. Why do I say that? Within the final days, as we see now, where this world ends and another breathes its first breaths of life, we are beginning to see the curtain fall; the immersion of our illusion is slowly drifting to sober realisation, and that the actors on the stage have discarded of their veneer. This is the age of revelation, where the illusory nature of our reality that we have been embroiled in, is beginning to become undone; and within the mad-dash for global dominion, the merchants of chaos have galvanised a sizeable enough number of the populace into pulling apart the threads of the fabric, of this matrix-like reality. This is the genesis-point, the primordial beginnings of a divergence within our species, that being the bifurcation between the vaccinated and the non-vaccinated will become more and more apparent. Accordingly, this is not just in terms of the potential physiological changes derived from the vaccines, but from the psychological changes witnessed within the vaccinated stemming from the lockdowns. Subsequently, they have shown themselves to be mere animal; lacking soul and reacting only to external stimuli, in the moment, as it is delivered to them via the media. They are the literal embodiment of the aptly titled "NPC": the living, breathing simulacrum of sentient-life but lacking all of the crucial components of sentience. We now see these people for who and what they are; the individuals who attack you for "not wearing your mask properly", the individuals who have snitched on you, and the ones one who will out you as a "non-vaccinated". These individuals have little substance to them, they are simply an animated corpse bereft of a soul.

For, it is that, a battle between the ones with souls and sentience and the ones who bear no soul. Thus, the soulless husks are terrified that their moral-compass will point somewhere else other than due North, to their cardinal point, where ensues the seeking of momentary pleasure at the expense of us all. That said, they fear death; even those among them who are ostensibly braced by religious conviction. This is an advantage to us, that you now know these people, you have met them, and now you can steer clear of them; do not engage in business with them, do not talk to them and to the best of your ability, detach yourself from these soulless entities. Encourage them also to take the vaccine, individuals who are not receptive to understanding the gravity of the situation, nor the evidence, have little merit in staying within this reality to wage this struggle against our tormentors. Conversely, the ones who remain must be our own intellectual kin, they must understand the situational variables that are arrayed against a free-humanity.

As another point, a solution that offers its hand to us all, is the fact that we can circumvent the system by simply growing our own food and engaging in a secondary- or grey-market structure. What does that look like when applied in practise, I hear you say? *Agorism*, as it is termed, and of which I have previously alluded to within this work, is as simple as growing your own potatoes, to as complex as creating systems of providing goods and services that is out with the remit of the system's taxing-tentacles. This may be crypto-currency based or barter-based, but it must deny sustenance to the system; that being, your productivity and labour through taxation and exchange of your services. This is far more practicable within the vast territories of North-America, but can see small-scale application within the European theatres and international scene, of which I am less familiar with I must admit. The growing of food will be integral in the days to come and, if the patterns stay consistent with what we are seeing, then the logistical apparatus of the state will begin breaking down. In this breakdown, the agriculturist will take on a powerful role within the community – historically, the first rise of "kings" could be traced back to this agricultural revolution within our species' history – and will be a veritable shepherd amongst a flock of lost sheep; this will ensure a localisation of power occurs into small states and counties, since the centralised government is without the means to enforce their will. These soulless individuals, of which I have alluded to, will instantly change their opinions upon the pandemic and centralised government if they dwell in these local principalities or inner-enclaves, so to say. However, if circumstance permits, they should be ostracised rather than aided due to the fact that they carry within them a "slave mentality" and as such are easily swayed by whoever wields the power of authority; this type of gullibility is dangerous and must be routed out from a civilised and liberty-loving society. Digressing, this logistical breakdown will most likely stem from the rising gasoline prices and the macro-economic effects of the current abnormalities, shall we say, in the bond markets; and the consequential effects that will be felt from that, resulting in higher inflation. These are naturally, to the perceptive, issues that compound the negative effects of each other. This will result in, most likely, an unravelment of society and this will lead the ruling-class to act in desperation; which always leads to some form of atrocity committed in an attempt to maintain power, thus insurgencies will spring forth and compel the government to focus on that, rather than solving the underlying systemic problem caused by their initial bureaucratisation and market manipulation.

To our brethren who dwell in the USA, of whom can bear arms, then it is a fairly prudent idea to stock up on said armaments and subsequent cartridges where lawfully possible, to ensure you can weather any potential civil breakdown; work within the law in your respective states or nations, internationally speaking, to ensure you can defend your property in the event of calamitous disorder, once society starts to unravel itself. Moreover, learn the skills that can sustain you in a state without modern amenities, for this is crucial beyond reproach, that you must become like your forebears did; hardy and enterprising. Furthermore, engage in preparatory action such as learning skills in electrical maintenance and repair, construction, plumbing, farming, rearing livestock, hunting, field-dressing and butchery, and fabrication of tools. Above all, your mind must become as sharp as a blade – it is a necessity that it must be able to cut through any false doctrine or artful lie that comes before it – it must understand its purpose and how to achieve it; this will allow you to cultivate and strengthen your resolve, and as such your sanity, which will be the most integral tool for your survival. Begin by reading *Marcus Aurelius, Meditations,* and understand his exhortations and reflections upon the transitory nature of life and eventually death; and contemplate your purpose in this existence and learn to relinquish the fear of your own mortality, for without this fear you will gradually fear nothing. Couple this with taking solace within your God or Gods, that after this life you may not wither to nothing be reborn anew, in a world beyond this; where you shall be rewarded for your diligence and dutifulness. If you are agnostic, then take solace in understanding that your essence and energy will be subsumed into the Whole, into nature, or providence, where it will live on for eternity and will breathe new life into this existence; just as your choices in life breathed life into the new expressions of divinity and beauty around you. Lastly, learn to harness the power of your body and to use it to best accomplish the challenges that will face you; begin with jumping rope every day for fifteen-minutes, then thirty-minutes and eventually, if time permits, begin to incorporate push-up and pull-up challenges within your routine. Above all, be agile on your feet and strong within your heart; be without fear of this world or the world beyond, it is how they enslave your lesser fellows, nonetheless; be in this world but not of it; and be the bedrock of a new and brighter future, through the new skills you will learn and develop.

In conclusion, use this opportunity afforded to you within this transitionary period wisely; forge alliances and found a brotherhood of fellowship with our common kin. Become kinder to your brethren and fellow countryman, of whom may be still brought to reason, but do not proselytise to them and do not seek hope within any worldly saviour; you must find that within yourself and of providence, which resides within us all. You must become a beacon of hope and strength to the world, you must proclaim that the Human spirit does not lie broken and bloodied, that it is alive and endures; and that the fires of this war will only temper our resolve to bring forth a better world for those that proceed us. You must decry the tyranny and corruption when you witness it, and you must never bend the knee no matter the pressure; for if you do, you will lose your soul and integrity, and without those life is merely existence. For with a thousand small actions of resistance, as I have explained, we can tear down this edifice of decay and supplant it with the hope of liberty for all. Stand tall compatriots, for a new day is dawning and like a phoenix rising, refreshed, from the ashes of despair, we shall lift our great nations to new heights in a world far beyond the reach of tyranny and decay. Hope is far from lost; it is simply awaiting its cue for entry.

THE PIPER COMES A CALLING

Lo, do hear the piper's Call.
Bustling and stirring from there out, the city walls.
The wrinkle of lip, the whistle of air,
The casting of you to the Demon's lair.
The Burghers, whom did not pay the sum,
Now heareth, the greedy scoundrels, the Siren's hum.
Their precious futures led torn astray,
By the merry piper's charming fay.

The current economic and political wrangling within the West, specifically the USA, is something akin to a child wishing to touch an open flame just to see what may happen. Naturally, to the rest of the adult world, we all understand what will be borne out of such a looming disaster. Thus, there is very much a compendium of issues to cover within the context of the present time and none of them shall bear any good fruits from their inevitable outcomes; unless you are China or one of the other rising powers in the East, of course. Conversely, news events such as the Suez Canal blocking, ostensibly accidental albeit, the continued lockdowns, and coming inflation and the signs of that within the bond market – to name but a few events – are all indicative of the proverbial sowing of the seeds of self-destruction. This section will not be brief, and will tackle major sequestered issues, at present, mainly concerning the subject of economics; and the future thereof.

To begin, if we may look at the current discombobulation within the bond markets, we see a sure-sign that the long-term economic outlook of the US is bleak and that the forty-year bull-market within bonds is most assuredly over. Many are stating, most notably the Bank of America, that within the next ten to twenty years, with the changing economic landscape, that the deflationary assets that were doing so well up to this point – bonds, government bonds, etc – will begin to subside, in terms of pitiful yield offerings, and inflationary assets such as commodities, real estate, etc will begin to eclipse these other aforementioned assets. Why is this? Well, the yields upon bonds are down and with the real inflation rates, of which are probably well into the 10-13% range at this point, and with the exponential credit expansion, will eat away at any potential yield derived from bonds. What does this mean for the economic outlook? It means that the low interest rates that allowed the US to expand credit in times of economic turmoil and fiscal issues, is gone and the room for decreasing the interest rates any lower is not there; unless, negative interest rates are devised but there are a multitude of issues with such an unprecedented concept. Digressing, the central banks around the globe have been instrumental in maintaining these artificially low interest rates, through the acquisition of these bonds, or currency in its infancy, through purchases conducted via credit expansion. However, this credit expansion typically does not trickle down into the other intermediary financial institutions and to the public, as we are seeing now with UBI and quarterly fiscal stimulus, thus it has negligible effect upon consumer inflation, but effects real-estate price and security price inflation, as we have seen. Once this artificial squeezing of interest rates is unable to be continued, due to the market demanding unattainable yields, proportional to perceived or real inflation, and the central banks unable to simply create credit into the system, to cover up the cracks (as we know, this central bank credit is naturally deflationary as per its low velocity), then we may see higher interest rates as a by-product of this breakdown in the bond market. If this occurs, that is higher interest rates are realised, then the entire global economy may as well pull the pin pre-emptively; because it will trigger massive sell-offs of US securities, I can imagine, and insolvency will hit the West and the East too. Of which the latter may emerge the last nation standing; though such a victory would be pyrrhic in nature.

This potential issue facing the West, economically, is one that is rooted in the *Thucydides' Trap* and we are beginning to see a more isolationist policy, both geopolitically and economically, from the US; the Chinese are responding in kind by beginning to move their economic reliance, on the US-China trade imbalance, to a more equitable arrangement that reflects more accurately their long-term interests. The US is further contracting in an ever-tangible sense, demographically and economically too. The excesses of the American public seem recalcitrant to contract though and we are seeing thus a strong push for the implementation of perpetual UBI; not quarterly, not monthly, but weekly, and in excessive amounts that would make the rest of the world's jaws collectively hit the floor in shock. Moreover, within the economic space of the digital-age, with the threat of overreaching and out-of-control government, we are seeing the divergence of the economic base with the advent and popularisation of cryptocurrency and block-chain. The new generation that is beginning to inherit this dishevelled and broken world are slowly turning away from the orthodox economic systems of their forebears, and instead are circumventing the power of the West by attacking its mainstay weapon; tax revenue and traceability of accounts. This creates a specific problem for government or Treasury bonds, as the main collateral backing them is a percentage portion of projected future tax revenue. Incidentally, we see that there are two options facing the US with these compounding of fiscal and economic issues; one is to rein in spending and to contract in the short-term to then compete with China industrially, in the long-term, or instead become belligerent and follow the predictable path of the trap of *Thucydides*. However, they have chosen the latter, as per Biden's recent threats to Putin and continued sanctions on the East. Thus, the US will undoubtedly lose this coming conflict with China and the East and I would strongly recommend the future individuals within that chaos, created as a by-product in that war-time scenario, use those prevailing circumstances wisely to topple the regime of Washington; and in its place, hopefully, a reinvigorated Republic stands tall once more.

As a diverging thought, we can see specifically with the Federal Reserve a strong and outward push to prop up the bond and securities market; for example, we see the perpetual UBI provided, of which I will discuss the importance of this in due time, and the balance sheet of the Federal Reserve rising to 22% as compared to last year's 13%. Moreover, income is up 14% from last year, funnily enough, and 20% of all income in the US is covered by the government; through the banking cartel, naturally. As a side note, the upper echelons of society who are receiving these stimulus cheques (income above $120,000 per annum), 79% of whom are using this fiscal receipt to speculate in the markets; as compared to the lower echelons (income below $30,000 per annum), 53% of whom, once food is covered use the rest on rent and energy. The inequalities are apparent obviously, but the point is that the stock market is going to explode in market capitalisation; it will literally be the biggest bubble to ever have been created in the history of bubbles; though central banks are "forever blowing bubbles", are they not? Furthermore, we see the smart-money starting to move into cryptocurrency, hence the meteoric rise in the price of Bitcoin, and the more patient smart-money is moving into gold and silver, respectively. As you can see, the central banks are busily trying to prop up this sinking ship with much the same failed policies, but it will be ultimately futile. In conjunction, we find that there is a vigorous and emergent push to cancel rents, student debt, mortgages, etc by the government – however, it will be the future projected tax revenue which will pay the lenders of these debts. Therefore, are you slowly starting to see what is occurring here? State-ownership of everything. I will detail this in parallel with what is beginning to be seen within the gene-altering technology witnessing applications on the populace, and the food supply; and where this is ultimately leading to.

As we see within the cartel-like, global Ponzi scheme, of the central banks there is a strong emphasis on maintaining the coordination of interest rate amendments and incremental credit expansion; we see what happens when an entity, be it political or financial, attempts to break away from the perceived monetary hegemony within the 2012 Libyan ousting of Ghaddafi. Thus, we find that this cooperation allows the central banks to collectively shield themselves from a unilateral collapse of the global order, as all of the various central banks are implementing the same policies and running their specific node of the racket in a similar fashion to all of the other neighbouring nodes. However, what is beginning to occur is a slow diverging of interests geopolitically and domestically; hence, this cooperation is slowly becoming eroded by competing interests that do not run in tandem with one another. Bitcoin and the rise of China are a stellar example of this, but many investors are beginning to see, with the furthering growth of the credit expansion, low interest rates at present and the increasingly optimistic view of inflationary assets long-term, the borrowing of low-interest credit in exchange for inflationary assets as a viable investing option long-term; cryptocurrency being a salient example of this. In conjunction, this causes real issues for the US economy and global economy as it enhances this divergence into other alternative forms of currency, that circumvents the central banks control; it is a speculative assault on the edifice of the global economic hegemony, in many ways. If one is deriving only, say, 1.6% yield on a bond then why hold that when cryptocurrency could yield hundreds of percent in a shorter time horizon? It is a no-brainer trade, naturally. Therefore, it would seem that the central banks, especially within the Western context, have created an impetus for investors to be bankrolled with credit in exchange for attacking the economic status quo of whom furnished that said credit; it is laughably paradoxical but nevertheless a predictable outcome. As mentioned, the central banks seem to be attacking themselves with this, as the more stimulus money poured into Bitcoin or Precious Metals, will only require further printing by the said central banks to stimulate increased currency velocity within the ailing economy. However, that said, I think they understand that the increased velocity of currency, coming out from this lockdown, will lead to huge increases in inflation, I will detail this soon. We are beginning to see this with durable good price increases and construction materials, in some capacity, widely fluctuating in price, week in and week out – thus making quotes and tenders difficult to accurately produce for clients – and within the Chapwood inflation index, inflation is not 1-2% but around 10-13%, as I have detailed prior.

Additionally, it would seem though that there is somewhat an implied desire by certain monied interests to actually artificially induce food shortages and increased consumer inflation. We see with the current Suez Canal event, and it seems suspiciously fabricated I might add, has led to a lowering of Bitcoin and an increased threat of inflation within the consumer market. Furthermore, during the beginning of this pandemic event we saw the drumming up within the media of fear about shortages; thus, the populace bought goods en masse that they did not actually require at that point in time. Moreover, it would seem that the bond markets are signalling, in response, that there will be very high inflation in the future; and it is not a case of if, it is a case of when. This will distort the geopolitical order and reshape it. I would state though, that it would seem a financial implosion is being slowly crafted and induced at this moment in time; for it seems to be known by the architects of the "Great Reset", that the only way to implement such a slave-system would be to create a state of affairs so monstrously threatening, to the average person, that they would gladly relinquish their freedoms and liberties for that small economic security; perceived or real. Thus, it may be that we find induced hyperinflation occurs as a pretext for the central banks, through the apparatus of the state and the puppet-leaders, to decree that if the populace would only adopt the digital currency, state-ownership of everything, gene-therapy through vaccinations, and increased controls upon capital movements within the economy, then they will be saved from this dire state of affairs. It is a potential option. Furthermore, we see a continuation of lockdown policy wholesale across the Western world – why is this? Simply put, economically speaking that is, if we were to come out of lockdown now and with all the saved-up capital and accrued profits from these various speculative investments, we would spend like madness had taken over us. This would drive consumer inflation to new heights through the abnormally steep rise in the velocity of currency; the supportive economic apparatus and logistical network would be stretched thin, due to the hit they took during the lockdown periods. The central banks, to deaccelerate this coming economic growth, which left unregulated would lead to a bubble or economic burnout, would be ultimately forced to raise interest rates. As I detailed previously, if interest rates were raised, as they should actually, then the US and global economy would implode due to the incidental difficulty in meeting the interest requirements of the debt; this would trigger a loss of confidence within the US and within the decade, wars would be waged by emerging nations set on forging a new unipolar world order.

Conversely, if I may elucidate upon the corporate aspect of this, we see that the corporate oligarchy that has been raised up within the Western world is one that increasingly wishes to maintain and strengthen its power, through means of patented technology and land acquisitions. See the huge landgrab that Bill Gates has conducted within the continental

US, it is mind-bogglingly nefarious. Moreover, these patents on these aforementioned technologies blur the line between product and person, or natural thing, in some cases. For example, Monsanto owns the food supply, de facto, through the mass-dissemination of its patented genetically modified grain; of which is not considered "natural" due to its genetically modified composition. Could a similar control be exerted by these corporations on the populace at large, with this gene-therapy through the vaccinations? That said, the vaccination does utilise CRISPR and mRNA technology to alter DNA, thus the question looms; does that make you a product of these companies, via your altered natural-DNA with a patented corporate formula? It is a strange conundrum, indeed. It would seem that, if true, it potentially may make of us direct serfs, instead of indirect wage-slaves; as per the collateral we become on certification of birth; a person in bondage, destined to produce revenue as collateral for the central banks.

In conclusion, this century will be dominated by China, as is going to be the case, and with that the US are slowly realigning their policy and governmental position to a Chinese-style one. Incidentally, this is largely not the US governments decision, but the decision of the corporations of whom own the US government; Socialism and totalitarianism is far more profitable and controllable for these corporations, you see. Hence, we are seeing large business interests slowly pick apart the carcass of the US – vast landgrabs and a scooping up of all of the available government wealth, through dubious vaccines and government contracts, though this will inevitably backfire on these corporations as most are asset-free conglomerates. Conversely, Chinese companies are very much tangibly driven and base their inherent value on production and manufactory. We will see a social credit system being implemented before the US empires eventual demise and we will also see, most likely, a more belligerent stance from the US on the geopolitical stage. Moreover, to maintain the status quo, a policy of smart-city integration and totalitarianism will begin to be phased in, but if this succeeds in being implemented prior to collapse, and the true ascension of China, is anyone's guess. I would suggest to anyone living within this period, and mind you this is not financial advice by any means, to take available assets and save them in an easily portable form; if the form is an asset that accrues value in this coming inflationary period, then all the better.

Alas, for like the Burghers of old, nestled in Hamlin town, unwilling to pay the piper, so too is the empire of the US unwilling to pay the price for their past errors in fiscal judgement, and so they too will hear the call of the infamous piper. Likewise, their future will be led from their view, from their immediate grasp, into the fiery jaws of oblivion of which penance will be thus rendered unto the child for the sins of the father. For everyone must pay the piper eventually, is it not so?

THE CULT OF COVID

> *For we endeavour to control the mind,*
> *The slow, methodical destruction of time,*
> *'Tis the story of how the cathedral falls, decked in fine gold and bejewelled in all.*
> *The casting out of the worldly foe; the cross, the crescent, the life we know. More and more our power doth surge, henceforth we collide with violent urge;*
> *The more that we do gain, the fewer that doth remain;*
> *A lingering testament of our destruction and reign*
> *We are the cult, the fanatic few, enthralled in superstition; thus, shall it be our glue.*
> *Bound in a desire to see this world burn; idols of filth and temporal spurn.*

The cult of Covid, the new demon and evil spirit running amok and tormenting the mortals of Earth, is very much an anathema to a mind capable of reasoned discernment. To what attributes can we most assuredly call COVID a cult, though? Well, within this section I will discuss the pertinent topic and its summary points as to why most conclusively COVID is a cult-like phenomenon and it very much has historical counterpoints within the phases of decline of other civilisations; most notably, and more familiarly, that of Rome.

I was brought to this idea surrounding COVID being incontestably a cult from a correspondence I received quite serendipitously, I might add, from an old friend concerning the re-opening of Edinburgh castle, in my original homeland, and it illustrated the various restrictions that would be present there. Least concerning, if one can remark that, was the use of QR codes and temperature checks. However, what piqued my interest the most was a picture surrounding the social distancing when watching the "One o'clock Gun", a firing of an artillery piece every day at one, post-meridian. The picture showed every one standing two-metres apart, six-feet, in these white circles. Now, my heterodoxic way of mind got me thinking, does this bear any resemblance to the magical circles poured by salt to ward of likewise evil spirits? It is a strange thing to ponder, that one may bring such a superstitious contra-example to the modern-era; although, one may conclude that we have re-entered such times of superstition again, of which plagued our ancestors; no pun intended of course. These people standing within these circles, or within the two-metre gaps between one another in general life, believe whole-heartedly that they are protected by the magical barrier of distance and the circle; that the evil spirit, I mean virus, suddenly stops traversing through the medium of air once it touches the perimeter of this powerful ward. This is akin to the same application and belief system surrounding the magical salt-circles; minus the foreboding incantations to boot, of course.

This entire thought experiment began the idea in my mind that this entire event, this virus-craze, is much like the same religious crazes of old - be it heresy or witchcraft – and that we are living within the genesis of a cult of sorts; will this last a century or a decade, like these crazes of old, who knows? However, what we do know is that what I discussed previously regarding the "Thousand Points of Light" section runs in parallel to this cult hypothesis, that is the manifestation of violence to the targeted group or minority is mainly sporadic and indiscriminate of guilt or innocence; one's membership of this targeted group is guilt enough. I will touch upon that last idea later on; it is a rather interesting theory, if I may add. Digressing, we find that the *Malleus Maleficarum*, or *Der Hexenhammer*, or *Hammer of the Witches*, written in 1487 by *Heinrich Kramer*, began this entire craze and was based, as per the denouncing by the Faculty of Cologne, comprised of top theologians and Inquisition members, as a book recommending unethical and illegal procedures, as well as being inconsistent with Catholic doctrines of demonology[475], as entirely unreliable and outright demonstrably false. However, the craze took off due to it being re-published everywhere and thus, it was popularised as sacrosanct gospel. Now, how does this tie in with the COVID crisis? Well, much like the PCR tests and other illogical misunderstandings of immunology and virology, such as mask wearing for example[476], we find that idiotic ideas have slowly become the consensus through media proliferation of said idiocy; moreover, anyone with eyes to see and a mind to reason can see that so much of the information and studies being conducted are not independent, they are either funded directly by the multinational pharmaceutical conglomerates or NGOs such as the Bill and Melinda Gates Foundation. Alas, this is the problem with modern science, that it is majority funded by monied financial interests who have ulterior motives and wish to utilise the findings for either the buttressing of a lie or for nefarious reasons; thus, it is largely a failing of the system that it has become so narrow-minded. For example, the Danish mask study that I cited, of which was critical of their efficacy, was almost blacklisted from being featured in any reputable journal, and they

---

[475] Jolly, Raudvere, & Peters(eds.), *Witchcraft and magic in Europe, Volume 3: The Middle Ages*, page 241, (2002)

[476] Henning Bundgaard, Johan Skov Bundgaard, Daniel Emil Tadeusz Raaschou-Pedersen, et al. *Effectiveness of Adding a Mask Recommendation to Other Public Health Measures to Prevent SARS-CoV-2 Infection in Danish Mask Wearers: A Randomized Controlled Trial.* Ann Intern Med.2021; 174:335-343. [Epub ahead of print 18 November 2020]. doi:10.7326/M20-6817

had to announce their conclusions from the study on social media; prior to luckily finding a journal that would include the study within their publication. This type of aversion from information that breaks from the popular consensus is nothing new within the Human experience, but it is a rather conclusive rebuttal to the impartiality myth of science. Diverging from that thought, we see that like the Faculty of Cologne denouncing the false doctrines and applications thereof by *Heinrich Kramer* within his magnum opus, *Malleus Maleficarum,* that too the modern example of PCR (Polymerase Chain Reaction) test being misused to determine RNA viruses present in the body, specifically COVID-19 of course, and one of the lead creators of the test, *Kary Mullins*, stating that "If they could find this virus within you at all, and with PCR, if you do it well, you can find almost anything in anybody…"[477]. This was in response to the amplification cycles. With the understanding that any number of cycles above thirty-five provide a "false-positive", and these "false-positives" account from anywhere between 70%-90% of the total number of positive cases[478]; hence, the disproportionately high number of asymptomatic cases, in relation to prior pandemic statistical patterns. This type of "false-positive" test, of which everyone considerably has the virus, is very much akin to the lacklustre and irrational testing for witches – of which almost always gave the inquisitor and the judicial laity a verdict of proven, in relation to the defendant being characteristically a witch. Clearly, some of the antiquated tests were as laughable as our own; and just as injurious as our own, likely one has heard of the laughable stories of the testing for the presence of witchcraft, so I will not dwell on this matter, for sake of time. Therefore, to conclude this point, we may

---

[477] James Herer, *"Coronavirus: The Truth about PCR Test Kit from the Inventor and Other Experts,"* Weblyf, https://www.weblyf.com/2020/05/coronavirus-the-truth-about-pcr-test-kit-from-the-inventor-and-other-experts/. Date accessed: 10/04/2021.

[478] Rita Jaafar, Sarah Aherfi, Nathalie Wurtz, Clio Grimaldier, Thuan Van Hoang, Philippe Colson, Didier Raoult, Bernard La Scola, *Correlation Between 3790 Quantitative Polymerase Chain Reaction–Positives Samples and Positive Cell Cultures, Including 1941 Severe Acute Respiratory Syndrome Coronavirus 2 Isolates, Clinical Infectious Diseases*, Volume 72, Issue 11, 1 June 2021, Page e921. https://doi.org/10.1093/cid/ciaa1491

acknowledge that this COVID-19 event either was entirely contrived, or was highly inflated for the purposes of social engineering and inducing a war-time scenario to corral the populace into a new social paradigm.[479]

Within the *Malleus Maleficarum*, it states also that "wherever women are, witches are also", it is much akin to our modern mantra of wherever air may be or people are, then the virus may also be; like witches, it is the invisible enemy, the evil incarnate that is incorporeal and undiscernible to the minds of man, but nevertheless presents a fearful shadow looming over our mortal heads. Much like the witch-craze was the erroneous aggregation of malicious gossip, natural phenomena such as animals and children dying, animals appearing near their houses, the use of traditional herbal remedies, and the exchange of cross words[480], the COVID-craze misidentifies naturally occurring deaths as the result of the demon of COVID by the falsely held standard of PCR testing, or, in the case of many a national legislation now, mere assumption by the coroner; of which is legally unchallengeable. This inflates the cases and thus the fear, much like the false confessions attested to as fact in the witch-craze in Europe, so too is our fear being bolstered to induce into the population hysteria; of which will allow the tyrants ample room and justification to impose social agendas, many a decade in the planning.

If we look moreover at the targeted demographic with that old campaign of witch-hunting, we find that over 80% of those convicted were women[481]; in fact, the *Malleus Maleficarum* states that "women are foolish" and when they are allowed to think alone "they think of evil", and this shows not just the personal view of *Kramer*, but of the Catholic

---

[479] DB. (2021). *"SARS-CoV-2 Has Not Been Proven to Exist: The Shocking Research of Christine Massey"*. Available: https://thenewabnormal513330780.wordpress.com/2021/01/27/sars-cov-2-has-not-been-proven-to-exist-the-shocking-research-of-christine-massey/. Last accessed 03/04/2020.
[480] Tim Flight. (2018). *12 Surprising Beliefs from the Malleus Maleficarum, the Witchfinder's Guidebook*. Available: https://historycollection.com/12-shocking-beliefs-from-the-malleus-maleficarum-the-witchfinders-guidebook/. Last accessed 02/04/2020.
[481] Ben-Yehuda, Nachman. *The European Witch Craze of the 14th to 17th Centuries: A Sociologist's Perspective*. American Journal of Sociology, vol. 86, no. 1, 1980, pp. 1–31. JSTOR, www.jstor.org/stable/2778849. Accessed 2 Apr. 2021.

church as a whole at that time. The church despised femininity for a very long time, this goes back to *Thomas Aquinas's* remarks on women, "The male sex is more noble than the female, and for this reason he [Jesus] took human nature in the male sex (*Summa Theologiæ* III:31:4 ad 1)." There was clearly a disdain for women and traditional medicinal and spiritual practises that still lingered within Europe, post-Christianisation. Now, this ultimately led to the singling out of the female of the society as all evil or to be suspected of evil; and this has a direct connection to our contemporary period. That is, just like the Catholic church ordered the hunting of women as witches, due to perceived opposition from them or disdain for them, so too is the COVID-craze an attempt by our contemporary rulers to root out dissidents and us all; of whom they hate and wish to manage more effectively. The witch-hunt, from the 14th to 17th century respectively, was not to kill all women but to subjugate them and to furthermore restrict the localised traditions and practises of others, to impose social disunity also, so that it would make others far more loyal to the state; it also had an aspect of inducing fear, as any natural phenomena, a death or a bad harvest, was actively blamed on the permeation of malevolence within society. This in turn, drew attention away from the governments of the time and their mismanaging of the sanitary conditions and the lack of proper land management for higher crop yield. Thus, in much the same vein, we find that any death or bad event in our time is attributed to COVID, it was attributed to terrorism prior but that lost steam rather quickly, thus the governments can divert attention away from their mismanaging of actual health and global crises – obesity, cancer, heart disease, overpowered corporate influence, etc – and blame the invisible enemy, accordingly. It is a tried-and-true method of many a state throughout history; we have to recall to, that the cabal who engineer these crises are masters of psychology and group manipulation and they use these skills to best affect, as we can bear witness to.

Additionally, if we take this discussion within another angle from the point of a cult, as to which I have prefaced thus far, then we can see some striking hallmarks indicative of the cult-like stratagem. If we assume, as I have previously touched upon, the idea that COVID is the evil spirit, the dualistic adversary of "The Good", that it is the devil or hell from a Christian perspective, then we begin to understand the broader and more holistic picture of this entire ruse. The media, the decriers of the gospel of COVID, sit piously upon their high horses, proclaiming the end of the world if sacrifices are not made by the adherents and relaying worryingly the rampant destruction the evil spirit has wrought upon the unsuspecting masses; defenceless from their outset and unable to fight this unseen and unknowing darkness, they require a saviour, they require the prophesised redeemer. Prophesised by whom you may ask? Prophesised by the leaders, the government, who have taken on the mantel of high-priest, or arch-theologian, and the only individuals capable of divining the signs and crafting the prophesy of this heralded saviour; all the whilst maintaining the darkness at bay, shepherding the flock of terrified and infantilised sheep. They deliver sermons each week from their pulpit, instructing the faithful in what to do to fend of the disembodied and unseen darkness; for if they only would submit, prostrate themselves before the saviour and relinquish their worldly belongings, property and rights all of this would simply go away. For whom is this saviour heralded, that I speak of? The vaccine. The vaccine is the saviour incarnate, that if you would only accept it into your heart, into your soul, that you would be purified and cleansed of this evil; for we must sacrifice our old self to be reborn anew, in a world beyond the abominably dangerous existence we find ourselves entrapped in; an everlasting life of pleasure and paradise. For only if you would accept it. For the ones who do not, then they are to be branded infidels – unbelievers – tainted by the tenebrosity of the world before, unwavering in their devotion to the old God, the old ways, and the old mode. They must be ostracised and demonised for permitting, through their reluctance to accept the saviour, the darkness and the devil to run amok within this earthly realm and afflict the faithful. Thus, halting the new world from being brought to realisation; they are evil-doers and godless miscreants, destined to doom the venerable adherents. For those who died, as martyrs for the new world, from the dark entity known as COVID, then shall we mark, as an anniversary, the day judgement was wrought upon us for our iniquitous and carnal ways; for it stemmed from us living life as we are now, and Humans, unaltered and natural, cannot be permitted to enter the new world after the darkness is cleansed. For the condition of man and nature is such that it is imperfect in the minds of our priestly-class. The glorious dead who sacrificed their mortal vessels for the prospect of a "Novus Mundus" for us who remain, shall be canonised as saints and pious people alike; the blood of the lambs shall wipe away the sin of this world.

The vaccine shall be seen as the "*Restitutor Orbis*", the "Restorer of the World", the *Sol Invictus*, the panacea of our troubles, and even the deaths accumulated from its ill-effects will be undeclared and shall henceforth go unnoticed; trivialised as the mere permeation of the deadly demon of COVID[482]. For COVID is a strange and unmoving beast, it contains within it many a variant, and it is immutable; being unable to be eradicated, until the great reset of our planet is thus complete. The variants that have ostensibly stemmed from this perfidious devilry are innumerable, "Our name is Legion, for we are many", and as such we have begun to fashion an atheneum on this novel form of demonology. Alas, let us look further into who may be susceptible to being afflicted by this blight, for we know that the symptoms number in the dozens[483], and that conceivably anyone may have it, as asymptomatic carriers are the main vector of transmission; anomalous indeed, in regards to all other prior transmission vectors within previous viral outbreaks. Though, this leads us back to the witch notion of *Kramer*, that "where there are many

---

[482] Tom Whipple, Science Editor. (2021). *Warning about coronavirus vaccine and clots is a sign that the system is working*. Available: https://www.thetimes.co.uk/article/warning-about-coronavirus-vaccine-and-clots-is-a-sign-that-the-system-is-working-x989rkjkt. Last accessed 10/04/2021.
[483] CDC. (2021). *Symptoms of Coronavirus*. Available: https://www.cdc.gov/coronavirus/2019-ncov/symptoms-testing/symptoms.html. Last accessed 03/04/2020.

women, there are many witches"[484], and as such this all-encompassing generalisation, for means of indiscriminate abuse of the target population, is present within this cult, too. Moreover, it is akin to the abstraction of the "original sin", that through no choice of your own or visible manifestation present to others without external influencing, you are declared a "sinner" or, in this case now, a "spreader", and as such you become incorporated into the mythology of culturally-spun fear; that if you do not abide by the priest-class's arbitrary diktats then you will burn in hell for all eternity. Much in the same vein, with the tantalisingly comedic intellectual overture, that if you do not abide by the modern priest-class's arbitrary diktats then you will die from COVID and, I love this caveat, that you will "kill granny" and all of your family, inadvertently too. The godless tricksters know no bounds, their psychological games are as old as time itself, but alas no one seems to notice the glaringly puerile nature of the lie. That said, the newly established priestly-class will project unto the minds of witless dolts, of whom comprise the majority, that the vaccine alone has the power to compel the COVID to be driven from the world; if only we would sacrifice upon the altar our inherent freedoms. This bears connection to the parable of Jesus traversing the desert for forty-days and forty-nights, and thence the devil appears to him – promising him the world, the material mundus, if he would but bow to him – but Jesus refused. For the metaphor present is one that states that if a man is guided, in decision-making, by material temptation and would forsake his soul by consequence, the spiritual fire conducive to all life that is, then all the earthly pleasures in the world would be unable to fill the void for where his soul once occupied; he would constantly be yearning for something more, something material could not provide; the metaphysical light, of which he erstwhile squandered. I will detail this further in another section entitled "Temptation, the Key to Power", later on within this work.

---

[484] Kalpana Jain. (2019). *Most witches are women, because witch hunts were all about persecuting the powerless*. Available: https://theconversation.com/most-witches-are-women-because-witch-hunts-were-all-about-persecuting-the-powerless-125427. Last accessed 03/04/2020.

We can look, with more depth, at the various rituals that have sprung up regarding this newly emergent cult as well; they merit discussion, very much so. If we begin by looking at the chef-d'œuvre of this cult, the focal point of the faithful's veneration, that being the vaccine or saving elixir of light, we find that this has taken on a quasi-religious significance within the peddlers of this absurdity and the frequenters of the fountain of said absurdity, then we find it is much akin to a baptism or to be born again within the light of the saviour; from Christian doctrine, naturally. The vaccine is almost being attested to as a cleanser of the soul, a panacea, a purifier of one's own fallible composition, and the ones who decline such an attestable marvel are met with vitriolic abuse and are ridiculed like those unbelievers within majority religious societies are. They are becoming slowly seen as the masses of the unclean, regarded as tainted and impure, and are declaimed as "anti-vaxxers", much like the term "antichrist", which brings with it a synonymity with evil and unnaturalness. Furthermore, to deviate from that topic now, we find that this evil spirit of COVID seems to be considered almost like a miasma of sorts, or an antiquated theory surrounding pathogens being primarily vectored via a "bad smell", or an evil pestilential spirit, or "pestilential odour". The evidence corroborating this is self-evident, from the use of masks of which is clear do little to mitigate the spread of the virus from the prevailing statistical infrequencies, the incessant circulation of air to the detriment of maintaining one's own proper bodily temperature, and the distancing of everyone indiscriminate of prior infection and recovery. This is a tropism that occurred during the great pestilence of the Black Death, where individuals believed it covered areas as a miasma. Funnily enough, they were somewhat correct in this assertion due to the bacterium being passed via a type sporous organic material via the bursting of the puss-filled nodules on the body. However, in our own contemporaneous era, this virus is not passed primarily via such vectors of transmissibility, officially according to formal virology, and it does not linger for as long as the bacterium of the Black Death did either; it is rather inefficient in its transmissibility, actually.

Chapter VIII

The Vaccine, the proclaimed saviour of all mankind, is ultimately a leap of faith forced tacitly by the barrel of a gun and all the force the state can muster. By its very existence the implication asserted is one that is a symbolic gesture unto the government of your blind obedience; it is the swearing of allegiance to the new paradigm, the new cult and ultimately is a baptism into the death-cult of COVID. Much like the "Heaven's Gate" cult, it promises a new world, but will deliver unto its followers, thenceforth, death. Shall you drink the cool-aid, or shall you take your chances in resisting this madness? I hereby swear to the latter. Thus, this ultimately denotes the true meaning of all of these pronounced ostensible "health" measures, that they are far more detrimental to one's constitution than the virus. That is, it is a form of self-flagellation, that the now theological state that has established its dominion demands one attack oneself in a blind act of allegiance to the archpriests of the state. The vaccine side-effects and unknown long-term effects, the mask wearing and impeding of one's own airways and further harmful effects that are beginning to come to light, and the freezing seen within leaving the windows open in the dead of winter within the northern hemisphere. This is similar in its scope or aims to the self-flagellation we witness in certain denominations of the Abrahamic faiths; such as Shia Islam and Catholicism. This type of mortification of the flesh or auto-sadism is typically exhibited as either devotion, or to endure what the prophet or holy people did, but more often than not is conducted as a mortification of the flesh and body to cleanse the soul of sin. A similar connotation is slowly becoming apparent in our present time during this emerging cult, as individuals are engaging in actions that may and often will self-harm, chemically-induced poisoning and slow asphyxiation, as a sign of penance and to experience, as an act of veneration, of the canonised dead during this purported "pandemic". Accordingly, individuals are engaged in, sometimes, twelve-hour shifts and they are wearing that mask during the entire time, usually five days a week. I do not care of the "official medical advice", this is the obstruction of one's most basic and fundamental actions essential for life; that being breathing; the expelling of carbon-dioxide and inhaling of air. Moreover, we have our ritualistic daily practises too, our saying of grace and our daily prayer, through the excessive and compulsive handwashing, mask-wearing and even the singing and clapping, thus the veneration, for the doctors and nurses. Of whom, might I add, have become the cloistered members of the new monastical order; the doctors have supplanted the monks, the nurses have supplanted the nuns, and the hospitals have became the monastical abbeys and cathedrals to this emblazoned cult of death. In conjunction, the mantras have been spun, too; "FACTS" is the Scottish variant I have heard of and Canada and the USA have similar childish mantras, too. This daily and compulsive symbolism is designed as a purification ritual of the demon or bad-spirit of COVID, alas we all know that excessive hand-washing, with white spirit unbelievably, does little to deter a supposed airborne respiratory virus; it simply dries out your hands and causes cracking and fissures on the skin to form; thus, allowing a pathway for infection, conceivably. Accordingly, we find too this cult has its own transubstantiation ritual or belief, that is being borne out in the media now, that the vaccine is to be considered a "ticket to freedom"; hence, the vaccine is being transubstantiated in front of your own eyes into the literal embodiment of freedom; a false freedom, mind you. This is akin, naturally, to the Catholic eucharist in which wine and bread is transubstantiated into the body and blood of Jesus; and other religions have similar customs and beliefs.

Moreover, one may look at the archpriests of this religion, the previous leaders and civil-servants of our various nations, and see them extoll the virtue of "our sacrifice" and that soon it will be over and our atonement complete. It is truly astounding that a population of whom champion scepticism, supposedly, fall for this colourful quasi-religious rhetoric; but they do, nonetheless. This very much mirrors the acts of self-flagellation, that being that our sacrifice is done in acts of self-harm, not just physically but mentally and spiritually too. We sacrifice, by the decrees of our leaders, as an act to restore the world; every tyranny in its ascension to power takes a similar route and power goes to the executive entirely; the executive or head-of-state becoming like a de facto religious leader of the nation. Conversely, every week we are being conditioned by the media through the reports of the COVID demons destruction being wrought upon us puny and impious creatures. Similar in vein to how the hysteria of the witch-craze was spun, that they would use "flying ointment on brooms" and one story exclaimed that a woman flew to a hillside on one of these magically-derived flying contraptions and sat atop the hill, raining down urine on an unsuspecting wedding taken place with the joyous congregation below; all people she disliked and whom in turn most likely disliked her; we know this as truth as the local shepherds bore witness to it. This is the same tone as to what we are going through right now, where one may ask crowds of individuals if they have experienced a death from COVID in the people they know and one will be met with either "no", or "I knew a person, that knew a person, that knew person and the person they knew died of COVID"; this is a game of "Chinese Whispers", that hysteria like this has trickled from the top and everyone seeks to virtue-signal regarding being beset by the new affliction; it is the pathology of crowds and mobs; it exists within the markets on a smaller-scale, of course. Forbye, it can be gleaned that we are the flock of sheep and the leaders are our shepherd, taking us through the shadow of the valley of death; however, they wish for us to fear the evil resolutely, even when the evil exists only within the shepherd's own soul. The leaders, religious now in nature, act as the intercessors between the apocalyptic times and the new world; the intercessor to the saviour that is the vaccine; As it is, "I am the way and the truth and the life. No one comes to the Father except through Me.", so sayeth our nefarious intercessors. The quintessential intolerance of new religions is present here and, as it has been seen, the attacks upon the unbelievers are intensifying. There will be two castes of people from now on, until this regime collapses, that of the vaccinated and that of the unvaccinated; as was foretold, in earnest, since those erstwhile days, the days of the beginning of this time of tribulation and turmoil, thence has it come to pass and so shall we behold it henceforth, the torturous overture of the infidel commenceth thusly. Lo, may Providence watch over us all in these days ahead.

As a conclusionary section upon this I will discuss the rise of the militant Nicene faith during the turbulent terminus of the Western-Roman Empire and the slowly gradual decline, from that point onwards, of the Eastern Roman Empire. I have touched upon this in a previous section, that being the idea of the Nicene faith slowly eclipsing both religiously and culturally its Graeco-Roman predecessor of old; and that during the declining phases of the empire it was witnessed that the Nicene faith burnt books, destroyed religious and historical monuments, murdered and maimed opposing personages and outlawed certain cultural traditions that went back millennia, once they had acquired total power and fear was likewise inflicted wholesale upon the populace that is[485]. The murder of *Hypatia* and the burning of secular texts within Alexandria was a startling event that occurred approximately during this rise of the Nicene faith. How did *Hypatia* die? She was torn from her carriage by a group of Christian fanatics, whilst they were enthralled to hysteria and hatred, they dragged her to a church, stripped her naked, beat and flayed her to death, tore off her limbs and burnt her remains. If you think this cannot happen now, then pray do tell where do you see this cult of COVID going when one declines the vaccination passport and subsequently becomes the similitude of a leper, in the minds of the fanatics? Prepare to defend your very life, lest you end up as *Hypatia* did; a martyr to a dying world, a world where reason and common-sense still prevailed nominally. *Prorsus credibile est, quia ineptum est; sic, alea iacta est*. Cometh forth the fury of the world, burden unto mine soul; for mine own soul from thence burden, shall beest rendered reinvigorated.

---

[485] Jordan, David P. *Gibbon and his Roman Empire*. (Chicago: University of Illinois Press, 1971), Pg. 213. "The insensible penetration of Christianity in the empire fatally undermined the genius of a great people."

Chapter VIII

The Children of Saturn

Power is a temptress akin to no other - she may set sail a thousand ships to war,
command men to their certain doom, or ensure they act on principles not wholly of their
nature. Brother versus Brother, Father versus Son, she can poison the mind of even the
best of man.
She may latch to them, like a leech latches to its host.
Thus, it may be said, power may lead man to delude himself that he is in direct control,
however, it is he who is the true pawn in such a doom-ridden arrangement.
Possessed by it, man becomes a mere puppet, a vehicle for the ruination of his soul; and
of the army of others also conspiring to consort directly with the bitch.

Let us understand, firstly, the myth of *Saturn*, or *Kronos*, in the Hellenic view, and how it rears its ugly head, amongst all conspiratorial fomentations throughout recorded history; the agitators, the rabble-rousers, and revolutionaries all; the pitifully power-mad conglomerations of men. All have succumbed to the same fate that befell *Saturn*'s children and so shall it be with this ambitious collection of conspiratorial oligarchs, hellbent on the formation of a world federated Empire.

Saturn, so fearful of the thought of his own children usurping him, ate them in a pre-emptive act to delay the inevitable. That being, the cleaving from his soul the parasite of power and thus the bestowing of the leech unto his eldest and wisest, that of *Jupiter*, or *Zeus*; in the Hellenic sense. Much akin to the children of revolutions, most notably that of the French variety, devouring each other in a fanatical drive towards purity of revolutionary thought and direction. Thus, what inevitably occurred was the demagoguism of *Napoleon Bonaparte*, the intellectual eldest and most inclined towards wise scheming, out of them all. Once a state of anarcho-tyranny is instituted in lieu of a changing world, that is the dispelling of nominal justice and rule of law, then we may begin to see the erstwhile shadowed despots rise to the occasion of the harvesting of power; the tricksters, those predisposed to schemes of intrigue and the addicts of power. Wherever overly ambitious machinations dwell, so does it draw likewise ambitious men together, in the pursuit of power; that is claimed to, once gained, be shared equally amongst them. However, what inevitably occurs is the slow eradication of the opposition and the greedily acquiring of all available power into a single, unitary body; the infamous tyrant. These tyrannies collapse speedily though, but the suffering experienced from such tyranny can be long-lasting and disruptive to the long-term recoverability of the nation.

What can we say of the attempt at the formation of this new world federated Empire? That the members, the cult, of this conspiracy, once power is achieved, will be somewhat upset, as all ambitious men are, at their measly share of the profits from their part. Additionally, do recall that these cult members, the conspirers, have laid their entire life on the line, their life has been enveloped and dedicated to the sole purpose of achieving a perfect, planned society. Would you, likewise, be content with just a small, but equal, share of the power? We may, but we are people of modest means and are not psychopathic like our hedonistic and megalomaniacal counterparts, who hold high positions. They are accustomed to the envelopment of luxury and pleasure unto them, they have never worked manually, nor do they hold to the virtue of empathy or sympathy. They crush the opposition and hold little in the way of remorse for doing so; they are pure pragmatists, clinical and calculated thinkers, who do not dwell on the past but harness all their available attention, to the problems required to be solved, in the present. They are the diametric opposite of us and as such, they see us as another species; as different from us as we see the cattle, grazing mindlessly, as different from ourselves. Once this age-old agenda is achieved and all opposition is vanquished, then as is the nature of humanity, and especially the psychopathic variety, they will invent new opposition; until all that remains is themselves; a God among mere mortals below. In conjunction, we can see the mindset of these individuals from the recent story concerning the blood of children, being commercially utilised, by entrepreneurial minds, in "Silicon Valley", for the application of reversing aging or at least slowing its effects. Do you really think such aristocrats think highly of your health, whence they are engaged in such foul acts? The answer is demonstrably no, naturally.

Thus, when this agenda of depopulation and strict resource management reaches its initial conclusion; through unilateral inventorisation of everything. The conspirators of this grand deception – the Gates', Bezos', Rockefellers and Rothschilds, and all of their political prostitutes of the world – will, whilst drunk on the lust for power, engage in a type of "Hunger Games" scenario, on a global-scale. We shall see the ambition of one of the ilk realised in the form of a short-lived, but first of its kind, global Empire; headed by a "King of the World", if you will. This will occur following on from a bloodbath of the cult, where each member will decimate one another in a sordid display of "Last Tyrant Standing". The personification of the *Ouroboros*; thus, shall the insatiable appetite of the Children of *Saturn* lead them to devour each other. So, shall it be, and if one thinks this ludicrous, then pray do tell when do individuals like this ever become contented with what they have, as we do? They do not and believe, within their twisted psyche, that all that they do survey should be rendered unto them; as theirs for all time. Hence, it can be said that this type of scenario, of internal decimation, is something that occurs within all societies and typically stems from the overly cumbersome bureaucracy that begins to act with impunity and above the yolk of the state. This was seen within the slow decline of the *Han* and the Roman Empire; where massively centralised states become brittle and inflexible; slowly making way for the manifestation of a disparate collection of warlords, enamoured with the prospect of realising a vast empire of their own, thenceforth cut from the carcass of the old. The cycle hence repeats, ad infinitum.

As a final concluding notion, tangential in nature somewhat, it can be said that to attempt to fight this tyranny from its outset is completely futile; this system will come forth into existence because of the majority's compliance with the agenda thus far. Moreover, it is the cycle of civilisations that tyrannies arise among weak and enfeebled populations; the predator provides preference to weaker prey, naturally. It is like we are aboard a ship with but a sail and no oars. We cannot steer the ship, nor input our own energy into fighting against the wind; thus, we can only sit back, and observe, while the dominant force of nature, takes us where she wills it. We can comment upon where we may be heading – to virgin land anew or the jagged cliff edge – but we only do this to brace our resolve for the possibilities. The majority and the irreversibly decaying civilisation are that aforesaid dominant force of nature, we find ourselves at the whim of.

Henceforth shall, "a nation of sheep, beget a government of wolves".

A Silent Overthrow

A silent *coup-d'état* is being waged as we speak; it is the overlord against the serf, the old against the emergent new, and freedom against slavery. It is a diametric struggle for the soul of Humanity – or at least what shall be left of Humanity – thus it is incumbent upon us to understand the manner in which this internalised struggle is being waged; its methods and its aims. The scope of this ousting of the old, via covert means, is one in which boggles the brain of the average, mindless lemming – the intellectual vagabonds of our time – and thus if we can endeavour to see it, then it certainly provides a holistic view of the enemy that is bearing down upon us; soon to be in the gates; alas though, it seems he is already. The serpent system is beginning to uncoil itself; to the onlookers bedazzled by its charming slither, it seems much like an entrancing

Chapter VIII

distraction; they, not sensing danger, see not the serpent's razor-sharp fangs hurtling towards them. By consequence, shall they be forever ensnared to its poison, once it is delivered. Thus, we must discuss this topic, of paramount importance, in haste.

We have been collectively hoodwinked by the invented threat of a virus for the sole reason of providing a smoke-screen and a justification for the imposition of a different governmental type; one entirely idiosyncratic to the previous traditions of the legal and political system. Thus, this system has not just changed, metamorphised into a new incarnation, it has been totally captured and in the place of the old has been supplanted the new. This is a new system and a new establishment. What evidence is there backing that claim? Well, if we look at the UK police, as of right now, there are alarming reports that a certain number of police constabularies, across many a county, are being contracted out to *G4S*, the infamous private security firm. This is naturally alarming for a number of reasons, least of which is the unwarranted power such a move transfers to that private organisation, of which would have a monopoly on the use of force within the society, at large. Moreover, policing or guarding is, what is termed, a "natural monopoly" which means that certain key sectors, industries or powers cannot be obtained by private monopolies as it would warrant them too much control over society; hence, they would begin to dawn the mantel of "state", in the previous state's stead. Although, moving forth in a different angle upon this, we see that the reports alleging this is the case – with photographic evidence to boot, mind you – do explain, quite convincingly, as to why this brand of brutal "policing", we are beginning to see across the globe, is occurring. Conversely, this ties very much into the "Stakeholder Capitalism" our near and dear friend, *Klaus Schwab*, affectionately propounds, ad nauseum; or, as we in the know like to entitle it, Corporatocracy.

Alas, there is a cataclysmic reshaping of society occurring and the new, collectivistic mantras of the regime have already begun springing forth from the faces of advertisements and the robotic babbling of the politicians – "we are all in this together", "stay apart so we can be together", and "The new normal". Orwellian double-speak, indeed. Seemingly, irrefutable drivel that is designed to chip away at one's resolve, one's own soul, to break you; much how like a rancher breaks in the obstinate stallion, still clinging to freedom, by a gradual process of breakage through repetitive instruction and coercion. Like the horse, we too will cease to exist solely for our own purposes and desires, we will thus be jumped upon by the shackles of the master, in which our existence shall be coloured by the needs and wants of the higher-tiered class; we will exist for a reason probably alien to our own, in which the turning of the wheel and the breaking of the rock shall be done for the purposes that our masters set down upon our backs. We shall wear the muzzle and cease communication with our fellow hierodules, lest we seek punishment by the divine kingly class; they will seek to not just break bone, but spirit also; for that, the stubborn shall be set upon by example-making, but do not let this quench the fires of freedom, you good fellows all. Digressing, this type of cataclysmic reshaping very much factors into the idea of the "Great Reset" and, rightly so, confirms my assertion that our various nations of old have been utterly captured, covertly mind you, by forces that still lurk to the shadows and cling to cover; too cowardly to have their presence be directly made aware to the public, in general. This entire state of affairs shows conclusively a shifting of direction to a more authoritarian state and if we look at the various anecdotal evidence surrounding this, for example, "Fortress DC", we see a new despotic state takeover in which paranoia and fear of the populace is rife; moreover, an intrepid move towards the use of outright and blatant propaganda, emotional manipulation en masse, has been adopted, supremely so. This is the culmination of the slow march through the institutions, the synthesis of the past decades and centuries of carefully crafted machinations in hopes of more power, and now we see the final end-game; the finale of all the prior years of infiltration and incremental control over everything.

Moreover, we see that the mask and social-distancing measures of this ostensible pandemic are not designed to lessen the extent of the virus, as they are still in place while the R-rate in some nations is officially below a rate necessary to propagate spread[486], but it is designed to lessen the spread of ideas; the dissemination of information pertaining to the death-inducing properties of the vaccine and the depopulation agenda required for the coming Technocracy. When one wears a mask and unsocially distances oneself from another, then that impedes communication almost interminably so. Amongst that fact is the glaringly insidious issue that the masks cause death, due to the encouraging of a multitude of gradually acquired respiratory issues, and this can be gleaned from the 2008 paper co-authored by *Anthony S. Fauci*[487], of which it is stated of the 1918 *Spanish Flu* pandemic that "Published pathologic and/or bacteriologic findings from the 1918–1919 influenza pandemic. Although the cause of influenza was disputed in 1918, there was almost universal agreement among experts [e.g., 20, 27–33] that deaths were virtually never caused by the unidentified etiologic agent itself, but resulted directly from severe secondary pneumonia caused by well-known bacterial "pneumo-pathogens"; that colonized the upper respiratory tract (predominantly pneumococci, streptococci, and staphylococci). Without this secondary bacterial pneumonia, experts generally believed that most patients would have recovered". This is exactly what has been found to be caused by long-term mask wearing in many a study, pre-pandemic[488][489]. Digressing,

---

[486] Emma Brazell. (2021). *Covid R rate drops as low as 0.7 across England.* Available: https://metro.co.uk/2021/04/16/covid-r-rate-drops-to-between-0-7-and-1-0-in-england-14421343/. Last accessed 16/04/2021.

[487] David M. Morens, Jeffery K. Taubenberger, Anthony S. Fauci, *Predominant Role of Bacterial Pneumonia as a Cause of Death in Pandemic Influenza: Implications for Pandemic Influenza Preparedness*, The Journal of Infectious Diseases, Volume 198, Issue 7, 1 October 2008, Pages 962–970, https://doi.org/10.1086/591708

[488] C.R. MacIntyre, H. Seale, T. C. Dung, N. T. Hien, P. T. Nga, A. A. Chughtai, B. Rahman, D. E. Dwyer, Q. Wang. *A cluster randomised trial of cloth masks compared with medical masks in healthcare workers.* BMJ Open, 2015; 5 (4): e006577 DOI: 10.1136/bmjopen-2014-006577

[489] University of New South Wales. *"Cloth masks: Dangerous to your health?".* ScienceDaily. www.sciencedaily.com/releases/2015/04/150422121724.htm (accessed April 15, 2021).

the state wishes to impose upon us their unipolar narrative of this event through stifling of contrary opinions and interpersonal communication between others and the surveillance of all indoor interaction, where possible as of right now. This ensures that the fear, that is a necessity for the promulgation of this invented crisis, is able to be prolonged for as long as required; until the fulfilment of the agenda, that is. Additionally, it is being seen within the UK propaganda-sphere, that the public is being fortuitously primed with the notion of SADS (Sudden Adult Death Syndrome/ Sudden Arrhythmic Death Syndrome) and with the high uptake of vaccinations, comparative to the rest of the developed world, it is suspicious that this term is being implanted within the minds of the British public; I think we can see where this is going, can we not? On the subject of Britain, we should discuss the leaked emails from Ministers surrounding the inefficacy of the lateral-flow tests; in which it has been stated within these emails that they are between two and ten percent accurate; so not accurate at all, naturally[490]. This begs a number of questions, if the test is useless, then we cannot validate nor verify the existence of this new Corona-virus accurately and additionally, what did the people, of whom were reported to have died from COVID, actually die from? This should be a scandal of monumental proportion, but alas I fear it shall be forgotten and swept under the rug; becoming dusty with time, until future generations thus find it and look at it with shock and disgust at the stupendous corruption that abounded in those long-ago times; those days of yore where their ancestors drunk and made merry at the expense of their civilisation's own future.

For it is clear, we have journeyed into a novel frontier, where it seems that the first stealth takeover of an entire global system, comprised of various governments and nominal nation-states, conducted by the banking cartel and oligopoly at large, has taken place before our very own eyes. The system acts differently, it behaves differently to the previous

---

[490] Lizzie Roberts. (2021). *Officials raised 'urgent' concerns about accuracy of quick Covid tests, leaked emails show.* Available: https://www.telegraph.co.uk/news/2021/04/15/mass-testing-rollout-hit-controversy-leaked-emails-show-officials/. Last accessed 16/04/2021.

incarnation, and it acts transparently within its own interest; it fears not the citizenry and is simply awaiting the expiring of the vast quantity of "dead-weight" that foolishly accepted the jab. We can bear witness to this type of uncaring attitude in potentially drawing the ire of the citizenry via the incessant lockdowns, forceable closure of businesses, and coercive tactics of denying treatment and medical services to individuals who will not comply with either the jab nor test. For *Socrates* once stated, in *The Republic* (Book I, 335C-335D), that "Well, do horsemen by horsemanship unfit men for dealing with horses?" "No." "By justice then do the just make men unjust, or in sum do the good by virtue make men bad?" "Nay, it is impossible." "It is not, I take it, the function of heat to chill but of its opposite." "Yes." "Nor of dryness to moisten but of its opposite." "Assuredly." "Nor yet of the good to harm but of its opposite." "So, it appears." "But the just man is good?" "Certainly." "It is not then the function of the just man, Polemarchus, to harm either friend or anyone else, but of his opposite." In this truth espoused by *Socrates*, vicariously spoken through the words of *Plato*, it is truth to speak that how can a man be just that wishes to harm, for justice's sake? For, if a just man is just, he must do good in deed and doing good in deed must be, by principle, the opposite of harm unto another. Likewise, we can extrapolate by the mere negotiating of logic, that if a state wishes to save you or ensure good health, by their own admission, then they cannot throw violent thugs at you and beat you to a bloody-pulp, if you do not wish to be helped and hence wish to go on with your daily life, unhindered; by masks and other intrusive measures, that is. Moreover, if a medicine is truly a medicine and, by such a definition, it would be required to impart a better or improved constitution upon the receiver of said medicine, then it would not subsequently elicit side-effects and death upon the said receivers, but that of its opposite; is it not so? Ergo then, if even one instance of the opposite effect of a medicine or "saviour" takes place, then that will, as such, dismantle the notion, by mere logic, that the entity is what it is claimed, or claims, to be. Elucidating upon that notion further, an entity or object must produce the effects from that which it claims to be, or it is not that which it claims to be and is fraudulent. Concluding that thought, the state must then be engaging in the opposite of safety and security and the jab must be the opposite of medicine, which is, thusly spoken, directly poison; it is a rather simple use of dialectical reasoning or deductive inquiry, but nevertheless glossed over by many in society.

"For when they shall say, Peace and Safety; then sudden destruction cometh upon them, as travail upon a woman with child; and they shall not escape" (1 *Thessalonians* 5:3).

JAHR NULL (YEAR ZERO)

Jahr Null, "year zero", is a socio-political theme throughout many a Utopian and Socialist regime, through history; in fact, one may say, it encompasses their entire domestic policy, upon the birth of their new idealistic state. Conjointly, we may look at *Pol Pot*, the bloodthirsty Cambodian dictator, of whom initiated a strict policy of "year zero" upon the establishment of his new tyrannical kingdom, in which he reigned supreme despot over all. We may travel a little further back and peruse at the liberality, if one can call it that, of the French revolution and the inversion of all that preceded that fateful societal cataclysm; they introduced a new state religion and set forth the calendar dates from *Anno Domini*, to the year of the revolution. Moreover, Islam and Christianity, even Judaism for that matter, had similar "year zero" policies, in which, once cultural dominance was established, the calendar dates were altered to originate from the prophets birth or a religiously significant event. However, the most salient question is still left thusly unanswered, why is this policy at the forefront of the domestic policy of these upstart ideologies and novel cultural phenomena? The answer is rather simple; they wish to utterly extirpate any potential resurgence of the old regime and the old culture; for it was in opposition to the new utopian ideals and was the problematic condition of the old world, of which they first rose against in revolt of. Accordingly, we are seeing a repeat of this reimagining of society, wholesale; we are seeing the birth pangs of "year zero" again; of which everything that proceeded the old paradigm has now made way for the "new normal".

Like all totalitarian regimes of old, a pseudo-reality has to be created – as described by James Lindsay – to fulfil the prerequisite of survival for the totalitarian ideology; namely, that of the distortion of truth and of perceivable reality is of the upmost importance because reality runs contrary to the totalitarian's aims[491]. To augment reality, so that the profligates, the serf-like subjects of the regime, see themselves as the enemy and the regime as the heralded saviour and reformer of the world; in its vast entirety. Thus, when they shall look out unto the world, they shall see what the regime wishes for them to see and when they breath, they breath unto a world reimagined in the likeness of the regime's pseudo-reality. Thus, this type of false reality, this lens of lies, can be seen within every narrative of today's rising global Technocracy; the race-baiting, the COVID scare, the inversion of normality, Anthropogenic climate change, etc. This is all designed to facilitate the regime's rise to power and utterly eradicate all that came before; for if one's mind does not hold to a naturally reasonable position, subordinate to truth, then one cannot possibly understand the paradigm that predated the regime's one. Thus, Man would be eternally entrapped within this hamster-wheel of surreal and unnatural thinking. Moreover, this can be aptly described as a cultural-reset and thus new symbols, slogans and cultural norms are instituted upon the advent of the establishment of the new regime of power. The detractors and resistors are ostracised and the next generation are inculcated with the new social norms via the compulsory education system, so that a new shift within consciousness and cognition takes place. Additionally, it has to be incessantly reinforced as any deviation

---

[491] James Lindsay. (2020). *Psychopathy and the Origins of Totalitarianism*. Available: https://newdiscourses.com/2020/12/psychopathy-origins-totalitarianism/. Last accessed 04/05/2021.

or letting up from this said reinforcement – via means of force, coercion and indoctrination – may lead the society to revert back to a more natural inclination; as the artificial pseudo-reality, or cultural-reset which is a part of this, is always unnatural and a perversion of truth.

Digressing, we can see that a great deal of regimes within the past who have instituted the "Jahr Null" concept, have ushered in their despotism with the sacrifice of blood. In an almost macabre-like ritual to an unseen evil, they wipe away, what they see, as the iniquitous abnormalities of the Human condition; where the regime can start anew and reshape Man into a likeness of obedience and predictability. This is akin to what is beginning now, through the avenue of stealth and the excuse of safety, where there will be massive depopulation – an artificially-induced extinction event – whence from shall arise the new Techno-Feudal overlords of their newly anointed cold, binary domain. The dissidents, the rabble-rousers, and the divergent minds shall all be smote by the proverbial sword of Damocles and thus the vengeance of those they inadvertently profaned against, the psychopathic egos and their shadowed deities, shall be wrought. As historical precedent would have it, following on from this cataclysmic event, the cold catalyst for the crowning utopia, there shall be dissidents abound and in that transitionary period where the new regime is not entirely formally established, there may be an overturning of the slow, slithering shadow of despotism. We can see that within the *White Russian* struggle, though in vain, did attempt to depose the mad-hatters of Bolshevism before their ensuing "purifying" of all of society. *Pol Pot* engaged in similar tactics and the playbook of extolled Socialist utopias are all the same. However, this new and emerging paradigm, or cult ideology, is not the same but it is similar in certain doctrinal views. For example, utopianism is expressed within the "Great Reset" and "Build Back Better" mantras and they have additionally made us hate ourselves, well the majority at least, in the peddling of the lie that carbon-based life causes climate change; a demonstrably transparent lie that goes against many observable laws of physics and embeds within itself paradoxical

CHAPTER VIII

deviations from empirical thermodynamic laws, though I digress[492][493]. Thusly, it was a carbon-copy, no pun intended, of the communistic ideologies prerequisite pseudo-reality, which stated that Human nature was imperfect and that it brought forth inequality; to amend this, the Communists/Marxists needed to be in control and enact radical policies of total reformation, lest we continue in this cycle of imperfection and inequality. You will understand, this is the same tenor of dogma from every radical and utopian position throughout recorded history; from religious radicalism to political cults, all are the same in tone.

If I may, I wish to look further into the devilish race-baiting being spewed forth from the media and what its reason for being perpetuated is. The recent Derek Chauvin case is the quintessential example of this and of the diversionary tactics utilised by tyrants. A tyrant, to take the public ire away from the outwardly visible destruction and dilapidation of the society and world at large, caused notably by his regime, must either draw the public's ire to existential threats or must drum-up some sort of diametric divide within society. Thus, we see the open advocation for the viewing of all of societies afflictions through the lens of race; and even gender and anything to contrast and play one side off against another. This is the ultimate reason multiculturalism was instituted, transgenderism, sexual unorthodoxy, and critical race theory. To make the parent culture, "whites", feel like they are under attack and for the incomers to feel as if the parent culture is attacking and oppressing them. Consequently, we see that this social dogma, since its injection within the fabric of society, has ensured that there is a sufficient amplifying of inward hatred and division, to allow this new paradigm shift to take place; with relative ease. This Derek Chauvin case and the BLM riots, were all fomented at this fortuitous time to distract the left-wing and

---

[492] Holmes, Robert. (2019). *On the Apparent Relationship Between Total Solar Irradiance and the Atmospheric Temperature at 1 Bar on Three Terrestrial-type Bodies.*
[493] Joe Postma; Joseph E. Postma. (2006). *Climate of Sophistry.* Available: https://climateofsophistry.com/2017/01/06/slayer-live-webcast-there-is-no-radiative-greenhouse-effect-jan-10-10am-mst/. Last accessed 29/04/2021.

right-wing contingents, each sub-divided into their own racial, sexual, gender and religious groups, with the frivolity of mindless hate for the other; all the while, the true oppressors of us all are busily bringing into place the conditions required to institute a Techno-Feudal world empire.

Post-dating the institution of this world empire and the "year-zero" policy, that being the formal and overt establishment of the "new normal", in addition to the stark but unreported population decline, we will begin to see a society that is unbearable for those who knew of a better world before. These individuals will seek safety within their memories of the old, or found new and parallel societies, hoping to be undisturbed by the encroaching tyranny. The debauchee elite of this new world will be entirely similar to the Parisian elite of the late 18th century, or much like the "Hunger Games" elite of district one; fabulously decked in ornate, but abstractly pompous fashion. This new world shall express the virtues of driving out the villain of inequality, but quietly behind the closed doors of their stately villas, they will be crafting policy to make the socio-economic divide even harsher for the survivors of the "deadlier variant of COVID/the Third-Wave"; the survivors shall be thus the ones who did not succumb to the vaccine's ill-effects, or did not take the vaccine and managed to procure false documents stating that they had; the black-markets shall be replete in this coming age, even with the centralised digital currency of the new state, people will find a way to circumvent such an obstacle.

To when can we conclusively state, without hesitation, the moment in which our various national governments and consortium of states fell to the grips of these shadowy architects of Western destruction? The Fabian Society, the Frankfurt School, and the endless horde of controlled radical fundamentalists who are arrayed against us, foaming at the mouth and baying for our collective destruction, as a free civilisation. It is hard to say and unlike the "year zeroes" of bygone ages, that wrought so much destruction, there seems to be no abrupt end to the prior paradigm, and the onset of the new one. Thus, the modus operandi of this diabolical

Chapter VIII

scheming, the long march through our halls of government, is gradual and the death of this civilisation will be conducted in the same protracted vein. The dissidents, the resistors of this duplicitous and callous agenda of our people's attempted eradication, are treated with the same disdain as the counter-revolutionaries and anti-revolutionaries of old

And in this new age, one will not be loyal to family or nation, but all loyalty and time will be offered unto the state in a forced act of admiration, for the pittance we may receive. We must resist, and resist we will, and with existential notions aside, we must understand that this is a simple choice of fight on your feet, or die on your knees. Thenceforth, the choice is naturally, do we as a nation throw into the dirt the gifts bestowed by our forefathers unto us – our nation, our ancient culture, and our freedoms, granted to us by grace – or do we stand and unite as one nation, under Providence's favour, and fight the horde of darkness that has come to steal away our future and blot out our own lineage? If we but stood as one and resisted, in the spirit of liberty and for our nation's own survival, we would be collectively unstoppable; we would not only overturn this state-of-affairs, but send the perpetrators back to the pits of hell from whence they came.

Alone we are few, but united we are many. Still, we endure and endure we must; for the truth that there will be a new tomorrow. A tomorrow where Man can chart the course of his own destiny unimpeded, secure in the notion that he shall be free from this day until his last; from his erstwhile birth, to his departing death. If we lose hope of that vision of the future, that vision that would see us charge into the thick of battle in defence of it, then what is the point in our struggle; our pursuit of gnosis at all costs, even if that pursuit may lead us into harm's way. Of the thousands of generations that have preceded us, none have been positioned upon such a crucial and contrasting crossroad of history – that between eternal darkness and perpetual light. For what we do in these dark days to come shall shape not just our own future, but the future of the next a thousand generations to descend forth from us. Shall the fable of history from henceforth this day, the songs and tales of the deeds of us, speak of the heroism and resoluteness of our struggle and eventual victory, in the face of insurmountable odds? Or, shall it speak of us as a mere footnote; in a hellscape beyond redemption? We are the harbingers of the future and we are the writers of our own destiny, and nothing is set-in-stone until every last one of us draws that final breathe of resistance; for our death shall be itself and act of defiance. We cannot be stopped, not by mere bullets, not by technological contraptions, or fanciful lies spoken from fork-tongue. We are the endless waves of the disenfranchised, downtrodden and dispossessed; and our day shall come.

On Propaganda

The riotous event within Hyde Park and Westfield Shopping-Centre/Mall, the one depicting the crowds turning violent against obvious rookie police officers, was set up to initiate counter-propaganda against the ongoing protests, opposing the tyrannical regime; to thus turn public opinion against the protesters. "They are anti-government radicals", "selfish killers of [insert contrived victim class, to stir emotions within the mindless plebeians] ", etc, and this is something that all tyrannies do; that is, to turn the domestic population against one another, inwards on itself, as a means of distracting from the regime's crimes and to vent anger at something other than the regime. As you can see from the films of the event, the police are not in their typical black, terror-inducing suits and are wearing white shirts and normal-duty attire. Neuro-programming and psychology, tells us that black is "serious or bad; to be feared" and white is "peaceful, passive, and the tone of the weaker party"[494]. This is intentional to project an image of the police, now the footmen of the tyrannical coup-d'état, as the victims in all of this. Hence, I predict, as regimes love to do after chaos, contrived or otherwise, which is to

---

[494] Kate Smith. (2019). *Meaning of Black: Color Psychology and Symbolism*. Available: https://www.sensationalcolor.com/meaning-of-black/. Last accessed 04/05/2021.

initiate sweeping draconian policies, on the justification of the prevalence of chaos, to further erode liberties and centralise more power within the hands of the regime; by means of empowering their enforcers with an ever more powerful licensed mandate.

It is all rather elementary; though, within a society that champions rampant stupidity for the lower orders, it can go unnoticed; as has been seen. This entire program of demonising the opposition and, by extension, the non-compliant, is the regime quietly preparing the ground for whipping up the sheeple into a frenzy; that they can, on the back of the frenzy, justify the eventual eradication of the minority dissident and non-compliant class. It is thus the sole reason for the fabrication of hysteria for invisible enemies and hatred towards minority classes; despotic regimes of old utilised it extensively, as did all Communist regimes and, as always, Capitalist regimes too. Now the Technocracies that are to come forth from this contrived event, of a pandemic, will utilise it in their infancy and presumably during their entire life-cycle, however short that may be.

On Escapism

The artificial destruction of the West through the propagation of mindless forms of escapism is rife. All the while, this tyranny, which is now coming into view, preys upon the apathy and stupidity of the drug- and alcohol-induced masses to bring forth a regime of perpetual enslavement. Of the docile and slumbering peons below, they suspect nothing and want for little but cheap thrills. For our swift acceptance of decadence, we have all inadvertently signed the death warrant of our civilisation and, for a vast quantity of us, ourselves. To the kowtowers to this tyranny, you shall enjoy the fruits of eternal enslavement; "where one will own nothing and be happy". Unless, we brave few who survive this cull exclaim "no!" and fight on for the sake of our very existence, as a free and independent people, then all hope shall be lost. I know of what I shall choose and that is the only choice anyone with a spine can make: that is, "give me liberty, or give me death".

The Global Plantation

The Berlin wall never came down, it simply migrated into the cerebral realm, to encircle the mind of Man. That if a thought, free of external conditioning, may attempt to expeditiously break forth from the vestiges of one's own mind, that the vigilant sentries, standing guard upon the constructed mental partition, will thence gun down the defenceless thought. Akin to how the immune system slaughters a foreign pathogen, or agent, upon entry to the body; viciously and without mercy.

You see, the Berlin Wall was never merely a physical emplacement to ward off defectors, attempting to cross the border to freedom, it was most acutely a psychological barrier, a monolithic symbol of oppression, to keep the domestic populace in line. It was the visible manifestation of control and was utilised to induce fear into the populace, by means of the implied threat of force and literal confinement. However, inevitably, the population grow weary of such "lock step" policies[495] and eventually the liminal barrier is broken and the fear of the regime is substituted with the fear of not having basic freedom and independence, from arbitrary diktats. Thus, the fear of death is trumped by the fear, of living a life, where one is already dead.

The Berlin Wall of the modern-era is seen within the corporate monopolisation of the public forum, the internet or social media, and the strict editorialization (censorship) of all the informational exchange that comes forth from that space. Not least to mention the siphoning of informational exchanges on the world-wide web, to collate them, and sell the data packets to state governments, is a ubiquitous practise now[496]. The

---

[495] The Rockefeller Foundation. (2010). *Scenarios for the Future of Technology and International Development*. Available: https://www.rockefellerfoundation.org/wp-content/uploads/Annual-Report-2010-1.pdf. Last accessed 04/05/2021.
[496] Catherine Thorbecke. (2019). *Facebook says government requests for user data have reached all-time high*. Available: https://abcnews.go.com/Business/facebook-government-

Gordian Knot of privacy and thus freedom has been struck and cut, in a simple yet violent fashion, and the aspiring global overlords are zealously cutting wounds into the last vestiges of freedom, ever more egregiously. Their determination is peerless in its relentless drive for a realisation of the singularity principle of politics. Conversely, they attempt to act as Gods among mere mortals, that they should be able to decide, like *Herod* of old, the children who should have the right to life. For instance, the jab rollout has been producing serious reports concerning miscarriages and infertility issues[497] and with the universal right to abort the unborn, with talks of post-birth abortions (definable infanticide)[498], how is this fact not apparent? For pregnant women are told not to eat shellfish, certain types of mould-ripened cheeses, raw fish, etc[499], but they may take into their body, by extension their unborn child's as well, an experimental vaccine of whose trial is still ongoing and will not entirely conclude until 2023. Does this seem logically sound? Of course, it does not, but it does if there is an ulterior agenda behind this incautious attitude, by the ostensible authorities within these fields.

Western nations are beginning to look like plantations, where we but live to work and, once our daily shift is complete, we are resigned to our abode or domestic cell; we have seen the conditioning to this engineered novel milieu, during these lockdowns. Concurrently, the government also owns one's property by implied right, via the paying of "council tax" proportionate to a property's value, or in the American context, the aptly titled "property tax"; in which one pays the government, again, a tax proportionate to the value of their real-estate. Therefore, these pieces

---

requests-user-data-reached-time-high/story?id=66981424. Last accessed 04/05/2021.
[497] Steven Li. (2021). *VAERS Data Shows Dozens of Miscarriages, Stillbirths After COVID-19 Vaccination, Link Unconfirmed*. Available: https://www.visiontimes.com/2021/03/08/covid-19-vaccine-miscarriage-stillbirth-concerns-for-mothers.html. Last accessed 04/05/2021.
[498] Giubilini A, Minerva F, *After-birth abortion: why should the baby live?* Journal of Medical Ethics 2013; 39:261-263.
[499] Adda Bjarnadottir, MS, RDN (Ice). (2020). *11 Foods and Beverages to Avoid During Pregnancy - What Not to Eat*. Available: https://www.healthline.com/nutrition/11-foods-to-avoid-during-pregnancy#9.-Unpasteurized-milk,-cheese,-and-fruit-juice. Last accessed 04/05/2021.

of "real-estate" are merely leased from the government and one does not own the land, but simply the ramshackle shack on top of it. We are for this reason, and this reason alone, serfs already, but the new system will overtly make us more than a serf; we shall be a slave, shackled to the digital chain-gang of forced conformity, via nano-bio-digital implants and the panopticon of surveillance everywhere we go. Accordingly, this new system will be more than a means of financial control over the individual, such a system, that we inhabit nominally now, is too fragile and open to the unpredictable condition of Man's free will. As such the new system must project social, psychological and cognitive control over the individual cog; the cog must be an interchangeable constituent of the machine, it must be a modish mimic of the collective in everything it says and does. It shall cease all autonomous functions, other than what is requisite for its purpose of existence, within the newborn dominion of the Technocrat. It will be justly likened to the tyre of a car, in that a tyre may seem to express the astounding power to change the direction of travel for the vehicle, from the outside and uneducated perspective, but on the other side of the blackened-out windows, it is purely acting upon the whimsical input of the driver. Such will be the nature of the newly anointed slave-class and its masters.

Continuing on with the concept of property, I believe that in this growing authoritarian society we are seeing a stranglehold of centralisation, where one is scarcely allowed to breathe; quite literally. In this novel petri-dish, of where anything may be cultured, a feudal society is being brought to bear upon the populace and it will, most likely, be induced via total economic and financial catastrophe. Within such a system, if hyperinflation occurs, banks and financial institutions will be reluctant to allow individuals to pay off their mortgages with hyper-devalued and a fluctuating currency, thus you may find that the government steps firmly in and redesignates, through legally questionable legislation, these mortgages as "indefinite lease agreements" with these said financial institutes; this will be further enforced as the irremediable and unaltering state-of-affairs per the introduction of a digital currency linked to some sort of vaccine or immunity ID system. Accordingly, like they have done all the way preceding such a move, this system will come in byway-of layer, upon layer, upon layer, until the fabric is so thick and intertwined that one cannot pull it apart or pierce it with the spear of resistance. Moreover, such a set of circumstances as mentioned above is probably unfathomable to you right now, but do recall that but two-years ago you would have thought this scenario entirely implausible and the receptivity at which it has been accepted as the new, unquestionable norm, hard to comprehend. Therefore, we must understand that when people are faced with a dire future and harrowingly prevailing circumstances, then they look for a saviour and a way out; they grab on to the first thing that seems to give them more breathing-room. In light of that, enter our would-be Technocrat with his promise of stability and his lie of "returning to normality", if we would but give up some of our freedoms; it is a lie we have heard all before, naturally. The people will swallow it, hook-line-and-sinker, and they will never understand the folly of their decision to acquiesce until it all too late.

This entire agenda, do recall, was brought swiftly along its upward trajectory to completion by the simple faint flicker of light from the shiny, marvellous screens brought to the apathetic classes; inter alia. Therefrom, they obediently lapped up every single instance of social programming and, due to the gradual and impalpable nature of the destruction, could not quite fathom the totalising manner of its conclusion.

The Postmodern "Meta-truth"

The post-modern Man does not wait for trials to be completed, he does not peruse the diverse landscape of scientific literature, nor does he glean from his own research of the facts surrounding the issue; he simply acts on his own impulses and discerns from this the "meta truth", via emotional deliberation. He appeals to authority and bases his entire understanding of the world around majority-held, cult-like narratives. He is a mere vessel, to be filled with lies masquerading as truth. Thus, this type of being, that may have predated postmodernism and existed within the historical periods of decline within other civilisations, nevertheless poses a beautiful opportunity to totalitarian ideologies. That being, it allows them to furnish the prerequisite state mythology, as *Plato* discussed, or the "pseudo-reality", as James Lindsay coined ingeniously. Thence, it is the reason as to why the seeds of blind obedience were sown so many years ago within the minds of the unsuspecting masses, and like all patient and studious farmers, the farmers of docility have tilled fertile ground, the collective Human psyche, to which they can plant their insidious seeds of obedience in. Consequently, with a little sun and water – analogous to the media and education system – the crops have begun to sprout and now the yield of a lifetime will soon be reaped; the souls of the damned await harvesting, likewise.

Digressing though, like all things within civilisations, it is thus a continuum. Tyrannies start with regulations to ensure safety from the contrived or real threat, then public ostracisation of those who won't comply, then this leads to isolation of the dissident class and then the extermination of that class. It has occurred a thousand times before and a thousand times from now it will thence happen again. However, what makes this different is that we are experiencing this and thus, within the haze of the present caused via the proximity of the issue to ourselves, we cannot or do not wish to see the repeatability of history and of the historically illiterate and naïve of mind fail to see the depraved nature of the "men of power"; the ones who gravitate towards the apex of the hierarchy and the ones who believe they make literally craft the future. However, these would-be benevolent dictators, in the fallible mind of all Man, fail stupendously to see the entire breadth of consequences, due to cause-and-effect, wrought by their radical policies to reshape the future in their own image; that being, these would-be dictators may directly or indirectly destroy not just others, but themselves.

Furthermore, as a final postulation upon this idea of post-modern, or more accurately post-civilisational meta-truth, or a self-referential narrative that proves its truthfulness through its own inarguable merit, thus we can say that these pseudo-realities crafted by these "men of power" do not have to be true; they only have to appear as truth, or be considered as such by the authorities who espouse it. Like all events we see within this sphere of reality, or on the screens that are infected with the babbling voices of the media telling us what to believe, none are reported within a truthful manner, nor are they mostly likely true from their source. However, it does not have to be true, it is simply a mythology crafted for a specific purpose; that being what the state wishes to impose upon the masses and this is typically reported as the only answer to the problem. For example, with "terrorism", the only answer was more surveillance. With illiteracy, it was compulsory education via a Prussian-style model. Thus, with the inflated COVID-scare it is to contrive societal mutual interdependency, which will, in turn, allow the government to legislate based on that presented answer, swallowed wholesale by the populace. The legislation will thus allow the government to take care of the noncompliant, dissident classes once and for all through abrogation of individualism at its source, that is the individual; once and for all. A collectivised hive-mind, for a collectivised state; working diligently and obediently for the hereditary Queen bee and her spawn. For that fact, this new system will resemble, in some ways, a hive of bees; an extremely simple model of hierarchy in which two classes exist; the royals and the drones.

Temptation, the Key to Power

Temptation can be rightfully understood as the key to power. It pervades through all plans of social engineering and of even military endeavours. It can be stated that individuals will only willingly engage in a direction, one wishes for them to take, if one tempts them with a reward. Like the stereotypically cliched lab-rat, we are very much led down funnels via the proverbial carrot-on-the-stick, by the ruling class whom, from our earliest formative years, moulded our malleable and impressionable minds into blind followers of authority. To seal the deal, as we say, if the authority is tempting one with the delicious cheese of freedom or money, at the end of the winding but unknown tunnel, the majority will thus venture forth into that uncharted territory in search of the said cheese, which they were so earnestly promised. However, like all games of temptation, one seldom receives what they were promised; the snake-oil does not provide a panacea to troubles, but it may just poison the intrepid recipient. Though, many "street-smart" individuals know that a salesman will promise the world, if you would only but buy his product, and once you buy his said product, his care for you will dissipate quicker than *Colin Powell's* credibility after that "weapons of mass-destruction" malarky, as *Biden* likes to remark so *passé*. Thus, temptation is merely to bring the potential recipient, the psychological prey, into line with an agenda; that could be a sale of products, business deals, or social engineering, etc.

Extrapolating that understanding out, onto the national and international level, we can see that populations are only ever brought into line with novel and emerging social agendas, favourable to the interests of the formulator of said agenda, by means of temptation; fear is only a catalyst to ensure the temptation, or bait, is seen and registered as a necessity by the target population. Evidently, the target population is only receptive to these types of "power plays" if they have been primed to follow or believe authority, unquestionably; this was the reason for the type of public-schooling system, compulsory education system, designed and implemented within the West, amongst the lower-orders at least; however, I will touch upon this later. Digressing, we can see the example of this type of deceptive temptation for fulfilment of the agenda, through this engineered crisis event, titled a "Pandemic". This event has been spun to deprive people of their freedom, through the guise of a health emergency, and enact lockdown policies to deprive them of social interaction and ensure they thoroughly go mad through torturous house-arrest; this is unequivocally "torture", of a mental variety designed for one to acquiesce to a third-party's demands, by the UN's standards of course[500]. The solution, to stop this state-imposed torture, blamed upon an unseen third-party, a malign entity, is to obediently acquiesce to the vaccine, immunity passport, testing, and the utter surveillance and tracking of all one does. To accept tyranny, the likes of which is all-pervasive and inescapable. Naturally, the justification for this is the emergency, which like all tyrannies, is inflated or fabricated totally and the solution provided, the fulfilment of the tyrant's agenda, is always projected in a light of keeping the populace safe; because they simply care for your wellbeing, of course they do. Continuing on, this indirect mandating of the solution is to provide the population with a sense of "choice" within the matter, that it is not being mandated directly, but is being indirectly implied as being a necessity, through the avenues of media, etc. Thus, individuals, almost instinctively, realise that if they wish to engage in their old luxuries once again – which they misidentify as "freedoms" – is only permitted once they have relinquished of their actual freedoms; bodily autonomy, right to property, right to privacy within one's abode, free speech, freedom to travel unimpeded, etc. It is largely a symbolic gesture of the final completion, which was started within the compulsory education system, of blind obedience.

I should discuss the Prussian-model of schooling, as I have alluded to it previously and many will be in the dark to what it actually is. The Prussian-model of education is very much the basis for the modern education systems we see across the Western world and the Prussian-model was championed by the 20th century pioneers of industry and finance, many you would know the name of today and we shall touch

---

[500] UN Human Rights, Office of the High Commissioner. (1984). *Convention against Torture and Other Cruel, Inhuman or Degrading Treatment or Punishment Adopted and opened for signature, ratification and accession by General Assembly resolution.* Available: https://www.ohchr.org/en/professionalinterest/pages/cat.aspx#:~:text=For%20the%20purposes%20of%20this,a%20third%20person%20has%20committed. Last accessed 10/05/2021.

upon the interwovenness of their efforts and of their sanguineous ties. The Prussian-model was developed by *Frederick the Great* with his decree of 1763, entitled *Generallandschulreglement*, which was written by *Johann Julius Hecker*, it went through many a development, but at the height of Prussia's military power it consisted of a compulsory attendance, formal training of teachers, a standardised curriculum, school year and a strict de rigueur or uniform. As stated by *Thomas Alexander*, in his 1918 literary work, titled "The Prussian Elementary School", "We believe, however, that a careful study of the Prussian school system will convince any unbiased reader that the Prussian citizen cannot be free to do and act for himself; that the Prussian is to a large measure enslaved through the medium of his school ; that his learning, instead of making him his own master, forges the chain by which he is held in servitude ; that the whole scheme of Prussian elementary education is shaped with the express purpose of making ninety-five out of every hundred citizens subservient to the ruling house and to the state. The elementary schools of Prussia have been fashioned so as to make spiritual and intellectual slaves of the lower classes."[501] Thus, what is described here is the developed *Volkschule*, which was what every industrial and oil tycoon from *Frederick T. Gates,* to *John D. Rockefeller,* to *Andrew Carnegie*, all invested heavily in the creation of forced education based on the system described above. This was centred around the *Rockefeller General Education Board* and *John D. Rockefeller* made an initial donation of $1Million in 1902, with aid for *Frederick T. Gates*. The stated goals were to fund higher education and medical schools within the USA. By 1903, this "Education Board" of *Rockefeller* would be incorporated, by the US government, most likely bought off by *Rockefeller*, and their goal changed to "the promotion of education throughout the US, without distinction to race, sex or creed"[502]. This

---

[501] Thomas Alexander (1918). *The Prussian elementary schools*. New York: Macmillan company. Preface, pg. V.
[502] U.S. Congress. (1903). *An Act To incorporate the General Education Board*. Available: https://www.loc.gov/law/help/statutes-at-large/57th-congress/session-2/c57s2ch91.pdf. Last accessed 10/05/2021.

Chapter VIII

Bill was supported by Senator *Nelson W. Aldrich*, a Senator from Rhode Island, coincidentally this Senator's daughter, *Abby*, was married to *John D. Rockefeller Jr.*, and it is a peculiar connection too that this Senator was also involved within the creation of the *Federal Reserve Act* of 1913. As I stated this entire agenda has been a slow process, carefully crafted for almost a century, and the characters are extremely interwoven, in familial terms. Digressing though, the *Rockefeller* family would furnish around $180Million to fund this incorporated board.

Why did they go to all this trouble to fund the enfranchisement of education, intellectualisation the lower classes and thus by consequence creating competition from such classes in the process? The reason being because it was not an intellectualisation of the lower classes, but a lobotomization and a stunting of intellectual growth of the lower orders. It was designed to destroy individualism and create more obedient workers; that were inculcated with the ideas that would be necessary for the formation of a planned society and, subsequent, planned population; this agenda was in its planning stages since at least the 19th century. *Frederick T. Gates*, an instrumental aid to *Rockefeller* in the creation of this plan for education within the USA, and potentially a man linked to the infamous software tycoon *Bill Gates* though such things are considered mere conjecture, stated within his 1913 literary work "The Country School of To-morrow" that, "In our dream, we have limitless resources, and the people yield themselves with perfect docility to our moulding hand. The present educational conventions fade from our minds; and, unhampered by tradition, we work our own good will upon a grateful and responsive rural folk. We shall not try to make these people or any of their children into philosophers or men of learning or of science. We are not to raise up from among them authors, orators, poets, or men of letters. We shall not search for embryo great artists, painters, musicians. Nor will we cherish even the humbler ambition to raise up from among them lawyers, doctors, preachers, politicians, statesmen, of whom we now have ample supply."[503] Thus, this is the system they wished for and the one they have now got. The educational system creates blind obedience to authority and one must memorise and regurgitate, memorise and regurgitate, if they wish to earn high grades; and high grades means a far better paying wage-slave position, of which one may gain some modicum of greater free time. Additionally, these individuals were "monopolists" and as such they wished to extend their monopolies they had created within their various sectors, over the entirety of society; an entire monopolisation of everything. They wish for no competition from the lower orders – like all merchant classes, that rise within the *age of Affluence*, they wish to create hereditary dynasties of power – and this is pompously put by *Frederick T. Gates* within the same piece of literature, where he states, "For the task that we set before ourselves is a very simple as well as a very beautiful one: to train these people as we find them for a perfectly ideal life just where they are". Their descendants edge ever closer to the realisation of this entire erstwhile ambition today.

To conclude, the state will thence utilise the mentality of servility instilled within the masses, via this compulsory education system, to ensure they can be made pliable to these "temptations" offered to them by the state. Since they have been made mentally meek, like children, they are thus emotionally and intellectually dependent upon the state; they will thenceforth do as the state bids them to do, for they have lost all agency. The state may suppress their freedoms and abuse them, on a societal scale, and then tempt them with gaining respite from this; only if they will conform to the demands of the emergent planned society. It is disgustingly sick, but nonetheless a brilliant and patient move by individuals who are beyond psychopathic; thus, beyond Human. It may be said that these fiends play the accursed devil, the daemon of enticement, that if only the rustics would bow before the new political paradigm, they would be remunerated with all manner of worldly

---

[503] Frederick T. Gates (1913). The Country School of To-morrow. New York City: General Education Board. Pg. 6.

pleasures; however, such pleasures come at a price and for one to cede their own soul in exchange for these promises, of which more than likely were made in bad faith, is a form of death in-an-of-itself. For if one relinquishes his sovereignty, his independence, for a pleasurable servitude; like perennial Lotus-Eaters, from birth to death.

> *"The tomb lies at the end of every path. Only the soul is immortal. Guard this treasure well. Your decaying husk is but a temporary vessel on an endless voyage."*
> —Willliam Hjortsberg

Fear, The Initiator of New Paradigms

Fear does not trounce hope, of which the main vehicle for hope is temptation. Subsequently, we must understand that the initiating stage within the infamous *Hegelian or Triadic Dialectic*, the thesis or problem, always has to be catalysed via the induction of fear or fear of a problem, perceived or real. However, fear cannot facilitate the full synthesisation of the thesis and antithesis, colloquially referred to as the "problem" and "reaction", thus this is why temptation or hope is really the coercive factor within this social engineering equation of the *Hegelian or Triadic Dialectic*; of which I have discussed previously. Consequently, it can be stated that in such a domesticated society, of which we find ourselves firmly in now, it can be stated that depriving the enfeebled masses of their precious luxuries is truly the far more effectual method of propelling an agenda of social-reengineering; as compared to a stratagem composed solely focused around the inducement of fear of an existential threat that cannot be controlled, and most notably, one that is unseen; or only able to be quantified by the initiator of agenda, or the authority figure in the situation. Fear can only be used as a primer, as such once it is employed as the staple facilitating mechanism within any agenda of social reengineering it will slowly lose its potency in propelling the agenda forward; hope, of whose vehicle is temptation, is thus far more efficacious in its resultant applied effects. Why is this the case? If a population has been slowly moulded into being mentally and spiritually, for lack of a better term, dependent upon the triviality of entertainment and amusement, they will thus become naturally distraught at the denial of those said objects of dependence. Like mindless addicts without narcotics and needles, they will seek to do the bidding of anyone – subjecting themselves to the lowest denominator – to simply acquire their next fix of inanity; naturally, to the supplier and denier of these fixes of inanity, it provides quite an advantageous position of which can be exploited to best effect, for the needs of social-reengineering. In conjunction, within our contemporary timeline, we find that the supplier and denier of these fixes is thus the state and this makes the states, at least within the Western sphere, omnipotent; soon-to-be omnipresent and omniscient; they wish to be God, like all mortals aspire to be. Thenceforth, from this understanding, from the priming of fear into the populace, the state can assuredly bring into lockstep an entire population of consumers by the simple action of turning on and off the tap of vacuous amusement; this is akin to taking away the toys of a child, as a means of behavioural correction.

Digressing though, what is becoming apparent within this present round of social-reengineering, with a chemical twist mind you, are that it seems with the slowing vaccination rates they are employing a three-fold strategy; with the echoing of fear throughout. The strategy of coercing the majority of the populace into accepting the vaccination and likewise the "new normal", is done within three stages of a continuum of pressure. Firstly, it begins with general denial of luxury, hope proceeding the adoption of the shot or "new normal", and social pressures. These pressures may amount to vilification of oneself within the public eye, shaming, ostracisation and a general feeling of being socially disenfranchised due to the denial of the touted social benefits of the adoption of these said vehicles of initiation into the "new world".

Chapter VIII

Secondly, within the continuum of escalation, we shall find that the state will seek to further buttress their initial foray into this agenda and then additionally include a type of door-to-door policy, in which medical and Police personnel will seek to enforce and "sell" the shot, and by extension, will utilise neurolinguistic-programming and manipulation of the ego to "convert" the hesitators; this is seen within a leaked NHS internal report[504]. Thirdly, once or if they reach the threshold of, what is looking right now across the global board, at around eight-percent, then they can initiate a broad and sweeping demonisation of the unconvertable, so to say. The third and final stage will be characterised by the pushing of both fear of variants and increased luxury denial, blaming it upon the remaining unconvertable; this will trigger a swathe of anger and resentment unto the non-compliant class, which will eventually, like all state-encouraged genocides, will result in the marginalisation and extermination of this class of people. Thus, this will be the *cassus belli* that will avail itself to the ruling class; if the agenda continues to its logical conclusion that is.

Continuing on with that theme of the current agenda at play, it can be said that the UBI (Universal Basic Income) that is starting to see pilot programs around the world[505], found its primordial stages within the rounds of stimulus cheques and government income support schemes. Consequently, this was a type of conditioning of the public to receiving currency for free and ensuring they become accustomed to this next level of state dependency. Many individuals, funnily enough, have now become so dependent upon the state and their four-walled abodes, that many are unable to leave their house; they have subsequently developed agoraphobic issues and, as such, they will have a very narrow window of

---

[504] NHS England and NHS Improvement. (2020). *Vaccination do's and don'ts by audience cohorts*. Available: https://www.local.gov.uk/sites/default/files/documents/Vaccination%20do%20and%20donts%20by%20audience%20cohorts.pdf. Last accessed 04/05/2021.

[505] Will Hayward. (2021). *Mark Drakeford approves universal basic income trial for Wales*. Available: https://www.walesonline.co.uk/news/wales-news/universal-basic-income-trial-work-20613496. Last accessed 19/05/2021.

information and viewpoints from which they can hear from. Pulling the discourse back to the main topic of UBI, we can see that, like China, this type of financial dependency upon the state will naturally be utilised for social control. That being, if one does not abide by all the new social policies coming forth – shots, mask-wearing, new social norms, universal application of QR Codes, etc – then they shall be denied their "basic citizen's income". Now, the disadvantages run far deeper than merely missing out on $5000-$7500, per annum; in present value terms. Naturally, in keeping with the inflationary effects that would arise from an unleashing of so much monetary stimulus onto society, universally, we would find that one's purchasing would be constantly eroded to the point that if one was not in receipt of this citizen's basic income, which would only grow in size and scope, then they would be at a severe financial disadvantage. Imagine it, if you will, a middle-class income being worth ten-percent or so less, in present value terms, if one was not in receipt of the UBI, strictly because of fact of prices rising and purchasing power falling parallel to the plenteous injection into society of copious credit conjured from thin-air; it would be economic terrorism on the unvaccinated; an artificial impoverishing of the dissident class. This will be financial fear, a sowing of terror into the hearts of the disbeliever of "progress", so to say. Fear of immeasurable suffering from the pangs of hunger and unavoidable homelessness; extortion of obedience.

Rerouting back to the main theme, as a conclusionary discussion, it can be justly said that fear must be sown and induced into the population prior to the initiation of an agenda of social-redirection, for if it is not then the said population will not be welcoming to such deprivation of liberty and luxury; as they obviously would see no justification for it, nor have their centres of reason and logic been disarmed thoroughly enough. A population not first paralysed by fear, is a population that may be led to engage their rational mind and, by virtue of that, what they will undoubtedly see, is the overreaching and intrusive predation of the state;

of which from they will consider two options; fight or flight. Naturally, both of these are undesirable to the state, or initiator of the agenda, in the boundless issues they may, by consequence, create. "Hope" and "Fear" can be summarised as the *lingua franca* of state-funded public relations.

The Panopticon Cometh Forth

The panopticon cometh forth, into a world bound in triviality;
and beckoned to momentary pleasure;
a world beyond the reach of reason and good judgement.
It cometh like a thunderbolt from the Gods above,
as a punishment unto the mortals, for their transgressions made in folly,
against the Mother of Order herself.
It is flame to cloth, a flail to skin; it renders all it touches
a mere depiction of dust.
Privacy; begone. Freewill; begone. Unmitigated
thought; begone.
The cold and steely gaze, of the prying eyes of modernity, creeps
lingeringly into the vestiges of one's own soul;
it will find one's deepest secrets and
darkest horrors and deliver it, as a weapon, unto the heart of their person.
It is a false, yet cruel God;
it is all-seeing, all-knowing and, ineludibly ever-present.
Lest we tread into its dark valley,
we should most assuredly turn away.

The surveillance state, in its infancy, we see slowly becoming constructed within this new and "progressive" age is very much in direct opposition to the old paradigms; it is not a natural progression, but a rewiring of the civilisational psyche into a neoterically puissant matrix. One of the main foundational pillars of this emerging matrix is that of currency reset; this will naturally be a requisite for the novel economic structure, that will subsume the old order in time. This currency reset thence stems from the unholy union of modern monetary theory with the emergent technology of blockchain. As with most new and powerful technologies, these can have positive and empowering applications for society, in a broad respect, or for a purely minority clique of rich robber-barons, who would hence prey upon that broader majority of society with their new tools of technological advantage. It would seem, unfortunately, that like much of history, blockchain is slowly falling victim to that latter category; as is the law of most of history, to the best of my knowledge. Additionally, this blockchain technology, that is ultimately a solution to the *Byzantine General's Problem* or the problem of establishing low-latency source congruency within an automated digital ledger, will be reversed engineered, so to say, to be applied solely to a centralised digital fiat system; which will utilise a modified form of blockchain technology for the essence of control and more stable manipulation of the prevailing economic structure, that will emerge out from this coming chaos. Effectively, it will usher in a bleak binary domain, where everyone is tracked and little is out of the way of the prying eyes of authority. To the discerning eye, one may conclude that this type of modified blockchain technology, will have other applications beyond mere unassailable economic and monetary control and that discerning eye would be utterly correct, but that is much too expansive of a concept to discuss in such a brief manner here and, as such, I feel inclined to deal with that in a future work of mine. Although, as a side-note, the ISO20022 framework seems to be the next vehicle for this furthering of monetary-cartel control, which is the theorised framework of the new interbank lending market that is seeing a slow uptake, really because for a long time the technology was absent to initiate it in a cost-effective manner, is beginning to come online, so to say, no pun intended; it is utilising centralised crypto-transfer protocols/systems such as Ripple (XRP), Stellar (XLM), Algorand, etc. Digressing however, now that we have thoroughly delineated the two paths that face the economic and wider world, in terms of the application of blockchain technology, we should also note that if that latter option – the centralised digital ledger (blockchain) – becomes applied to society in a broader context, such as a social-credit system, then everyone can kiss their lives goodbye, genuinely. Why is this? Simply put, if society is merged into a digital protocol, where all actions and structures, micro and macro, are inescapably surveilled and the logistics systems are thoroughly into this framework, then every single person will be at the mercy of this centralised control-grid if they wish to eat or live; couple, this with a potential bio-digital fusion amongst every person, so that every person is a living and breathing bio-digital embodiment of the centralised protocol and you begin to see the implications for liberty and living free from the clutches of control. Conformity would be strictly regulated via direct infusing into the bio-digital mainframe of the person, who in all actuality would be more machine than man by this point, a bio-digital construct distorted by the minds of mad-hat techno-feudal overlords. This shall thus be the finale of this currency reset, which underpins the entire "Great Reset" agenda; that being, without the reset of the economic apparatus, there can be no congruent direction of control on the global stage; the parity of serf could not be maintained; the social and economic mobility of the lower castes could be satisfactorily induced.

Concordantly, we may also remark upon the idea of the "Great Reset" and its technological underpinnings being wrapped up in an innate desire by the ruling-class and their hubris in defying the natural cycles of civilisational decay and entropy; they wish to disarm the law of entropy of power within this world; they can accurately be described as the world's most fantastical control-freaks. Thusly, they are attempting actively right now to stave of the inevitable decline of their monetary and, by extension, political hold of the planet by means of invalidating nature via technology. Although, the odds are not within their favour, this could be the first civilisation in history to artificially stave-off collapse via technological means; however, at what cost does this come, though? Well, it requires a digitisation and binarization of all of humanity, postdating a mass-cull of the herd for reasons of manageability; followed by a partially induced collapse for ease of rebuilding from the premise of an enfeebled and population pleading for order to the contrived chaos. The revitalisation of the ailing monopoly of the ruling class will thus be ushered in, as all their nascent protocols are, on the back of fear and the predetermined hope of a solution. The cost will thusly be too high, for the ordinary man and woman, but they will know not this truth until it is too late; such is the folly of the human mind captivated by fear and consequently disarmed of the ability laterally reason. Thus, if we accept this digital currency, which will precede a forced bio-digital interconnectedness, an "internet of things", which will be sold as convenience and "enhancement" of one's self, then we shall be forever imprisoned by means of possession to the demons of the digital abyss; the Abaddonic realm realised in the tenebrious milieu of digital purgatory. Thus, all of our liberties eroded entirely, our ability of social mobility rendered void, and an entire monopolisation, by an indomitable monopolist class, of not just the economic and monetary sectors but of human nature entirely; down to the very individual's natural composition and his personnel thoughts; everything shall be assimilated into this collectivist interconnected web.

The cost is too high and I think, if everyone took a moment to think about this clearly, they would see that it does not benefit the ordinary Man to empower the necro-economists with reanimating a zombie economy, rather it only benefits them and their maintaining of monopolistic control over the main object, which is undivided power; of whose wielders are reticent to share even but a crumb of.

Another topic I wished to discuss was the idea of "Social Primers". Social Primers, unlike "predictive programming", is very much a tangible concept in which one can easily see the hallmarks of the social conditioning that preceded it, and how it laid the foundational pillars that sit atop the new structure of lies that is busily being constructed. "Predictive programming" would be indicative of a type of visual familiarisation with a future, planned event; on the other hand, Social Primers are a

Chapter VIII

slow continuum of various, seemingly unconnected emergent social norms, that leads to acclimation to an absurd or unorthodox new social paradigm; in our contemporary world, this is acclimation to societally visible absurdities in the form of social-media-driven and media events. For example, we see the social experiment of the Ghost Watch hysteria, within the UK, within the 1990s and comparatively, this was seen within the War of the Worlds hysteria, within the infamous radio broadcast, which was all used to gauge the public's willingness to believe, blindly, absurd narratives in a stupendously eccentric fashion. Thus, from these Social Primers and social experimentation, has a sort of bizarro world come forth where contemporary academia and media are embroiled in the process of discussing the topic of "can males give birth?", or "should the term Mother be banned?" Thence, this mass perturbation within the regular social character has loosened the constraints upon the stability of the societal pathway and, as such, society has become almost cancerous in nature; that being, highly mutagenic and spontaneously self-pernicious. The "Ice-bucket" and "Cinnamon" challenges were another modern example of this; with the added angle of "nomination" and thus social conformity on the command of one's peers."

Social Primers are absolutely crucial for a ruling class, if it wishes to, within a larger agenda, to introduce the traditionally level-headed public to social norms and cultural beliefs that are antithetical to their interests and the maintaining of natural inclinations. It is largely for means of inducing chaos into the system, in which the public will feel entirely atomised by this chaos that, for the normal person, offers little solution at resolve; in this mentally enfeebled state, they will look to the state for the answers and blind obedience will be induced, ergo. Contemporarily, this induced absurdity of blind obedience to, what logically can only be, a planned depopulation measure in the form of an immunisation shot. This has stemmed from the insatiable desire of the ruling class to foist upon the unvigilant populace, a gradually intensifying set of unpropitious social norms through media and invented "stars" of the day. What we have seen since the swinging 1920's and, what started as anything but gradual, but faded into a gradualist approach, was a sexualisation of the youth and a promotion of promiscuous tendencies through invented popular music, drink, drugs and lewd dancing. This was to push on and eventually break down the barriers of acceptable cultural practises, via the supplanting of traditional folk music, that had always accompanied youth dances before, with crude and alien "pop-music"; that was solely controlled, in direction, via a cartel of record-labels. Moreover, this music would contain sexual themes and references, that would be sold as "harmless fun", as a means of covertly infiltrating society and priming it for destruction via the gradual, multigenerational tainting of its youth. Continuing on, through the bulwark of lewd music, also came the lewd sexual-icons and pop-stars and the inventing of those for the purposes of promoting sexual promiscuity and cultural decay; for example, Elvis the pelvis, as he was described as after shockingly shaking his pelvis in a sexually provocative way, as he was instructed to do by the record-labels. This, naturally, generated intense anger within the public sphere and the youth, seeing the dismay of their parents to this, and as youth generally are, wished to be independent; so, they copied this, like monkey-see-monkey-do, and rebelled against the cultural traditions. Now, we see that clip of Elvis acting provocatively as nothing and we find the traditional sensibilities utterly outdated and almost laughable. However, that is because we are the resultant product of the multigenerational taint that stemmed forth from that type of promoted sickness and, as such, we are by consequence mentally sick ourselves. Alas, we have Miley Cyrus and other disgusting "artists", and their profanity abound today; it is a slow degradation and has been since the advent of dances like the Charleston and Fox trot of the swinging '20s. Within this type of music too, was a familiarisation of the teachings of Marx; wherein, naturally intellectually devoid political ideologies garnered clout and promoted a further set of absurd tenets onto the cultural framework of the country; equality, sexual

Chapter VIII

liberation, equality of the sexes, dismantling of the traditional family unit, etc.

These types of absurdities were designed to facilitate what we have now and the blind obedience, coupled with an affrighting apathy, within the masses. How did it do this? Generally, it promoted atomisation and a subtle demolishment of the national glue that held these communities strong; whilst dressing this demolishment in finely, embroidered silk and bright and colourful adornments to attract the target populations; to have them partake in actions that were detrimental to the long-term survival of their line and themselves. Militarily speaking, to clarify the ruling class's rationale on this, how would one break apart a densely packed formation of an interlocked and shielded pike formation? One would sow chaos within the ranks, firing volleys of missiles from a distant safety, breaking apart its formation and consequently extirpate its cohesion; only then is it vulnerable. Alas, in contrast, the assault of the West could not be done in a full-frontal charge; it had to be slow, methodical and pick apart the population until it was sliced up into its constituent parts, each divided against the other. Only then could the ruling-class destroy them and control the social direction entirely; gaslighting them, through the instituting of absurd notions of "colonialism" from the imperial stock and "sexual and gender non-conformity", so that they would be unable to discern correctly the natural order and world around them; to taint their minds and intoxicate them upon harried delusion. Digressing and touching upon another aspect of this question, one may ask: why did they do this? Simple. Sexual desire is a powerful force and is one that must tempered for the long-term promulgation of a prosperous civilisation; that being, both sexes must agree to temper their sexual desires to create strong family units and use those energies for the good of the group; naturally, as I have previously discussed, a group who is embroiled in the frivolity of pursuing rampant sexual desires typically experiences a breakdown in the social fabric and a birth-rate that destroys their future;

this stems from the weakness or lack of families that abound in such social circumstances. Thus, it has furthermore been found that if one engages in rampant promiscuity, that with the ever-greater number of sexual partners one has, past having zero before your wedding night that is, increases the statistical average of divorce[506]. This was seen comparatively within parralled the moral and thence demographic decline of Rome, of which I described in a previous section. Hence, if the family is weak then the main frontline defence of the civilisation shall be in disarray and susceptible to assimilation by foreign adversarial thinking and ludicrous new social norms; it is also fantastic for tyrannies to arise, as you can see, as the population have no tribe to defend them, they thus succumb to capitulation to the new tyrannical paradigm.

Naturally, this entire collection of intentional maiming to the body of the West has coalesced to create the evolved poison of "Wokeism". This is the synthesis of all that has came before and is the final form of the social viper that is gripped onto our necks, and is slowly sizing us up for consumption. The reason for the perversion of the natural culture, within this current phase, is due to the need to confuse the public as to what they are and who they are. If the public are in incessant debate on whether a man can have a vagina, get pregnant, or have a menstrual cycle, then they are utterly despondent of fixed logic and thus an understanding of their place in the world and within society. Subsequently, they will be seriously displaced, mentally, by the torrent of fluctuating and ever-changing social norms and even, what should be, the observable natural world and its laws. Thenceforth, can the tyrant play upon this immobilising confusion and cognitive dissonance in the individual, who will have become a *Tabla Rassa* by this point, a malleable "blank slate" if you will, and thus he can project obedience onto the individual's psyche because they know not

---

[506] Nicholas H. Wolfinger. (2016). *Counterintuitive Trends in the Link Between Premarital Sex and Marital Stability*. Available: https://ifstudies.org/blog/counterintuitive-trends-in-the-link-between-premarital-sex-and-marital-stability#:~:text=Even%20so%2C%20premarital%20sex%20with,increases%20the%20odds%20of%20divorce.&text=T. Last accessed 26/05/2021.

how to chart a course through this daunting novel frontier; as such, they relinquish their thinking to what they perceive to be their betters; the tyrant and his subordinate army of professed "experts".

Thus, it can be said, that this incremental distortion of the natural order and of civility itself, has led to the unfathomable descent into mass madness we see today; "clown world", as it is comically described. Alas, this has led to the conditioning of instinctive obedience to an ever-changing and complex social paradigm – by design obviously - that differs extensively from the natural order; the human mind is adaptable to what it perceives to be the consensus on sensibilities. In conclusion, as *Voltaire* stated, "those that can make you believe absurdities, can make you commit atrocities". Likewise, we find ourselves on the precipice of mass suicide as a national and intercultural form; the conclusion of the concatenated self-mutilation of the culture; conducted at the hands of a blinded and debilitated population, drunk on the lust for the ludicrous and profane; revelling in sin and captivated by the unfolding of ever more unnatural horrors. Consequently, as we can see now with the bifurcation of the newly emergent species, the vaccinated and unvaccinated, the obedient are very much sated in the pursuit of protecting the four-walled confines of their prison cells. The four-walls being; Consumerism, Conformity, Safety and Pleasure. They care for nothing else and wish for little more. The crumbs of these satisfy their base sensory needs and they go back to a life of grazing, mindlessly; even if one was to discuss the evident potentials of, say, this perceived cure to this not-so-deadly disease, then they would still take that leap-of-faith for the promise of maintaining those four-walls. Without the walls, they are nothing; without the safety provided by the word of the master, they are lost. Henceforth, human slavery continues to propagate itself silently.

"The propitious smiles of heaven can never be expected on a nation that disregard the eternal rules of order and right, which Heaven itself has ordained." - *George Washington*.

Incremental Digitisation

This will be somewhat of a continuation in principle to the last section, but will more acutely discuss the technological, as opposed to psychological, means of the furthering of this agenda. As we can see from the past two decades, there is strong emphasis on the digitisation of all life to the point that one, certainly presently, cannot live without the internet and a smart phone. What was seemingly sold to us as convenience has become an oubliette, from which we cannot escape from the vertical funnel we were chucked down so many years ago. We rot in the dark, with the faint flicker of a light that we cannot put down, cannot relinquish and are required to always have with us if we wish to enter a wide arrange of establishments. Convenience and safety, the creed of slaves and the justification of tyrants; it would seem.

Thus, the slow incline towards digitisation, *en masse*, of the various facets of modern human existence, through the forcible conditioning of the public into the viewing of these "smart-phones" and other such devices – ostensibly designed for convenience in mind – as a necessity to life; social, financial, etc. Through this unshakable view of necessity, we find that the newly emerging political regime can use these devices, this grid of control if you will, to survey, micro-manage and better control the population. Permitting the managerial classes of all of society to control large numbers and direct them with ease. Subsequently, as the smartphone is almost a portable access point for the ruling-class to bombard one's psyche with incessant messaging from their media and programming the behavioural pattern of the individual via the constant hammering of a false view of the world and of the consensus; an individual can thus be psychologically moulded, non-invasively and undetectably. For example, look at the slow decline of grammar, diction and general conversational speech from the advent of the mass-telecommunicated media, that being the TV, but it seems to have taken a sharp, parabolic downturn since the mass-adoption of the smartphone. You see, this is not simply a device

Chapter VIII

of surveillance, no of course not, the ruling-class prefer popularised mechanisms of population management to be multipurpose, and as such it is a potent device of manipulation. Let us discuss that fact of decreased vocabulary and the lack of expression of the younger generations, though this has been a successively degrading problem. Thus, we can see that this has been a product of applications, colloquially termed "apps", such as snapchat, SMS texts that have migrated to applications such as Messenger, WhatsApp, etc, and this has infused into the mind of the modern youth an abbreviated and narrow form of applied English; in that, the mind has been infected with the inability to form coherent and persuadable arguments, interesting sentences and a lack of vocabulary to exchange ideas efficiently. Similes are incorrectly accounted for within sentences and the timbre of speech is obtuse and repulsive; though this type of degradation of culture has infected every aspect of art and expression, it is most acutely visible within the intermediary of intellect, that being language and linguistic.

Par exemple, we find that there is a distinct lack of the attention span that has sprung forth from this type of devolution in language, spurred on by SMS-style writing, that has ensured a reduction in the number of people who read and read well. Why is this an issue for a body of citizenry? That being, if the vast proportion of the populace fail to enjoy reading or do it regularly, this will only further erode the language standards and if the language standards erode broadly, then we will begin to see, as we are now, a stupefaction of the populace. Hence, from this degradation of reading, a more easily manipulatable prey species will evolve; a lack of absorbing of new and challenging information, coupled with a laxer grasp of one's native language, will hinder the development of an individual's mastery of logic and rational-mind and will only embolden a type of emotional and one-dimensional pathology, as we are seeing now. That is, individuals now will subscribe to absurdity on the sole reason that it makes them feel good; essentially, the empathic nature of the individual has been strengthened to an unnatural extent, via a dumbing-down of their cognition, and weaponised into a pathological form of gullibility and feel-good mania. That being, we can see why people are scrambling to inject themselves with an unknown and experimental substance to "save Grandma"; even though, according to official immunology, if Grandma is vaccinated then the transmissibility stops with her, unquestionably. Furthermore, this is the reason for the development of "virtue-signalling"; the sanctimonious advertisement of one's own goodwill and altruism for enhancement of social status. As you can see, these are some of the main psychological reasons for the proliferation of the smartphone to the masses, by the ruling-class.

Edward Snowden discussed and still discusses these outward developments, from this technology, of a toolkit of tyranny. He discussed that these types of devices, that have been intentionally made a necessity within our lives, is very much a step towards the "social-credit system" of which we see in China. That being, if the government, in real-time, like not any of your purchases, associates, travel history, etc, then you are barred from engaging in these privileges and, are such, labelled a dissident, an outcast. This type of government control, he states, will be increasingly decided by algorithms and these algorithms will be "be fuelled by the innocent data that are devices are creating all of the time; constantly, invisibly, quietly right now." These devices are thus a casting, a mark if you will, of our real-time activity to the government of whom will in turn, as governments by nature do, will use that data nefariously and for the purposes of ever tighter control of the citizenry. These records, *Snowden* also remarks, "that in aggregate seem very innocent" but when collated, create a precise picture of your identity as an individual and every dirty secret, every potentially blackmailable part of you, all at the disposal and view of the government; it is total control, much like the sway they hold over the political prostitutes on their payroll. Even right now, directly incriminating material is not exactly needed, the government can collect, within the USA, without a warrant, the metadata; the location of calls, the contact you called, etc, for example. Thus, we are already

Chapter VIII

on the legal road to the social-credit system of China, where everyone will be tracked, traced and dealt with if they dissent against the state. The *Social Primer* of this is the "Track and Trace" and "Contact Tracing" apps that are being unveiled for use by the public, some are even being mandated by government; this is the "Architecture of Oppression", as *Snowden* described it, is being created before our very eyes and is being done under the guise of a supposed medical emergency. Remember, a state of emergency declaration is simply government declaring more emergent powers for themselves; there is no real threat, but the threat of encroaching tyranny.

What is about to be ushered in is a total surveillance state, it is the literal realisation of the "Big Brother" concept of *Orwell's* "1984". It will be a bleak dystopia, full of fear and people clamouring to make ends meet. I think this entire agenda is a response, or solution if you will, by the Western powers to the inevitability of collapse and decline within the cyclical nature of their civilisation; this aforesaid solution is thus being advised to them by external powerbrokers and monied interests, of whom are preying upon their wish to circumvent civilisational death; these external powerbrokers and monied interests naturally hold blackmail and financial dominion over these various Western powers, too. Thus, they believe, to outrun this civilisational death, they must artificially collapse it and from the ashes impose a predictable and clinical world; where the mechanism of collapse, the citizenry, is tightly controlled within a brittle, top-down approach with the aid of technology. Naturally, brittle, top-down approaches – tyranny – never work in the long-term, but they clearly believe it will with the technology they possess. This technology, as I have outlined, allows them the ability to remotely control and micro-manage the populace through coercion, denial of basic amenities, and social exile; those are only the ones that we know of and can visibly see come into view at present, naturally. However, it could be several avenues of control they exert upon the populace through the means of technology; only time will tell. However, they are actively attempting to rewrite the course of human history, to remake Man in their own image and play God in a perverse and ever fallible way; it is not unlike the spirit of evil to be so brazen, but for the good to do nothing is certainly a surprise. The social-credit system is the only natural progression of the current applications of this type of technology; it is a grave mistake to acquiesce to such a future shaped by these devious digital assassins, cloaked in shadow and prone to evil. Do you trust the wielders of this technology? You would be foolish, if you did.

> *"Hide not thy poison with such sug'red words.*
> *Lay not thy hands on me; forbear, I say!*
> *Their touch affrights me as a serpent's sting.*
> *Thou baleful messenger, out of my sight!*
> *Upon thy eyeballs murderous tyranny*
> *Sits in grim majesty, to fright the world."*
> —Shakespeare, Henry VI, Part II

THE ATLANTEAN MYTH

The *Richat Structure* may very well be the Capital of the old kingdom of King Atlas; the mythological Atlantis and there is good evidence purporting to that fact. One is met with tantalisingly ponderous wonders within finding the artifacts that, if the *Richat Structure* is that of Atlantis, would have been washed away to the Eastern-most Atlantic. Historically that location within Mauretania and up to the North to *Gades* (Modern-day Cadiz) was the fabled Atlantean Empire of extreme pre-history. However, let us put questions about historical authenticity aside, and discuss the idea of Atlantis, as a cautionary tale of the greed and immoral pursuits of an advanced utopia. Of whom, attempting to become like Gods, were smote by fire and earthquake by the natural powers and sunk into the sea, where time rusted and distorted their very memory. The story has parallels to many cultures and shares similarities

Chapter VIII

with the Abrahamic *Sodom and Gomorrah* tale, even the tale of *Noah*, and every other flood and catastrophe myth that proceeds from human folly is very much concurrent; the legendary city of *Ys* in Breton mythology, for example, is another example. This conceptual ember, that is cross-cultural, has been passed down between civilisations - from Kemetic to Hellenic, and so on - about the "world before the world"; the precursor civilisation that reached its imperial and technological zenith, bearing no other rivals bar its own hubris, and of the natural world it angered so. The understanding being, that when Man reaches a point of extreme technological or civilisational might that, in accordance with Man's intrinsic nature, will most undoubtedly engage in self-destructive behaviour that will eventually lead to the total demise of the said great civilisation. Accordingly, one may equate it to the understanding of the cycles of civilisation or the constant force of entropy upon the world and its inhabitants; even if this is not exhibited in the external environment, it may rear its ugly head within the ruling class's pathology.

The Atlantean myth if real though, and the cross-cultural fable of these similar legendary empires and cities may attest to this fact, may be alluding to the precursor civilisation that came before the Hellenes and the Kemetic (Ancient Egyptian) civilisation. The civilisation that predated all recorded and conserved history, and it may have been advanced as described by *Plato* – who heard from a fourth-hand source of whose ancestor heard it from an Egyptian priest – but it is all conjecture. What is interesting though, is that the *Richat Structure* was one of the locations in which the CIA, with the aid of the Marine Core and Geophysicists, conducted airborne geomagnetic surveys, in 1967; of which the data recovered from this is redacted within the ostensibly declassified report[507]. This raises many questions and with other attributable evidence, geological in nature, linking this site to the Atlantis tale, it can be very compelling to a lover of history, but it is not conclusive and leaves us

---

[507] General CIA Records. (1967). *CIA-RDP79B01709A000500030003-2*. Available: https://www.cia.gov/readingroom/document/cia-rdp79b01709a000500030003-2. Last accessed 31/05/2021.

with more questions than answers unfortunately. Although, from what we can glean from the fable of Atlantis, the moral of the entire thing is far more valuable than any historical accuracy. Thus, we seem to be going through the same hubristic phase within our civilisation, or at least our pompous ruling-class are, and as such with our contemporary global civilisation contending for the mantle of Godhood, as the story of Atlantis teaches, Providence or nature will always restore the equilibrium and summon back the upstarts of Man to their rightful place within the natural order. However, this cautionary tale we have forgot and thus we must be reminded of the reason for antiquities caution in travailing nature too much with the unbridled ambition of Man; excess pride begets abundant humility; nature is thus a cruel disciplinarian.

We may conclude that since eleven-thousand BC, approximately speaking, when the shining and unassailable brass and Orichalcum walls stood imposingly, looking upon a vast maritime empire, a true thalassocracy of antiquity, they thought not they would perish and be sunken into the watery prison of the Atlantic; their tale to be told and retold, distorting in truthful essence, with each successive retelling throughout the generations. Thus, Atlantis, in its true form, can never be truly known and the once mighty people are now subject to the imagination of lesser peoples. In all actuality, within our time, they do not exist anymore and have been supplanted by convoluted conjecture and fantastical suppositions. Thus, shall we share the same fate as an advanced civilisation, or so we think in our obnoxious view of our perceived greatness; Atlantis is now no more real, within the collective memory, than we will be in three-millennia proceeding this collapse.

> *"But afterwards there occurred violent earthquakes*
> *and floods; and in a single day and night of misfortune*
> *all your warlike men in a body sank into the earth,*
> *and the island of Atlantis in like manner disappeared in the depths of the sea."*
>
> Plato, *Timaeus and Critias; Timaeus.*

CHAPTER VIII

SILENT WEAPONS FOR QUIET WARS

"One Ring to rule them all,
One Ring to find them,
One Ring to bring them all
and in the darkness bind them."
– J.R.R. Tolkien

This shall be the penultimate section prior to my concluding coda of thought and, as such, I wish to unify the previous points of discussion, that has been approximately a years' worth of observations, into what I think will now occur within the future from here on out. With the constant threat of food shortages, "digital pandemics"[508] [509] as discussed by Mr. Schwab and prepared within the "Cyber Polygon" training event (much akin to *Event 201*), the perpetual pandemic, the growing tide of authoritarianism, and the ever-present danger of the "Great Reset" looming over our heads, it can be very confusing in attempting to see the forest for the many trees that have been intentionally planted in front of us; intended to obfuscate our view. The realisation that is required to overcome this march to a dystopian horizon, is for the population to collectively see the formula for control and to resist it. Simply put, crisis after crisis is put forward as a ploy to induce into the population fear, to grease the wheels societally, for the implementation of specific agendas that solve the fear-inducing crisis; that is the currency of the political class, the only ace up their sleeve; the *Triadic Dialectic*. It is the main tool for their feverish dream of a future where the implementation of a system of *Social Automation* becomes a reality, which is a term that really does encapsulate, what they would call, the benevolent slave system to come.

---

[508] Ice Age Farmer Resources. (2020). *Klaus Schwab: Cyberattack Worse than COVID-19 Crisis - Power Grid Down, Banking Offline*. Available: https://www.youtube.com/watch?v=0D-KRvS-C04o. Last accessed 01/06/2021.
[509] Tim Hinchliffe. (2021). *Prepping for a cyber pandemic: Cyber Polygon 2021 to stage supply chain attack simulation*. Available: https://sociable.co/technology/prepping-cyber-pandemic-cyber-polygon-stage-supply-chain-attack-simulation/. Last accessed 01/06/2021.

This slavery will be so unorthodox to any system that has preceded it, it will find no common counterpoint within history and will be the first of its kind, in scale and methodology. It is a slavery that will be universal and inescapable, if it comes to pass, and it shall be a reformation of society that will be so unbelievably insidious in its scope and final realisation that all other dictatorships in history, combined, will pale in comparison to it. This *Social Automation* will make of Man a machine-like creature and will infuse within him a predisposition towards obedience, either through chemical or digital means. Thus, with that said, I will discuss the potential pathways that this system will come about, the "silent weapons" that are being utilised against us in this "quiet war", and how they will coalesce to provide impetus for the osmosis of this paradigmatic shift. Remember too, that everything that is fed to you upon the establishment channels is crafted as a narrative and, like a narrative, it contains the same, predictable devices and elements contained within narrative writing. That is, to move the fictional plot, emblazoned as reality, forward to its logical resolution or denouement.

The pandemic is the initiator of this new paradigm shift, in that it has set the precedent for many things; it has acted as a *Social Primer*, if you will. The precedents it has set range in scale, but all are designed to coalesce to change the societal fabric and the conscious barriers of the acceptability of the uncontrolled exercise of authoritative power. The first and most glaringly obvious precedent set is the slow diffusing of authoritarianism throughout the various political systems of the world, and for the public to look solely to the executive for what it should and should not be doing within its respective daily functions. Thus, this aids in the eventual adoption of a type of top-down social-credit system, the mass-injection plays a specific function in this too, but I will touch upon that later, and the nascent steps towards an aristocratic shift in governmental structure; with a global mandate and unbridled control over a predictable and manipulatable economy and social landscape. Circling back around, we can detail as to how this came along and what

Chapter VIII

stages in the remote past led to this formulation of the social and cultural conditions required to necessitate, what could aptly be described, as a breeding ground of domestication and reposited despotism; the blind belief of the individual in a class of ostensible experts revelling in the warm waters of the *ad verecundiam* fallacy; of whom look upon us insignificant lab-rats, those verminous beings that are to be studied and manipulated to the likening of the syndicate. This idea has somewhat a peculiar familiarity to *Lyotard's* ideas of *Legitimation by Paralogy*, within his work "The Postmodern Condition", where he seems to see traditional reason and logic as mental constructs that should be mutable and in opposition to the established fashion of reason; we can see the application of this today within this current pandemic and the emotional, rather than logical, suppositions of the severity of the disease; anecdotes are utilised in the stead of logical statistical comparisons with death-rates from other years, for example.

We may look at *Aldous Huxley* or *George Orwell* and discuss their ideas of the future, of whom the former was inclined in an almost sociopathic manner and the other somewhat reviled by the notion of the planned future and planned society waiting within it. "*Brave New World*", written by *Aldous Huxley*, is the system that we are in now, with slight caveats of modification here and there. Within this pandemic and within the larger "Great Reset" agenda, we see that the populace is kept caged within a labyrinthian like cacophony of drugs and distractions – which act as rewards – utilised to control the psyche and keep the individuals perpetually chained to their prison. Why are tides of wilfully ignorant troglodytes drooling at the mouth to receive their shot? Naturally, with what is tantamount to a leap of faith within experts claiming they can "resurrect normality from its deathly slumber" through their blasted necromancy, and unquestionable and incomprehensible magic; thence, the mentally deficient masses must relinquish their agency to higher authorities, they know best of course. Yes, that shall be the saving grace and "resurrect the normal". However, what is the "normal" everyone wishes for? The normal they speak of, is what *Huxley* envisioned; mental necrosis masquerading as life; a society where the individual members are entirely unwitting "junkies", addicted to the drugs, pastimes and other forms of hypnosis which are designed to anaesthetise them and coax them into "loving their own servitude". As you can see today, with the lines of individuals willing to blindly do anything to get back to the bars, clubs, sports games, and every other external pleasure - that they require to provide for them a false actualisation of self - it is self-evident that we inhabit a brave new world. Clearly, the mob require for their very existence the steady supply of vacuous and shallow pursuits, in abundance; they will partake in a mass-Jonestown-event for it, as we are seeing. Thus, within this state of learned helplessness, all the state is required to do when it wishes to mobilise the populace into the next stage of the societal plan, going forward, is to turn off the tap. To starve them and through the torture of deprivation are they primed to unquestionably accept any demand. Naturally, like addicts, they will do anything and everything to ensure their supply of "the fix" is intact; that means that everyone who accepted the shot to "get back to normal" (which is code for "get back to my next fix") should be considered dangerous and deadly as they can be easily lulled into blind obedience for that elusive fix; these lotus-eaters will turn murderous if instructed to.

Conversely, *Huxley*'s brother, *Julian Huxley*, was involved directly with the *Roundtable Society*, and he was an evolutionary biologist and open eugenicist; he was the premiere Director-General of UNESCO. Naturally he seemed to have relayed something of a plan to *Aldous* as he wrote in a fictional sense of what his brother, *Julian*, within his own work, wrote matter-of-factly about. *Julian* was the coiner of the term, "Transhumanist" and wrote extensively upon the coming future, of which we seem to be drifting into now, and naturally paints a picture much like that of *Brave New World*. *Julian* stated emphatically, "I believe in transhumanism: once there are enough people who can truly say that the human species will be on the threshold of a new kind of existence, as different from ours as ours is from that of Peking man. It will at last be consciously fulfilling its real destiny." (*New Bottles for New Wine*, pp 13-17). *Aldous* was clearly inspired by his brother's vision of the future, but he had the natural flare for authorship and as such weaved these ideas into his seminal works; this has parallels to the development of cybernetics and sociocybernetics which was theoretically formalised in the *Macy Conference* between 1946 and 1953, but I shall discuss this later. Candidly speaking also, to the astute observer, the world seems to be fitting right in line with *Aldous* and *Julian's* vision; that of society becoming a mere laboratory experiment, one that can better engineer the conditions to facilitate the formation of a grand scientific dictatorship, that will be like an immovable emplacement on Earth; immortal and unmitigated in its exercise of pure power to alter the very evolutionary pattern of Man.

This is the world we now traverse into, and the narratives drawn from the application of cybernetics or sociocybernetics, from *Norbert Wiener's* definition, would produce a continuum that would portray accurately *Aldous'* imagined, ostensibly fictitious future. *Wiener*, in response to his development of the *Cybernetic Loop*, which was a type of feedback loop that had an array of real-world applications of control, stated "Cybernetics, which I derived from the Greek word κυβερνητικός, or steersman, the same Greek word from which we eventually derive our word governor". Technocracy is the political and economic evolution of the cybernetic and sociocybernetic hypothesis on efficient "steersmanship" of systems; of evolution too, of which I shall discuss later. The singularity is another part of this, popularised by *Ray Kurzweil*, but initially discussed by *I.J. Good* in 1965, and *Good's* understanding and definition influenced the "Transhumanist" movement which *Julian Huxley*, as I previously discussed, laid the foundations for. Although, one may wonder, is this simply to control and steer politico-economic systems? Well, yes and no. As you see, it is designed to do just that but, with the understanding of controlling and steering these systems by taking away the randomness of natural evolution and putting that power, to steer it, into the hands of the "helmsman"; the minority of individuals, at the apex of this conspiracy, who have a view of the whole. This can be outlined by *Pierre Elliot Trudeau's* comments in the conference on Cybernetics in Government, in November 1969, *Trudeau* said: "We are aware that the many techniques of cybernetics, by transforming the control function and the manipulation of information, will transform our whole society. With this knowledge, we are wide awake, alert, capable of action; no longer are we blind, inert powers of fate." *Pierre* is the father of *Justin Trudeau*, the current Prime-Minister of Canada, and was integral in radically reforming the Canadian social and political system in the vision of the cyberneticists during his reign of terror from 1968-1972. Another major conceptual step forward for this conspiratorial ideology, that of cybernetics and its evolved counterparts, was discussed within the *Limits of Growth* report, which the *Club of Rome* produced; this brought forth the long-refuted idea of the Malthusian nightmare, as a justification for population decline and restructuring. *Wiener* also discussed the idea that, "where a man's word goes and where his power of perception goes, to that point his control and in a sense his physical existence is extended. To see and to give commands to the whole world is almost the same as being everywhere." Thus, one can perceive quite easily the advantages cybernetics and its system could offer to a conspiracy for a scientific dictatorship, hellbent on utilising technology to become a God; such a system, once developed and in place, would be theoretically unassailable to the subordinates. The injection is either the initial preparatory stages of this coming transition from natural humans to artificial and evolutionarily flexible ones – a human that can be moulded and changed to the whims of the "helmsmen", so to say – or it is a massive depopulation drive to destroy the old, so that the new can be born from its corpse; either way, it is antithetical to our interests and must be resisted until death or our total victory.

Digressing though, it seems just like the dialogues of *Plato, Mores,* and *Campanella* hid the true loyalty these individuals had to such ideas,

Chapter VIII

Aldous Huxley too disseminated brazenly despotic ideas within the context of innocent literature; such dissemination is memetic in nature, it is a subtle infiltration of the societal subconscious and thus the sprouting of a sapling that leads to our eventual collective enslavement. As his brother, *Julian*, stated, "make the unthinkable become thinkable". One can ponder too upon the idea of the chemical lobotomization of society, as it appears in "Brave New World", in the form of "Soma" - the drug designed to ensure "happiness" and disable one's capacity to think – and the potential for this within the now emerging, what seems to be, eternal routine of injection and booster shot; is this the real-world application of that "Soma" pill spoken of by *Huxley*? Only time will tell, naturally, but it certainly arouses suspicion in the informed observer. Suspicion though, is all we have, as the system is designed to perform thusly: that we are all upon a large boat, where only the helmsman is required to have an idea of the whole. All the subordinates below him, however, need only understand their local compartmentalised roles, a system of semi-permeable, concentric societal circles. Digressing somewhat, one of *Aldous Huxley*'s most poignant and descriptive quotes, I strongly believe, is contained within his work detailing psychedelics and his experience, through letters and correspondences upon the subject, entitled *Moksha* (Letter, 115); he states:

> "*No more Mammy, no more Pappy:*
> *Ain't we lucky, ain't we happy?*
> *Everybody's oh so happy.*
> *Everybody's happy now!*
>
> *Sex galore, but no more marriages;*
> *No more pushing baby carriages;*
> *No one has to change a nappy—*
> *Ain't we lucky, ain't we happy:*
> *Everybody's happy now.*

Dope for tea and dope for dinner.
Fun all night, and love and laughter;
No remorse, no morning after.
Where's the sin, and who's the sinner?
Everybody's happy now.

Girls pneumatic, girls exotic.
Girls ecstatic, girls erotic-
Hug me. Baby; make it snappy.
Everybody's oh so happy,
Everybody's happy now.

Lots to eat and hours for drinking
Soma cocktails— no more thinking.
NO MORE THINKING, NO MORE THINKING!
Everybody's happy now."

How does the ostensible injection or shot play into this particular type of narrative design, the novel framework of pandemic? Simple, it is a plot device utilised within this narrative to push the plot forward and bring it to its resolution or denouement. It is a type of *Deus Ex Machina* ("A God from the Machine"), that being it is the solution to the irresolvable dilemma posed within the narrative; the great saviour of the hero of the tale, that being humanity, against the tireless and unstoppable villain, the demonic and invisible killer virus. I will discuss the resolution this plot device is intended to bring very soon, but another characteristic of narrative writing is the writers need to suspend the disbelief of the audience. This can be achieved by a varying degree of means, but the simplest way within this specific plot would be the inducement of fear and proximity of the problem; horror stories utilise a similar means, by playing on our deep-rooted, psychological fears. Thus, we see the reason for the low-cut "B-roll" that was rehashed and recycled around the various news networks of the overcrowded, busy and disaster-hit hospitals; along with scary graphics and statistics, to boot, showing exponential and parabolic lines of death, if policies of lockdown were not implemented and this fictional narrative was not taken seriously. However, now that we understand this, then we must answer the question as to why the plot device is utilised and why it is so important in the resolution stage of the fictional narrative. The answer is relatively simple, that is, since we are marching forward to a "Brave New World" resembling a form of aristocratic despotism, in which the citizenry is to be treated like cattle, then for cattle to work and be ordered efficiently – without issue and unrest – conformity must be instilled within the populace. How is this conformity instilled easily, though? The easiest way, and this is utilised in parenting and the educational system, is to shame the disobedient by collective punishment; the disobedient will be shamed, attacked and ostracised from the group for, seemingly, bringing punishment upon them all for the individual's lack of team-spirit and conformity to the prescribed action. This plot device, as we can see, facilitates such a function in an exemplary manner. As we are beginning to see from the political class, the next stage of the narrative being developed, is that "the vaccine is effective and we need one-hundred percent of people to get their double-dose, to be brought out of these lockdowns and tiered-lockdowns. As such, the reason for the continued lockdowns and restrictions is due to the "no-shows" and lack of uptake in the vaccine". Thus, this is the reason for the plot device, it is a tool of driving forward conformity to the desired resolution to the fictionally derived problem; the resolution being mass-dosing of whatever this is for a reason that we can only speculate, but it is unlikely that it is benevolent. Most likely, it is to induce a population decline via sterilisation or incremental death to facilitate a more manageable population coming into this new global system; or it is a tracking device that will be connected to some sort of digital-grid, and this may be connected to the towers that sprang up during the initial lockdowns. For one only must ask themselves the most fundamental question? If they are forcing a high percentage of the population to take this shot through financial coercion, social ostracisation, collective punishment, and outright intimidation then do you think the supposed solution is any more benevolent, in its application, than the tools they utilised to attempt to foist it onto you in the first place? The answer is obvious. Judge by deeds and the fruits borne of those deeds will be likewise. I will discuss later within this section how they will eventually force the unvaccinated either out of society or engage in the final phase of the vaccine implementation agenda, the use of direct force and tactics tantamount to genocide.

Continuing forward with discussing the precedents set via this pandemic, we can see that the idea of a pandemic (the problem) and the vaccine (the solution) being now familiarised characters or elements within the narrative of crisis. Thus, they have been redefined and moulded into a malleable form of narrative-clay, in which the new crisis can simply inscribe its specific parametric terminology unto the already familiar problem and solution dualism. For example, the "digital pandemic" to come, which will be the rise in cyberattacks and debilitating cyber-criminality, which we have seen within the Colonial Pipeline ransom-ware attack and the recent attack upon the JBS meat processing giant[510], thus this will bring general systemic shock to the world and induce panic and fear; due to aggregate or global supply-chain breakdown, consequential spikes in consumer inflation, major civil strife, disruption to financial services, and energy-grid shutdowns. It will, most likely, create a plentiful supply of fear to ensure sufficient pressure is faced upon the populace to accept a solution; the "digital vaccine", which will most likely be, as *Klaus Schwab* states, a fusion of the physical, digital, and biological identities; this will be justified to better regulate the citizen's movements and digital presence to mitigate hacker activity within society. Mark my words, the populace will be crying out for this transhumanist fusion for

---

[510] Tom Polansek, Jeff Mason. (2021). *U.S. says ransomware attack on meatpacker JBS likely from Russia*. Available: https://www.reuters.com/world/us/some-us-meat-plants-stop-operating-after-jbs-cyber-attack-2021-06-01/. Last accessed 01/06/2021.

the return of the familiar comforts of the society the know; this is akin to the reasoning of the vaccine. However, the society everyone knows is dead and gone, never to return. This cyber pandemic is being *Socially Primed* within the psyche of the populace right now, through the various events in recent months and via the discussions and scenario planning of the WEF (World Economic Forum), conducted within the "Cyber Polygon" scenario and report[511]. The world is being primed for cataclysm the likes of which, as *Schwab* states, "will make the COVID-19 crisis look like a minor disturbance"; we are facing what seems like an artificially induced collapse for means of "building back better" with a compliant populace of terrified, confused, and, when it comes, emaciated dependents. Moreover, by this time, it may create another means of leverage to force the experimental shot upon the populace faced with a situation beyond their comprehension; many in the global sphere, especially in the West, have been conditioned via generational domestication to wish for a life free of hardship and replete with the accessibility of pleasure; thus, they are prime targets for the denial of this as a form of coercive ransom.

This coming cyber-attack will also allow many other subset agendas to be brought to their synthesis or conclusion, too. The agenda for a "meatless" world, where the populace will be unable to buy meat due to its outright banning or by them being simply priced out of the market; via artificial inflation of the price or as a supposed consequence of the hit being felt within secondary, supportive industries. For example, within this current global meat-production industry meltdown and cyber-attack on JBS, we are seeing that the corn and grain industry – utilised naturally to feed the cattle and livestock – has increased in price so dramatically that it has transferred such pressures to the meat-production industries and poultry and cattle farmers. More so, we must remember that this, much like the rising gas prices, is a *Social Primer* as well; it is priming the public and psychologically familiarising them with the prospect

---

[511] WEF/Cyber Polygon. (2020). *Cyber Polygon: International online training for raising global cyber resilience*. Available: https://cyberpolygon.com/. Last accessed 01/06/2021.

of slowly increased prices for necessities and especially food and fuel. Thus, the system that will come to pass in future, if it continues on its current unchallenged trajectory, will impose a system of terrible austerity onto the populace via high prices for travel and living; this ensures that the populace cannot travel great distances, thus keeping them localised and manageable, and it also ensures they do not have an abundance of readily available capital as to potentially start businesses and rival the monopolist's oligopoly. However, one may ask the question, typically revolution and rebellion has been sparked when food prices account, on average, for 40% of most of the populace's weekly income. This is true, but in the coming system, technology will hold the citizen in the grip of bondage and for the citizen to rebel would be as unthinkable as a fish migrating to dry land; the system to come will also be instituted on the back of hunger, famine, disease, death – as you can see the introductory stages of right now – and as such the populace will be so demoralised and despondent that miserable routine will be preferable to relinquishing even the vestiges of the old society's yolk. Domesticated populaces, especially frightened and terrified populaces who have been scarred by the whip of chaos, wish for fences and barbed wire; they know nothing more than their servitude and are happy as long as they are shielded from the ravages of the true chaos of nature.

We can further Segway this discussion, from that point, into the previous point alluded to regarding how they will force the unvaccinated out of society or garner public support for a policy of forced vaccination. As I described above, such inconceivable crises, as the ones we are beginning to see right now, cause extreme social pressures and individual stress, to such a point, that the populace will be more open to governmental policies they would be previously repulsed by. Thus, for the citizenry in the hopes of clawing back their freedom, they will do the bidding of anyone; as has been seen through this pandemic. They will take into their vein concoctions from long-term criminal pharmaceutical conglomerates, they will engage in the most unhygienic and outright

Chapter VIII

ridiculous rituals to protect against the evil force in the world that effects negligible numbers, and they will take swabs, dipped in one of the most carcinogenic substances known to Man, all the way up to their blood-brain barrier. Therefore, with that in mind, do you think it a stretch for them to go along with a policy of eliminating the unvaccinated and dissident classes of society? No, I think not, and all the government need do is announce that the unvaccinated are depriving the vaccinated of their freedom and the irrational majority will spring madly into action; of course, the irony is terribly good. Concurrently, they are setting the stage for that at present, and are engaged in polarising and segregating society into its vaccinated and unvaccinated parts; of the latter class, it will begin with social stigma and end in state-orchestrated genocide as I will detail. It is a fantastically pragmatic strategy to almost weed and root out the disobedient and rabble-rousing strata of society, of which the state will have plausible deniability because the killings and massacres will be carried out by the frenzied masses of the vaccinated, yearning for their freedom and luxury once again. Naturally, they understand that, like most genocides, most of the targeted population will attempt to flee, however in a situation where variants are running amok and further justification is provided to the state for the continuity of restrictions, most notably travel, then this will gift the opportunity of corralling the target populations within their localities and homes. In such an event, the dissident class, the unvaccinated, will be easy pickings for rabid mobs aided by state-enforcers; this coming genocide will be justified via the good of the collective health and the narrative of the unvaccinated are unclean and selfish; their actions are harming and killing others.

You will see, mark my words, the longer this goes on the more you will see terms intended to dehumanise the dissident; "refuser", "anti-vaxxer", "normalcy deniers", etc; anything to question their status as human and to turn them into, within the minds of the genocidal mob, an incarnation of evil. Thus, the question may be raised, why am I insisting this will occur? Simply put, because genocide is predictable within certain social conditions and the conditions at present are more than apt. This is detailed within the "eight stages of genocide", of which the stages are predictable but not inexorable and the main orchestrator of genocide, throughout history, are states[512]; rarely terrorist groups are initiators also, but the line between states and terrorists is always extremely blurred. The eight stages, in order as they appear from the source cited, are: Classification, Symbolisation, Dehumanisation, Organisation, Polarisation, Preparation, Extermination, and finally, Denial. From my own interpretation of these eight stages, I believe that each of these stages can be categorised into two groups: the covert and overt elements. Thus, the covert elements are Classification, Symbolisation, Dehumanisation, and Polarisation; while the overt elements are subsequently Organisation, Preparation and Extermination. These various stages, as previously stated, do not need to occur in any sequential order, but the covert stages obviously occur prior to the overt stages. Genocide is thus a slow incline, a gradual process, where the society is divided apart, and the apparatus of the state is utilised to infuse hatred for the target population. The target population is classified, meaning that they are rendered as different within the media and societal space; this will naturally build in pace towards symbolisation, meaning they are visually marked as different, and then eventually dehumanisation. Polarisation will occur then, thusly meaning that the target population are entirely differentiated, legally and socially, from the population at large; this eventually will lead in a crescendo to organisation, preparation and eventual extermination; these overt stages will logically occur in rather quick succession, as to facilitate efficiency of the disposal of the target population by means of the element of surprise, so to say.

We can see at present, a media campaign within its infancy that is now seeking to construct a lexicon of derogatory terms and societal attitudes towards the unvaccinated and non-compliant strata. Though

---

[512] Dr. Gregory H. Stanton, President, Genocide Watch. (1998). *EIGHT STAGES OF GENOCIDE*. Available: www.genocidewatch.org. Last accessed 01/06/2021.

this has been a slow process that has been occurring for decades, all the way back to the MMR vaccine and the invention of the demonising term "anti-vaxxer"; of which, is designed to equip the compliant segment of the populace with a dismissive term to ensure they feel superior in intelligence and morality to the non-compliant segment; naturally, this is to dispel of challenges to this establishmentarian panacea that is now seeing an evolution and broadening in definition, within this current mRNA variant. Eventually, the terms of classification, which is what they are, will become far more vitriolic and organisation will occur, within the media and political channels, to physically attack the unvaccinated; this will be legitimised by either a preceding false-flag or media-driven event designed to demonise this segment of society and thus set into motion their final removal from society through genocidal methodology. This is the antecedence to the new world that the overlapping corporate and political interests are attempting create right now; dissidents and detractors cannot be permitted to come into such a top-down global system, as such a system will most likely be inflexible to such unpredictable elements. Hence, disposal is the only solution.

Why do they require the death of the dissident and the thinning of the herd, through chemical concoction? Simply put, they wish for a system of *Social Automation*. That is, a system in which, through digital means, they can create and update a population of pure automatons; this will be almost like a singularity, as discussed by *Ray Kurzweil*, where the human population will be merged bio-digitally with an AI mechanism. Naturally, such a seismic shift in the pathway of the species must be predated by an equally seismic shift in the political and social landscape; the only way to facilitate this equally seismic shift, in a controlled fashion, is to ensure a manageable population is constructed. Moreover, to then further facilitate the manageable population left into this new bio-digital automatonlike existence, an existence where rebellion will never arise, is to ensure they are tracked every moment, of everyday; hence, the *Social Primers* of "track and trace" and "contact tracing", along with the ingrained usage and culture surrounding the smartphone. Accordingly, this current event being perpetrated by the ruling class, a consolidation of their power for all time, is a high-wire act and will be until the sort of all-encompassing totalitarian system – the first totalitarian system that is total in scope – is instituted. Of course, what better way to institute it than via a fear-inducing pandemic that foists the population into a "state of war", into perpetuity; perpetuity because, conceivably, new variants can be created ad infinitum and absolutely no one will decry the continuation of lockdown as it makes logical sense; and no one would wish to be an "anti-vaxxer" or, God-forbid, a selfish "anti-lockdowner". What is being constituted, for both the vaccinated and unvaccinated, the dualistic divide busily being fashioned at present, is a social environment which is a killing ground for the vast majority. Like the shrewd hunters of the mammoth, these new ingenious stalkers of the human masses, are funnelling us all into a trap; a funnel flanked by high cliffs on either side, metaphorically speaking. The walls are closing in and the net, designed to hold us in place while the missiles of these new hunters hurtle towards us, are being brought down over us all. We are being entrapped, both vaccinated and unvaccinated, and we are being led to the slaughter ground in large part.

Although, one may ask, how has the human, the cleverest of all the known animals, been so easily hoodwinked into their own demise? By their one innate advantage; adaptability. Adaptability has been utilised as the cudgel to which we have been beaten into submission. Thusly speaking, our adaptability makes us predictable, in that if we are faced by a consensus of change – contrived or natural information – then the path of least resistance and our natural inclination would lead us to adapt to it rather than resist it. Our own nature has been subverted and turned against us. This hoodwinking was slow, methodical, it started at birth and progressed through to compulsory education and was accompanied through it all with the constant shadow of media. The method utilised was not so much bothered in changing the individual at the source, it was intended to change society and then change the majority through deceptively bringing forth a conscious perception that the consensus on issues had changed; this contrived consensus would then, considering our tribal mentality and inclination to adapt, would produce social conformity to the said false consensus. From this simple concept and approach, Man has been led to his own doom and to this, will engage in foul and horrendous acts to the non-compliant; the inadaptable, so to say. Subsequently, we may conclude that the unvaccinated are acting in opposite to the normal, the predictable parameters of Man's nature, and as such must be highly inquisitive and curious to act against their natural inclination towards adaptability and thus conformity.

From this technological merging of Man and machine, one can then beg the question, can Man then be patentable? Accordingly, can humans through the genetic, or altered genetic, patterns be commodified; thence controlled? This leads invariably to questions of *de facto* chattel slavery being implemented through technological means. This entire technological pathology seems predestined towards furnishing the avenue to power, and its means, to a ruling-class dominated by a mental subservience to psychopathy. Thus, the Technocratic age, for which the road to it seems to be being paved by the bodies of the sacrificed, will be unorthodox to our common shared view of Western consumeristic life. Conversely, this supposed pandemic has fortuitously sprung forth in a time where it would be needed most by a ruling-class hellbent on the realisation on this aforementioned new system of control; a time where the technological capabilities were there to ensure mass-automation and thus, economically speaking, a justification of a more profitable system of exploitation of the human and natural resources available; one beyond mere predatory and consumeristic Capitalism.

The candid approach and speed in which this was pursued really does lead me to believe that they have the capabilities available, weaponry and such, to easily quash a rebellion of the masses; they seem to not even be actively hiding the agenda anymore and thus this stems forth from an understanding, as well, that the brainlessness of the masses renders potential open rebellion, to them, entirely unlikely. This system will not be overthrown in its present state and with the accompanying lobotomization they have successfully conducted upon the public, *en masse*, it is unlikely the disaster that will stem forth from these injections will be avertable. Billions will die and, from their blood, shall a new regime arise; one of whose Crown will be black and its pinnacles adorned with rods of iron. It may attest to a futurist outlook, but it will be as primitively brutal as the rest of the despotisms of old. It will be a system predicated on the unwaveringness in bringing forth a world of anti-life, anti-love and anti-human; on the one hand it will say it professes its care for classes below, and on the other it will inflict slaughter and merciless exploitation on them. A system of cohabiting opposites and confusing reality, schizophrenic, hiding its true intent through prevarication and fanciful platitudes. It will make of the citizenry slaves and claim emancipation has been rendered unto them; it is a system where the man, woman and the family do not exist and are regarded as a misguided and forgotten remnant, of a long-dead past. They shall claim these new systems of control are augmentations to one's body, and expediency and convenience come from such marvels of science, but these marvels will ultimately decimate the small fragment of humanity left in the bio-digital vestments of the, by then, techno-slave class. Naturally, once full-automation becomes achievable, one where the means of production can be outsourced from Man to machine, in its totality, then shall you see an outright disposal of the unrequired, remaining human resources; through bio-weaponry, poisoning, or some other devious method of disposal. The system of "Turnkey Totalitarianism", as *James Corbett* remarks, is nigh; the era of Man is ending, and the era of the Techno-Feudalist has just begun.

"People will come to love their oppression, to adore the technologies that undo their capacities to think."—*Aldous Huxley*

Chapter VIII

On Control Functions Within Society

Fear is a control function. Society can be understood as a (negative) feedback loop, as described in Cybernetics. Consequently, like any informational system, to control the wild oscillations in the variability of input and output (in this case the opinions of the populace, unrest, or divergent thinking, etc), it is necessary to input an aperture, an effector, in the path of this input; to narrow and control more tightly those oscillations that will be witnessed within the output. Eventually though, like most negative feedback loops (inhibitory loops) and the control functions within them, in their desire to control the input, they thus become the input. Accordingly, within our society, fear has become the main input, the central driver, and as such it will lead us into an irreversible logarithmic decline as we see now. However, one could argue too, that the main control function is not fear, but the media who proliferate it. In this regard, such an assertion would be correct - although, fear and the media are synonymous terms in all actuality. Just as fire produces smoke, it is safe to say through inductive reasoning, that if you see smoke on the horizon then fire has thenceforth produced it. Apropos that prior statement, if you see fear and hysteria rife within society, then it is safe to say the media is generating it and for that specific function of tantalising control, as I outlined above in the feedback loop analogy.

"The future science of government should be called "la cybernétique"."
—André-Marie Ampère

"Besides electrical engineering theory of the transmission of messages, there is a larger field [cybernetics] which includes not only the study of language but the study of messages as a means of controlling machinery and society, the development of computing machines and other such automata, certain reflections upon psychology and the nervous system, and a tentative new theory of scientific method."
—Norbert Wiener

The Cybernetic Truth

The truth of cybernetics and the relation it potentially has to the injection should send a chill up your spine. I am beginning, considering my present investigation into cybernetics and its modern applications, to see the big picture surrounding this pandemic event and the real reason for the injections. It can be summarised by the creation of a hive-mind, literally. However, I will delve further into this and discuss the ideas surrounding cybernetics and how it ties in with eugenics; of which ties into transhumanism, the singularity principle, and of AI. Eugenics is not merely concerned with the genetic hygiene of the species and depopulation, that is a sub-goal of the larger agenda which is the self-direction of human evolution itself; utilising technology to take away the arbitrariness of nature, in terms of how it propels forward evolution, and placing the power to propel and steer evolution within the hands of the expert class.

Cybernetics can be understood as "the communications and automatic control systems in both machines and living things." However, you can see already the implications of this within the creation of something akin to a self-perpetuating tyrannical system, if it were applied socially. Cybernetics also has applications within computer science; due to it being a control theory, a theory surrounding the management and regulation of variables within feedback loops, common or contrived. As such, Cybernetics as a transdisciplinary science may be entirely benign right now, but its formation and its intellectual patriarchs were developing it for anything but benign reasons as I shall detail further on. The dream system of sociocybernetics is the realisation of *Autopoiesis* (or a social organism that functions in equilibrium amongst all its component parts and is self-ordering and self-perpetuating, basically a hive-mind)[513]. As *Fremont-Smith*, introducing the Systems of Cybernetics Conference of 1948, stated "the concept of teleological mechanisms...may be viewed

---

[513] Kamran, Q. (2020). *Strategic Value Chain Management: Models for Competitive Advantage*. Kogan Page. Pg. 186

as an attempt to escape from...old, mechanistic formulations that now appear inadequate, and to provide new and more fruitful conceptions and more effective methodologies for studying self-regulating processes, self-orienting systems and organisms, and self-directing personalities..." (*Frank et al.*, 1948). Now, "Teleology" is very important within this discussion, but I have not the space to cover that within here; as such, all you must understand is that teleology, within a Cybernetic context, is concerned with the end-state that has come about by controlled feedback for a purpose of control of a critical resource[514]; I will discuss feedback and negative feedback loops shortly. This very much ties in with the notion of cybernetic immortality – which is seeing practical applications within the "Neuro-Link" concept of *Elon Musk* – and though the immortality concept could very well have individually-driven applications, it is referring very much to an immortal memetic system; or a system where people within society perpetually mimic each other with the aid of a technological system of regulation and control[515]. Essentially, a more accurate and predictable form of direct mind-control through technology; as opposed to the resource-heavy control mechanisms of media, education, and political theatre, etc. They are desirous of a "wind it up and let it go" society, a self-regulating system of enslavement. Ultimately, it may be approached in an alternative view, Cybernetic modification of the human-being makes information and its communication the key to control of the said human-being; the nervous system is the way in which we interpret and perceive reality, so if one interjects a control function that can manipulate this nerval stimuli, then one can control the being directly. This simple idea naturally stems from the fundamental belief of Cybernetics, that human-beings are informational systems based on feedback loops, inputs and outputs, much like computers, and the two

---

[514] Rosenblueth, Arturo, et al. *"Behaviour, Purpose and Teleology."* Philosophy of Science, vol. 10, no. 1, 1943, Pg. 18–24. JSTOR, www.jstor.org/stable/184878. Accessed 12 June 2021.
[515] Elan Moritz (1995) *Metasystem transitions, memes, and cybernetic immortality*, World Futures, 45:1-4, 155-171, DOI: 10.1080/02604027.1995.9972558

thence share a compatibility with one another. Therefore, as was discussed within the *Macy Conference on Cybernetics*[516], a type of interfacing of the brain and computer was sought and theorised to be possible; upon those mechanistic principles they all subscribed, too.

In terms of this concept of the hive-mind; a similar concept is underwritten within *Aldous Huxley*'s *Brave New World*. However, *Huxley* makes a distinction in terms within *Brave New World Revisited*, in which it is stated, "For the individual termite, service to the termitary is perfect freedom. But human beings are not completely social; they are only moderately gregarious. Their societies are not organisms, like the hive or the anthill; they are organizations, in other words, ad hoc machines for collective living." (*Brave New World Revisited*, pg. 127). Therefore, Cybernetics could be described as the expediting of the "organisation" of Man to a more perfect depiction of that of the hive or anthill; it is the engineering of a society built upon the individual members being entirely subordinate, within their very being, to the service of the hierarchy; this is the crux of Transhumanism and even Cybernetics, and as *Valentin Turchin*, a Cybernetic thinker, asserted that *metasystem transition* is required to produce a higher control level to allow the system to progress[517]. The term *metasystem transition*, within modern Cybernetic Theory, can be summarised as thus: "Metasystem transition is the formation of a new level of control, when systems of a certain kind become integrated as subsystems of an emerging metasystem. The main tenet of the theory is that the major steps of evolution—both biological and cultural—are metasystem transitions at various system levels. Metasystem transitions are thus seen as quanta of evolution."[518] The terms "systems" and "control" have specific meanings within the modern conceptualisation of *Cybernetic Theory*; the term "system" can be understood as the Cybernetic

---

[516] Steve Joshua Heims (1991). *The Cybernetics Group*. Cambridge, Massachusetts London, England: The MIT Press. Pg. 12.
[517] Heylighen and Joslyn, *"Cybernetics and Second Order Cybernetics,"*. Pg. 18.
[518] Valentin F. Turchin (1995) *A dialogue on Metasystem transition*, World Futures, 45:1-4, 5-57, DOI: 10.1080/02604027.1995.9972553

or feedback loop, which is inherent in most aspects of human and machine function. However, to understand "control" it is best to utilise the marrying of the two terms into the "control system", which engenders the conditions for the specific cybernetic "control". The "control system" is composed of say two elements: the controller and the controlled. The feedback, or Cybernetic, loop that is produced from this would be, for example, the controller exercises a change of state or action upon the controlled. Naturally, the controlled can either be conducive to the suggestion of that change of state or not, either way it shall reciprocate back to the controller a perception of its now either altered or unchanged state. The input of the controller, the change of the target's state, is the specifically defined "control" concept in Cybernetics. Do you see as to the principles being discussed here? It involves a great deal of discussion surrounding neurology, control systems, and how to apply closed-loop feedback patterns to change the states of human and machine systems – and their respective substrates. Consequently, effecting change upon the internal and external environments of these aforesaid systems more efficiently, accelerating the acquisition of the means of the artificial directing of evolution, like so. Hence, the creation of the human societal organism; the hive-mind.

Digressing however, upon our main point of how these potentially tie into this crisis event and the ostensible solution, that being the injection, the speculative hypothesis I have come to is that the injection is a pharmacological primer which will implant, within the injection site (which will be dispersed throughout the body via magnetofection (transfection)), a type of nanobioelectronic receptor which will act as a translator and receiver of Electro-Frequency or Electromagnetic Frequency (EMF) from the falsely named "5G" towers; this grid of towers, of which were erected during the lockdowns, will emit commands, through the medium of EMF, which will then be received by the receptor, which will act as a circuit modulator of sorts, and will almost hijack one's central processes and proceeding electrical stimuli, to then reprocess them within the targets physiology and neurology using, as a basis, the EMF-type Frequency emitted; this will imperceptibly alter the behaviour of the target. The genius of this system is that the target shall believe their alteration of behaviour is being entirely done of their own volition. This will be utilised for purposes antithetical to our interests, naturally, and may be utilised to induce mass-suicide, mass-conformity, or mass-murder; as we shall see from the academic quotes discussing this technology, further on. This can be understood as mind-control on a mass-scale – the transhuman concept of something beyond human. Furthermore, this is the reason for the magnetisation at the injection site and, peculiarly, the probable reason for the constant boosters, there will most likely be an eternal regime of injections and boosters, is due to fact the magnetic nanoplatforms, that will act as a receptor for the EMF (ELF or EHF) signal, are biodegradable and non-durable. The study titled "Biodegradable polymer iron oxide nanocomposites: the future of biocompatible magnetism" clarifies this by stating, "Superparamagnetic iron oxide nanoparticles (SPIONs)... The superparamagnetic properties of these nanoparticles enable their magnetic manipulation of biological targets such as cells, proteins and nucleic acids...by treating the SPIONs as a cargo to be loaded into larger biodegradable polymeric nanostructures, new nanocomposites can be created to unite the beneficial features of paramagnetism and controlled drug release into one single nanoparticle."[519] Magnetic manipulation of biological targets, down to the cellular level, is very much what is intended by the utilising of nanoplatforms such as SPIONs; I believe these are within the shot, hence the magnetisation effects postdating injection. As a clarification too, "Superparamagnetic" refers to nanoparticles that, with sufficient temperature above *Curie*, the magnetic pole or direction can flip. However, the biomedical applications of this are realised in the fact that the iron oxide nanoparticles can be formed into an aqueous solution (a liquid), a *ferrofluid*, which will not have the appearance of

---

[519] Meyer, R. A., & Green, J. J. (2015). *Biodegradable polymer iron oxide nanocomposites: the future of biocompatible magnetism.* Nanomedicine (London, England), 10(23), 3421–3425. https://doi.org/10.2217/nnm.15.165

CHAPTER VIII

magnetisation until an external magnet or magnetic field is introduced onto it; hence the magnetisation when a magnet is put over the injection site[520]. Moreover, the reason superparamagnetic nanoparticles are utilised is because they have very high magnetic susceptibility, or the property of a material becoming magnetised by an external field[521]; hence why a small fridge magnet can generate a very strong magnetic hold to the injection site. Are you beginning to understand what this nanoparticle technology will potentially be used for? Thus, I can only theorise as to what will happen when the towers are turned on and the external EMFs are emitted to the injected, will it cause behavioural modification? I suspect it may. As *Klaus Schwab* remarked, "we must prepare for an angrier world" at the end of this year; will this be created via this new magnetic nanoplatform control system? However, all of the various quotes from *Klaus Schwab*, *Bill Gates*, etc predicting certain issues with great accuracy – cyber-attacks and viral pandemics for example - would lead one to believe that they are indeed to be taken seriously when they discuss these issues. Their wealth affords them access to information that is beyond our reach, unless we land lucky through mere speculation.

Alas, this is an obviously radical working hypothesis I have developed here, but there is a great deal of evidence purporting to this type of "Remote Influencing Technology" being available to the status quo[522]. Therefore, I am naturally inclined to bring this to your attention, and it fits entirely in with Cybernetics and this dream of engendering "Homeostasis" (the controlling of Man's internal processes and the establishment of permanent memetic stability) within the internal and external environment; that being, the dream *Norbert Wiener* spoke of which is the "fight against entropy"; or the inextricable drive of the organic towards disorder and decay. Hence, this fits in with the cycles

---

[520] Pedro M. Enriquez-Navas, Maria L. Garcia-Martin, *in Frontiers of Nanoscience*, 2012
[521] Vahak Marghussian, *in Nano-Glass Ceramics*, 2015
[522] U.S. Army (Defence Intelligence Agency), Office of the Surgeon General, Medical Intelligence Office (1975). *Controlled Offensive Behaviour - USSR (U)*. U.S.A.: DST-18105-387-75. Part V. Accessed here: chrome-extension:///oemmndcbldboiebfnladdacbdfmadadm/ https://www.cia.gov/readingroom/docs/CIA-RDP96-00792R000500730002-1.pdf

of civilisation discussed within this book; given that this cycle deals with the natural inclination towards decay, or entropy, and thus if one wished to ensure a world-empire this would be required to be abolished or mitigated beyond principal action. That being, the way to abolish entropy is, the fulfilling of the dream of universal *Social Automation*, or the establishing of the conditions to facilitate the predictability of Man via the artificial steering of evolution, through technological control of Man's direct capacities of thinking. Thenceforth, this inevitably ties Eugenics, bioethics, Cybernetics, AI, and Transhumanism together as purely ideological fomentations cut from the same cloth. It has been found within nature, an electric sense that enables certain animals to detect voltage gradients as low as 0.01 µV/cm within the frequency range of direct current (DC) up to about 8 Hz - this is linked naturally to migratory patterns in these animals – and special receptors are required to detect and incorporate this electro-frequency stimuli into their neurology[523]; keep this in mind. Moreover, it has been found that in studies with ELF fields suggest that behaviour can be influenced by exposure to either magnetic or these aforesaid electric fields[524]. This study reported that prenatal exposure of rats to 0.5-Hz, 0.05-to 3-mT fields, resulted in changes in juvenile or adult rats' emotionality and ability to perform a conditioned-suppression test (a stimulus test). Furthermore, another study found that prenatal exposure of rats to a 60-Hz field at 3.5 kV/m caused changes in open-field activity (this is a test that is designed to assess the curiosity within animals)[525]. Another such instance of an academic discussing this type of bioelectromagnetic control technology

---

[523] Kalmijn A.J. (1978) *Experimental Evidence of Geomagnetic Orientation in Elasmobranch Fishes*. In: Schmidt-Koenig K., Keeton W.T. (eds) Animal Migration, Navigation, and Homing. Proceedings in Life Sciences. Springer, Berlin, Heidelberg. https://doi.org/10.1007/978-3-662-11147-5_34

[524] Persinger MA. *Open-field behavior in rats exposed prenatally to a low intensity-low frequency, rotating magnetic field*. Dev Psychobiol. 1969;2(3):168-71. doi: 10.1002/dev.420020307. PMID: 5407665.

[525] Frey, A. H. 1982. *Neural and behavioural consequences of prenatal exposure to 3.5 kV/m 60 Hz fields*. Abstr. 4th Annual Meeting Bioelectromagnetics Society, Los Angeles, California.

CHAPTER VIII

is *Amin A. Muhammad Gadit*, M.D., a Psychiatrist from the Memorial University of Newfoundland, St. John's, and it stated within a paper he wrote in 2009, titled "Terrorism and Mental Health: The issue of psychological fragility": "Of late, there are reports of a new and dreadful invention of weapons of violence that are called Bio-electromagnetic Weapons…Through this form of terrorism, it is possible to persuade subjects that their mind is being read; their intellectual property is being plundered and can even motivate suicide or murder…Manifestations of the effects of these occult weapons can mimic mental ill health and add further to the misery of the victims. The potential threat from use of biological warfare agents is more devastating as they are not detectable before the attack and can lead the possible victims to a state of constant vigilance and anxiety."[526] Now, with the passage of time and consequential progress of technology, if the military and state had access to technologies such as this back in 2009, then how far advanced have they become within this field now? Such questions would only lead to speculation, rather than answers because the state is instinctively driven towards secrecy, and they obviously sequester their plans to the prying eyes of the general public.

I hope that you, the reader, are beginning to see more vividly the picture I am painting of the technology that they have available at their disposal and of which I speculate is being utilised, for the purposes of reshaping society into a rigid system of top-down control. Now that I have went over some of the small breadcrumbs of information pertaining to the applications and effects of this technology, I wish to discuss the exponents of the ideology behind this reshaping of the human system and of their long-held collective aspirations, of the path, progress should take to bring forth a type of final revolution for the species. Within our contemporary period, the leading luminaries and magnates of wealth and

---

[526] Amin A. Muhammad Gadit (Discipline of Psychiatry, Memorial University of Newfoundland, St. John's, NL A1B 3V6 Canada.), *Terrorism and Mental Health: The issue of psychological fragility*, JPMA (October 2009, Volume 59, Issue 10), Last Accessed: 11/06/2021, URL: https://jpma.org.pk/article-details/1837?article_id=1837

prestige such as *Ray Kurzweil*, *Elon Musk*, and *Klaus Schwab* all talk ad nauseum upon this concept of a synthesis of man and machine; that we must complete this synthesis "for us to stay relevant within the next stage of our evolution"; all have been drawn into the orbit of what is termed the "Great Reset" or "Fourth Industrial Revolution" (the "Final Revolution"). All of these concept's stem from the ideologues of the 20th and 19th century respectively, and they can be put into three distinct phases that brought about the genesis of this type of deterministic faith, in the binary reduction of humankind into a Borg-like entity: inhabiting a clinically predictable world. The first category stems from *Charles Darwin* and his naturalist and natural history theses upon the origins of species and of natural selection; as you can tell today, such academic discoveries had social and political applications, as well. This subsequently spawned the *X-Club* headed by *Thomas Henry Huxley*, nicknamed "Darwin's Bulldog", he was a steadfast proponent and defender of the *Theory of Evolution*. The Club he headed was a social network of friends who held great sway and influence within the scientific scene of London, at the latter part of the 19th century; they pushed greatly the theory of evolution. You may be familiar with Thomas's surname, that of Huxley, well *Thomas Henry Huxley* just so happens to be the grandfather of *Julian* and *Aldous Huxley*; as you can see, this is a multigenerational aspiration of sorts. Carrying on, the second category is that of *Bertrand Russel, David Hilbert, Aldous,* and *Julian Huxley*. The two former characters being mathematicians, who were linked with the redirecting of science in the early 20th century, and they would be integral, on a purely axiological standpoint, in the evolving of evolution into the branches of eugenics, cybernetics and transhumanism; all of which are concurrent with one another. The third generation, being that of *Norbert Wiener, John von Neumann* and *W. Ross Ashby* who would go onto fundamentally create and develop cybernetics and, what could be described as, proto-*Social-Automation* and sociocybernetics which would spawn a whole host of various other ideologies; just as the theory of evolution had done so too in the past. As a sidenote too, *Norbert Wiener* was a protégé of *Hilbert* and *Russel*.

Bertrand Russel would famously state that the scientific dictatorship would make children believe "snow is black"; with the bioelectromagnetic technology I describe above, it seems that they may well achieve this impossible feat. *Russel* famously stated too, "The scientific rulers will provide one kind of education for ordinary men and women, and another for those who are to become holders of scientific power. Ordinary men and women will be expected to be docile, industrious, punctual, thoughtless, and contented. Of these qualities probably contentment will be considered the most important. In order to produce it, all the researchers of psychoanalysis, behaviourism, and biochemistry will be brought into play…. All the boys and girls will learn from an early age to be what is called 'co-operative,' i.e., to do exactly what everybody is doing. Initiative will be discouraged in these children, and insubordination, without being punished, will be scientifically trained out of them." Digressing, we now find ourselves in the fourth phase of this conspiracy, the transitionary or conclusionary phase, in which the sum of the other three phases of thinking and planning shall come to total fruition: the *Partibus Summa* of tyranny. We are treading into the world that has been planned for us, for a very long time, and so many are rolling up their sleeves and treading willingly to their potential doom.

These cast of characters, from the advent of the theory of evolution, believe in the quasi-humanist tenet that the human mind was a concoction of bestial impulses guided by feedback loop machine logic and that, like computers, we are but informational systems of whom possess no soul; we are simply that of a series of electrical impulses. Thus, *Wiener* would refer to Humans, within his writings, as "animals"; such thinking, you can imagine, leads to an amoral world view from which pure pragmatism can be exercised, without care for the pain wrought upon the innocent. I have previously discussed *Wiener* being the coiner of the term "Cybernetics", which derives from Greek and means "steersman" or "governor", and as such I will simply mention it in passing. Continuing, these individuals – fuelled by an unwavering view of Social Darwinism – would go on to forecast the inevitability of systems of global information control and, by consequence, political control. You see, because they believed inherently that the human mind was merely an informational system, like any other, within an age of information it too was fair game to be exploited and reprogrammed. *Wiener* stated, "where a man's word goes and where his power of perception goes, to that point his control and in a sense his physical existence is extended. To see and to give commands to the whole world is almost the same as being everywhere." Thus, Cybernetics was more than compatible, if not a requisite component, of a future scientific dictatorship that had full-spectrum dominance over the population below; I theorise that this will now see applications in direct control via EMF wave and the Cybernetic loop created by the implanted receptor, and these innumerable towers. Upon this type of closed-loop system, the general idea behind this within Cybernetics, at least in *Wiener*'s idea, was to echo in a practical sense what his teacher, *Bertrand Russel*, worked upon in a theoretical sense; *Russel*'s personal philosophy was one of misanthropy, and a belief upon the idea of entropy ruling the destiny of everything. Hence, the system of cybernetics, in a twisted sense, seeks to outrun entropy or degradation in the organism, by mechanising and digitising it, rendering it transhuman or beyond human. The central issue or theme in Cybernetics is thusly the control of entropy. *Wiener* identified that the mechanism of feedback is the function by which machines can control the mechanical tendency toward disorganisation; accordingly, one can see the attraction of tyranny to this. You see, it boils down to this precept, that the reason tyranny has failed in the past is the condition of Man – that of freewill – which leads to an inevitable disintegration of the said tyranny. Thence, Man must be changed and thus mechanised in some way to spur on a resistance to entropy – that of negentropy. *Wiener* states, regarding the Cybernetic loop in the context of Man/machine as: "a sequence of events in time which, though in itself has a certain contingency, strives to hold back nature's tendency towards disorder by adjusting its parts to various purposive ends" (*Human Use of Human Beings*, pg. 27).

I should also discuss feedback loops and negative feedbacks which are extremely important in Cybernetics and comprise one of the most integral units of the study. In Cybernetics, the understanding of the circular loop of feedback is applied to facilitate a system of control, through which a critical resource is held at the desired level by a self-regulating mechanism. The critical resource within my working hypothesis is that of the human-being and its mind; the self-regulating mechanism (the control function) being the commands absorbed and translated by the receptor, within the injection site, to then imperceptibly affect the behaviour of the human-being. In Cybernetics, there are two types of feedback loops, negative and positive, for the scope of this discussion we do not have to discuss positive feedbacks; but negative feedback loops are essential to understand this agenda. This quote shall provide an in-depth overview of negative feedback loops as it relates to a system of control: "The term "self-regulation," developed in this context by Carver and Scheier (1982, 2011), refers to the "sense of purposive processes, the sense that self-corrective adjustments are taking place as needed to stay on track for the purpose being served" (Carver and Scheier, 2011, p. 3). The key cybernetic unit is "the negative feedback loop" (Carver and Scheier, 1982). The "negative" refers to its function to reduce discrepancy between the current state and the desired end-state. The loop is comprised of four functional elements: a reference point, a comparator, input, and output functions. A goal within a negative feedback loop is the reference point one desires or intends to achieve (Carver and Scheier, 1982). The role of the input function is to identify one's current state in respect to that goal. Finally, the comparator continuously compares (monitors) the input function and the reference value. The result of the comparison determines the output function—the behaviour that seems appropriate to reduce the gap between the current state and the desired end-state. The output function—through the selected behaviour—affects the environment and consequently the perceived input changes until the gap is nullified (Carver and Scheier, 1982, 2011; Miller et al., 1960)."[527] Thus, within the context I have outlined above, that being mass mind-control, it can be naturally delineated by the above statement. As a sidenote too, we have seen a great deal of contemporary examples of government attempts at, what is termed, either psychotronic, bioelectromagnetic, or "frequency remote influencing" within the UK and within the entire Western world[528][529]; this has been pervasive leading up to this pandemic event and is a rather large clue that this system they are unveiling now, through the guise of a medical injection to fight a pandemic (collectivised morality mixed with a fear-inducing narrative, creating a desired systemic feedback), is the final culmination of the systems and principles I am outlining throughout this section and the last one.

I wish to discuss this idea of the resistance of entropy through mechanisation and how it ties in with the cycle of civilisations; thus, this is the reason why they are engaged in, what can only be described as, the mass-scale perfection of *MK-ULTRA*[530] [531]. Keep in mind too, in

---

[527] O. Nafcha, E.T. Higgins, B. Eitam, *Chapter 3 - Control feedback as the motivational force behind habitual behaviour*, Editor(s): Bettina Studer, Stefan Knecht, Progress in Brain Research, Elsevier, Volume 229, 2016, Pages 49-68, ISSN 0079-6123, ISBN 9780444637017, https://doi.org/10.1016/bs.pbr.2016.06.008. (https://www.sciencedirect.com/science/article/pii/S0079612316300942)

[528] *"MICROWAVE MIND CONTROL by Tim Rifat: UK INTELLIGENCE FORCES AND MICROWAVE MIND CONTROL MIND CONTROL."* (2008). URL: https://www.semanticscholar.org/paper/MICROWAVE-MIND-CONTROL-by-Tim-Rifat-UK-INTELLIGENCE/2b0f109dd90dba39e08975a4701ac80d5019b965#references

[529] Rauscher, E.A.; Bise, W.L. *1999 Response of physiological parameters to low frequency and low intensity pulsed magnetic fields.* The Free Library (September, 22), https://www.thefreelibrary.com/Response of physiological parameters to low frequency and low...-a0163331989 (accessed June 12 2021)

[530] Lipton, E. L. *The amytal interview. A review.* Amer. Practit. Digest Treat.,1950, 1, pg. 148-163

[531] UNITED STATES. (1977). *Project MKULTRA, the CIA's program of research in be-*

recent times the governments of the world have been trying to perfect this remote engineering of the human-being for purposes of creating a planned society. For example, *PROJECT ARTICHOKE (MK-ULTRA)*, which was preceded by *Project Bluebird*, stated surprisingly within its declassified documents, "Can we get control of an individual to the point where he will do our bidding against his will and even against fundamental laws of nature such as self-preservation?"[532] Thus, as you can see the reason surrounding this is to extract the freewill from the Man, to create a more predictable situation throughout the system. As I have been stating, to some disapprobation by others, the cycle of civilisational rise and fall is what this expert-class is trying to undo, with this notion of mind-control; to escape the orbit of civilisational death and to have an everlasting system that cannot be overthrown. They wish for a planned system, a system of *Social Automation*, in which humans are little more than remotely controlled automatons; whilst the reimagined society they shall dwell in will be an entirely engineered one. These injections are designed to create a feedback-loop of control, from the origin of input (the towers/central-node) to the receptor - proprioceptor, biologically speaking - in one's arm (hence, the magnetisation at the injection site). Consequently, it will facilitate the total control of the human mind and the transforming of the human into a transhuman; something beyond man; the Cybernetic, the steered or piloted, man. They would be able to command individuals to do anything as was discussed within these military experiments such as *Project Bluebird* and *PROJECT ARTICHOKE*[533]; along with many others that we only hear rumours of here and there. The technological reshaping of man, the completion of the final revolution. The cold and binary world where the

---

havioural modification: joint hearing before the Select Committee on Intelligence and the Subcommittee on Health and Scientific Research of the Committee on Human Resources, United States Senate, Ninety-fifth Congress, first session, August 3, 1977. Washington, U.S. Govt. Print. Off.

[532] Estabrooks, G.H. *Hypnosis comes of age*. Science Digest, 44–50, April 1971.

[533] Scheflin, A.W., & Opton, E.M. *The Mind manipulators*. New York: Paddington Press, 1978.

prototypical *MK-ULTRA* has been totally perfected and shall allow the fundamental concept of Eugenics to be fulfilled; that of the self-direction of human evolution. Tangentially too, it must be understood that some of the rumours surrounding this use of bioelectromagnetic control of a target's neurology, via the implanting of a receptor under the guise of some medical device, goes back to the rumoured *"PROJECT CRIMSON MIST"* conducted in Rwanda, which was speculated to have inflamed the genocide; the reported physicist and paraphysicist working upon its *Elizabeth A. Rauscher* was indeed working on behavioural modification by means of electromagnetic frequency; simply a coincidence I wish to share, but only mere conjecture [534]. However, this type of serious investigation by the various apparatuses of the state, the tendrils of the military and intelligence agencies most acutely, into the idea of mind-control by many means was done in the hopes of bringing about the wish for a system of pure efficiency and permanency[535] [536].

Norbert Wiener spoke of this also, in primitive terms of course, as he was writing within the early- to mid-twentieth century. *W. Ross Ashby* was another Cyberneticist who spoke to this concept as I have outlined above. I will thus provide some quotes from them and then comment upon the implications of their statements, considering our current thematic narrative of remote command-and-control via frequency. *Wiener*, within his work *Human Use for Human Beings*, stated that "Of course, we assume that the instruments which act as sense organs record not only the original state of the work, but also the result of all the previous processes. Thus, the machine may

---

[534] W. Van Bise and E.A. Rauscher, *"Multiple Extremely Low Frequency Magnetic and Electromagnetic Field Effects on Human Electroencephalogram and Behaviour,"* Pg. 57-58, the Annual Review of Research on Biological Effects of Electric and Magnetic Fields from the Generation, Delivery and use of Electricity, DOE, EPRI, and the U.S. National Institute of Environmental Health Sciences, Tucson, AZ, September 1998.
[535] Keeler, Anna *"Remote Mind Control Technology" Reprinted from Secret and Suppressed: Banned Ideas and Hidden History* (Portland, OR: Feral House, 1993)
[536] WHALE. Dr Ross Adey. Available: http://www.whale.to/b/adey.html. Last accessed: 13/06/2021.

carry out feedback operations, either those of the simple type now so thoroughly understood, or those involving more complicated processes of discrimination, regulated by the central control as a logical or mathematical system. In other words, the all-over system will correspond to the complete animal with sense organs, effectors, and proprioceptors, and not, as in the ultra-rapid computing machine, but to an isolated brain, dependent for its experiences and for its effectiveness on our intervention." (*Human Use of Human Beings*, pg.156). The terminology surrounding sense organs and proprioceptors is one that mirrors the biology of the nervous system and the feedback loop it expresses; the proprioceptor is a specific biological term, it is the receptor that receives the electrical stimuli and then processes it, eventually feeding back a reciprocated electrical impulse to the origin point or input. Hence, what *Wiener* is alluding to here, is a future where from a central control point, that with a human (that he calls "animal") with a receptor, will interact with this "all-over system"; to the human's isolated brain, it will be dependent upon the external intervention, that being the electrical stimuli, from that central control, for the experiences and effectiveness. This excerpt is rather direct in its allusion to mind-control, but in most of the quotes I will share here it is rather ambiguous in its context as they are discussing concepts that have a wide-range of applications.

Wiener asserts, "On the one hand, it receives its detailed instructions from elements of the nature of sense organs, such as photoelectric cells…In other words, such factories should be under a regime rather like that of the interlocking signals and switches of the railroad signal-tower." (*Human Use of Human Beings*, pg. 157-158). As you can see, the prototypical terminology of "tower" and "photoelectric cells" as a receptor – which exist in the injected now I postulate - were already being utilised by *Wiener* as a conceptualisation of a theoretical paradigm of control. Interestingly, the usage of the analogy of the railroad echoes the work of *Donald MacKay*, another Cyberneticist from Britain, in which he stated that - and I am paraphrasing - that the train is a perfect cybernetic control system in that it needs no steering wheel, as all the forces required to correct for the buffeting of wind and sway are all automatically provided for by the sideways reaction of the wheel-flanges upon the rails. Thus, this is a perfect self-regulating control system, you see. As a final note on this excerpt, look at the usage of the factory environment to apply this type of imagined system of technological control; that being, the factory is implicitly linked to the idea of the "means of production" and the "means of production" is implicitly linked to the human because that is the main means of production at present; which *Wiener* asserts is imperfectly organised. Hence, a helmsman is required as a control function which shall mitigate the wild oscillatory patterns of a society left to its own devices; that being an expert class, or a self-regulating system of direct mind-control, or a brain-computer interface via receptors; the *IoT* (The Internet of Things); "a fusion between our biological, digital and physical identities", you see.

The next statements by *Wiener*, from the same book of course, are regarding this future "steering or governing machine", which I think is about to be revealed soon once the vast majority are implanted with this nanoplatform receptor, "The *machines a gouverner* (the steering or governing machine) will define the State as the best-informed player at each particular level; and the State is the only supreme co-ordinator of all partial decisions. These are enormous privileges; if they are acquired scientifically, they will permit the State under all circumstances to beat every player of a human game other than itself by offering this dilemma: either immediate ruin or planned co-operation. This will be the consequences of the game itself without outside violence. The lovers of the best of worlds have something indeed to dream of!" (*Human Use of Human Beings*, pg. 179). What is being discussed here is the idea that *Artificial Intelligence* or a direct control network, it is unclear as to

Chapter VIII

which, should indubitably comprise the mechanism of control within the state; this is clearly framed from the work of *Von Neumann*, titled *Theory of Games and Economic Behaviour*. Pay close attention also to the binary and threatening choice the human player is thus provided with: "immediate ruin or planned co-operation". Naturally, this purports to the dictatorship of terror they wish to implement, where one will either succumb to the "planned co-operation", in which the "planned" part translates to direct control from an external source, or henceforth death. The idea of the "steering or governing machine" is discussed a few times within that particular work of *Wiener*, but I wish to draw to your attention another quote regarding it; I feel it paramount in light of our current tribulating times. *Wiener* states "Despite all this, and perhaps fortunately, the machine a gouverner is not ready for a very near tomorrow. For outside of the very serious problems which the volume of information to be collected and to be treated rapidly still put, the problems of the stability of prediction remain beyond what we can seriously dream of controlling." (*Human Use of Human* Beings, pg.158-159). Indeed, *Wiener* saw clearly, almost prophetically, that to create this steering or governing machine that it would conceivably take a serious advancement in computational technology, one that could process and collect all of this data to be used against the human players within society. As a final quote, this indeed is another prophetically twisted one: *Wiener* write, "Progress imposes not only new possibilities for the future but new restrictions. It seems almost as if progress itself and our fight against the increase of entropy intrinsically must end in the downhill path from which we are trying to escape." (*Human Use of Human Beings*, pg. 48). Naturally, the phraseology, that progress imposes new restrictions is very eerily reminiscent of our current dilemma; was this all entirely planned from as long ago as 1950? It is hard to conclusively say, but he alludes to this idea of "entropy" or decay and the fight against it and the need to "escape it"; as I have been stating with my anacyclosis or the cycles of civilisation discussions. However, he sees the truth of the matter, that they cannot escape it in the end and, though *Wiener* still pursued it, he expresses doubt as to the fulfilment of this agenda of extracting from tyranny its characteristic trait of impermanence. Although, I believe they feel they have, as they are now engaging all of the available resources at their disposal, to realise that old desire of the father of Cybernetics, *Norbert Wiener*, and of his teachers, *Russel* and *Hilbert*, of controlling people most thoroughly. This will alleviate the general tendency towards internal disintegration of human systems, or so they believe. However, I believe it will probably collapse from the top in such a Techno-feudal system.

They wish to escape the orbit of civilisational death and to have an everlasting system that cannot be overthrown. They wish for a planned system, a system of *Social Automation*, in which humans are little more than automatons, robotic servants, and the society they shall dwell in will be an entirely engineered one. These injections are designed to create a feedback loop of control from the input device (the towers/central node) to the receptor (proprioceptor or artificial sense organ, as stated by *Wiener*) in the arm, thus it will facilitate the total control of the human mind and the transforming of a human into a transhuman; something beyond man and machine. They can command individuals to do anything; it is a frighteningly close future. The technological reshaping of man and the completion of the final revolution; the cold and binary world where the prototypical forays into *MK-ULTRA* have been totally perfected on a mass-scale. More so, it is the bridging of the perceived gap between the organic and the inorganic; the cybernetic man we shall become in this dystopia; not cybernetic in terms of the technological augmentation, but cybernetic in terms of the Greek etymology of the word, κυβερνητικός, meaning steered or governed man. A man connected to a hive-mind, that is controlled remotely. As discussed within a presentation by *Dr. Robert*

Chapter VIII

Duncan, titled, "Intelligent Systems of Control"; he states quite clearly that the idea of the "Cybernetic Hive Mind" is actually old technology, which has been around since the 1960's.

I wish to end on a final note, regarding how this fundamental transhuman concept of becoming cybernetic – or controlled – will be sold to us. Right now, the bio-digital fusion of the human is being touted as "you could be superhuman" if you were transhuman or a "Cybernetic man"; or, in terms of bringing about an equally impoverished servile class, they state "we need to create a fairer world, where your basic needs are met and inequality is less". They thus market it, like all snake-oil salesman, as them selflessly helping you; for nothing more than the good of you. However, as is always the case, the truth is so far departed from the illusion. In the case of the "we need to create a fairer world, where your basic needs are met" line. Well, in prison such a system exists; where one's needs are met and there is fairness, through the inmates having an equal position in terms of wealth. However, the wardens and the enforcers have an equally greater position than the inmates; they control them and have set in place a system where the inmate's routine is created for them; their behaviours somewhat dictated by the series of psychological prompts (force, sounds, fear, etc). Moreover, to achieve this "fairer world", like a prison, one must relinquish their freedom and their right to social and financial mobility; the authoritarian does not say that though and he simply tells you the skewed "benefits" of the system. The "fairer and more equal world" really means a world resembling a prison and a population resembling the inmates. Naturally, this is synthesised within the "you will own nothing and be happy" concept of the World Economic Forum. However, think about it for but a moment, what society or group of people would be content with "owning nothing"; why would a shrewd ruling class believe they could pull off such a daring heist of everyone's freedom and yet, still live to tell the tale at the end of it? The only way to explain their confidence in realising such an unprecedented goal – which would, in any other period or setting, cause a cataclysmic collapse of the society via civil unrest – is to understand the Cyberneticist's future, of which I have outlined in this section, and the machinations that have been spun by the proponents of Cybernetics and of which originally emanated from its progenitor schools of thought. You must understand the methodical nature of this all and the meticulous zealotry, in bringing about the conditions in which human evolution can be self-directed and mass-enfeeblement made thorough and impervious to any potential external challengers.

Epilogue

This book, of which is my first foray into writing literature on this grand a scale, is very multitudinous in the concepts it presents and it strays into many ideas and themes, throughout. Upon that note, I hope the reader can digest all of these and can take value from what is presented herein this book; in hopes it provides at least a hint of a greater mystery afoot within all these seemingly unconnected happenings, occurring within this unique period of civilisational development. As you may well understand, since I began writing this book, around eleven-months ago, many changes have become apparent within our social environment and civilisation; of which led me to take strange twists to the information I presented within this piece of literature. Naturally, I was planning on including some of the information I discuss within this book, specifically that contained within the "Conclusionary Thoughts" section, within other books I was planning on writing. However, as is to be expected time is running rather short in this civilisational cycle and, it seems to be that I will not have enough time to create another book of this scale; with the walls closing in so swiftly and mercilessly, so to speak. As such, what I write here, taken holistically, can provide a good point of reference to understand where we are and, most likely, where we are going.

Alas, with that said, it is my earnest desire to point out another major takeaway from the overarching theme of this book. The overarching theme being civilisational entropy and the ever-present orbit of the celestial body of decline, naturally; in its literal and subtly memetic forms, of course. Adding on to that, it can be gleaned from history, that all empires, civilisations, and large conglomerates of tribes seem, within their end states, at least within the upper echelons of the hierarchy, to identify somewhat the patterns of decline from the past. From this, the leadership, in an attempt to protect their privilege in assuming the mantle of power, seek to reverse this assured trajectory via inventive ways of, what always boils down to, tyranny of some form or another. Thus, the main congruent element they identify from the various patterns of decline, the element that is to be controlled and mitigated from corroding civilisation any further, is that of Man himself. I did delve into this point within the "Problematic Condition of Man" section, but it bears reiteration as it is a vitally important point within all of this. That said, the present swift move towards a type of "Hive-Mind", or control of the human thought process, is, ironically, another strong, observable element of this cycle of civilisational decline; one that consistently repeats itself at the terminus of any given civilisational cycle. To take a for instance, let us peer back in time, to the era of *Constantine the Great* and his likewise policies that was a striving in this direction of control and mitigation of the nature of Man. Now, to be very brief in my prior preamble remark to this, to ensure we understand the defined variables we are discussing here, when I state the "nature of Man", what I really mean is the sentience and freewill of Man; his everchanging thought pattern, his uncontrolled ambitious nature, his determinacy to firstly understand and then redefine the world around him, etc. Thus, we can understand as to why exactly this would be a most grave problem for maintaining the cohesion of a civilisation and ensure that the oligarchy maintained the lifeblood of their grip on power; that being, monopolistic control. Therefore, with that out of the way, we can begin discussing the policies of *Constantine* and how they tie most accurately in with the contemporary attempt to thwart the nature of Man.

Chapter VIII

As you may well be aware, *Constantine the Great* was an ambitious man who led the Roman Empire through a transitionary phase of unbridled centralisation and cultural modification; a time not of renewal of the old, but of a new course of gradual assimilation of it into something new. *Constantine* laid the foundation for the mass-Christianisation of the Roman Empire by the end of his life. Why did he engage in such a risqué policy of alienation through unification of the, still, largely pagan and multi-faith empire? The answer is rather simple, *Constantine* was striving to unify the sundry assortment of different faiths and modes of thinking into a single, monolithic structure of control; a nexus point for the centrally-administered direction of the behaviour and thinking of Man. Likewise, within our current Constantinian policy of cultural and cognitive regulation-driven osmosis, we find that the technology that is potentially being developed and unveiled will create, what all of the antiquated forms, like *Constantine* and Christianity, sought to create, a persistent control over the minds of Man – which is the main destroyer of civilisation and of itself, inevitably – and a supplanting of the traditional mutually-cooperative structure of society, by a social-organism akin to a hive or termitary. It is a rather simple concept and it always, logically of course, will result in a tyrannical exertion of unwarranted power by the central state; just like the forced Christian baptisms, the new state will deal with the current resistors, of this new form of baptism by injection, in a similar envenomed way. Thus, concluding this point, we may now understand that the entropic principle and its identification by the elite of a society, of its presence being pervasive within that society, shall lead to an attempt to control the main vector of entropy within the civilisation. That being, the unpredictable condition of Man and thus, once mitigated beyond principal effect, it then sets the stage for a greater degree of predictability and steerability within the civilisational arena, so to say; this, the oligarchy or monopolists of power hope, will ensure an interminable empire (See the section: "Belief in Eternal Pre-eminence").

Continuing on, I wish to provide attention to the almost memoir-like nature of this piece of literature. I must confess, I had no real plan, nor timeline for completion when I began writing this over eleven-months ago and, as such, I let the research take me where it willed it. Therefore, with that in mind, I wish for you to very much see the arc of development within my thinking throughout this book as the various unprecedented events, throughout this tumultuous eleven-months, played out in real-time. My thinking upon matters changed very much and, though I am somewhat trapped within the perfectionist spiral, I feel it very germane to leave the thoughts as I wrote them intact; as not just a memoir of my real-time postulations upon the events, but as a chronicle, for future generations, of a civilisation in the throes of decline. Undoubtedly, they will draw parallels to their own contemporary civilisation, as anacylcosis is a never-ending cycle, naturally.

Moreover, as another somewhat tangential sidenote, within the "Conclusionary Thoughts" section, I have attempted to bring forward my explanations of the current medical crisis – the reasons for it and the capitalisation of it, within a larger historical arc – and of the reasons for, what seems to be, the artificial inducement of controlled catastrophe within the system. This is all naturally being done in hopes of political expediency for hidden and partially-hidden aims. However, though this may seem quite an unorthodox departure from my previous analysis upon the decline of civilisation, present and past, it is nonetheless very much entwined and carries the betwixt constant of life, and thus its outgrowth of civilisation; its decay and its unnerving drive towards its own cycle of destruction and creation.

Thus, if we may, we could very well extrapolate this idea further and discuss the peculiar nature of our existence and its twisted sense of poetic irony, within its dualistic feedbacks. What do I mean? Look at it this way, death is the terminus of life and the reverse is true, in that death begets life; destruction is the terminus of creation and the reverse heralds truth, in that creation eventually begets destruction; barbarism and tribalism

Chapter VIII

beget civilisation and civilisation has its terminus within a return to barbarism and tribalism. So on and so forth. Hence, we may look upon the thematic forces of existence, the ever-present constants that permeate our mind, the informational receptor from which our image of the world is decoded therefrom, and see that the dualistic opposite of each said thematic force is existent within the other. Naturally, they are siblings of the same mother, fated to be locked in perpetual, attritive struggle until the end of time. However, without each other, each respective thematic force would be devoid of meaning within this existential realm; for if life was undying, or civilisation unending, then how could change and thus motion prevail? Existence would be in stagnation and the expansion and contraction of the universe would be utterly invalidated; cause and effect would have no meaning; the laws of the universe would be mere subjections to vanishment; the universe itself would be inextricable from that of the concept of nothingness; meaning would not have meaning; nothing would be, itself, nothing; inertia indistinguishable from motion. Therefore, depending upon one's opinion, that being if the universe is or is not acting upon principles of meaning, one must still conclude that without the dualistic feedback of these natural occurrences - life and death, civilisation and barbarism, creation and destruction – then the wheels of motion, the constant feedback between these dualisms that breaks the default state of inertia, would cease and thus life and existence would cease. Accordingly, it is the main reason as to why tyrannies and despotisms always fail, as they wish to constrain motion into a predictable and controllable series of pulsations of activity. As they learn the hard way, like a child that plays with fire only to get burnt, existence does not function in such a way and this feedback of motion between dualistic forces cannot be halted or reversed. Motion is life, and life is a force of indifference.

I hope I have made you, the reader, at least contemplate the nature of all that is going on here in our current time. Though, this book is nebulous and wild in its various twists and turns, I hope, that if it is taken holistically and absorbed as such, then one may be provided with somewhat a greater degree of understanding of where historical precedent dictates our course from here on out. I have alluded to several theories myself, dictated from that aforementioned shadow of historical precedence, however I always stand to be corrected and I very much hope I provide an impetus, an intellectual coaxing to you, the reader, to delve further into these various subjects presented and doing just that; correcting me and, in turn, informing me of other avenues of thinking and of knowledge. For, to sup of the waters of knowledge and wisdom is to drink from an everlasting spring, from which each partaking of it bears a new and intriguing taste upon the drinker's intellectual tastebuds. Always recall, *Non est auctoritatis, solum ipse*: "there is no authority, only self". Moreover, imperfect freedom is always preferrable to perfected slavery and the "safety and security" it claims it can grant you; if you would only bow and pay homage, that is.

I thank you all for reading this book for which I crafted with the idealistic hopes of aiding and informing others of the grave trajectory we are on. In the end, as is the tyrant's folly, one cannot stop the motion of the aforesaid wheels, but one may warn others so that they may jump from the cart; of which the wheels indifferently carry forward. Inevitably, I believe this is the intention of this book and was my intention in persevering to write this piece of literature. In any which way, it has been a pleasure to hopefully provide for you an insightful read and information you may have been otherwise unaware of. My friends, I bid you adieu and may many good and glorious blessings go with you, in all you endeavour to do justly in the world.

Igne Natura Renovatur Integra – "Through fire, is the Earth reborn whole".

BIBLIOGRAPHY

Alexander, T. (1918). *The Prussian Elementary Schools.* New York: Macmillan Company.

Al-Munajjid, S. a.-D. (1975). *Al-Hayah al-Jinsiyyah 'ind al-'Arab, min al-Jahiliyyah ila Awakhir al-Qarn al-Rabii' al-Hijri [The Sexual Life of the Arabs: Since Jahiliyyah until the End of the Fourth Century A.H.].* Beirut: Dar al-Kitab al-Jadid.

Ammianus, M., & Yonge, C. D. (1862). *The Roman history of Ammianus Marcellinus: During the reigns of the emperors Constantius, Julian, Jovianus, Valentinian, and Valens.*

Aquinatis, T. (n.d.). *Summa Theologiæ Part III.*

Ashby, R. W. (1956). *An Introduction to Cybernetics.* London: Chapman & Hall.

Asquith, G., & Bräutigam, M. (2019). *Engaging Ethically in a Strange New World: A View from Down Under.* Wipf and Stock Publishers.

Azmon, G. (2017). *Being in time: A post-political manifesto.*

Bacon, F. (1992). *New Atlantis.* Kila, MT: Kessinger.

Balsdon, J. P. (1979). *Romans and Aliens.* Chapel Hill: University of North Carolina Press.

Batra, R. (1978). *The Downfall of Capitalism and Communism: A New Study of History.* London: McMillan.

Bauman, R. (1999). *Human Rights in Ancient Rome.* .

Bernardi, A. (1970). *The Economic Problems of the Roman Empire at the Time of its Decline.* (C. M. Cipolla, Ed.) London: Methuen & Co. Ltd.

Birnie, A. (1958). *The History and Ethics of Interest.* London: William Hodge & Co.

Blickle, P. (1981). *The Revolution of 1525: The German Peasants' War from a New Perspective.* Baltimore, Maryland: Johns Hopkins University Press.

Bork, R. H. (1996). *Slouching towards Gomorrah : modern liberalism and American decline.* New York: Regan Books.

Bosworth, C. e., & al, e. (1986). *"Liwat" The Encyclopedia of Islam.* E.J. Brill.

Burnett, A. (1984). *Clipped Siliquae and the End of Roman Britain. Britannia.* Society for the Promotion of Roman Studies.

Bury, J. (1923). *"The Nika Revolt", The History of the Later Roman Empire.*

Cameron, A. (1976). *Circus factions: Blues and Greens at Rome and Byzantium.* Oxford: Clarendon Press.

Cameron, A. (1976). *Circus Factions: Blues and Greens at Rome and Byzantium.* Oxford: Clarendon Press.

Carcopino, J., In Rowell, H. T., & Lorimer, E. O. (1956). *Daily life in ancient Rome: The people and the city at the height of the empire.* Harmondsworth, Middlesex: Penguin Books.

Chopra, P. N. (2003). *A Comprehensive History Of Ancient India (3 Vol. Set).* Sterling Publishers Pvt. Ltd.

Churchill, W. S. (1978). *The Second World War: The Hinge of Fate* (Vol. 4). New York: Houghton Mifflin Company.

Cicero, M. T., & Occidentalium, C. T. (n.d.). *Epistulae ad Atticum.* Turnhout: Brepols Publishers.

Cicero, M. T., Kerin, R. C., & Allcroft, A. H. (1890). *Cicero: Pro Plancio.* London: W.B. Clive.

Clarke, J. (1998, 2001). *Looking at Lovemaking: Constructions of Sexuality in Roman Art 100 B.C. - A.D. 250.* University of California Press.

Cowan M.D., T., & Morell, S. F. (2020). *The Contagion Myth: Why Viruses (including "Coronavirus") Are Not the Cause of Disease.* Skyhorse.

Craies, W. F. (1911). *Treason (Encyclopædia Britannica)* (11 ed., Vol. 27). (H. Chisholm, Ed.) Cambridge: Cambridge University Press.

Cramer, F. (1945). *Bookburning and Censorship in Ancient Rome: A Chapter from the History of Freedom of Speech.* (2 ed., Vol. 6). Journal of the History of Ideas.

Dawson, C. (1950). *Religion and the rise of Western culture.* New York: Sheed & Ward.

de la Torre, C. (Ed.). (2018). *Routledge Handbook of Global Populism* (1st ed.). Routledge.

Deggans, E. (2012). *Race-baiter: How the media wields dangerous words to divide a nation.* New York, NY: : Palgrave Macmillan.

Development, U. N. (1993). *Agenda 21: programme of action for sustainable development; Rio Declaration on Environment and Development.* New York, NY: United Nations Dept. of Public Information.

Dio, C. (n.d.). *Roman History - Epitome of Book LXII*. Chicago: University of Chicago.

El-Feki, S. (2013). *Sex and the Citadel: Intimate Life in a Changing Arab World*. North Sydney, N.S.W.: Vintage Books.

Erdkamp, P. (1980). *The Food Supply of the Capital*. Cambridge: Cambridge University Press; The Cambridge Companion to Ancient Rome .

Ferrill, A. (1986). *The Fall of the Roman Empire: The Military Explanation*. London: Thames and Hudson.

Fitzgerald, W. (2007). *Martial: The Wolrd of Epigram*. Chicago: University of Chicago Press.

Foucault, M. (1979). *The History of Sexuality* (Vol. I). London: Allen Lane.

Friedman, M. (1990). *Free to choose: a personal statement*. Houghton Mifflin Harcourt.

Gabriel, R. A. (2008). *Scipio Africanus: Rome's Greatest General*. Washington: Potomac Books Inc.

Gates, F. T. (1913). *The Country School of To-morrow*. New York: General Education Board.

Geitz, H., Heideking, J., Herbst, J., & German Historical Institute (Washington, D. (2006). *German influences on education in the United States to 1917*. Washington, D.C: German Historical Institute.

Gentili, A., & Antonius, W. (1607). *Alberici Gentilis Iurisconsulti, Professoris Regii, In titulos codicis si quis imperatori maledixerit, ad legem Iuliam maiestatis, disputationes decem*. Hanouiae: Apud Guilielmum Antonium.

Gibbon, E. (1867). *The History of the Decline and Fall of the Roman Empire*. London: Bell & Daldy.

Gibbon, E., & Bury, J. (1914). *The History of the Decline and Fall of the Roman Empire*. New York: Macmillan.

Glubb, J. (1978). *The Fate of Empires and Search for Survival*. Edinburgh: Blackwood.

Goethe, J. W., & Miller, G. L. (2009). *The metamorphosis of plants*. Cambridge, Massachusetts: MIT Press.

Grant, M. (1990). *The Fall of the Roman Empire*. London: Weidenfeld and Nicolson.

GRIFFIN, G. E. (1995). *The creature from Jekyll Island: a second look at the Federal Reserve.* Appleton, Wisc: American Opinion.

Griffin, J., & Orwell, G. (1989). *Animal Farm.* Harlow: Longman.

Grousset, R. (1970). *The Empire of the Steppes.* New Brunswick, New Jersey: Rutgers University Press.

Habermas, J. (1987). *"The Entwinement of Myth and Enlightenment: Horkheimer and Adorno." In The Philosophical Discourse of Modernity: Twelve Lectures.* (F. Lawrence, Trans.) Cambridge, MA: MIT Press.

Habermas, J. (1987). *"The Entwinement of Myth and Enlightenment: Horkheimer and Adorno." In The Philosophical Discourse of Modernity: Twelve Lectures,* translated by F. Lawrence. Cambridge, MA: MIT Press.

Hall, E. T. (1966). *The Hidden Dimension: An Anthropologist Examines Humans' Use of Space in Public and in Private.* New York: Anchor Books.

Hamilton, E. J. (1938). *Revisions in Economic History: VIII.-The Decline of Spain* (2nd ed., Vol. 8). Economic History Review.

Harb, F., & In J. Ashtiany, T. J. (1990). *Wine poetry (khamriyyāt); Abbasid Belles Lettres (The Cambridge History of Arabic Literature).* Cambridge: Cambridge University Press.

Heather, P. (2005). *The Fall of the Roman Empire.* London: Pan Books.

Heather, P. (2006). *The Fall of the Roman Empire: A New History of Rome and the Barbarians. Oxford University Press.* Oxford: Oxford University Press.

Heather, P. J. (2018). *Rome resurgent: war and empire in the age of Justinian.* New York, NY.

Heims, S. J. (1991). *The Cybernetics Group.* Cambridge, Massachusetts: MIT Press.

Hess, K. (1995). *Community technology.* Port Townsend, WA: Loompanics Unlimited.

Hibbs, T. (2012). *Shows about Nothing: Nihilism in Popular Culture* (2nd ed.). Waco: Baylor University Press.

Hinsch, B. (1990). *Passions of the Cut Sleeve.* University of California Press.

Hobbes, T. (1651). *Leviathan.* Penguin Books: Baltimore.

Holland, T. (2003). *Rubicon: The last years of the Roman Republic.* New York: Doubleday.

Hoppe, H.-H. (2001). *Democracy - The God That Failed: The Economics and Politics of Monarchy, Democracy and Natural Order.* Routledge.

Howell, P. e. (1995). *Martial: The Epigrams, Book V.* Liverpool: Liverpool University Press.

Hubbard, T. K. (2003). *Homosexuality in Greece and Rome: A Sourcebook of Basic Documents (1st ed.).* University of California Press.

Hughes, I. (2010). *Stilicho: The Vandal Who Saved Rome.* Barnsley: Pen & Sword Military.

Hughes, P. (1949). *A History of the Church, I (rev. ed.).* Sheed & Ward.

Huxley, A. (1932). *Brave New World.* New York: Harper Brothers.

Huxley, A. (1954). *The Doors of Perception.* New York: Harper & Brothers.

Huxley, A., & Hitchens, C. (2005). *Brave New World: and, Brave New World Revisited.*

Huxley, A., Horowitz, M., & Palmer, C. (1999). *Moksha: Aldous Huxley's classic writings on psychedelics and the visionary experience.* Rochester, VT: Park Street Press.

Huxley, J. (1957). *New Bottles for New Wine.* London: Chatto & Windus.

Huxley, J. (1968). *Transhumanism.* Journal of Humanistic Psychology.

Innes, M. (2004). *The Credit Theory of Money.* Edward Elgar Publishing.

Jones, A. H. (1964). *The Later Roman Empire, 284–602: A Social, Economic, and Administrative Survey* (Vol. 1). Basil Blackwell Ltd.

Jones, A. H. (1986). *The Later Roman Empire, 286-602: A Social, Economic and Administrative Survey.* Taylor & Francis.

Jordan, D. P. (1971). *Gibbon and his Roman Empire.* Chicago: University of Illinois Press.

Jowett M.A., B. (1892). *The Dialogues of Plato translated into English with Analyses and Introductions.* London: Oxford Press.

Juvenal, & translation by Ramsay, G. (1918). *The Satires of Juvenal.* London.

Kaegi, W. E. (1981). *Byzantine Military Unrest, 471–843: An Interpretation.* Amsterdam: Adolf M. Hakkert.

Kamran, Q. (2020). *Strategic Value Chain Management: Models for Competitive Advantage.* Kogan Page.

Kim, H. J. (2016). *The Huns.* Milton Park, Abingdon, Oxon: Routledge.

Kirchubel, M. A. (2010). *Vile acts of evil: Banking in America.* Charleston, SC.

Kirklees. (2001). *Kirklees' Agenda 21 Action Plan: 2000.* Huddersfield: Kirklees Environment Unit.

Kroll, J. &. (1993). *The Greek Coins.* The Athenian Agora (Vol. 26).

Le, R. P. (2003). *Le Haut-Empire romain en Occident: D'Auguste aux Sévères, 31 av. J.-C. - 235 apr. J.-C. .* Paris: Ed. du Seuil.

Lenski, N. (2002). *Failure of Empire: Valens and the Roman State in the Fourth Century A.D. .* University of California Press.

Livy. (1924). *The History of Rome.* (B. O. Foster, Ed.) Cambridge, Massachusetts, USA: Harvard University Press.

Locke, J. (1663). *Essays on the Law of Nature.*

Locke, J. (1980). *Second treatise of government.* (C. B. Macpherson, Ed.) Hackett Publishing.

Locke, J., & Nidditch, P. H. (1979). *An essay concerning human understanding.* Oxford: Clarendon Press.

Lyotard, J.-F. (1984). *The Postmodern Condition.* Manchester, England: University Press.

Machiavelli, N., Mansfield, H. C., & Tarcov, N. (1996). *Discourses on Livy.* Chicago: University of Chicago Press.

MacIntyre, A. C. (1984). *After Virtue: A Study in Moral Theory.* Notre Dame, Ind: University of Notre Dame Press.

MacMullen, R. (1988). *Corruption and the decline of Rome.* New Haven: Yale University Press.

Marshall, B. A. (1976). *Crassus: A political biography.* Amsterdam: A.M. Hakkert.

Massad, J. A. (2008). *Desiring Arabs.* Chicago: The University of Chicago Press.

Meadows, D. H., Meadows, D. L., Randers, J., Behrens, W., & Rome, &. C. (1972). *The Limits to growth: A report for the Club of Rome's project on the predicament of mankind.* New York: Universe Books.

Meyer, G. J. (2006). *A World Undone: The story of the Great War, 1914-1918.* New York: Delacorte Press.

Middlefort, E. (2011). *The Hammer of the Witches: A Complete Translation of the Malleus Maleficarum.* Catholic Historical Review.

Mohr, G. (1982). *Brain-washing (mind-changing): A synthesis of a Russian textbook on mass mind-control (psychopolitics)*. Phoenix, Ariz: Distributed by Lord's Covenant Church, America's Promise Broadcasts.

Mommsen, T. (1992). *A History of Rome under the Emperors*. London.

Mores, T. (1949). *Utopia*. New York: Appleton-Century-Crofts.

Müntzer, T. (1988). *The Collected Works of Thomas Müntzer*. (P. Matheson, Ed.) Edinburgh: T&T Clark.

Murphy, R. P. (2020). *review of The Deficit Myth: Modern Monetary Theory and the Birth of the People's Economy, by Stephanie Kelton*. Quarterly Journal of Austrian Economics 23, no. 2 (Summer 2020): 232–51.

Mussolini, B. (1928). *Discorsi del 1927*. Milano, Alpes.

Neesen, L. (1981). *The Revenues of Rome* (Vol. 71). The Journal of Roman Studies.

Nietzsche, F. W. (1974). *The Gay Science; with a Prelude in Rhymes and an Appendix of Songs*. New York: Vintage Books.

Nietzsche, F. W. (2006). *Thus Spoke Zarathustra*. Cambridge: Cambridge University Press.

Nietzsche, F. W., & Large, D. (1998). *Twilight of the Idols, Or, How to Philosophize with a Hammer*. Oxford: Oxford University Press.

Northedge, F. S., & Edwards, P. (1967). *Peace, War and Philosophy* (Vol. 6). The Encyclopaedia of Philosophy: Collier Macmillan.

Nuwas, A. (1994). *al-Nusus al-Muharramah [Abu Nuwas: The Forbidden Texts]*. London: Riyad al-Rayyis.

Orlov, D. (2013). *The Five Stages of Collapse: Survivors' Toolkit*. Gabriola, BC, Canada: New Society Publishers.

Orwell, G. (1950). *1984*. New York: Signet Classic.

Plato. (1937). *Plato's Cosmology; The Timaeus of Plato*. London: Harcourt, Brace, K.Paul, Trench, Trubner & Co. ltd.

Plato, & Lee, H. (1977). *Timaeus and Critias*. Harmondsworth, England: Penguin Books.

Plato, & Shorey, P. (1930). *The Republic, Book 3*. Loeb.

Plato, Lane, M., & Desmond, L. (2007). *The Republic*. London: Penguin Classics.

Polybius. (1889). *The Histories*. (E. Shuckburgh, Trans.) Macmillan.

Procopius, & Dewing, H. B. (1914). *History of the Wars, Book III*. London: W. Heinemann.

Procopius, & Mihaescu, H. (1972). *Historia Arcana*. Bucharest: Editio Academiae Reipublicae Socialis Romaniae.

Putnam, R. D. (2000). *Bowling Alone: The Collapse and Revival of American Community*. New York: Simon & Schuster.

Quigley, C. (2010). *Tragedy and hope: A history of the world in our time*. Cheyenne, WY: Dauphin Publications Inc.

Rathbone, D. (2009). *Quantifying the Roman Economy: Methods and Problems*. (A. Bowman, & A. Wilson, Eds.) Oxford University Press.

Rebenich, S., & In Rousseau, P. (. (2012). *6 Late Antiquity in Modern Eyes; In Rousseau, Philip (ed.). A Companion to Late Antiquity*. John Wiley & Sons.

Reinert, S. W. (2002). *Fragmentation (1204–1453), In. Mango, Cyril (ed.)*. Oxford and New York: Oxford University Press.

Renna, T. (1999). *Campanella's City of the Sun and the Late Renaissance Italy*. Utopian Studies, vol.10, no.1.

Richard A. Werner. (2014). *Can banks individually create money out of nothing? — The theories and the empirical evidence*. International Review of Financial Analysis, Volume 36.

Roberts, A. (1999). *Salisbury: Victorian titan. London: Weidenfeld & Nicolson*. London: Weidenfeld & Nicolson.

Robinson, N. A. (1993). *Agenda 21: Earth's action plan annotated*. New York: Oceana Publications.

Robinson, N. A. (2004). *Strategies toward sustainable development: Implementing Agenda 21*. Dobbs Ferry, N.Y: Oceana Publications.

Rogers, R. (1959). *The Emperor's Displeasure-Amicitiam Renuntiare* (Vol. 90). Transactions and Proceedings of the American Philological Association: The Johns Hopkins University Press.

Rowson, E. K. (2012). *Homosexuality II. In Islamic Law*. New York: Columbia University, Encyclopaedia Iranica.

Rudich, V. (2016). *Navigating the Uncertain: Literature and Censorship in the Early Roman Empire*. (Series 3 ed., Vol. 14). Boston: Arion: A Journal of Humanities and the Classics.

Rushdie, S. (2005). *Shalimar the clown: A novel.* London: Jonathan Cape.

Russel, B. (1931). *The Scientific Outlook.* Routledge.

Schwab, K. (2017). *The fourth industrial revolution.*

Schweizer, P. (2015). *Clinton cash: The untold story of how and why foreign governments and businesses helped make Bill and Hillary rich.*

Scott, A. G. (2018). *Emperors and Usurpers: An Historical Commentary on Cassius Dio's Roman History.* Oxford, UK: Oxford University Press.

Seneca, L. A. (1917). *Ad Lucilium Epistulae Morales* (Vol. 1). (R. M. Gummere, Trans.) London: William Heinemann.

Seneca, L. A., & Campbell, R. (1969). *Letters from a Stoic: Epistulae morales ad Lucilium.* Penguin Books.

Smith, J. (2019). *Irrationality: A History of the Dark Side of Reason.* Princeton: Princeton University Press.

Southern, P. (2014). *The Roman Army: A History 753 BC - AD 476.* London: Amberley Publishing.

Southern, P., & Dixon, K. (1996). *The Late Roman Army.* London.

Spengler, O. (1932). *The Decline of the West* (Vol. Abridged). (H. Werner, A. Helps, Eds., & C. F. Atkinson, Trans.) New York: Oxford University Press.

Spengler, O. (2021). *The Decline of the West: Perspectives of World-History.* La Vergne: Arktos Media Ltd.

Spengler, O., & Atkinson, C. (1926). *The Decline of the West.* New York: A.A. Knopf.

Spring, P. (2015). *Great Walls and Linear Barriers.* Pen and Sword.

Staveley, E. S. (1972). *Greek and Roman voting and elections.* London: Thames and Hudson.

Steed, H. W. (1924). *"Through Thirty Years 1892–1922 A personal narrative"* (Vol. II). New York: Doubleday Page and Co.

Storr, A. (1971). *Human Aggression.* London: Penguin Books Ltd: British Journal of Psychiatry.

Strauss, B. (2013). *Masters of Command: Alexander, Hannibal, Caesar, and the Genius of Leadership.* Simon and Schuster.

Sun-tzu, & Griffith, a. S. (1964). *The Art of War.* Oxford: Clarendon Press.

Tacitus, C. (1939). *The Annals of Tacitus, Book XV.* London: Methuen & Co, Ltd.

Tacitus, C., & Robinson, R. P. (1935). *The Germania of Tacitus.* Middletown, CT: American Philological Association.

Thompson, L. (1994). *The Clinton Body Count: Coincidence Or the Kiss of Death?*

Thornburg, T. (2001). *CliffsNotes: Republic.* New York, N.Y: Wiley Publishing.

Thucydides, & R, W. (1968). *History of the Peloponnesian War.* Baltimore, Md: Penguin Books.

Toner, J. P. (1995). *Leisure and ancient Rome .* Cambridge, England: Polity Press.

Turchin, P. (2006). *War and peace and war: the life cycles of imperial nations.* New York: Pi Press.

Turchin, V. (1977). *The Phenomenon of Science: A Cybernetic Approach to Human Evolution.* New York: Columbia University Press.

Valturio, R. (1472). *De re militari.* Uerona: Johannes ex Uerona.

Voltaire. (1765). *Les Philosophes: The Philosophers of the Enlightenment and Modern Democracy.* (N. L. Torrey, Trans.) Capricorn Books.

Von Neumman, J., & Morgenstern, O. (1944). *Theory of Games and Economic Behaviour.* Princeton University Press.

Ward, G. C., & Burns, K. (2017). *The Vietnam War: an intimate history (Abridged).* New York: Penguin Random House Audio Publishing.

Watson, A. (2010). *The Digest of Justinian: Volume 2.* University of Pennsylvania Press.

Watson, R. T. (1996). *Global biodiversity assessment: Summary for policy-makers.* New York: Cambridge University Press.

Watts, E. J., & Kugler, M. (2018). *Mortal republic: How Rome fell into tyranny.*

Wells, H. G. (2002). *The shape of things to come.* Thirsk: House of Stratus.

West, L. C. (1932). *The Economic Collapse of the Roman Empire* (Vol. 2). The Classical Journal.

White, C. (2018). *The emergence of complex political organisation; In. A HISTORY OF THE GLOBAL ECONOMY.* Cheltenham, UK: Edward Elgar Publishing.

Wiedemann, T. (1980). *Greek and Roman Slavery* (1st ed.). Routledge.

Wiener, N. (1954). *The Human Use of Human Beings: Cybernetics and Society.* Garden Cit, New York: Doubleday.

Wiener, N. (1961). *Cybernetics; or Control and Communication in the animal and the machine.* New York: M.I.T. Press.

Williams, C. (2010). *Roman Homosexuality (2nd Ed.).* New York: Oxford University Press.

Williams, S., & Friell, G. (n.d.). *Theodosius: The Empire at Bay.* Yale University Press.

Xenophon, & Brownson, C. L. (1922). *Anabasis: Books IV-VII.* London: W. Heinemann.

Zimmerman, C. C. (1947). *Family and civilization.* New York.

www.ingramcontent.com/pod-product-compliance
Lightning Source LLC
Chambersburg PA
CBHW030433190426
43202CB00035B/40